CONSUMING YOUTH

ROB LATHAM

CONSUMING
YOUTH

VAMPIRES, CYBORGS, AND THE
CULTURE OF CONSUMPTION

THE UNIVERSITY OF CHICAGO PRESS • CHICAGO & LONDON

Rob Latham is associate professor of English and American studies at the University of Iowa, where he also directs the Sexuality Studies Program. In addition to publishing numerous articles, he has edited, with Robert A. Collins, a collection of essays, *Modes of the Fantastic,* and four volumes of *The Science Fiction and Fantasy Book Review Annual.* He is a coeditor of the journal *Science Fiction Studies.*

The University of Chicago Press, Chicago 60637
The University of Chicago Press, Ltd., London
© 2002 by The University of Chicago
All rights reserved. Published 2002
Printed in the United States of America
11 10 09 08 07 06 05 04 03 02   1 2 3 4 5

ISBN: 0-226-46891-7 (cloth)
ISBN: 0-226-46892-5 (paper)

Library of Congress Cataloging-in-Publication Data

Latham, Rob, 1959–
    Consuming youth : vampires, cyborgs, and the culture of consumption / Rob Latham.
        p. cm.
    Includes index.
    ISBN 0-226-46891-7 (cloth : alk. paper) — ISBN 0-226-46892-5 (paper : alk. paper)
        1. Consumer behavior—United States.   2. Young adult consumers—United
    States—Attitudes.   I. Title.

    HCI10.C6   2002
    658.8'34'0842—dc21   2001037803

♾ The paper used in this publication meets the minimum requirements of the American National Standard for Information Sciences—Permanence of Paper for Printed Library Materials, ANSI Z39.48-1992.

C O N T E N T S

ILLUSTRATIONS

ACKNOWLEDGMENTS

This book has had a long gestation and has benefited, along the way, from the generous input of a number of fine scholars and even finer friends. In particular I would like to thank Michael Antonucci, Margaret Bass, Shay Brawn, Phil Brodd, John Brogan, Dwight Codr, Corey Creekmur, Kathleen Diffley, Stefan Dziemianowicz, Kim Gillespie, Joan Gordon, Jon Hansen, Kate Hayles, Veronica Hollinger, Miranda Joseph, Brooks Landon, Fernando Luera, Joss Marsh, Lee Medovoi, Patty McLain, Ray Mescallado, Abby Metcalf, Diane Nelson, Hilton Obenzinger, Andy Parker, Marjorie Perloff, Ben Robinson, and Gil Sorrentino, all of whom read portions of the manuscript at various stages and provided valuable feedback. I would also like to thank the audiences at the Berkeley Symposium on Interdisciplinary Approaches to Visual Representation, the California American Studies Association Conference, the International Conference on the Fantastic in the Arts, the Modern Language Association's discussion group in science fiction and utopian literature, and the Science Fiction Research Association Conference for their helpful comments on sections presented as public talks. Moreover, I am grateful to the students in my classes on the vampire in literature and film, on cyborg culture, and on youth subculture studies for indulging me as I developed readings and tested out ideas that eventually found their way into this book.

A fellowship at the Stanford Humanities Center in 1992–93 allowed me to commence work on this project, while the University of Iowa provided an Old Gold Summer Fellowship in 1997 and a flexible load leave assignment in 1998–99 that enabled me to complete it. Trent University's Centre for the Study of Theory, Culture, and Politics, in Ontario, also provided support in the form of a visiting lectureship in 1999. The English Department at Iowa has been unstinting in its provision of research assistance, and I am grateful to Damon Franke, Susan Hwang, Kathy Lyons, Tara McLellan, Angela Nepodal, and Mimi Van Ausdall for their kind help along the way.

The editorial staff at the University of Chicago have been warmly supportive of my work, and I would particularly like to thank Doug Mitchell and Robert Devens, for their solid and unstinting advice, and

Sandy Hazel, for her superbly proficient and patient supervision of the manuscript. The book that you hold in your hands owes an enormous debt to their collective expertise.

Sections of this book have been published previously, and I am thankful to the following venues for permission to reprint. An abridged form of chapter 1 appeared in the anthology *Blood Read: The Vampire as Metaphor in Contemporary Culture*, edited by Joan Gordon and Veronica Hollinger (Philadelphia: University of Pennsylvania Press, 1997). Copyright © 1997 University of Pennsylvania Press. Reprinted with permission of the publisher. Portions of chapters 3 and 4 were featured in two collections of conference proceedings: *Imaginative Futures: Proceedings of the 1993 Science Fiction Research Association Conference*, edited by Milton T. Wolf and Daryl F. Mallett (San Bernadino, Calif.: Borgo, 1994), and *Trajectories of the Fantastic: Selected Essays from the Fourteenth International Association on the Fantastic in the Arts*, edited by Michael A. Morrison (Westport, Conn.: Greenwood, 1997). Small sections of chapters 2, 3, 5, and 6 were originally published, in very different form, as book reviews in *The New York Review of Science Fiction* and *Necrofile: The Review of Horror Literature*.

Finally, I would like to dedicate this book, with affection and gratitude, to Jen and Dave, true citizens of Cythera.

INTRODUCTION

THE CYBERNETIC VAMPIRE OF CONSUMER YOUTH CULTURE

From the novels of Anne Rice to *The Lost Boys*, from *The Terminator* to cyberpunk science fiction, vampires and cyborgs have become, over the last two decades, strikingly visible figures within American popular culture, especially popular youth culture. During this same period, literary and cultural critics ranging from Nina Auerbach to Donna Haraway, Sue-Ellen Case to Scott Bukatman have argued for the vampire and cyborg as privileged metaphors possessing an uncanny ability to evoke the psychological and social experience—the relationships of desire and power—characteristic of postmodernist culture. Given these twin developments, this book seeks to answer the following question: What are the implications for contemporary youth, especially for their practices of consumption, of this unprecedented pop-cultural and critical mobilization of vampires and cyborgs?

To state my thesis in brief, I believe that these figures metaphorically embody the libidinal-political dynamics of the consumerist ethos to which young people have been systematically habituated during the contemporary period. The vampire is literally an insatiable consumer driven by a hunger for perpetual youth, while the cyborg has incorporated the machineries of consumption into its juvenescent flesh. Indeed, the conspicuous unnaturalness of both figures, their frankly mutant character, serves to point up how deeply youth has come to be defined by its ensnarement in the norms and ideologies of consumption, rather than by more conventional measures of identity rooted in the structures of family life. The vampire and the cyborg thus provide fruitful models for apprehending the forms of cultural activity—of labor and of leisure—that contemporary capitalist society has staked out for American youth, offering a potent meditation on the promises and perils inherent in youth consumption.

But why *connect* the vampire and the cyborg? Aren't these fundamentally inimical creatures—the former a survival of the Gothic past, the latter a harbinger of our high-tech future? And don't they circulate within entirely separate fictive and critical traditions? While it is certainly true that most of the texts and critics mentioned above have tended to focus on these figures in relative isolation, more recent work—both popular-cultural and theoretical—has begun to consider them together. British novelist Richard Calder's *Dead* trilogy, for example, unites vampires and cyborgs in a provocative meditation specifically on youth-culture issues, while critics such as Haraway and Allucquère Rosanne Stone have lately sought to conflate these figures in order to assess the ideological complexities of the postmodern world. While Stone defends both vampires and cyborgs as "boundary creatures" that permit the cultural theorist to construct "thought experiment[s]" exploring conditions of liminality characteristic of contemporary subjectivity, Haraway extrapolates her influential vision of the cyborg to encompass the vampire as well, conceived as a figure "who effects category transformations" and thus provokes "uninvited associations and dissociations" that prove useful in the critique of cultural hierarchies.[1] Such arguments are essentially analogical in nature: vampires and cyborgs are seen as metaphorically or conceptually similar but are not necessarily linked historically.

Yet the vampire and the cyborg are indeed historically connected: they share a genealogy that transcends their seemingly fortuitous convergence in contemporary cultural theory. Moreover, this genealogy offers a more powerful means for analyzing and critiquing the postmodern condition—especially as it relates to youth consumption—than a merely analogical model allows. In order to trace this genealogy, we must explore a series of contexts and issues that may at first seem rather remote from contemporary youth-culture concerns, yet this background is crucial to an understanding of the contradictory possibilities inherent in youth consumption. While this book may be read simply as a series of case studies of youth-culture texts prominently featuring vampires and cyborgs, the following discussion unveils its underlying assumptions and thus provides the argumentative backbone that underlies and unites the succeeding chapters. In fact, this study is concerned as much with consumption as a socioeconomic and cultural practice as it is with youthful consumers in particular. So let us now turn to an examination of what vampires and cyborgs have to say about consumption generally, before proceeding to their mobilization specifically within contemporary youth culture.

THE FACTORY OF THE CODE

The historical roots of the theoretical connection between the vampire and the cyborg can be found in Karl Marx's *Capital*, where he develops his understanding of industrial automation as the objectification of human labor—a process that, as he envisions it, is both prosthetic and predatory. According to Marx, "In the factory we have a lifeless mechanism which is independent of the workers, who are incorporated into it as its living appendages. . . . Owing to its conversion into an automaton, the instrument of labour confronts the worker during the labour-process in the shape of capital, of dead labour, which dominates and soaks up living labour-power."[2] In the process of its conversion into fixed capital, the fluid dynamism of labor is congealed into a technological simulacrum that confronts the working class as a seemingly autonomous system with its own powers and demands. Estranged from the material embodiment of their labor, workers find themselves integrated into the factory system as cogs in the productive apparatus their own energies have spawned, forced "to adapt [their] . . . movements to the uniform and unceasing motion of an automaton" (1:546). "[T]he self-valorization of capital by means of the machine" (1:557) permits the capitalist to extract surplus value from workers at an increasingly intensive rate, at the same time that the capacity of machinery to replace labor power exposes the proletariat thoroughly and pitilessly to competitive market forces;[3] laborers thus experience the industrial apparatus not as the crystallization of their creative skills but as an "inimical" alien power (1:562).

What I wish to highlight in this argument is not merely its political-economic critique of capitalist social relations but, just as important, the metaphorical system Marx deploys to elaborate it. In brief, capital is "dead labor which, vampire-like, lives only by sucking living labour, and lives the more, the more labour it sucks" (1:342). For Marx, the capitalist factory system is a regime of avid vampirism whose victims are transformed into undead extensions of its own vast, insensate, endlessly feeding body. "The automaton itself is the subject, and the workers are merely conscious organs, co-ordinated with the unconscious organs of the automaton, and together with the latter subordinated to the central moving force" of capitalist production (1:544–45). The worker essentially becomes a cybernetic organism—a cyborg—prosthetically linked to a despotic, ravening apparatus.

Marx's understanding of the vampire figure owes little to the suave aristocrat popularized earlier in the nineteenth century by John Polidori's unflattering portrait of Byron; rather, it derives from the darker, more brutal figure of central European folklore, a monster driven by what Marx more than once refers to as a "werewolf hunger."[4] Yet its form of embodiment is nonetheless "modern": it literally *is* the factory system, dead labor risen up as undead capital to batten on the workers, draining their vital energies and incorporating them into itself. Thus, unlike its construction in the recent critical work of Stone and Haraway, the vampire-cyborg is not merely an analogical system but a perfect *dialectical* image in which unprecedented technical progress and primitive, inhuman exploitation coexist in a structure of profound contradiction. The immense productive potential of human labor, congealed in the machineries of capital, becomes the very means of the worker's subjugation, at least under the capitalist relations of production that prevail in the factory system. This last proviso is crucial, since for Marx the problem was not machinery per se but rather its specific existence as fixed capital, as alienated labor power; under a socialist regime of production, industrial technology would not absorb, in predatory fashion, the worker's energies but would instead free them for creative self-realization. There is thus, for Marx, a progressive potential latent in cyborgization, if this aspect of the worker-machine relation can be detached from its subordination to an economic logic of vampirism.

I believe that Marx's arresting central metaphor, because of its dialectical complexity, provides a better critical guide to our contemporary context than the vaguely analogical models of more recent critics. In essence, what my book does is to reactivate and resituate Marx's image of the vampire-cyborg, arguing that this ambivalent figure can be extended to comprehend the technical modalities of consumption considered as a form of objectified cultural labor. Contemporary American youth culture can profitably be studied in terms of a dialectic of exploitation and empowerment rooted in youth's practices of consumption, practices that are enabled by and contained within specific technologies, primarily electronic ones (videogames, television, music videos, computers, etc.).

The complex figurative logic of the vampire-cyborg has achieved literal substance over the last two decades in a series of youth-culture texts—principally though not exclusively literary and filmic—that have overtly deployed the vampire and the cyborg as resonant popular icons. These texts form the specific focus of my study. I read them as materializations of potent cultural anxieties related to the shifting social position of youth during the period—anxieties that are connected to the waning of a Fordist and the emergence of a post-Fordist form of socioeconomic organization since the mid-1970s (a transition I analyze at greater length below). During this moment of widespread crisis and retrenchment for postwar capitalism, contemporary youth-culture texts featuring vampires and cyborgs reflected the telling cultural contradictions embodied in youth consumption as a form of social labor.

Remarking the complexities of this fraught situation, the title of my text, *Consuming Youth*, should be read as a pun indicating three separate, though intertwined, dimensions of analysis. It refers to (1) an empirical youth culture of consumption, literal young people and their consumerist values and practices; (2) an appetitive impulse to (metaphorically) consume youth, through images and other commodities; and (3) a general cultural obsession, bespeaking an ideological project (as in capitalist society is "consumed by youth"). Thus, the vampire and cyborg texts I examine in this book not only depict youthful consumers, they also interrogate the fetishization of youth as a desired/desiring substance at play within the collective activity of consumption. The baby boom generation remains deeply invested in this libidinally charged image of youth, even as the socioeconomic base that gave rise to and supported it has begun to fragment and crumble. The widely discussed cultural tension between this generation and what has variously been called Generation X, the Baby Bust, and the 13th Generation—basically, children and teenagers who have been raised amid the ruins of a Fordist economy and culture—is in large part the fallout of these ongoing transformations in postwar capitalism.

Before proceeding to a discussion of what is at stake for youth consumption in the emergence of a post-Fordist system, I need to address how my argument develops Marx's central metaphor—a metaphor, after all, designed to describe nineteenth-century industrialism, not contemporary consumer culture. Above all, I want to explain why I feel Marx's powerful dialectical image may be understood to encode a cybernetic logic—why, in short, the cyborg metaphor is not as anachronistic as it might initially appear. Of course, when Marx wrote *Capital*, the path-breaking work of Norbert Wiener, the founder of cybernetics theory, lay nearly a century in the future; yet as James R. Beniger has shown in his book *The Control Revolution*, nineteenth-century capitalism may fruitfully be envisioned as a protocybernetic system.[5]

According to Beniger, the immense productive energies unleashed by industrialization led to a series of crises in the planning and management of commodity production and distribution—crises essentially of communication and control, to use the foundational terms of cybernetics discourse as conceived by Wiener—which necessitated automation measures that now seem less industrial than implicitly cybernetic in form: "attention to regularity in data collection, to formalization of information processing and decision rules, and to standardization of communication with feedback" (p. 224). The vampiric automaton of fixed capital into which Marx's laborers were prosthetically inserted was thus composed not merely of the machinic hardware of the physical plant, but also of a complexly ramifying "software" of continuous-processing technologies, operations research, and managerial bureaucracies. Indeed, as Beniger observes, the potential for literally programming production was realized as early as 1801 with the invention of the punch-card system for the Jacquard loom, a model that led Charles Babbage in the 1830s to his pioneering blueprints for the steam-driven Analytical Engine, the world's first universal computing machine.[6]

What is significant here is that Beniger's argument allows us to view Marx's factory as both vampiric *and* cybernetic—indeed, to see the two metaphors as crucially linked. Moreover, Beniger provides a bridge to the consideration of consumer culture specifically, showing how the "cybernetic" streamlining of industrial production in the late nineteenth century soon led to "a crisis in the control of consumption" (p. 269) which required that consumer demand be systematically stimulated to keep pace with the rapidly expanding forces of supply. With continuous-processing technologies laying the groundwork for full-fledged assembly-line production, new mechanisms were required for ensuring the uninterrupted distribution and sale of the resultant mass-produced commodities. In his discussion of the evolution of these mechanisms, Beniger provides a fascinating viewpoint on the origins of mass marketing techniques as implicitly cybernetic strategies.

Alongside the evolution of modern print and broadcast media, which allowed for "messages to attract, hold, and imprint the mass attention" (p. 271), a "new infrastructure developed for mass control of consumption via national advertising and market feedback" (p. 273). Trade-marked brands, large-scale promotional campaigns, audience research, new service institutions such as department stores and mail-order houses, came to form the hardware and software of an evolving consumer society that Beniger depicts as a "generalized information processor"—marking "a trend toward integration of informational goods and services, media and content, that has continued unabated to this day" (p. 280). As a result, "new control crises have appeared and been resolved throughout the twentieth century at levels of control increasingly removed from the processing of matter and energy" in production (p. 292); automation has achieved a "system-level rationality" (p. 295) that involves the programming and processing, not merely of industrial inputs and outputs, but of consumer desire and demand itself.

This vision of total integration is, for Beniger, little more than an inspiring story of irksome bottlenecks confronted and eliminated by brilliant businessmen and protocyberneticians. Though his argument deploys a quasi-marxist rhetoric of socioeconomic crisis, the systemic instabilities he identifies tend, finally, to derive from contingent limitations amenable to managerial-technical problem solving, rather than from inherent structural contradictions or conflicts among divergent social interests. Beniger, essentially a cybernetician himself, tends to view historical capitalism as an evolving, self-reforming system, rather than as a fundamentally agonistic, rupturing process.[7] On the other hand, neomarxist thinkers, from the Frankfurt school onward, have not quailed at drawing out the totalitarian implications of Beniger's "system-level rationality," frequently deploying in the process a metaphorology that, like Marx's, links vampire and cyborg images. While I describe and critique this tradition more fully in chapter 1, I would like to summarize its main thrust here, principally by means of an interrogation of the early work of Jean Baudrillard, who shares many of Beniger's cybernetic assumptions but pushes them in a more critical (not to say paranoid) direction.

In *For a Critique of the Political Economy of the Sign*, Baudrillard argues that, in the postwar "affluent society" of consumer goods and services, the economy has increasingly come to be driven by what he calls "consummativity": "an indefinite calculus of growth rooted in the abstraction of [human] needs."[8] The ability of the socioeconomic system to instill consumer demand, moreover to delude consumers into conceiving these demands as their own autonomous expression, is the very motor of contemporary capitalism, the new source of its self-valorization. In an explicit contrast with Marx, Baudrillard argues, "During the phase of industrialization, the last pennyworth of labor power was extorted without compunction. To extract surplus value, it was hardly necessary to prime the pump with needs. Then capital, confronted by its own contradictions (over-production, falling rate of profit) . . . unearth[ed] the individual *qua* consumer." This consumer "was no longer simply the slave as labor power," subjected to the factory's machines, but rather "a new kind of serf: the individual as consumption power" (p. 85), subjected to the general mechanisms of consumer society: advertising, product design, the fashion system.

These diverse mechanisms find their coherence in what Baudrillard calls "the code," a force of structural integration so powerful that it

constitutes a "totalitarian logic" (p. 86) in which "everything is reproduced, from the outset, immediately, as an element of the system, as an
integrated variable" (p. 87). Cybernetics discourse and communications
theory provide the code at once with its ideology and its operational
rationale, constituting "a gigantic ramification of human and social engineering" that involves "the autonomization of the entire universe of
practices and forms, from the everyday to the architectural, from the
discursive to the gestural and the political, as a sector of operations and
calculation" (p. 202).

In a later work, *Symbolic Exchange and Death*, Baudrillard extrapolates
Marx's arguments even further by conceiving this vast social software of
the code as a form of dead labor.[9] Yet now he explicitly rejects the marxist emphasis on economic production as the determining social moment, alleging that it has given way entirely to the code's cultural *re-*
production, "collapsing into the sphere of 'consumption,' understood as
the sphere of a generalised axiomatic, a coded exchange of signs, a general lifestyle" (p. 14). According to Baudrillard, this possibility was already latent in the factory system, in the "crystallized social relations
incarnated in dead labour, weighing down on society in its entirety as
the code of domination itself." In Baudrillard's view, "Marx's greatest
error was to have retained a belief in the innocence of machines, the
technical process and science—all of which were supposedly capable
of becoming living social labour once the system of capital was liqui-
dated, despite the fact that this is precisely what the system is based on.
This pious hope springs from having underestimated death in dead labour" (p. 15).

In other words, Marx too credulously believed that the threat posed
by industrial (and, by extension, every other kind of) machinery was
merely its contingent historical existence as fixed capital and not its very
form as congealed human labor. This reservoir of past labor, stored up
in the machine, could be liberated by a socialist revolution to serve the
ends of the workers: the enemy was thus the vampire of capital and not
the industrial automaton itself. Or so Marx supposed. In fact, according
to Baudrillard, machines are far from innocent; rather they are the "direct and immediate operational signs of the social relation to death on
which capital is nourished" (p. 13). Industrial machinery merely prefigured the generalized, abstract, cybernetic machine of the code, which
emerges as its historical perfection—so much so that "society as a whole
takes on the appearance of a factory" (p. 18) in which we are all, as consumers, subjected.[10]

In short, Marx wanted to salvage the industrial automaton from its conscription by the vampire of capital, without recognizing that the automaton, in its capacity at once to replace and to integrate (i.e., cyborgize) living labor, was itself the genuine vampire. Unlike in Marx, Baudrillard's cybernetic vampire is an emphatically *non*dialectical image: here the term expresses no structural contradiction between technical progress and primitive exploitation that awaits its historical supersession in a higher form of social organization. Rather, progress *is* exploitation: the perfection of technological means serves the sole end of cementing the reign of the code. Indeed, Baudrillard explicitly abandons Marx's dialectical method as outmoded: "With the hegemony of dead labour over living labour, the whole dialectic of production collapses" (p. 16) and we are left only with the unceasing reproduction, via consumption, of a system moored in nothing and driven by nothing but "the omnipotence of operational simulation" (p. 22). In this immense social factory, we are all the victims of the code's cybernetic vampirism, and our very pleasure in consumption expresses nothing more than "the ritual rationalization of . . . a social injunction" to consume.[11]

While I find this extrapolation-cum-critique of Marx's central metaphor useful in that it shows the way toward a construction of consumer practices as modes of cultural labor, I feel that Baudrillard's rejection of dialectics is premature and, consequently, his account of the code too abstractly totalizing. Deriving largely from his theoretical debts to structuralism, Baudrillard hypostatizes the code as a dictatorial system that precedes and structures human expression in its minutest particulars. There is a paranoid, almost masochistic glee in Baudrillard's monolithic depiction of the code, which at times he personifies as an almost conscious force for domination. As Douglas Kellner has observed, Baudrillard's argument proceeds from the perspective of the code itself and not from the more divided and agonistic viewpoints of the diverse social classes engaged in enacting—and perhaps contesting—the manifold activities of consumption;[12] indeed, all agency has been evacuated from human subjects and invested in the cybernetic regime that purportedly regulates them.

Yet such nightmarish visions of what Nick Dyer-Witheford calls the "necrotic apogee of capitalist control" fail to acknowledge crucial "countervailing tendencies"—alternative trends in which the "prosthesis of labor and machine . . . loosens capital's unilateral control of technology" by enabling short circuits and subversions of the regulating system.[13] A truly adequate account of consumer culture developed from marxist premises requires, I think, a much more deeply situated analysis of the complex interplay of global forms of domination with local complicities and resistances, one that does not take refuge in reified visions of an abstract totality but that instead seeks to trace the concrete relations of force that constitute contemporary capitalism's social hegemony. To this end, I believe a dialectical construction of the image of the vampire-cyborg is essential, since it allows for a sense of the contradictory promises and dangers inherent in consumption as a mode of social integration and personal expression—a point of particular relevance when it comes to a consideration of youth consumption in the contemporary period.

FORDISM, POST-FORDISM, AND YOUTH

Such a dialectical approach—one centrally focused on an analysis of postwar capitalism—is offered in the theory of a Fordist socioeconomic system articulated in the work of the French Regulation school.[14] The chief value of this approach, in my view, lies in its attempt to theorize precisely the problem of integration between the spheres of capitalist production and consumption that Beniger and Baudrillard address, but in a way that is considerably more dialectical than Beniger's feedback model and Baudrillard's quasi-structuralist code.

In contrast with these more static visions, Regulation theory deploys the notion of a "regime of accumulation," which, according to Alain Lipietz in *Mirages and Miracles*, "can be defined as a *schema of reproduction*" designed to "ensure a certain adequation between transformations of conditions of production and transformations of conditions of consumption."[15] This "adequation" cannot be presumed to be seamless or faultlessly efficient, especially since it describes a system in process— moreover one that, following Marx, is prone to crisis due to the persistent development of structural contradictions. The regime of accumulation manages these periods of crisis as best it can (indeed, its ability to sustain a relative equilibrium over an extended period is what marks it out as a regime of accumulation), but this management falls far short of the cybernetic perfection posited, in their different ways, by both Beniger and Baudrillard. Indeed, a regime of accumulation operates with no guarantees and can easily fail at a global level when its management strategies prove inadequate to historical realities.

The primary agency by means of which a regime of accumulation ensures its reproduction is the "mode of regulation," which is essentially the regime of accumulation realized at the level of institutional norms and everyday practices. This realization, however, is far from a process of bloodless cybernetic programming, since the concept of a mode of regulation refers ultimately, as Lipietz has suggested, to "*a hegemonic sys-*

tem in Gramsci's sense of the term" (p. 70; emphasis in original): in other words, to the always fraught and uneasy compromise of social interests, forged in the spheres of politics and culture, that ensures the ongoing rule of a dominant class. This hegemony is neither automatic nor guaranteed, but must itself be reproduced: the consent of the dominated classes has continually to be won, and while the resulting consensus may last for decades, it remains exposed to the social fallout of economic crises and other historical contingencies, which may lead to cultural-political crises of legitimation that can fatally undermine the entire system. What all this means, in other words, is that it is crucial to grasp the *contextual specificity* of how a regime of accumulation and a mode of regulation are dialectically articulated at any given moment rather than assuming a purely formal, serenely functional homeostasis.

The Regulation school's debts to Gramsci can also be discerned in the name they selected for the regime of accumulation to which the bulk of their analysis to date has been devoted: basically, Regulation theory amounts to a systematic development of Gramsci's seminal but elliptical writings on Fordism. This term, for Gramsci, referred not only to Henry Ford's epochal renovations of mass production but also to his attempts to regulate the private lives of his workers, including especially their domestic arrangements—a situation that prefigured, in Gramsci's view, a new model of relationship between the spheres of economy and culture.[16] As Regulation theory develops the argument, what Fordism achieves in its mature phase—variously dated, but certainly at its peak during the two decades following the Second World War—is a growing articulation of mass production with a new ethos of mass consumption through the agency of an implicit compact (the "postwar consensus") between labor and capital that cemented the latter's hegemony. On the terms of this unwritten contract, workers eschewed divisive strikes in favor of institutionalized bargaining over wages and benefits (mediated finally by the state, whose social-welfare safety net, government-insured loan programs, and Keynesian fiscal strategies offered further impetus to class compromise), while capitalists provided affordable mass-produced commodities and a general rise in living standards. This regime of accumulation was supported by a mode of regulation that engendered a consumerist ethos in working-class households by means of widespread new technologies (especially television) and powerful social discourses (especially advertising). The resultant "affluent society" saw a massive growth in the middle classes, including the rise of new class formations linked to burgeoning technological and managerial sectors; mature Fordism was also an unprecedented boon for the capitalist class, whose profits remained strong from the early 1950s to the late 1960s. Indeed, this period has been dubbed by some "the Golden Age of Capitalism."[17]

By the early 1970s, however, Fordism had clearly entered a period of structural crisis due to a confluence of factors both economic and cultural-political. Economically, the system was hamstrung, ironically by its own success: so thoroughly and effectively had it inculcated an ethos of consumption that it ran up against natural barriers in the saturation of markets for consumer durables; most households owned televisions, other major appliances, automobiles, and so forth, so that the omnipresent lure of advertising (even combined with these products' planned obsolescence) had reached a limit in its ability to provoke demand (Regulation theory refers to this as a "crisis of overaccumulation").[18] This situation—exacerbated by a series of external crises culminating in the OPEC oil embargo of the early 1970s—began systematically to erode productivity and profits,[19] forcing capitalists to retrench their social position in ways that had major implications for the capital-labor relationship. As Martyn Lee argues, the "contract which brought together the agencies of capital and labour into a pragmatic acceptance of each other's position was underwritten by the tacit agreement that wage-claim restraint would become the necessary corollary to falling productivity. For a workforce socialized over many years into the expectation of constantly improved returns in exchange for their labour-power, the small print of the . . . contract was hard to accept and . . . easy to resist."[20] The results of the shattering of the postwar compact were diverse, ranging from fractious strikes, to an inflationary spiral that eroded living standards, to systemic deindustrialization and capital flight as capitalists internationalized production, permitting them to exploit less evolved and resistant labor markets—developments I will discuss, especially in terms of their cultural fallout, more fully in the following chapters.

What I would like to stress here is a point Lee makes in passing regarding youth culture as the site of Fordism's most pronounced and telling *cultural* contradiction, one that led to a major crisis of legitimation in its mode of regulation during the 1960s. Lee builds on—and effectively historicizes—Daniel Bell's influential analysis of the powerful tension in postwar capitalism between an ascetic ethos of production and a hedonistic ethos of consumption—between the competing demands of work and of leisure—a contradiction Lee sees played out with particular force in the nascent domain of popular youth culture. According to Lee, Fordism essentially "developed and defined the social category of youth which became the most prominent materialisation of the

new mass consumption ethic," in the process "open[ing] up fertile teenage markets and ma[king] available for youth the now familiar material
and symbolic objects by which they could objectify a common structure
of feeling." This structure of feeling found its coherence principally
within the sphere of consumption, where subcultural fashion "provided
a rich source of potentially subversive cultural resources" that allowed
young people to establish "a critical social distance from, and negation
of, the values that were espoused by their parent culture—values such as
work, sobriety and moderation which were of course co-terminous with
those of the social system into which youth was to be integrated and
eventually asked to serve."[21] On the one hand, Fordist society saw in
youth the crystallization of its deep-seated imperative to consumerist
pleasure; on the other hand, it had somehow to integrate youth, as empirical social subjects, into the responsibly "adult" system of economic
production and profit seeking. In Lee's view, the subcultural youth
movements and student uprisings of the 1960s were a manifestation of
this cultural contradiction in the mode of regulation.

This contemporary crisis of legitimation was the culmination of a
long history of twentieth-century capitalism's libidinal-political fetishization of youth. As Stuart Ewen has shown, youth had become a site
where contradictions between the spheres of production and consumption could be modeled and ideologically "resolved" as early as the 1920s
and 1930s. During that period, youth began to be depicted throughout
popular culture as an "industrial ideal": such skills as quick reflexes, endurance, and adaptability, nominally associated with youth, came to be
valued by a nascent Fordist regime engaged in the Taylorization of the
production process. Traditional values such as experience and maturity
were no longer essential on a heavily mechanized work floor, where rou-
tinized integration into the technological apparatus counted for more
than cumulative know-how. The resultant cultural valorization of youth,
in Ewen's analysis, found its voice in the expanding realm of advertising,
which in this period not only began explicitly to target youth markets
but also mobilized an ideology of youth as the organizing principle and
ultimate goal of mass consumption: "As youth appeared [to be] the
means to industrial survival, its promulgation as something to be
achieved by production provided a bridge between people's need for satisfaction and the increased corporate priorities of mass distribution and
worker endurance."[22]

In other words, youth, valued as a physical commodity in the labor
process, came to be articulated during the early decades of this century
as a cultural commodity available for exchange. The organization of

consumption around an ideology of youth provided the promise of achieving precisely those values—innocence, openness to possibility, physical dexterity—mandated by the new regime of production. In Ewen's words, "corporations which demanded youth on the production line now offered that same youth through their products."[23] Thus, Fordist capitalism from its origins saw in "consuming youth" a potential for cementing the increasingly fractured activities of labor and of leisure, yet this "resolution" did not eliminate the ethical contradiction between these realms that would in the postwar period become a source of profound cultural crisis.

An important corollary to Ewen's arguments is the fact that, implicitly, Fordism had begun to conceive of youth not merely as an empirical category but as an ideological abstraction, in a way that erased distinctions between youthful bodies and machinic processes. In his book *Bodies and Machines*, Mark Seltzer has detailed how the industrial paradigm of Fordist Taylorization conflated bodies and technologies: the new production system valorized the youthful body not as a natural object but as a set of properties—flexibility, durability, and so forth—that could, at least in principle, be aped by machines or by complex human-machine interfaces. Seltzer cites Henry Ford himself, whose renovations of production gave the greatest impetus to Taylorization:

> The production of the Model T required 7882 distinct work operations, but, Ford notes, only 12% of these tasks—only 949 operations—required "strong, able-bodied, and practically physically perfect men." Of the remainder . . . "we found that 670 could be filled by legless men, 2,637 by one-legged men, two by armless men, 715 by one-armed men, and ten by blind men." If from one point of view such a fantasy projects a violent dismemberment of the natural body and an emptying out of human agency, from another it projects a transcendence of the natural body and the extension of human agency through the forms of technology that represent it.[24]

Seltzer refers to this vision as a "logic of prosthesis," and he finds it at work not so much in the process of production (where it remains largely a fantasy) but in consumption. Youth, by this analysis, had begun to function within the emergent domain of mass consumer culture as a prosthesis, a site of integration between the natural body (variously aged and abled) and the newly mechanized labor process. Obviously, much was being invested in youth—in both the financial-speculative and libidinal-political senses of the term—as a crucial ideological underpinning of Fordism's maturing mode of regulation: working-class consent to Fordist hegemony was largely won by gaining acceptance of "youth" as an ideal to be realized through the practices of mass consumption.

To summarize, "youth," in the Fordist industrial-cultural regime, ceased to be a quality inextricably attached to quantifiably aged bodies and instead became a set of values desirable both as the means of production and the end of consumption. Further, these values inhered in bodies no longer as purely natural properties, but as artificially attached prostheses facilitating incorporation into a techno-economic system. Thus, from the outset of modern consumer culture, youth was implicitly a cyborg identity.

In the postwar period, this latent cyborgization of youth was complexly articulated with the demographic explosion of the baby boom. Since prewar industrial culture had valorized youth as a privileged subject-position, it could only be expected that a thronging generation of young people would come to claim it for cultural and political purposes. The apparent result was an emphatic naturalization of youth as a social category, since the sheer visibility of young people—literally adolescent bodies—seemed legitimately to represent the social subject industrial culture had valorized.

The situation was more complex than this, however, since the perceived homogeneity and mutuality of interests across divides of difference—regional, racial, and so forth—that seemed to link young people as "youth" was an entirely artificial construction. Most obviously, it stemmed from the rituals of mass consumption that had produced youth as a coherent social category; it was only because prewar industrial culture had manufactured youth as a corporate ideal, sustained through the practices of mass consumption, that the postwar generation could hope to lay claim to it. Indeed, as Lawrence Grossberg has argued, the seemingly monolithic character of "youth" may have begun to fragment with the graying of the baby boom: "Youth . . . has become a battlefield on which the current generations of adolescents, baby boomers, parents and corporate media interests are fighting for control of its meanings, investments and powers, fighting to articulate and thereby construct its experiences, identities, discourses and social differences."[25]

The salient point for my argument here is that the baby boom did not dispel the logic of prosthesis that had defined consuming youth in the prewar period, installing instead a generation of authentically "youthed" bodies. Rather, it helped to exacerbate that logic immeasurably, not least by providing vivid images of "lived youth" that were readily recuperated as commodities available for consumption. As I argue in chapter 3, youthful bodies became the festive sites where mass culture modeled "youth" as a consumable substance, as a style: beginning with Pop, virtually every aesthetic formation in popular culture has been complicit with this mass-market fetishization of youth. More than ever, youth became prosthetic, a point of intersection between the individual body and the technologies of the fashion system.

More important, the sorts of technologies that came to predominate in the postwar period brought the cyborgization of youth to an unprecedented level of cultural self-consciousness. Prewar high technology had centered on industrial production, but the postwar period has seen the rise of so-called postindustrial technologies of information that have further collapsed distinctions between human and machine. Not only does cybernetic science conflate these entities in a general study of information-processing systems, but the dissemination of information technologies throughout the social body has made for a heightened intimacy of contact and interaction with machinery. Technologies like television, VCRs, and camcorders suture everyday life into a mediated image continuum, and interface with computers—whether overt in the form of PC units, or less obvious in the form of data banks and other regulative and surveillance systems—is a prosthetic connection within the labor and leisure practices of virtually everyone. Appropriately enough, it is Baudrillard who has summed up the resulting situation, arguing that the contemporary individual seems to subsist "as a terminal of multiple networks . . . endowed with telematic power—that is, with the capability of regulating everything from a distance, including work . . . , consumption, play, social relations and leisure." [26] As interface with such informational networks increasingly comes to define the substance of social interaction, contemporary experience becomes an ongoing acculturation into cyborg possibility. And in this progressive cyborgization, youth have been and remain on the front lines, as I hope to show in what follows.

What my book does, therefore, is to press these various arguments about youth's persistent imbrication with capitalist culture forward beyond the initial period of Fordist crisis in the 1960s and early 1970s, in order to examine how the socioeconomic system's ideological construction of youth as a privileged site of consumption responds to subsequent transformations in the struggling Fordist system. In the process, I am going to beg the question—a hotly debated one within Regulation school theory—of whether these transformations constitute mere retrenchments within a period of "late" Fordism or if they signal a wholesale movement beyond Fordism into a new regime of capital accumulation.[27] Since I cannot hope to resolve this deeply vexed issue, I should perhaps clarify exactly what I mean when I use the term *post*-Fordism.

Perhaps the most ambitious account of the growth and spread of an entirely new socioeconomic system is offered in the work of the New Times Project associated with the British journal *Marxism Today*, which summarizes the post-Fordist regime as follows:

> A shift to the new "information technologies": more flexible, de-centralised forms of labour-process and work organization; decline of the old manufacturing base and the growth of the "sunrise," computer-based industries; the hiving-off or contracting-out of functions and services; a greater emphasis on choice and product differentiation, on marketing, packaging and design, on the "tar-geting" of consumers by lifestyle, taste and culture rather than by . . . categories of social class; a decline in the proportion of the skilled, male, manual working-class, the rise of the service and white-collar classes and the "feminisation" of the workforce; an economy dominated by the multinationals, with their interna-tional division of labour and their greater autonomy from nation-state control; the "globalisation" of the new financial markets, linked by the communications revolution, and the new forms of the spatial organisation of social processes.[28]

This account of post-Fordism is similar to the one offered in David Harvey's *Condition of Postmodernity*, yet Harvey warns against assuming its accomplished hegemony, remarking "the danger of confusing the transitory and the ephemeral with more fundamental transformations in political-economic life."[29] For Harvey, this new regime coexists with residual, yet still quite socially powerful, Fordist structures, and argu-ments such as those offered by the New Times Project have to be un-derstood as describing an idealized vision of a system that is at present only partially and unevenly developed. Some critics allege that post-Fordist transformations have really only occurred within the sphere of economic production and have yet to generate and sustain a political-cultural "mode of regulation" alternative to the traditional Fordist model.[30]

Yet Harvey's work suggests otherwise, as he analyzes not only the transformations in the production-consumption complex that bespeak a new regime of accumulation, but also the hesitant emergence and gradual consolidation of a fresh set of norms and practices that indicates the entry onto the cultural stage of a new mode of regulation. Harvey describes the post-Fordist regime as one of "flexible accumulation," re-

ferring above all to the increasing social and global mobility of capital
that has permitted it to radically restructure labor markets—through
extensive subcontracting and the proliferation of temporary employment—and to begin to transform industrial organization, de-emphasiz-
ing assembly-line mass production of identical commodities in favor of
"batch production" of more specialized and differentiated consumer
goods.[31] On the consumption side, flexible accumulation is characterized by a transition from a stable and expanding mass market to rapidly
shifting niche markets, allowing for "a much greater attention to quick-
changing fashions and the mobilization of all the artifices of need inducement and cultural transformation that this implies."[32] Harvey connects this transition with an emerging culture of postmodernism, which
he identifies as being based on "difference, ephemerality, spectacle, fashion, and the commodification of cultural forms" (p. 156). Thus, to the
extent that one can understand postmodernism as a historically unique
ensemble of values and practices, then it can be seen to indicate the
growing consolidation of a new mode of regulation suited to the cultural demands of the post-Fordist regime of flexible accumulation.[33] Of
course, as Harvey stresses, post-Fordism is as unevenly developed in the
cultural arena as in the economic sphere, and what in fact prevails is a
"complex mix" of modernist and postmodernist forces, "swaying back
and forth between centralization and decentralization, between authority and deconstruction, between hierarchy and anarchy, between permanence and flexibility" (p. 339).

A similar argument is advanced by Scott Lash and John Urry in their
book *The End of Organized Capitalism*.[34] While they do not use the specific terminology of Regulation theory, Lash and Urry, like Harvey, see
postmodernism as the characteristic cultural expression of a new socioeconomic system, one that they refer to as "disorganized capitalism."
(Their understanding of this system converges in major particulars with
influential accounts of post-Fordism, but as their alternative term suggests, they do not see this new regime as having yet attained an autonomous, fully stable structure.) Moreover, Lash and Urry, drawing on the
sociological work of Pierre Bourdieu, identify this postmodernist sensibility with the growing consolidation of a new cultural-political hegemony associated with the rise of a new middle class and related class
factions—groups aligned predominantly with the burgeoning service
industries and defined principally through their strategies of consumption. While I think it is still too soon to say whether the classic Fordist
hegemony, based on the capital-labor-state compact, has definitively
given way to a well-established post-Fordist form, Lash and Urry's iden-

tification of these newly enfranchised classes, with their burgeoning life-styles and practices, certainly suggests that fresh structures and relations are developing amid the ruins of Fordism, albeit in a disorganized state.

CONSUMING YOUTH

I have obviously heavily abbreviated a set of wide-ranging and compli-cated arguments, and subsequent chapters of this study will touch base with their animating assumptions in a more developed fashion (for ex-ample, I discuss the rise of the new middle classes at length in chapter 2). For the moment, what I would like to underline are the implications for contemporary youth and youth culture of this incomplete historical trajectory from Fordism to post-Fordism. If, as Martyn Lee argues, youth can be seen as the ideal representative, socially and ideologically, of Fordism's strategic enshrinement of consumption, and at the same time as its most telling site of cultural contradiction (since the devotion to consumption exists in tension with productivist imperatives), how does the structural crisis of Fordism and the advent of a regime of flex-ible accumulation impact youth both as a social subject and as an ideo-logical figure? This is the central question that my book addresses.

To do so, it analyzes a series of youth-culture texts—texts centrally featuring vampire and cyborg images—that have emerged during this fraught period of transition. These texts, I argue, provocatively address the construction of youth as a privileged consumer identity and as a sig-nificant ideological code within the domain of consumption generally. Moreover, as the postwar "affluent society" petered out in the 1970s and 1980s and Fordism's equation of youth with a hedonistic lifestyle of con-sumption ran up against the nascent structures (and strictures) of post-Fordism, the cultural contradiction embodied in youth only became more pointed. The vampire and cyborg texts discussed in this book serve powerfully to embody and work through this contradiction.

Following Baudrillard, these texts engage consumption as a powerful mechanism of social integration, but one whose function in terms of youth is shifting due to the ongoing transition from Fordism to post-Fordism. However, they generally depict the situation with a greater dialectical complexity than Baudrillard's model allows. They do this de-spite the fact that, in the vast majority of them, it is *either* the vampire *or* the cyborg that is foregrounded, and not both together. As we saw in Marx, the power of the cybernetic vampire as metaphor lay precisely in its fusion of the contradictory elements of technological progress and primitive horror: the machineries of industrial capitalism preyed upon the worker while at the same time auguring a utopian transformation.

Although the metaphor is split in most of the texts I canvass, the separate figures—because of their mutual implication in issues related to youth and consumption—strongly evoke their dialectical counterparts: the vampire texts that I discuss in my first three chapters operate within a broadly cybernetic context, especially in their thematic foregrounding of consumer technologies, while the cyborg texts that I treat in chapters 4 through 6 are generally dark in tone and often feature relationships of brutal exploitation. Both textual systems thus have positive and negative valences: bloodthirsty vampires evince utopian longings, while powerful cyborgs move within a dystopian social horizon. My final chapter also examines a recent spate of texts that draw the two figures back into a fresh, if uneasy, fusion particularly appropriate to the post-Fordist moment.

Moreover, during these two decades, the vampire-cyborg as a twinned metaphor for youth consumption appeared not only in works of fiction but in a variety of discourses that centrally addressed issues related to youth, technology, and consumer culture. My readings of pop-culture texts, therefore, mobilize a number of discursive systems in which vampires and cyborgs operate not as overt icons but as organizing tropes, showing how, since the 1970s, these figures have provided suggestive and influential ways for understanding the social values implicit in—and the changing role of youth in relation to—a consumerist lifestyle. In each chapter I situate my "primary" texts within a broad theoretical-cultural horizon where the vampire-cyborg can be seen to circulate as a figurative construction, attending especially to discourses related to consumer technologies, since (following Marx and Baudrillard) it is precisely in and by means of these apparatuses that individual labor/desire is mobilized and put to work. The electronic and microelectronic technologies I focus on in this book thus materialize all three meanings of *consuming youth:* they constitute young people as subjects of consumption, inculcating shared values and fostering specific practices; they disseminate consumable images of youth, thus provoking consumer appetite within society generally; and they help to forge the cultural ideology of consumption in which youth functions as a privileged, almost mythic figure. Given all this, it should come as no surprise that the cultural discourses that have historically subtended these technologies, whether promoting them or critically interrogating their social function, have consistently been marked by the metaphor of the vampire-cyborg.

Chapter 1 begins with a more detailed critique of the monolithically negative view of consumption characteristic of Baudrillard, showing how it has spawned a compensatory, yet equally undialectical, defense of consumerist values and practices in some branches of contemporary cultural studies. Throughout this discussion, I attend to how youth has been consistently mobilized as a privileged figure within the major theoretical debates about consumption. I then offer a large-scale historical-cultural sketch of how the postwar Fordist regime enfranchised youth as consumers, creating both a widespread image of young people as consuming subjects as well as a series of politicized critiques of this construction. These popular critiques served to point up the social contradiction youth represented for Fordist culture, evincing a concern that the very notion of responsible adulthood was under siege, radically transformed by a system that identified consumption with the achievement of perpetual youth—a view that still retains much of its cultural power, despite the fact that Fordism itself is in the widespread process of decay.

This first chapter highlights the popular Fordist construction of "consuming youth" that texts covered in subsequent chapters will develop, react against, and subvert. It thus draws out an ideal image of youth consumption, enshrined under Fordism, that continues to give off a powerful charge, even as it has begun to fray and fragment in recent decades. This chapter also elicits the ambivalent situation of youth as consumers—at once exploited and empowered—that continues throughout the transition from Fordism to post-Fordism (a trajectory discussed in more detail in the following chapters). Finally, this chapter takes as emblem and central site of youth consumption the video arcade—and, more generally, the shopping mall, a characteristic Fordist institution whose technological seductions seemed blatantly vampiric to many critics—culminating with close readings of two texts that contain powerful portraits of mall-culture, youth-consumer vampirism: S. P. Somtow's novel *Vampire Junction* (1985) and the popular film *The Lost Boys* (1987).

Chapter 2 moves to a consideration of how the ideal Fordist image of youth consumption has been impacted by the socioeconomic realities of post-Fordism. Broadly, it distinguishes two main trends of development that have formed an ongoing dialectic in youth-culture vampire texts since the mid-1970s: on the one hand, the emergence of the "slacker" vampire, first descried in George A. Romero's film *Martin* (1977), which chronicles the response of working-class youth consumers to the effects of rampant deindustrialization; on the other hand, the rise to prominence of the "yuppie" vampire, initially evoked in Anne Rice's novel *Interview with the Vampire* (1976), which depicts the enfranchisement of new bourgeois consumption classes linked to emergent technologies, professional identities, and processes of urban gentrification. Following culturally situated readings of Romero's and Rice's works, I track the twin traditions they have spawned as they mature in overt counterpoint with, and critique of, each other. Taken together, these opposed sub-genres of the contemporary vampire story indicate the consolidation of new class identities against the backdrop of a struggling Fordist system.

In chapter 3 I move to a consideration of how the class issues fore-grounded in the yuppie and slacker traditions are further inflected by gender concerns. Specifically, I focus on the "homosexual panic" aroused by Rice's vampires—a panic that also informed contemporaneous cri-tiques of youth consumption, especially in the areas of lifestyle advertis-ing and music-video culture. What the critics were attacking was a visual regime of homoerotic narcissism that emerged within 1960s subcul-tures, in particular the one associated with the Factory aesthetic of Andy Warhol—a regime that achieved potent expression in popular advertise-ments of the 1980s oriented toward youth consumption. I close the chapter with readings of the film *The Hunger* (1983), Rice's best-selling novel *The Vampire Lestat* (1985), and Poppy Z. Brite's novel *Lost Souls* (1992) in relation to the cultural discourses surrounding the MTV Net-work as an orchestrator of youth-consumer practices and lifestyles dur-ing the 1980s and 1990s. All three of these texts powerfully mobilize homoerotic imagery, yet the cultural implications of this process differ on the basis of the new class alignments each attempts to negotiate.

Chapter 4 shifts the focus from youth-culture texts that deploy the vampire icon to those featuring the cyborg, though my general analysis continues to attend to the ways in which these two figures are dialecti-cally related. In this chapter, I address the question of whether post-Fordism constitutes a truly postindustrial socioeconomic formation; in the process, I consider how the various theorists of postindustrialism in the 1970s and 1980s mobilized a rhetoric of youth to describe major features of the new regime: its purported openness, streamlined form, adaptiveness, and flexibility. I then trace the emergence of a new eco-nomic paradigm responsible for building the technological infrastruc-ture of a nascent post-Fordism: venture capitalism, associated preemi-nently with centers of computer hardware and software production such as Silicon Valley in northern California. By means of a synthetic reading of the discourses of venture capitalism—focusing particularly on jour-nalistic coverage of the rise of "sunshine industries" run by youthful entrepreneurs—I explore the consolidation of an ideology of the micro-electronics corporation as radically innovative and creatively liberating, allegedly undoing in its managerial and social structures the vampiric predation of labor elaborated by Marx in *Capital*. As counterpoint to this idyllic portrait, which deploys a rhetoric of youth to cement its claims, I consider the actual situation of youthful labor within this new system, which is considerably less rosy than the apologists for venture capitalism suggest. I then move to a detailed reading of Douglas Coupland's novel *Microserfs* (1995), which explores many of these issues related to postindustrial culture and computer industries in a way that opens questions regarding the possibilities of a "posthuman" consumer identity.

Chapter 5 canvasses the cultural discourses surrounding the so-called Information Superhighway, a vast engineering project conceived on a par with the Fordist construction of the literal superhighway system in the 1950s. I attend above all to what the projected I-Way portends as a mode of cultural participation for youth, aligned with but different from traditional practices of consumption; in particular, I review arguments by proponents of a nascent digital culture that suggest a radically participatory mode of agency will soon become available to consumers as a result of the Infobahn. This interactive capacity, which is consistently contrasted with the passive absorption characteristic of broadcast television, is already evolving, so these critics claim, within the domain of contemporary youth culture. I address this claim by exploring the relationship between two discursive systems: journalistic and other popular evocations of contemporary youth as "Generation X"—a horde of apathetic slackers aimlessly cruising the circuits of mass-media culture—and popular road narratives of the mid-1990s that, I argue, offer powerful commentary on the cyborgization of experience portended by the Infobahn. These new "information road narratives" are, however, unable to disentangle the empowering prosthetic consciousness heralded by the prophets of digital culture from the traditional sedentary pleasures of televisual spectatorship, an extrapolation that is left to the more science-fictional and utopian treatments I discuss in my final chapter.

While chapters 4 and 5 deal with texts and critical traditions in which the cyborg functions mostly as a metaphorical construction rather than a literal entity, chapter 6 explores the cyberpunk subcultures of the 1980s and 1990s, where bold figurations of youth-machine hybrids explicitly emerged. This chapter extends my consideration of the cautionary cultural portraits of Generation X to encompass popular constructions of the underground ethos of computer hacking, an activity I read as evoking a fresh youth-consumer identity in which the possibilities of cybernetic empowerment begin to outweigh the tendencies toward vampiric exploitation. This utopian potential has had to work against powerful cultural forces seeking to recuperate its energies, such as the journalistic coverage that has depicted teenage hackers as everything from computer addicts to youth-gang saboteurs. Yet even these critiques have implicitly mobilized a logic of prosthesis to suggest the illicit empowerment hacking seems to allow, an image of activist consumption that also figures in novels and movies featuring teen hackers as central characters, such as Poppy Z. Brite's *Drawing Blood* (1993) and Iain Softley's film *Hackers* (1995).

The chapter then moves to a discussion of cyberpunk subculture as the site where a more overt recognition of the growing cyborgization of youth by information technologies predominates—a development this subculture, despite its embrace of hacking as a veritable model of cultural agency, tends to view with deep ambivalence. This ambivalence, often expressed in neo-Gothic and quasi-occult thematics, is most readily discerned in cyberpunk novels and stories where youthful consumption is the central topic, such as Marc Laidlaw's novel *Kalifornia* (1993) and the work of Pat Cadigan, in particular her short story "Pretty Boy Crossover" (1986) and her novel *Tea from an Empty Cup* (1998). These texts collectively provide a complex vision of the imbrication of youth with the technical apparatuses of post-Fordism—especially virtual reality technologies—one that is at once celebratory and dystopian. My reading of these texts builds upon the debates about postindustrialism and venture capitalism canvassed in chapter 4 to show how, refocused through the lens of cyberpunk science fiction, they have generated a critique of a corporate-dominated near-future in which youthful practices of labor and leisure have been radically transformed; it also pursues my investigation, in chapter 5, of contemporary information road narratives into the twisted circuits of cyberspace.

Chapter 6 closes with a discussion of the work of British science-fiction author Richard Calder, whose *Dead* trilogy (1992–97) offers a decadent retro-futuristic vision actually featuring teenage cyborg vampires. Thus, Calder's work directly combines Marx's two central metaphors in a context that displays their significance for youth-culture concerns: his refractory teen-rebel creatures move through a hallucinatory cybernetic wasteland dominated by the kitschy detritus of rampant consumerism. This decadent "hypercapitalist" future, for all its numerous cyborg enhancements, has essentially regressed to primitive forms of exploitation and control; yet at the same time, in a compensating move (already implicit in Marx's dialectical image), it still contains utopian aspirations for an epochal revolutionizing and redemption of the historical project of consumption. This vision of libidinal-political liberation finds it most potent expression in Calder's novel *Cythera* (1998), which envisions a futuristic realm in which the autonomous agency of youthful consumers is finally (if ambiguously) realized.

This final chapter shows how powerfully Marx's dialectical image continues to grasp the basic logic of capitalist automation, whether industrial or cybernetic in form. Indeed, in its implications for issues of social agency, the vampire-cyborg is such a potent figure that contemporary youth culture has virtually come to understand itself, albeit unconsciously, in its terms; popular vampire and cyborg texts effectively materialize the basic framework of Marx's dialectical critique of capitalist automation, now exported from the public site of the factory into the private domain of consumption and "lifestyle." Whereas, for Marx, the realities of factory life—"the horrors of this sphere, in which capital conducts its exploitation against the background of largescale industry"—fundamentally "surpass[ed] the most loathsome fantasies of the [Gothic] novelists,"[35] the situation of youth consumption as a mode of cultural labor is, I feel, effectively captured, if often in a distorted or heavily allegorized form, in the popular fantasies of contemporary vampire and cyborg texts. This is not to say that I believe Marx's socioeconomic model provides a commanding blueprint for subsequent history, but rather that his central metaphor of the cybernetic vampire retains its freshness and potency even when the evolution of modern capitalism has far outstripped his more specific predictive claims. Indeed, it is precisely the changeful and protean quality of capitalism as an economic and cultural system that the image of the vampire-cyborg registers so profoundly.

YOUTH FETISHISM: THE LOST BOYS CRUISE MALLWORLD

THE DUAL METAPHORICS OF CONSUMER VAMPIRISM

In my introduction I focused principally on the political-economic implications of Marx's metaphor of the vampire-cyborg: how it allows a critique of the capitalist factory as an undead machine that feeds upon and incorporates workers' living substance. In this chapter I would like to shift my attention more explicitly to the *libidinal* economy of this complex figure, the model of desire it encodes. If one attends carefully to Marx's rhetoric, it is clear that what he finds most terrible about the factory is not that it is a lifeless mechanism leeching surplus value, but that this activity gives it an eerie semblance of life: avid for the accumulation of profit, the factory seems driven by a remorseless hunger that resembles a corrupt form of human desire. In Marx's words, "the capitalist devours the labour-power of the worker, or appropriates his living labour as the life-blood of capitalism. . . . By incorporating living labour-power into the material constituents of capital [i.e., the factory], the latter becomes an animated monster and it starts to act 'as if consumed by love.'" [1]

Marx's allusion here is to Göethe's *Faust*, specifically to the refrain of a drinking song about a corpulent rat that is poisoned by a cook and becomes wildly maddened, "as if"—in Walter Kaufman's translation—"love gnawed his vitals." [2] The desire Marx speaks of here is, then, only a parody of amorousness; in reality, it is gluttony transformed into tortured death throes. Through this sly allusion, Marx implies that capital's uncontrollable lust for self-valorization will be its undoing, that the vampiric hunger of capital will culminate in a paroxysm of self-consuming destruction. The valiant proletarian cook will slay the demonic capitalist rat, thus freeing the forces of production to nourish truly human needs.

Much of twentieth-century marxist thought has involved attempts to explain why this outcome was forestalled, why the vampire of capital has managed again and again to rise from the grave of economic crisis to batten on the living. Marxist critics—often tutored by Freudians of one stripe or another—have been compelled to admit that the desire animating capitalism is more complex than mindless gluttony, that the vampiric relationship between capital and labor involves a libidinal investment, an erotic complicity. As with Lucy Westenra in Bram Stoker's novel *Dracula* (1897), the laborer-victim seems in some measure to *will* the capitalist-vampire's parasitical aggression, to take pleasure in the surrender of substance and identity to a remorseless force. This is a possibility Marx himself never expressly acknowledged, yet it is often implicit in his rhetoric, which persistently returns to metaphors of seduction to describe the capital-labor relationship.[3] Of course, this sexualized language is intended satirically: after all, how could workers ever truly be seduced by the vision of an undead machine lusting after them body and soul?

As I noted in my introduction, Marx's concept of the vampire is basically the hideous animate corpse of central European folklore—"dripping from head to toe, from every pore, with blood and dirt"[4]—not the playful seducer of the literary tradition. What drives Marx's vampire is pure and simple bloodlust, and its seeming amorousness is only a sham, a coy pretense that cannot disguise its exploitative aims. Given the miserable conditions under which the bulk of the industrial proletariat lived and worked during Marx's time, these assumptions are unsurprising; one would surely be hard pressed to imagine the Victorian factory as a site of quasi-erotic courtship. More interesting from our contemporary perspective is the fact that Marx evokes the arena of the marketplace in libidinal terms as well: in his discussion of how profit is realized in monetary exchange, Marx refers to prices as "those wooing glances cast at money by commodities" (1:205). Indulging again his penchant for literary allusion (this time to Shakespeare), Marx comments, "commodities are in love with money, but . . . 'the course of true love never did run smooth'" (1:202). His purpose in this passage is to lay bare the contradiction between use value and exchange value that informs every mundane act of buying and selling. Although his erotic vocabulary continues to serve essentially satiric ends, his remarks take on added significance in light of modern advertising campaigns, with their more or less explicitly eroticized appeals to consumer appetite and pleasure seeking. In the century since Marx wrote, the capitalist marketplace has become quite brazen in its tactics of seduction—to the frank exasperation of marxist critics, who have generally seen this development as a ploy to ensure the continuing docility of the working class.

The notion of the libidinous complicity of labor in its own subjection has informed analyses of consumer institutions and practices written from a leftist perspective since at least the work of the Frankfurt school. Stuart Ewen's influential historical studies of the evolution of an American mass market, for example, argue that this self-surrendering desire was meticulously produced through the image-based apparatuses of product design, fashion, and advertising and directed toward an endless project of consumption, thus effecting what Richard Hoggart has called (in a similar analysis of the British context) the "consumerization" of the working class.[5] In brief, the capitalist-vampire made willing accomplices of its laborer-victims by soliciting their desire with seductive promises—for example, perpetual youth—and profitably attaching that desire to an ever-expanding realm of commodities, thus installing a capitalist logic of accumulation within working-class hearts and households. Note the vampiric metaphors built into Ewen's description of the results, in his book *Channels of Desire:* "Consumerism engendered passivity and conformity within this supposedly ever-expanding realm . . . which put leisure, beauty, and pleasure in the reach of all. . . . [T]he logic of consumption . . . is embroiled in our intimacies; tattooed upon our hopes; *demanding of our energies.* . . . The *insatiable urge* for new things . . . "[6] As I detailed in my introduction, Ewen's work contends that since the 1920s the figure of youth has functioned as the perfect emblem of this rampant consumerist ethos; indeed, the "symbolic ascendancy of youth represents the corporate infiltration of daily life and the creation of a family structure that might be ruled through the young, or through people's acceptance of a youthful ideal."[7]

Building on such views, Sut Jhally has argued in *The Codes of Advertising* that the extraction of surplus value in contemporary capitalism extends beyond the factory into the realm of popular leisure, encompassing everyday interactions with consumer technologies. For Jhally, the mechanisms of mass media, especially television advertising, are directly analogous in their operations and effects to the marxist factory system, and in fact (in an argument similar to Baudrillard's, reviewed in my introduction) constitute "a *higher* stage in the development of the value-form of capital."[8] Capital's self-valorization, accomplished in the factory through the incorporation of workers' labor into machinery, is effected in contemporary consumer culture through the conscription of viewing by the televisual apparatus: viewing becomes "watching-labour," a consumption of advertising messages that is ultimately productive of profit. Thus, "the process of consciousness becomes valorised" (p. 121), and desirous subjectivity is preyed upon in much the same way as the objective exertions of muscles and nerves are vampirized in the factory. In Jhally's words, "The movement of value *invades* the symbolic/material processes of human needing" itself (p. 205; emphasis in original).

The result is a new kind of commodity fetishism in which the use value of viewing—its capacity to generate meanings from coded messages—is subsumed and subordinated by its exchange value—its profitability within a system of market relations. Viewing becomes fetishized, a kind of alienated "compulsion," an "*enforced participation*" (p. 186; emphasis in original) that only *seems* a freely chosen exercise of one's leisure time. Like wage labor in Marx's analysis, "watching is formally free but practically compelled" (p. 188), and "the search for meaning [is] directed towards the marketplace as the only means of meaning-fulfilment" (p. 204). Significantly for my youth-cultural focus here, the most highly perfected institutional form of this fetishized consciousness is, for Jhally, the Music Television Network (MTV):

> On MTV the "blurring" of the content between programs [use value] and advertising [exchange value] is complete on both the objective and subjective levels. On the *objective* level we can see that, viewed from an economic perspective, everything on MTV is a commercial. Videos are promotional pieces for record albums while the commercials that appear between these are promotions for other commodities. . . . [Subjectively, in] the actual viewing of the messages transmitted by MTV it is sometimes impossible to distinguish between programming and non-programming, between video and advertisements. Style, pacing, visual techniques, fantasies and desires are all interchangeable. (pp. 96–97)

The effect is of a "pure environment" (p. 101) saturated with the ethos of consumption, in which exchange value has triumphed over use value and fetishized, compulsive viewing reigns supreme ("I Want My MTV").[9]

The broader ethical-political implications of such an argument have been drawn out by W. F. Haug. Further deploying and updating Marx's concept of commodity fetishism, Haug alleges that, in advertising, the actual use value of a product is systematically replaced by its "promise of use-value,"[10] its appealingly designed and fashionably constructed appearance, which functions as a kind of sensual bait for the consumer. "Sensuality in this context becomes the vehicle of an . . . economically functional fascination" (p. 17) that permits exchange value to assert its priority over use value and thus to usurp and distort the very structure of human needs, producing an "addicted buyer who rushes headlong after mere images" (p. 35). The manifold apparatuses of advertising thus incarnate a "technocracy of sensuality" in which "the fascinated individual is dominated by his or her own senses" (p. 45), by the incorporation of psychic impulses toward aesthetic and sensual gratification into a gigantic economic machine of capital accumulation. The result is a transformation of humanity at a virtually anthropological level: "The corrupting use-value [use value as mere appearance] feeds back to the needs-structure of the consumers, whom it brings down to a corrupt standpoint of use-value. . . . People seem to have had their consciousnesses bought off" (p. 53). Thus, as in Baudrillard, progress in technical means dovetails with the capacity for social domination, conspiring "to warp the progressive tendency in human instincts" (p. 53) into a "compulsive fixation [that] threatens to cut off completely the possibility of direct pleasure" (p. 55), substituting instead mass-produced desires and their prepackaged satisfaction. Even human sexuality is compromised by this invasive, colonizing system, since commodity aesthetics' quasi-erotic appeal to consumers, its tactics of seduction, is not a liberation of repressed desires but a technique of manipulation, "a means of solving certain problems in valorization and capital realization" (p. 54).[11]

Again, as with Ewen and Jhally, youth culture becomes a prominent site of advertisement's social hegemony. In Haug's analysis, a major strategy of commodity aesthetics is the sensual appeal of aesthetic innovation, in which an economic goal of exchange value (the necessity for a rapid turnover of goods) is manifested as a (seeming) psychological use value in the consciousness of consumers (a desire for new and fashionable objects). Thus, commodities themselves come to follow a generational logic in which their "determining aim is the outdating of what exists, its denunciation, devaluation, and replacement" (p. 42). The result Haug calls "youth fetishism"—a notion that, as he develops it, closely resembles the three meanings of *consuming youth* adumbrated in my introduction. Youth fetishism refers at once to (1) "the compulsive character of the young"—that is, the specific consumerist practices of young people, their tendency both to set and follow fashion; (2) sensualized images of youth that serve to provoke consumer appetite; and (3) a pervasive ideology of youthfulness, which "subjects the whole world of useful things, in which people articulate their needs in the language of commercial products, to an incessant aesthetic revolution" (p. 44). Thus, youth as aesthetic innovation constitutes "a moment of direct anthropological power and influence, in that it continually changes humankind as a species in their sensual organization, in their real orientation and material lifestyle" (p. 44). For Haug, then, youth is the perfect image of consumption envisioned as a form of vampirism: a figure of invasion, infection, corruption, and transformation that, like Dracula himself, "becomes completely disembodied and drifts unencumbered . . . into every household. . . . No one is safe any longer from its amorous glances" (p. 50)—save perhaps for those rare few who refuse to invite it inside because they don't own television sets, listen to radios, surf the Web, or buy magazines.

In these various analyses, the individual laborer has been irreversibly penetrated by and infected with consumerist desire, an unquenchable, acquisitive lust at once sustained by and sustaining of the institutions of consumer culture. Among the most important of these institutions, one that has become the lightning rod for much of the neomarxist critique of consumption (and one that I will foreground in the balance of this chapter) is the shopping mall, perhaps the most characteristic architectural form of Fordist capitalism. The basics of the marxist argument against the shopping mall have recently been rehearsed by Mark Gottdiener and Lauren Langman. Claiming that malls are designed "to disguise the instrumental exchange relation between producer and consumer," Gottdiener critiques the mall structure as "an integrated facade which facilitates consumption acts by the stimulation of consumer fantasies"—fantasies that "are primed by years of conditioning deriving from exposure to advertising and the mass media."[12] Langman, following Haug, draws a more cutting inference, alleging that the very desires and emotions of consumers "are now mass produced and distributed in the shops, theatres and food centres of shopping malls," which, like television and other consumer apparatuses, have come to "control norms of affective gratification . . . in everyday life." Unsurprisingly, Langman deploys an implicitly vampiric metaphor to describe the process: "everyday life in amusement society proceeds within a dialectic of enfeeblement and empowerment"—enfeeblement because the vampiric regime has usurped the autonomy of individual experience, empowerment because consumption becomes the sole driving motivation.[13] Thus, to return to Marx, the gluttonous capitalist rat has been transformed, under Fordism, into an army of consuming mallrats, denizens of what Langman—updating Max Weber for the postmodern era—calls the "neon cages" of consumer society.

This transformation has been cleverly staged, appropriately enough, in Francis Ford Coppola's popular film *Bram Stoker's Dracula*, wherein the master vampire converts himself into a multitude of rodents to elude capture. This visually arresting image culminates a scene in which Dracula—whose association with mass culture has already been established in earlier scenes set at Castle Dracula, a site dominated by filmic trickery,

Figure 1. The youthful consumer as capital's erotic accomplice. Video still from Francis Ford Coppola's *Bram Stoker's Dracula*.

and in a cinematograph theater—promises Mina Harker an eternal life of pathological consumption, an ambivalent empowerment/curse that the young woman avidly seeks. Indeed, she even has to persuade Dracula of her committed desire, a major change from Stoker's original, where she was his meek, passive victim. For the mallrats watching Coppola's film (a staple of mall multiplexes in the summer of 1992), seeing teen idol Winona Ryder (fig. 1) as Mina affirm her libidinal complicity with consumer capitalism could only, from the draconian critical perspective outlined above, serve to damn them to a similar fate.

This sort of judgment illustrates the extent to which the rigid neo-marxist view of the culture of consumption partakes of what Fredric Jameson has identified as "left puritanism"; the problem becomes "Who is to break the news to them [consumers] that their conscious experience of leisure products—their conscious 'pleasure' in consumption—is in reality nothing but false consciousness?"[14] In other words, who is to drive the stake of critique through the vile, undead heart of consumerist desire? For all their surface acknowledgement of the commodity's libidinous appeal, indictments of consumer culture such as those canvassed above ultimately endorse Marx's sternly negative image of the vampire as bloodsucking beast; indeed, its erotic attraction is now pre-

cisely the problem, and consumers must—like poor Mina in *Dracula*—
be saved from its amorous clutches. Unable any longer to experience
autonomous desire, to distinguish a mere fantasy of use value (the men-
dacious "satisfaction guaranteed" of commodity culture) from authentic
happiness, consumers must be shielded from their own pleasures—or,
better, from the very impulse to pleasure seeking, which has been compromised and corrupted at its roots. While Marx could rest secure that
workers would never be tempted by the ratlike, undead machine of the
factory, against which their instincts would naturally rebel, contemporary marxist critics seem less confident of popular resistance to the suave
seductions of consumer society.[15]

Perhaps in reaction to this puritanical negativism, a competing trend
in contemporary left discourse—especially within the burgeoning domain of cultural studies—has attempted critically to redeem the pleasure taken in consumption. Annette Kuhn has succinctly formulated the
conviction animating this mode of criticism: "pleasure is an area of analysis in its own right. 'Naive' pleasure, then, becomes admissible. And
the acts of analysis, of deconstruction and of reading 'against the grain'
offer an additional pleasure—the pleasure of resistance, of saying 'no':
not to 'unsophisticated' enjoyment, by ourselves and others, of culturally
dominant images, but to the structures of power which ask us to consume them uncritically and in highly circumscribed ways."[16] Indeed,
much of the recent work in this area has alleged that the modalities of
consumer culture—and the forms of subjectivity they enable—do not
necessarily integrate seamlessly into the capitalist society that has mobilized them but may instead be potentially subversive of its purposes.
For example, recent feminist investigations of the evolution of the fashion system and the culture of shopping[17] have argued that consumerism historically provided genuine empowerment, however limited, for
women—an agency that, according to Elizabeth Wilson, generated
profound anxieties about gender relations in bourgeois society: "The
presence of women [in turn-of-the-century department stores] created
a special and ambiguous atmosphere in these zones, which were public,
yet aimed at the intimacy of the private interior.... [B]ourgeois consumerism invaded the public sphere, and the very spaces that were permitted
to respectable women were in many cases devoted to purchase and sale
rather than to morally more elevated activities. There, women looked,
as well as being looked at."[18] Similarly, Anne Friedberg argues for the
construction, within the public sites of consumption (culminating in
the contemporary shopping mall, "a historical endpoint of increasing
female empowerment"), of a female gaze quite different in its structure

and effects from Jhally's exploited watching-labor. For Friedberg, this
gaze was that of the mobilized window-shopper whose pleasure in the
inspection of commodities was active rather than passive, calculating
rather than uncritical—though, as she stresses, women were still, as
a class, economically dependent on men and still, in their consumer
choices, subject to "a constructed desire." [19]

Kathy Peiss, while fully supporting Friedberg's crucial demurrals,
also suggests a potentially subversive aspect to consumerism: "Leisure
institutions played an intricate game of mediation in which the lines between cultural oppositions—female and male, domestic and public, re-
spectability and disrepute, sexual purity and sensual playfulness—were
shifting and indeed blurred." [20] This shifting and blurring, however, for
all the anxieties it produced in bourgeois culture, was not radically inimical to the ongoing capitalist project of commodification; after all,
economic capital is not historically coterminous with the institutions of
capitalist society and may in fact be profoundly unsettling of bourgeois
norms and assumptions (as Marx himself well knew). Indeed, what the
work of these critics suggests is that consumption may now be the terrain where contradictions between the economic forces and the ideological forms of capitalism are highlighted, negotiated, and contested,
and that the public spaces of consumer culture stage these contradictions
most forcefully. This sort of analysis builds upon a left tradition, extending back at least to Walter Benjamin, that views the marketplace as the
"dream world" of capitalism, where mass fantasy is activated as a potentially critical-utopian force; like Benjamin, these feminist critics have recourse to Charles Baudelaire's image of the *flâneur*, the urban stroller
whose aimless browsings inspire not preprogrammed, but restless and
inchoate, pleasures. [21] As Don Slater has argued, "the market as a place
of desire without obligation, of intimate fantasy in the midst of imper-
sonal anonymity, of spectacle, entertainment and play, as a place where
dreams can flow across a multitude of objects without yet being fixed
permanently on any one probably still provides the single most potent
space in Western societies in which one dreams alternative futures and
is released (utopicly) from the unthinking reproduction of daily life." [22]

Given such a viewpoint, it should hardly be surprising that the mallrat
has been explicitly thematized—indeed, frankly celebrated—in recent
cultural studies, and that this celebration has reversed the metaphorics
of vampirism characteristic of "left puritan" discourse. In her discussion
of the shifty pleasures of *flânerie*, Friedberg argues that "the fluid subjectivity of the spectator-shopper" potentially allows for the performative
enactment of labile identities under the aegis of "the commodity's trans-

formative power"—a power that, like the shape-shifting vampire's, is protean, but not necessarily demonic.[23] In a related discussion, Susan Buck-Morss, building on the work of Benjamin, has elaborated a "politics of loitering" in which "the fantasies which populate the reveries of the *flâneur* are also a form of resistance," a kind of "strike" against the instrumentalization of leisure.[24] John Fiske goes further, depicting malls as "key arenas of struggle" where shoppers "inflict a running series of wounds upon the strategic power" of capitalist calculation, "where the art and tricks of the weak" can overcome the "interests of the powerful"[25]—a total reversal of the predatory relationship imagined by Ewen, Jhally, and Haug. By this analysis, the vile capitalist rat has not surreptitiously dissolved into the mass of consumers, infecting them in the process; instead, mallrats constitute an autonomous faction infesting the capitalist's factories of consumption with their insubordinate presence.

Fiske's view both neatly encapsulates this alternative tradition and amounts to a reductio ad absurdum of it. Resisting the monolithic, manipulative system decried by the left puritans, Fiske asserts, I think quite rightly, that the "conditions of production of any cultural system are not the same as, and do not predetermine, the conditions of its use or consumption" (p. 24). Consumers are not mere drones whose only choice is either to ratify the decisions already made for them by capitalists or else opt out of consumption entirely; instead, they are conscious actors within a complex and contradictory system of power relations. But instead of going on to show how production and consumption are in fact articulated at specific historical moments or under specific conditions, Fiske entirely dissevers the two spheres: production is the site of economic calculation, driven by the profit-seeking motives of capitalists, while consumption is the space where cultural meanings are created by consumers for themselves. The two have rather little to do with each other, beyond the former providing the raw material—the commodities—that the latter appropriates and subverts. Thus, from a position that sees consumers as mere dupes whose very desires are not their own, Fiske has moved to an equally extreme position that sees them as guerilla warriors whose choices automatically generate pleasure and validate identity.

What is of specific interest to me here is that Fiske turns, for revelatory examples, to contemporary youth-culture practices. His discussion of shopping, for instance, builds upon the work of sociologist Mike Presdee, who closely studied the consumer practices of working-class and unemployed youth in Elizabeth, South Australia. According to Presdee, these youth "cut off from normal consumer power" invade by night "the space of those with consumer power," an invasion that boldly lays claim to "the possession of consumer space where their very presence challenges, offends and resists. . . . They parade for several hours, not buying, but presenting, visually, all the contradictions of employment and unemployment" (quoted on p. 16). This passive-aggressive territorialism rattles the stolid bourgeois going about their business of consumption, invites the wary attention of mall security, and terrorizes and infuriates the shopkeepers. Presdee dubs their obstinate strategy "proletarian shopping," which Fiske glosses as the consumption of "images and space instead of commodities, a kind of sensuous consumption that [does] not create profits . . . an oppositional cultural practice" (p. 17). If Presdee's marauding mallrats also toted around raucous boom boxes, Dracula himself might be moved to remark, "Listen to them, the children of the night. What music they make."

Perhaps unsurprisingly, this articulation of a subversive vision of consumer vampirism has been a project not only for contemporary cultural studies but for several recent vampire texts, in which Presdee's scene of cruising youthful terrorists has been explicitly staged. In Poppy Z. Brite's novel *Lost Souls* (1992), a master vampire passes a nightclub where a swarm of punkish kids "postured on the sidewalk, waving their spidery hands," tracking him "with their black-smudged eyes"; catching a snatch of their music—appropriately enough, British Goth-rock band Bauhaus's song "Bela Lugosi's Dead"—the vampire makes an ironic allusion to "children of the night."[26] In the Joel Schumacher film *The Lost Boys* (1987), the eponymous pack of adolescent vampires wanders sullenly through a crowd of boardwalk shoppers, prompting the owner of a video parlor to throw them out of his store and a security guard to chase them away (much more on this film below).

The competing strands in left cultural analysis canvassed above may thus be said to mobilize contrasting vampire metaphors. Those who argue for a totalizing system, in which fixed desires are imposed, through the apparatuses of mass culture, on a passive audience of consumers for the dovetailing purposes of capital accumulation and social reproduction, deploy a metaphorics of ruthless predation and dictatorial control. Those who believe rather in a less efficient regime, in which desire is relatively fluid, the audience active and even resistant, and economic capital less seamlessly articulated with social institutions, have recourse to a metaphorics of playful aggression and changeful identity. In short, the choice is between Marx's parasitic vampire-rat, a verminous beast deserving only of extermination, and Fiske's mischievous mallrats, rebellious creatures avidly indulging their cravings and caprices.

My purpose in this chapter is not to decide between these options, since I feel they condition, reinforce, and sustain each other. Indeed, this is precisely the problem: this dual metaphorics is evidence of a sundered dialectic in which critics have tended to stress either an omnipotent total system on the one hand or a subversively "free" subjectivity on the other. Despite their various protestations of fidelity to marxist premises, neither tradition is sufficiently dialectical in its analysis of consumption; neither, in short, fully grasps the contradictory force of the vampire-cyborg, in which exploitation and empowerment function and develop together. As Jameson has observed, "Marx powerfully urges us to do the impossible, namely, to think this development positively and negatively all at once; to achieve, in other words, a type of thinking that would be capable of grasping the demonstrably baleful features of capitalism along with its extraordinary and liberating dynamism simultaneously."[27] Rather than make a critically limiting choice, therefore, I propose to deploy, dialectically, both metaphors of vampiric consumption—one foregrounding a controlling system, the other a voluntaristic self-fashioning—in my analysis of youth-culture vampire texts.

THE TRAUMA OF CONSUMPTION

To see how such a dialectical analysis operates, let's look briefly at one such text, Somtow Sucharitkul's science fiction novel *Mallworld* (1984). Set predominantly on a "thirty-kilometer-long shopping center that floats in the loneliness between the asteroids and Jupiter,"[28] the story consists of a sequence of episodes given coherence by their common setting and stitched together with bridging passages narrated by an extraterrestrial observer. The broadly satiric portrayal of consumerist values and practices is sharpened by *Mallworld*'s futuristic milieu, which permits fantastic exaggerations of contemporary realities. Here, for example, is a description of the mall's interior: "level upon level of corkscrew corridors and gravi-looped walkways, tier upon tier of brash shops festooned with color-screeching holo-ads, sensuous androids selling sex, rambunctious robots peddling insurance, flying auto-shopping-carts that disbursed free samples of deodorants, expectorants, and autosuggestible sycophants, demat-booths that popped you in and out" (p. 164). The structure is so monumentally vast that it contains, transplanted from Earth, Mount Rushmore and the Pyramid of Giza. The Muzak filling this wonderland consists of "layer upon layer of erotic sighs and sweet nothings" (p. 261)—the aural equivalent of Marx's "wooing glances" cast at customers' pocketbooks by commodities. Indeed, one of the many attractions of Mallworld is the Disneyesque enclave Copuland, a "theme

brothel" (p. 262) that brings together "two proven high-market entertainment concepts—the sex-mart and the amusement park" (p. 254);
here, synesthetic drugs and piped-in aphrodisiacs produce a general atmosphere of "aleatory eroticism" (p. 258) that promotes dreamy shopping experiences. In Mallworld, Haug's dire technocracy of sensuality
would seem to have achieved its galactic apotheosis.

In fact, Somtow's novel reads at times like an extrapolation—if not a
reductio ad absurdum—of Haug's arguments. Haug's claim that the influence of advertising constitutes "a moment of direct anthropological
power and influence" achieves particular resonance in this future world,
where the dictates of the fashion system are literally written onto the
body: clothing designs "changed every twenty-four hours and were
regulated by android proctors who would spray the new clothes on you
on the spot" (p. 155). More avid mavens of haute couture resort to extremes of physical transformation: members of the "minimalist" cult, for
instance, undergo radical "somatectomies," their severed heads floating
around on platters, while the "maximalists" respond by grafting multiple
limbs onto their torsos. Consumer credit is tracked by thumbprint, and
veteran shoppers are referred to as "well-thumbed" (p. 164). These gro-
tesqueries—and others too numerous to mention—have given rise to
reactionary political and religious movements manifesting the puritanical attitudes remarked by Fredric Jameson: the "League of Sensual Standards," for example, inveighs against Mallworld's "kitschification" of
sexuality and its "Disnefying of the meaning of life" (p. 254), while the
"copout sect" denounces Mallworld as a new Babylon and attempts to
shun it entirely. While these movements are themselves satirized in the
novel—the league's periodic "Sensual Interdicts" are routinely flouted
by Mallworld's denizens, and the copout sect's views are described as an
"anachronistic disdain for commercialism" (p. 163)—there can be little
doubt that their ethical outrage is a quite understandable reaction to this
wanton scene of consumerist frenzy.

That Mallworld is not quite the paradise it seems is indicated by the
fact that one of its more successful franchises is the Way Out Corporation, which operates suicide booths throughout the mall. "TIRED OF
LIFE?" croons one of its talking signs in "a mellow father-image sort of
voice. WHY NOT . . . KILL YOURSELF? 300 WAYS POSSIBLE. . . .
MONEY BACK GUARANTEE IF STILL ALIVE AFTER PRO-
CESSING!" (p. 88) These self-immolation parlors localize—and speak
to—a general feeling of exhaustion and ennui that periodically grips
many of the novel's characters, a sense that the human project has
reached its moral nadir if not its evolutionary dead end. This attitude is

reinforced by the quarantining of Mallworld, along with the rest of the solar system, by the alien Selespridar due to its ineradicable barbarousness; forcibly sealed off in their tiny corner of the cosmos, humans can no longer even see the stars, and the result is a lingering claustrophobia and a barely suppressed self-hatred. It is on feelings such as these that the Way Out Corporation (literally) capitalizes.

It should perhaps come as no surprise that this company's most visible representative is a vampire: "the Vampire of Mallworld. A psychopath of unknown origin, this vampire came to The Way Out Corp. wishing for a release from life. Today, instead, he has earned a permanent place to live out his dread fantasies . . . all his victims are our customers. All the death scenes are genuine" (pp. 89–90). So intones a smarmy announcer just before the vampire, decked out in classic Bela Lugosi regalia, proceeds to dismember and feast upon a flock of would-be suicides, to the edification of a studio audience contemplating a similar fate. It would seem as if the living-dead labor of consumption has found its perfect incarnation in this undead monster, who turns upon consumers their own pent-up, alienated lusts, now deformed into something horrible.

But, it transpires, the Vampire of Mallworld is not a supernatural entity at all. Actually, he is a rather sad, shabby figure, the scion of a wealthy family who has fallen from grace due to his peculiar psychosis, and whom the Way Out Corporation is "milking . . . for all he was worth, paying him peanuts" (p. 96). This "little man, childlike and torn by uncontrollable desires" (p. 94), begs to be cured of his addiction to blood, and following a lengthy psychoanalysis, the roots of his vampirism are discovered. Apparently, during his weaning in a popular baby factory known as Storkways, he had teethed on a defective pacifier: "The plastiflesh had broken off, rotted away somehow, revealing the pointed steel of the milk-injector underneath, sharp and ugly" (p. 113). Confronted with this revelation—that his vampirism is the result of a trauma in which he had accidentally imbibed his own blood instead of mother's milk—the vampire is cured.[29] The last we see of him he is "being chased everywhere by an army of amorous groupies begging for a gentle nip on the neck in memory of the old days" (p. 116).

It would be easy for Jameson's left puritans to dismiss this outcome as a bourgeois recuperation of the novel's negative critique of consumer culture: instead of pursuing a truly collective solution—in which the vampire, emblematizing the dead labor of all consumers, is valiantly resisted and slain—the story resolves him into an empathetic individual whose purely personal pathology can be magically effaced. Yet this sort of reading, it seems to me, would be too one-sided—in other words, undialectical. For, following the logic of arguments such as Haug's to their inevitable conclusion, the critical problem of consumption is precisely that its social imperative now resides in the depths of the individual: it is not an external force weighing down upon and incorporating otherwise autonomous subjects, but rather is experienced, in some basic sense, as an expression of their own desire. What Somtow's "Vampire in Mallworld" episode shows, I think quite brilliantly, is the way external system and internal self, capital and libido, are socially mediated, their opposed forces mixed in the same way that blood and milk are confused in the Storkways' malfunctioning nursery apparatus. A technical modality of consumption links system and subject in an inextricable, yet profoundly contradictory, relation.

The relation is contradictory because the machinery of consumption, which should ideally function to nourish the individual, has been distorted from this aim. Instead, it generates a psychic wound that compels individuals to enact the vampirism they have themselves undergone. That the story's particular vampire is not the only one of Mallworld's denizens to have suffered this fate is indicated by the fact that the malfunctioning apparatus remains in operation decades after his birth. Clearly, the situation is one not of individual but of social trauma: a system that should exist to feed human hungers has instead transformed those appetites into a vampiric addiction. The problem is not the machine itself, but the social relation through which it operates. And while the capitalist rat does indeed survive and multiply in the growing horde of mallrats, slaying such a beast becomes vastly problematic when it has taken refuge in the most intimate psychic recesses of every proletarian cook and consumer.

Let me stress that by this argument I am not endorsing Haug's claim that our "needs-structure" has been systematically deformed by consumer culture's technocracy of sensuality. The problem with this idea is that it assumes human needs are static, that they take an essentialist form, and that commodities whose appeal reaches beyond these bottom-line, pregiven needs must evince a "corrupting use-value," a lying promise of satisfaction. Mallrats are the victims of vampirism, not because their "real" needs have been "bought off" by the capitalist rat, who manages them via the puppet strings of their "false" needs, but because the technical apparatus that exists to satisfy their needs—which are always historically constructed and variable—is not in their immediate control. In other words, the social interests that this apparatus serves are not those of the consumers whose labor it incarnates. While I reject the notion that shoppers must resist the evil siren song of Mallworld, refusing the manifold pleasures it proffers in order to keep their "needs-structure" pure, I do believe that for their pleasures to be freely willed, they must directly determine how its technical apparatus is organized. This is why I find Fiske's vision of radically empowered mallrats laughing in the face of capital equally unconvincing: absent consumers' control of the mechanisms of commodity production and exchange, the forms of agency inhering in consumption, must necessarily be experienced, for all their real empowerments, as ideologically and practically constrained.

This is especially true given the radical new technologies of consciousness with which the landscape of Mallworld is littered: "audio-video-tacto-olfacto projection devices" (p. 109), psionic amplifiers that tap into unconscious images and channel them musically (p. 53), "fantasizing palaces" where one's secret dreams take on virtually real form (p. 241). This vast cybernetic apparatus of futurity is latent with utopian possibility, capable of provoking a passionate longing for happiness; but so long as it is structured by the contradictory relation between a profit-seeking system and a desire-driven subject, its full human potential will go unrealized. Indeed, its legitimate opportunities for sensual pleasure and aesthetic self-creation will coexist with a profound malaise and a general sense of frustrated energies. As one of the novel's characters comments, "it has been said that when one is tired of Mallworld one is tired of life. I was tired of life" (p. 179). This is the dialectical paradox at the heart of Fordist consumer culture: its capacity to unleash the most powerful, exhilarating desires, and its inability finally to satisfy the epochal hungers it has itself invoked. The cynical blandishments of the Way Out Corporation thus express, in negative form, the utopian impulse that the consumerist paradise of Mallworld both enshrines and entombs.

Mallworld is an important text for my argument not only because of its dialectical critique of consumption and its prominent deployment of vampires (and cyborgs), but also because of its explicit linking of consumption, as an ethical norm and an ensemble of practices, specifically with youth and youth culture. Indeed, the novel—and the Mallworld itself—potently illustrates the three meanings of *consuming youth* defined in my introduction: it is crammed with teenage characters, from the middle-class kids playing "human pinball" in the game arcades to the gangs of feral runaways inhabiting the mall's interstices; its shops sell not only commodities but youthful images, cosmetic rejuvenation being a common practice; and it is animated by a general ideology of youthfulness, which finds its culminating expression in an "Institute for

Eternal Youth Research" (p. 178). Mallworld is Fordist capitalism, with its consuming-youth ethos, extrapolated into outer space. But if this is the imagined future of Fordism, this worldwide mall thronging with literal and figurative youth, what are the material and ideological conditions that paved the way for its extravagant science-fictional vision?

VIDKIDS GO MALLING

With regard to the first meaning of *consuming youth*, the Fordist enshrinement of young people as *subjects* of consumption could never have been accomplished without the singular demographics of the baby boom. The postwar period saw a growth in the number of Americans under the age of 25 from roughly 62 million in 1950 to almost 80 million in 1960 and about 94 million in 1970 and 1980.[30] In the decade between 1963 and 1974, 46 million new Americans were born, which made the under-25 cohort almost equal in numbers to their elders during this period.[31] This demographic bulge coincided with a period of relative affluence unique in U.S. history: from the mid-1950s through the early 1970s, median incomes rose steadily for full-time workers in all age classes.[32] As Lawrence Grossberg has observed, these demographic and economic trends together generated an extraordinary expansion of social consumption "not only by creating a huge demand for all sorts of products to service the needs of the children . . . , but also by creating an entirely new market. By 1957, the juvenile market was worth over $30 billion a year. This was the first generation of children isolated by business (and especially by advertising and marketing agencies) as an identifiable market."[33]

Though Grossberg underestimates the extent to which previous generations of youth were targeted by advertisers,[34] he is certainly correct that the postwar period—the period of mature Fordism—saw an exacerbation of this process to an unprecedented level of intensity and cultural obviousness. If youth was, as Stuart Ewen has argued, the perfect ideological image for consumption in the prewar era, it had become by the 1960s its literal incarnation, something palpable and measurable. Indeed, the statistical objectification of youth—of their tastes, values, and discretionary spending patterns—is a uniquely contemporary enterprise, a testament not only to their inescapable social presence but to the profit-seeking motives of consumer capitalism. During the 1960s advertising firms with names like Youth Concepts made fortunes vending their putative youth-culture savvy; by 1970, a book by the president of an advertising agency was enthusiastically proclaiming the youth market to be a $50-billion opportunity for adventuresome marketers and their lucky clients, while a decade later a corporate research firm was calling young adults "market pacesetters," a "Superclass . . . who have a concentration of buying power that is unique." In 1987, a book called *Youth-trends* (whose title alone suggested that teens had come to constitute an advance guard for marketers) estimated this superclass to be solvent to the tune of some 200 billion dollars.[35] More recently, the emergence of so-called Generation X has spurred a new wave of advertising frenzy.

Not surprisingly, given the negative metaphorics of consumer vampirism outlined above, this postwar consumerization of youth spawned cautionary diatribes—frequently of conservative, as opposed to left-wing, provenance—that mobilized vampire metaphors. These critiques ranged, chronologically, from Fredric Wertham's notorious 1954 polemic against comic books, *Seduction of the Innocent;* to Ron Goulart's synoptic 1969 indictment, *The Assault on Childhood;* to Neil Postman's 1982 lament over *The Disappearance of Childhood;* to the 1991 study *Dancing in the Dark.*[36] For all their manifold differences of context and emphasis, these texts shared a fierce sense of outrage at the calculated manipulation of young people by the apparatuses of consumer capitalism. At times, their rhetoric implied that the characteristically "seductive" appeal of commodity culture amounted, when its targets were preadult, to an insidious form of sexual abuse. In essence, these polemics recapitulated the logic of the left-puritan critique of consumption, now focused explicitly on youth culture.

Goulart, for instance, writing at the very peak of Fordism, lambasted the "kid business" for vampirizing youthful leisure, for cynically turning aimless pleasure into avid profit. In essence, his argument amounted to a quasi-marxist critique of the conscription of young people as cultural laborers, proletarian shoppers whose desires were no longer their own but Madison Avenue's and Walt Disney's. *The Assault on Childhood* was designed to warn parents that their children were gradually being lured into a commercial relation with faceless outsiders whose motives deserved close scrutiny. Goulart knew whereof he spoke, since he had worked in the advertising industry during the late 1950s and early 1960s, and so was conversant with the trade journals in which the strategy and tactics of the kid business were first articulated. For example, in his book he cautioned parents about research questionnaires direct-mailed to children by marketers eager for a profile of their household earnings; not only were mechanisms like these disturbingly intrusive, he argued, but responding to their lures—or others, from premium promotions to magazine subscriptions—functioned to turn children into the virtual "possession of the people who have their name and address."[37]

Judging from Goulart's alarmist rhetoric, this form of "possession" was more than merely economic, but verged on the sexual and even the demonic. In language seemingly geared to spur parental anxieties about a secret society of lurking pedophiles, he claimed that the marketing industry, in the "locker room" privacy of its trade publications, openly "flaunts its felt ownership" of kids (p. 13). Parents should be worried at permitting their children to "be talked to by strangers who have all the oily harshness of used car dealers" (p. 9)—predatory hucksters casting lustful glances at the money in their pockets. Kids who surrendered to this crass seduction became all but literally possessed. In a hyperbolic tone befitting this later author of science-fiction satires,[38] Goulart alleged that the consumerization of youth had spawned "an increasingly evident type—a person who is not a kid any more, but who is not really an adolescent or an adult either"—in short, an almost supernaturally transfigured being (Goulart called it "Superkid") that devoured everything in its path: "He graduates from kid consumer to affluent teenage consumer to young married consumer. He goes from having 2.6 billion dollars worth of toys bought for him each year to spending 20 billion dollars a year on lingerie, surfboards, motorcycles, deodorants, hamburgers, skis, mouthwash, eye makeup, phonograph records, used cars, movies, etc., to being 100 million dollars in debt through installment buying" (p. 4). These Superkids lived eternally in a "cold antiseptic magic kingdom" of consumption, a "vast Disneyland" (p. 95).

Goulart's indictment of the vampirism latent in Disney's commercial appeal to youth was subsequently glossed in a work of vampire fiction: Robert R. McCammon's novel *They Thirst* (1981). An epic tale that depicts the vampiric takeover of that capital of consumer fantasies, Los Angeles, the novel introduces its master vampire—"a dark-haired young man wearing a black velvet suit, Gucci loafers, and a light blue Beach Boys T-shirt"—at Disneyland. The theme park is closed for the night, but the vampire uses his powers to activate one of the rides, thus suggesting a crucial convergence between their respective magics. Watching "the grinning Dumbos bouncing gently up and down," the vampire "smiled, entranced, wishing that someday he could meet the one who had built this magnificent place; he thought that if he owned this place, he would never grow tired of playing here, not in the whole eternity of existence that lay before him."[39] Given Goulart's scathing portrait of Disney, the two would have had much in common: "Disney's greatest disservice to children was the persistent imposition of his lifeless dream on them"[40]—akin to the endless pall of vampire existence.[41]

More recent texts continue this basic line of argument. *Dancing in the*

Dark depicts modern youth as unmoored from traditional sources of community by the lures and snares of mass culture, united instead as "citizens in a new, commercially prescribed electronic culture,"[42] entry into which is arranged by "ritual induction" into consumerism.[43] Indeed, the very possibility of seeing youth as a unique "community" is predicated on the consumer and media apparatuses that organize and orchestrate their collective desires and opinions—apparatuses more interested in inculcating the ethical norms of the fashion industry than in developing children's moral or spiritual qualities. While one might expect this sort of critique from religious conservatives (the book was sponsored by the Calvin Center for Christian Scholarship), its animating assumptions have been common on the Left as well. Jacques Attali's critique of the commodification of popular music offers a similar view of the "confinement of youth" in "a separate . . . society with its own interests and its own culture"; in Attali's analysis, "socialization through identity of consumption"[44] has produced a "channelization of childhood" that propels youth toward the "huge anonymous retail outlets where mass production is shamelessly displayed, where children come, fascinated by the Pied Piper of Hamelin."[45]

These visions of swarming, feeding mallrats were more than the paranoiac fantasies of mass culture critics; they were observable realities. For the consumerization of youth under Fordist capitalism was facilitated not only by advertising strategies and media appeals, but—as Attali's reference to "huge anonymous retail outlets" suggests—by an epochal mutation in the spatial forms of consumer culture. In 1956, the first enclosed mall opened; between 1964 and 1982, the number of shopping centers—including strip malls as well as enclosed malls—increased 300 percent, from 7,600 to more than 23,000.[46] By 1985, there were, as William Kowinski's *Malling of America* details, "more enclosed malls than cities, four-year colleges, or television stations," and Americans spent "more time in malls than anywhere except home, job, or school."[47] A Rutgers University study conducted in the 1970s found that a substantial number of suburban adolescents tended to locate their homes geographically as, for example, "Three miles from the Oxford Valley Mall" or "Near Quaker Bridge Mall"[48]—an unsurprising fact given the eagerness with which young people took to malljamming from the beginning. A study commissioned by the International Council of Shopping Centers concluded that "teenagers in suburban centers are bored and come to shopping centers mainly as a place to go"—a recourse the study advised management to encourage. Mall festivities, including the annexation of cinema culture into multiplexes, combined with the widespread tendency of parents to use the mall as a babysitter, led rapidly to the rise of a distinctive mall culture through which, in Kowinski's words, teen-agers were "educated in consumption."[49]

One particularly deplorable result, in the eyes of the critics, of this mass-consumerization of youth was its radical destabilization of the adult-child polarity, leading to the development of a cultural dialectic in which the opposed sides began to exchange properties. In the words of media analyst Joshua Meyerowitz, American culture was witnessing the simultaneous production of "the adultlike child and the childlike adult": children were becoming prematurely sophisticated while adults were be-ing juvenilized.[50] On the one hand, the critics evinced deep anxiety that the collective confinement of youth in walled consumerist enclaves was producing a generation of precociously jaded hedonists and cynical de-linquents: Kowinski cites psychologist David Elkin's concept of "'the hurried child': kids who are exposed to too much of the adult world too quickly," while Jerry Jacobs, in his book on malls, deploys sociologist Georg Simmel's notion of "the blasé attitude" to describe the cruising hordes.[51] According to Lauren Langman, teenagers had come to find in the "high-tech dystopia" of shopping malls a quasi-adult autonomy, an illusory "empowerment through hyper-real gratification" more valuable to them than the childish pastimes of home or school.[52]

On the other hand, the regime of mall culture was allegedly produc-ing a new sort of "adult," one suffering from what Goulart diagnosed as a Peter-Pan complex: the enveloping power of consumerist paradigms imbibed in youth had bred an entire generation that was "growing up falsely, or never growing up fully at all."[53] Basically, adults had become little more than overgrown Superkids, their tastes molded by rampant youth fetishism; as Grossberg has observed, for the baby boom genera-tion youth is "something to be held on to by cultural and physical ef-fort," an immortality promised by the seductive apparatuses of fashion and advertising, where youth is iconically displayed, modeled, and mar-keted.[54] In the sour view of the *Dancing in the Dark* authors, "Increasing years seem to breed not acceptance of mortality or the pursuit of wis-dom," but "rapidly changing patterns of adult consumption, lifestyles, and leisure activities, all pursued in the hope of recovering adolescent bliss."[55] For Meyerowitz, even adults' form of dress has become indis-tinguishable from that of children: "jeans, Mickey-Mouse or Superman T-shirts, and sneakers."[56]

In essence, these various critiques implicitly deployed my three mean-ings of *consuming youth:* the concept of premature sophistication regis-tered an awareness of the growing social presence of young consumers

determinedly pursuing their own pleasures, while that of incipient juvenilization acknowledged the powerful influence of youthful imagery
and values on adult desires and decisions. The third meaning of consuming youth is crystallized in the Calvin Center study, where the result
of the collapsing of the adult-child polarity is depicted as a generalized
"youthification," a "state of arrested development" that "encourages everyone, including adults and young children, to think and act like adolescents." [57] Thus, from the perspective of these critics, the consumer—
whether adult, adolescent, or child—is, like the vampire, trapped in a
stasis of perpetual youth, an ongoing *Teenage Tyranny* (as the title of a
1963 polemic put it) [58] whose reign is as endless as the capacity of capitalism to generate ever-new, ever-youthful commodities. Like Mephistopheles, consumer culture seems to offer a Faustian bargain, a vampiric
promise of undying youth that transforms its initiates into voracious
consumers.

The cultural anxieties informing these popular critiques frequently
crystallized, especially during the 1980s, around that rallying point of
mall youth culture, the video arcade—an institution that, by 1981, was
generating five billion dollars in revenue annually. [59] Not only were these
parlors sources of concern in the relative murkiness of their interiors—
which made them potential sites for drug transactions—but teenagers'
visceral absorption in the games was often attacked as a kind of addiction, a vampiric hunger. In 1982, Surgeon General C. Everett Koop
declared that young people were in thrall "body and soul" to videogame
playing, which caused "aberrations in childhood behavior." Psychoanalytic critic Martin Klein agreed, arguing—in an article called "The Bite
of Pac-Man"—that videogames appealed to the oral-sadistic drive in adolescents, the very drive Ernest Jones, in his influential Freudian study
On the Nightmare, identified with the vampire. In the hysterical vision of
novelist Martin Amis, the denizens of the arcades became subhuman
fiends, a "blank-screen generation" moving through a hellish neon landscape: "Who are these that haunt the electronic grottoes . . . these proletarian triffids, these darkness-worshippers?" Jacobs summed up the
dystopian world constructed in gaming scenarios in terms of a stark,
vampiric choice: "one is either the victim or victimizer. One eats or is
eaten." [60] Following analyses such as these, exposure to the apparatus of
video not only ethically deformed but radically denatured the experience
of childhood, causing what Marsha Kinder has called an "acceleration of
the child's ripening process." [61] In short, videogames not only effectively
emblematized, but contributed directly to causing, the premature sophistication of youth deplored by the critics.

But kids were not alone in suffering the depredations of this gaming regime: adults, too, were being compromised and corrupted. Kinder argues that the influence of videogames may no longer stop with adolescence, suggesting that they have become a major medium of socialization through consumption for Americans at all life stages. Furthermore, just as the Fordist project of consuming youth was effectively emblematized in the mall, Tracy Davis argues that the videogame can be perceived as a microcosm of the malling experience itself, its spectacularization of perception and affect mirroring the shopper's experience of the entire glitzy, ersatz environment [62] (a metaphor *Mallworld* literalizes in its "human pinball" arcade). Thus, for adults as well as for kids, participation in this vast machine of consumption, of desire inducement and gratification, was akin to negotiating the exhilarating mazes and scrapes of game scenarios; literally and figuratively, videogames functioned as a technical system by means of which consumer appetite and attention were stimulated, mobilized, and put to work. According to the critics, the result was to juvenilize the adults who interacted with it.

Yet despite the alarmist tone of these critiques, they often tended to evince a bemused fascination with Fordism's consuming-youth project, a fascination linked to the fresh, startling powers assumed to inhere in it. While these potencies were ultimately seen as being merely the outcome of a vampiric exploitation—one that made all consumers, in effect, undead puppets of the capitalist master vampire—they also bespoke a growing process of cyborgization that was implicitly envisioned by the critics as radically empowering. Kinder's notion of the "interactive spectatorship" stimulated by videogame playing is a case in point: while on the one hand the possible "spectator positions" made available by the games "are preprogrammed to make youngsters feel empowered" [63] in ways that promote essentially capitalist imperatives (consumption, competition, etc.), ramifying finally into a "supersystem" (p. 122) of commodified objects and pleasures, on the other hand they augment and accelerate children's perceptual-cognitive development in strikingly new ways, "requiring sensorimotor eye-hand coordination and processing of visual information from multiple perspectives" and "developing skills in iconic-spatial representation once restricted to elite technical occupations (such as pilots and engineers)" (p. 115). As the title of Eugene Provenzo's (otherwise scathing) study of Nintendo, *Video Kids*, suggests, the critics seemed to be heralding the advent of a new youth entity indistinguishable from the technical apparatus with which it was entwined. [64]

Thus, against their overt intent, a latent utopianism, linked to the potentialities of cyborgization, haunted all the dystopian critiques of youth-consumer vampirism canvassed above. Like the views of the left puritans discussed in the first section of this chapter, these jeremiads have tended to stress only the negative side of the dialectic of consumption, whereby youth are transformed into passive objects to be manipulated by a controlling system; however, the opposing face of this process, involving the subjective empowerment of youthful consumers, could not be entirely suppressed. And just as the left-puritan position regarding consumption spawned a compensatory reaction within contemporary cultural studies—a response that was equally one-sided in its affirmation of an autonomous agency—so the youth-culture critiques have generated passionate defenses of teenagers' empowering connection with consumer technologies, especially videogames. These arguments have legitimately sought to combat the overwhelmingly draconian perspective of Goulart and his ilk, but at the price of downplaying if not ignoring entirely the real forms of exploitation that inhere in consumer technologies.

These more affirmative visions have ranged from early 1980s studies such as Geoffrey and Elizabeth Loftus's *Mind at Play* and David Sudnow's *Pilgrim in the Microworld* up to J. C. Herz's *Joystick Nation* and Douglas Rushkoff's *Playing the Future* in the 1990s.[65] Not only have these texts been concerned to defend youth-culture practices—especially videogame playing—against their harsher critics, in the process drawing out the logic of cyborgization those detractors had only implicitly acknowledged, but they have also at times adopted an almost evangelical tone, evoking contemporary youth as a potent technological and social avant-garde. Rather than seeing teenagers' absorption in videogames as a mere passive addiction, thus invoking the negative metaphorics of consumer vampirism, these studies have generally constructed the relation as active and empowering, transforming young people in profound and valuable ways. In essence, they have invoked the logic of playful mutation and rebellious self-fashioning that characterized the cultural-studies vision of the mallrat, but with an added apocalyptic twist. In the words of Rushkoff, teenagers playing videogames have come to represent "our test sample—our advance scouts . . . the thing that we must become" if only we can "carry on beyond the end of our world, into theirs."[66]

This celebratory attitude is more pronounced in the later studies, those produced during the early 1980s tending to be rather more careful and ambivalent. This difference in tone represents a generational division: the earlier works explicitly spoke in a voice of parental authority, as adults attempting to weigh responsibly the social impact of videogames, whereas the late-1990s texts expressed the views of a younger generation, one that has actually grown up with the technology. Moreover, this generational shift also illustrates Meyerowitz's thesis about the contemporary culture of youth: Sudnow's book specifically shows how adults might be, if not exactly juvenilized, then powerfully rejuvenated through video interaction, while Herz's and Rushkoff's works explore the forms of social and technological sophistication kids have achieved through their videogame playing.

Pilgrim in the Microworld opens with a classic 1980s scene: a parent—the author himself—entering a video arcade "to retrieve my teenager."[67] Fascinated by this "new species of public place" where "[s]omething vital is being dispensed" (p. 4), Sudnow decides to test his own skills in the video arena; purchasing an Atari VCS (Video Computer System) for his home, he launches into a rigorous regimen of Breakout!, a game in which the player manipulates an on-screen paddle to send a ball shooting into massed rows of electronic bricks. Frustrated by his first attempts at the game, Sudnow begins to suspect that his abilities may be innately limited by comparison with his teenage son, young people being perhaps more prepared for the febrile prosthetic consciousness videogames seem both to demand and to promote; after all, his son had "grown up with several hours of television a day. For all I knew extensive tube time trained micromuscles for neuroathletic competition and I was thus irrevocably consigned to the video boondocks" (p. 36). But patient daily application leads Sudnow to gradual mastery and, in the process, to a transformed perception and invigorated reflexes. "Called upon to heighten its powers of observation, my gaze rose to the task" (p. 47); soon, "I was hitting fast shots with the slightest little upbeat twist, a zestful flick of the fingers" (pp. 49–50). This newfound youthful ability finds its most powerful expression in an ecstatic game session all but erotic in its intensity: "here I am with my first authentic video experience, going for the last brick like any kid in an arcade, palms wet, pulse racing, mouth dry, nerve endings interfaced in nanoseconds, the knob itself throbbing, electronic reflections going straight for my spinal cord" (p. 59). Attempting to describe the "electric anticipation" of this "beckoning desire," Sudnow resorts not only to psychoanalytic terminology—videogames, he says, promote "object cathexis"—but also to a rhetoric of avid consumption: "Come on, Atari bricks you. I'm gonna gobble you" (p. 60). Unleashing, through the agency of video, these juvenile consumerist tendencies promises to youthen adults in both body and mind.

Yet for all the positive value of this experience, and for all the glowing language deployed to evoke it, Sudnow's views are informed by a sharp strain of skepticism. Like the critics of videogames discussed above, he often uses the metaphor of addiction to capture the compelling nature of their interactivity: "Just hook up, plug yourself in till you reach the right dosage. . . . Perhaps they had called them video 'games' to avoid troubles with the Food and Drug Administration" (pp. 60–61). More interestingly, his attraction to the technology is tempered by a sense of its manipulative economic agenda. "Precisely engineered to maximize profits, it was a 'game' whose entire internal structure was calculated to both establish and respond to the value for a coin. . . . [W]hat an extraordinarily pure instance of the very essence of a commodity" (p. 176). Indeed, though he never cites Marx directly, Sudnow's critique of how videogames hanker lustfully after the "[l]oose change in the pockets of human bodies" (p. 179) strikes a familiar note; like a vampire, the game is driven by the goal of "sucking [the player] into its quarterizing mentality" (p. 198).

Sudnow gives Marx's basic point an even more sinister twist, since the vampiric arcade machines metaphorically conceive of teenagers not only in terms of their disposable cash, but also as "trillions of nerve endings walking by" (p. 167), whose deepest instincts for pleasurable exercise and aesthetic gratification can be cynically capitalized upon.[68] The result is what Sudnow imaginatively dubs a "neuroeconomic" regime (p. 153), involving both a "truly refined marketing phenomenology" (p. 157) and a complexly ramifying prosthetic technology that shackles human consciousness to preprogrammed skills and gratifications: "Competence is possible only when action is motivated in those ways the game itself motivates it, and the game motivates action in ways proven to be most profitable in a rapid coin turnover scheme" (p. 163). Thus, just as Marx's factory is the incarnation of workers' own dead labor turned vampirically against them, so the videogame is a congealed form of alienated will and desire to which players are linked in a one-sided, exploitative relation.

Yet Sudnow never draws the dialectical conclusion implied by this thesis: instead of calling for the liberation of videogames, with their clear utopian potential, from enthrallment to the imperatives of capital, he radically distinguishes, à la Fiske, the authority of the overarching system from the quasi-anarchic activities of distributed consumers, celebrating the latter's "playful pattern switching" (p. 197) and improvisational tactics of resistance as voluntaristic alternatives to the programmed pleasures dictated by Atari et al.[69] Moreover, Sudnow ultimately shortcircuits his critique by *naturalizing* video, evoking it as "a commodity in

the midst of uncertain neuroeconomic evolution" (p. 156)—an evolution that promotes a "mutated form of touch" between humans and
their technological apparatuses (p. 202). While he seems at times ambivalent about the effects of this mutative process on contemporary
youth, his book concludes on a hopeful note, with a fleeting daydream
about his teenager as a "software entrepreneur" (p. 220), one who can
perhaps "make sure the interface stays flexible" (p. 226) and thus assuage
his father's anxieties over "the eerie implications" of these powerful machines (p. 223).[70]

Strategies of naturalization—specifically through a rhetoric of evolutionary process—also mark Herz's *Joystick Nation* and Rushkoff's *Playing the Future*, studies that are considerably more upbeat regarding the
relationship between the video regime and its youthful consumers. For
both authors, the past two decades of interaction between young people
and videogames can best be understood as a fruitful co-evolution, in
which teens and technology have crossbred and developed together.
Both authors deploy hybrid terms—"vidkids" (Herz), "screenagers"
(Rushkoff)—to suggest the prosthetic transformations effected by the
imbrication of adolescents with the video system. These new mutants
have embraced advances in consumer technologies avidly and fearlessly,
making them an adaptive success in a social environment that fosters and
mandates unceasing change. According to Rushkoff, the screenager of
today "is interacting with his world in at least as dramatically altered a
fashion from his grandfather as the first sighted creature did from his
blind ancestors, or a winged one from his earthbound forebears."[71] In
Herz's words, "ten years, in the computer universe, is a geologic era
riven by massive earthquakes, volcanic eruptions, and tectonic shifts,"[72]
and to prove the point her second chapter traces a "Natural History of
Videogames" punctuated by evolutionary leaps in technology, from the
Pre-Pong Era to the Atari Era and so on.[73] For both authors, teens stand
out as the social group best suited to weather these rapid-fire technocli-
matic changes, emerging as "our evolutionary future," "the latest model
of human being, . . . equipped with a whole lot of new features."[74]

These features include a heightened capacity to recognize and respond to patterns of high-speed data, a skill Rushkoff dubs "multi-
tiered scanning" and which, he argues, will be essential to thrive in the
coming information millennium.[75] Indeed, video interaction has made
kids impatient with traditional modes of data transfer, such as the passive
absorption of broadcast television, as well as with the settled media hierarchy of specialized knowledge that makes consumers mere receivers

of information rather than active participants in the construction of their leisure-time pleasures. As Herz demonstrates, teenagers who play home videogames religiously often develop programming skills that allow them to write their own code, "creat[ing] custom soundscapes, tweak[ing] the game's configurations, or even creat[ing] new levels, entire episodes of the game."[76] According to Rushkoff, this sort of hands-on, interventionist attitude has, by reciprocal influence, fed back into the structure of gameworlds themselves, which have "progress[ed] from objectified viewpoints to increasingly participatory ones."[77] The result, in his view, is an entirely new way of viewing the contemporary mediascape: not as a domain of commercial manipulation or passive entertainment, but as a "cooperative dream, made up of the combined projections of everyone who takes part."[78]

While I would certainly agree that the forms of participatory play cited by Herz and Rushkoff tend to disprove the more extreme versions of the addiction hypothesis, showing that young people's interactions with video are considerably more complex than these negative visions allow,[79] I also feel that they, like the cultural-studies advocates of the mallrat-*flâneur* discussed in the first section of this chapter, go too far in the opposite direction, seeing teens' leisure activities as essentially delinked from determinative structures of social power. For Rushkoff, screenagers playing videogames manifest nothing less than an epochal paradigm shift in popular consciousness, since by "understanding what a world without hierarchy looks like, and learning how to navigate it," they assert themselves as "empowered cybernaut[s]"[80] negotiating a decentralized mediaspace, rather than simply accepting their roles as passive consumers. For her part, Herz at least *acknowledges* the significant efforts at control exercised by videogame marketers—for example, huge advertising budgets designed to stimulate demand, limited initial supplies of games geared to provoke frenzied rushes at stores, and so on—but she finally defends a voluntarist system in which the decisions reside ultimately with the kids themselves: "A kid will evaluate the latest software firsthand, determine, in a very empirical way, what's cool and what sucks, and make a hardware decision on that basis. Kids have a ruthless set of criteria for separating great games from the dross . . . [and] will unequivocally trash a bad game, regardless of the marketing fanfare."[81] This "ruthless set of criteria" is presumably innate, a natural pleasure in the challenging exercise of cognitive and motor faculties, and the technology is merely a prop to assist its evolution "further up the slope of a long neurological crescendo" (p. 141).

Given this affirmative view of the vidkids' universe, it is curious that so many of the videogames discussed by Rushkoff and Herz are consistently dark in tone, with violence—enacted and endured—the main form of narrative action and the player's vicarious death the abrupt culmination. In Herz's breathless description, players cling, euphorically, to their "last desperate grasp for survival": "you were within seconds of everything going black. You're gonna die in three seconds. You're gonna die at this instant. You're dying. You're dead" (p. 64). She devotes an entire chapter to a discussion of the mid-1990s sensation, Doom, in which the player inhabits a claustrophobic gamescape besieged by high-tech monsters: "everything that flies at you seems to combine medieval demonology with advanced robotics: Revenants (skeletal robodemons with combat armor), Arachnotrons (cybernetic spiders engineered in the Hell Department of Robotics), and Cyberdemons (missile-launching leviathans with goat legs)" (p. 87). As she observes, "videogames are where technology melts into the occult" (p. 169)—where, in short, the cyborg meets the vampire, in some cases quite literally (for example, the 1993 Microprose game BloodNet, billed as "a Cyberpunk Gothic," installs the player as a vampire hacker in a world dominated equally by advanced machinery and supernatural powers). This persistent thread of darkness suggests that the world reflected in videogames is hardly the utopia celebrated by Rushkoff, but is rather a strikingly apt performative allegory of the alienated skills—the "dead" labor of consumption—encoded in the game programs. Yet at the same time, I think Rushkoff and Herz are correct to see in teenagers' growing sense of their collective prosthetic empowerment a harbinger of more genuinely participatory cultural possibilities.

What all this indicates is that Marx's dialectical image of the vampire-cyborg remains a more compelling metaphor for youth consumption than either the vampire or the cyborg considered by themselves. The former merely captures the exploitation effected by the youth-consumer regime, the conscription of young people's physical skills and psychic processes into the "dead labor" of the capitalist apparatus, without adequately acknowledging the immense potential of this epochal mobilization of youthful desire and energy. Thus, the "positive" metaphorics of consumer vampirism, with its valorization of the legitimate (if limited) empowerment provided by the sites and practices of consumption, is both a recognition of this submerged cyborg strain and a necessary corrective to the "negative" metaphorics that would view consumption as mere exploitation. But at the same time, this utopic view, if de-linked from its negative complement, can generate its own naive extreme, wherein consumption is seen as an automatic license of autonomy and pleasure.

In the concluding section of this chapter, I read two youth-culture vampire texts of the mid-1980s—S. P. Somtow's novel *Vampire Junction* (1984) and the film *The Lost Boys* (1987)—in terms of this dual metaphorics, conceived as a genuine dialectic rather than a static opposition. These texts offer compelling insight into teenagers' interactions with the structures and mechanisms of consumer culture, especially video-games and shopping malls. If their judgments about the political implications of the youth-consumer system are ultimately ambivalent, this is only fitting, since no work of fiction could hope to resolve the deep-seated contradiction youth has represented within Fordist culture.

TEEN IDOLS, FASHION VICTIMS, AND
PROLETARIAN SHOPPERS

Somtow's *Vampire Junction* is the tale of a two-thousand-year-old vampire named—at least in his contemporary incarnation—Timmy Valentine.[82] Perpetually frozen as a boy of twelve (that being the age at which he was originally transformed), Timmy has shrewdly parleyed his youth—along with his preternatural, androgynous good looks and his ethereal singing voice—into a successful career as a pop star. Worshipped by throngs of "weeny-bopper" fans, Timmy's face is plastered across the pages of *Idol* magazine, and his "inhumanly beautiful" voice throbs from every radio, singing "song[s] of alienation, of despair" with "such wounded innocence, such ancient grief" (p. 12). While the emotional pain is genuine, the result of Timmy's centuries of battle against human prejudice and cruelty, the fan press is quick to package it as a fashionable pose, the alluring ennui of "the cutest teen hunk in the whole world" (p. 249). Timmy himself is not above feeding this commercial cycle, having crafted his most recent hit, "Vampire Junction," "by running all the most popular love songs of the previous year into a Cuisinart, thus ensuring its success" (p. 234). Still, beneath this slickly commodified surface, Timmy suffers the lingering doom of a timeworn spirit trapped in a juvenile body; he is, in short, a classic example of Meyerowitz's adultlike child: in appearance "a typical suburban kid" (p. 74), his eager immersion in consumer culture coexists with "the bitter cynicism of immortality" (p. 98).

Like the Vampire of Mallworld, Timmy is a reluctant predator, the tool of a corporate empire over which he has little control; and the expression of his bloodlust is tied directly to an apparatus of consumption—the extensive media and technological system that links him and his fans in a mutually exploitative relation. Though in fact undead, he chafes at the marketing of his image in typical Dracula regalia, as in this ironic exchange with a representative of his record company, Stupendous Sounds Systems:

> "Why do they always make me look like a vampire?"
> "Well, the market experts say we should capitalize on that big hit of yours, you know. They think we can milk it for another album or two."
> "What bloodsuckers!" said Timmy. (p. 95)

Quite aware that he is "there to be exploited and to exploit other children in their turn" (p. 22), Timmy is also curiously naive, finding himself on the short end of contracts—"We make the deals, Timmy-boy, and we split the take sixty-forty. Our favor" (p. 146)—and allowing himself to be manipulated when it comes to spin-off properties.

The most prominent of these spin-offs is an arcade videogame called, appropriately enough, Bloodsucker. In this game, the player, controlling a miniature vampire, preys upon travelers on a passenger train while at the same time evading vampire hunters armed with wooden stakes. "It's more than a Pac-Man clone," boasts a corporate representative, "it's got something for everyone! . . . And with every machine they produce, kid, royalties! Fat fucking royalties!" (p. 146) The marketing structure of the game perfectly illustrates the complexly ramifying commodity system in which Timmy finds himself emplaced. On the one hand, Bloodsucker is designed to promote Timmy's music: the game actually croons the hit "Vampire Junction" during key moments of play, thus "insinuating [the tune] . . . into the unconscious mind of every trigger-happy kid in the country" (p. 146); on the other hand, the game itself provides eye-catching, hyperkinetic imagery for a series of music videos broadcast on the company's television network, Stupendous Cable (p. 212). High scorers on Bloodsucker in selected arcades receive free tickets to Timmy's next concert (p. 170), while the concert itself features holographic imagery and laser effects designed to simulate the game (p. 234). Profits circulate throughout this corporate supersystem like the stolen blood in Timmy's bloodstream, making one wonder which, finally, is the genuine vampire.

The videogame functions throughout the novel as a microcosm of this larger consumer system. Several key scenes are set in video arcades as teens interface, via joysticks, with the marketing phenomenon that is Timmy Valentine. The first such scene is conveyed through the point of view of a would-be vampire hunter, Brian Zottoli, who has good reason to be wary of the game's calculating seductions; yet even he is drawn in by its thrilling scenario and spectacular effects. Observing a group of boisterous teens playing the game avidly, Brian muses, "I need this like I need a hole in the head. But he went on watching fascinated. . . . What a morbid game, he thought. But he couldn't get the tune out of his mind. . . . He clutched his unspent quarters in his pocket and went to the door. . . . What if this whole rock star thing, with all its exploitation merchandise, its arcade games . . . was a front for—" (pp. 170–71). Brian's ambivalence is instructive: while he recognizes the mercenary nature of the game, equating its metaphorical hunger for his loose change with the literal bloodlust of the vampire he seeks to slay; he cannot deny the game's sensory and visceral appeal.

This appeal is even more pronounced for those who routinely play Bloodsucker, as subsequent scenes set in an arcade in Junction, Idaho (the site of the novel's culminating action), indicate. There, a group of teenagers—brothers David and Terry Gish and their half-Shoshone friend, PJ—are transfixed by the game, playing it over and over. PJ in particular has become something of an expert, managing to get through seven screens, "wriggling the joystick with the lightest wristflick, tapping casually at the garlic control button and the crucifix shield button and the coffin lid control" (p. 247). Typical vidkids, the pleasure they take in the game involves the challenging enhancement of their sensory and motor skills, a growing prosthetic mastery; their enactment of the Timmy Valentine role in the game scenario mobilizes the positive metaphorics of consumer vampirism, the experience of playful empowerment that is the dialectical counterpart of Brian's apprehension of cynical exploitation. Yet this sense of empowerment comes, literally, at a price, as the boys are perpetually begging quarters in order to access it.

There is a larger social price as well, a lurking dark side to teen consumption, as Somtow makes clear at the climax of the novel, when the town of Junction succumbs to a rampant plague of vampirism. Amidst the developing crisis, which has seen David Gish and his younger sister Alice transformed into vampires, PJ and Terry attempt to maintain a sense of normalcy by playing Bloodsucker; however, when they arrive at the arcade, a grisly scene confronts them:

> Glimmers in the gloom: a purple lightning flash, a grid of darting phosphorlines, a blue spiral dissolving into darkness . . . the machines were running. But where were the players? Terry couldn't see anyone at first. Then he saw something move behind

the Ms. Pac-Man. Who was it? "Alice!" A girl giggled. He saw her now. Her face, powderwhite, reflected the pink of the Ms. Pac-Man maze. She had blood on her mouth. . . .

There was a body slumped beside the machine, and several figures were bent over it. It was Mr. Schwabauer, the man who ran the arcade. There was a lot of blood. . . .

The thing that had once been Alice giggled hysterically; then she bent down and daintily lapped at a wound in Mr. Schwabauer's groin, her tongue slithering in and out like a snake's. Terry saw the fangs. They glittered electric blue in the glow of a Tempest game next to the Ms. Pac-Man.

"Play you Bloodsucker?" a familiar voice.

Terry whipped round to see, perched on the Bloodsucker, his legs dangling over the demo display—

"David!"

"Big brother. Wanna play?" (pp. 300–301)

The festive scene of youth consumption has suddenly become a nightmare of bloodletting and chaos. Yet this world of horror is clearly linked to the everyday norms and modalities of consumer youth culture: the vampires are depicted almost as reflections of the arcade environment—their faces "so pale, so luminous, you could see every high-resolution line of the Ms. Pac-Man maze superimposed like a pink window's veil over their features" (p. 302)—and their undead devotion to the master vampire merely restates their earlier teen-idol worship: "'Timmy Valentine,' she [Alice] said, and she uttered his name with that half-choked prepubescent longing she always used to have when she was leafing through interminable weeny-bopper magazines" (p. 301). Echoing throughout this scene of horror, the arcade machines continue their hungering appeals, "blinking, flashing, whooshing, booming, demanding quarters in insistent electronic voices" (p. 337).

At the end of the novel, when the vampire hunters arrive at Timmy Valentine's mansion in the hills above the town, they find themselves enmeshed literally *within* the Bloodsucker scenario, bombarded by "inane electronic pingpinging music" and signs "strobing on-off on-off" (p. 345). The house itself has become the maze of the game, and what once were playful "funhouse shrieks and shivery evil voices [and] skeletons popping up from trapdoors" (p. 345) are now dire, genuine threats. This final, phantasmagoric confusion of microcosm and macrocosm suggests that the apparatus of consumer youth culture has come to dominate the social field so totally as to demand its apocalyptic destruction—which indeed occurs, and the book closes with images of moonlight "glisten[ing] on the marbled innards of arcade games, . . . piled up at the bottom of Main Street" (p. 360).

That the seductions of the games constitute a genuine threat to youth is underlined by the novel's equation of the video arcade not only with Timmy's mansion but with Bluebeard's Castle, conceived as both a fairy-tale house of horrors and an actual site: a lengthy subplot details Timmy's encounter with the historical Bluebeard, fourteenth-century French nobleman Gilles de Rais, an infamous seducer and murderer of children. This subplot cements the notion that the regime of consumer youth culture is little more than a medieval monstrosity in high-tech guise, a modernized version of Bluebeard's pedophilic predations. Just as that wanton fiend lusted after pubescent bodies, so the apparatus of consumption is avid for youthful souls—and not only their souls: as the barely concealed eroticism of *Idol* magazine suggests, the marketing system exploits teen bodies in an all but sexual way. Thanks in part to his numerous pin-ups (e.g., "Photograph A: Timmy serious, borderline preppy, staring soulfully at the looker" [p. 176]), twelve-year-old Timmy Valentine has become the object of rampant consumer desire and is perpetually fending off—even as he feeds upon—his fans' leering attentions. The novel suggests that it is only a short step from this swooning weeny-bopper lust to Bluebeard's pederastic frenzies.[83] And, just as medieval villagers "cease[d] to allow their children to wander alone" in order that Bluebeard "might be forbidden his games" (p. 272), so Somtow would seem to be calling for a vigorous monitoring of teens' leisure practices lest they fall prey to the lures of scoundrels, of bloodsucking corporate hucksters selling *"the latest, greatest video game"* to kids too credulous to resist (p. 170; emphasis in original). In short, a consistent thread running through *Vampire Junction* seems to indict consumer youth culture in terms that strongly echo the conservative critiques reviewed earlier in this chapter.

Yet this negative judgment is far from monolithic and is consistently balanced by the novel's more affirmative depictions. As noted above, PJ and the Gish brothers derive a strong sense of prosthetic mastery from their interface with Bloodsucker, an empowerment that enables them to confront the undead horde in Timmy's mansion; indeed, their prowess with a joystick carries over to their use of wooden stakes, and as they dispatch waves of vampires, signs pop up "flashing BONUS 20,000 POINTS BONUS BONUS YOU HAVE COMPLETED THE FIRST

SCREEN" (p. 345). What this suggests is that the knowledge and skill acquired through playing videogames—and, by extension, through the practices of consumption generally—may potentially be turned against the exploitative system that has constructed and mobilized them.

Moreover, the pleasure teenagers take in consumption, although it is often satirized as a mere "weeny-bopper" compulsion manipulated by fan-idol industries, also appears at times as a positive force. Indeed, the novel contrasts the easily channeled desires and activities of mindless fans with the more autonomous, cultivated amusements of the buff, a theme crystallized in Timmy Valentine's obsession with his model train collection. While Timmy is openly contemptuous of fannish consumerism (the novel opens with him murdering a prying reporter for *Idol* magazine), he dotes on the toys provided him by Phil Preis, the proprietor of a New York hobby shop, whom he protects from the depredations of his vampire minions. Phil's unpretentious Magical Greenwich Village Junction—hidden away in "a converted brownstone on a side street, tucked between rival undertakers" (p. 37)—emerges in the novel as a redemptive utopian alternative to the endless glitz and cynical hype of Stupendous Sound Systems. While this valorization of face-to-face exchange in a small-shop setting is in part merely a petit-bourgeois reaction to the soulless anonymity of corporate commodity culture, it also shows that consumer pleasure is not in and of itself irremediably corrupt. One of the few touching scenes in this rather gruesome novel features Timmy sitting on his bedroom floor, surrounded by lines of track and piles of *Model Railroader* magazine, absorbed in childish play.[84]

Timmy's role as the center of readerly identification and empathy in the novel (indeed, the story chronicles the process of his gradual humanization, his acquisition of feelings of compassion and love) suggests an important distinction between the playful vampirism he represents and the more predatory kind exercised by Stupendous Sound Systems—a commercial regime in which Timmy, too, is ultimately a pawn. This corporate empire may be seen as the novel's genuine master vampire, its central force for domination—though one with which Timmy is, finally, obscurely complicit. *Vampire Junction* thus enacts a dialectic in which youthful desire and pleasure are conscripted by an apparatus of consumption that both prosthetically empowers young people and preys upon them financially and spiritually. In this dialectic, Timmy is the crucial site of contradiction. The most powerful figure in the book—his senses finely honed instruments, his shape-shifting skills protean—he is also its most exploited: scene after scene depicts him as manipulated and abused, a pathetic figure of "lost innocence" (p. 75). Literally unable to grow up—a perpetual orphan, haunted and lonely—he "seems frozen in the moment between childhood and puberty, like Peter Pan" (p. 38). His music, for all its triteness, captures this sense of abandonment with its attendant longings, and its popularity among teenagers suggests that his experience is far from unique. The painful irony, of course, is that his youthful fans are forced to buy back their own alienation and pain from a consumer system that has made of them wildly profitable commodities.

Similar ironies and contradictions—as well as echoes of *Peter Pan*—mark the other youth-culture vampire text I consider here, the film *The Lost Boys*. Set in the fictitious California town of Santa Carla,[85] the story centers on a family—Lucy and her two sons, Michael (roughly seventeen) and Sam (perhaps thirteen)—who have moved from Phoenix following a difficult divorce to stay with the boys' maternal grandfather, a crusty curmudgeon who lives a bucolic hermit's life in a rambling farmhouse on the outskirts of the town. While Lucy takes a job working at a video store in the boardwalk mall that is owned by the suave Max (whom she also begins to date), her sons fall in with the local teenagers—Michael with a pack of leather-clad motorcycle punks led by the charismatic David, Sam with a pair of survivalist weirdos, the Frog Brothers (Edgar and Alan). While David's gang lures Michael into a nocturnal life of drugs and dangerous thrill-seeking, the Frog Brothers proceed to fill Sam's head with comic-book fantasies of exterminating the confederacy of vampires that, so they claim, secretly infests Santa Carla.

Of course, this undead coterie is David's gang, who are attempting to initiate Michael into their ranks. Indicating the linked empowerments and addictions of consumption, Michael is persuaded to drink from a decanter containing David's blood, which gives him the ability to fly but also infects him with an incipient bloodlust. When David and his crew finally reveal their true natures to Michael by butchering a competing youth gang and urging him to join in the slaughter (in a scene of chaotic horror similar to the arcade bloodbath in *Vampire Junction*), Michael tries to escape from their control and, in the process, to save the lives of two other initiate vampires—Star, a teenage girl with whom he has fallen in love, and Laddie, her preadolescent friend. Armed with improvised weapons (homemade crossbows, holy-water squirt guns) and knowledge provided by the Frog Brothers (e.g., that initiate—or "half"—vampires will become human again if the "head" vampire is slain), Sam comes to Michael's aid, and they mount a pitched battle with David's gang that destroys the latter entirely. Michael, Star, and Laddie, however, do not revert to normal but continue to display vampiric qualities (fangs, glowing eyes, feral appetites), which indicates that the true head vampire has yet to be dispatched. This villain turns out to be Max, who not only has been insinuating himself into Lucy's good graces but also has been secretly stage-managing David's efforts to draw Michael into his own undead "family"—his ultimate goal being to secure a mother for his footloose brood of bloodsuckers. Just as it appears Lucy is about to break down and accept his proposal, her crusty old dad appears and saves the day, staking Max and releasing the family from his clutches.

What Max represents, beyond the obvious threat of a usurper trying to supplant the boys' absent father, is the incarnate power of consumer culture itself, a localized version of *Vampire Junction*'s Stupendous Sounds Systems. His glitzy video parlor vends mass fantasy to all of Santa Carla, a fact of which he is notably proud: "How may I help you this evening?" he asks Lucy when she first enters his establishment; "we have it all" (fig. 2). When he makes this remark, Max is positioned directly in front of a solid wall of televisions, seeming almost to loom out of the massed screens at Lucy (and the viewer). Significantly, Lucy's father, who thwarts Max's plot in the end, does not—indeed refuses to— own a TV set, a refusal that is part of a hippie-style rejection of modern consumer society. This society is represented by the figure of slick yuppie Max, the master vampire who holds the puppet strings to every household that owns a VCR; his wooing of Lucy involves an infiltration of the domestic space of the home, a privatization of consumption that Lucy's children fully expect to enjoy.[86] Not only is Michael the one who literally invites the vampire inside when he arrives at their house for a date with Lucy, but, more tellingly, Sam is anguished by his grandfather's banishment of television, because he now has no access to MTV, the national organon of mass youth culture (though he is not entirely happy about its personification in Max, whose designs on his mother disturb the boy). Sam more than anyone is marked as a dutiful consumer, with his connoisseur's knowledge of Superman, his already quite settled sense of his own tastes ("I don't like horror comics"), and the movie posters adorning his closet door—a closet that also contains a strikingly colorful and diverse wardrobe. Implicitly deploying Haug's concept of the technocracy of sensuality, the much grungier Frog Brothers identify him on sight as a "fashion victim."

That Max stands in for MTV and its consumer-youth project is proven by the appearance and lifestyle of his vampire brood. Max's minions, David and his black-clad gang of heavy-metal punks, are living their own ersatz fantasy of 1960s Dionysiac revels in a music video–style cavern decked out with a giant poster of Jim Morrison. This lifestyle,

Figure 2. The ingratiating master vampire of consumer capitalism. Video still from Joel Schumacher's *Lost Boys*.

for all its seductive appeal to Michael (and, by implication, to the teen-age audience of the film itself), is ultimately depicted as a wantonly de-structive fantasy manipulated by a cynical agency of power; it is Max's local version of MTV, a glitzy dream of illusory adolescent autonomy. Against this vampiric cooptation of a rock-and-roll ethos, the film coun-terpoints not simply the grandfather's literal autonomy—a rural idyll disconnected from the mass "channels of desire"—but, more generally, an "innocent" version of the 1960s, ultimately represented by Laddie, who runs around throughout the film wearing a Sgt. Pepper jacket and whose salvation from vampiric takeover becomes a central motivation of the plot. Basically, Michael, Star, and Laddie emerge at the end as a per-fect neohippie family purified of the taint of teen-cult vampirism vended by the mercenary Max.

By contrast, the members of the original 1960s generation are de-picted as either naively complicit with power or blind to its effects, an easy-going generation of neglectful parents who have left their children ill equipped to resist the suave blandishments of mass culture. Lucy, an erstwhile flower child who thinks that the only real difference between her youth and David's gang is that the latter "dress better," readily falls under the spell of Max, and her father prefers to ignore the spread of vampirism throughout the region, intervening only when it intrudes into his own home. The militant Frog Brothers have been fighting the vampires virtually alone, while their parents—a stereotypical pair of tie-dyed dopers—snooze behind the counter of the family comic book store. The film's title can thus be taken to refer not only to David's crew, but also to the Frog Brothers, to Michael and Sam—indeed, to the entire contemporary generation, seduced and abandoned in a garish teenage wasteland presided over by a vampiric image-apparatus that has become a kind of surrogate father. That the sixties generation is hopelessly muddleheaded in the face of this evolution is suggested early on as Lucy, driving her sons into Santa Carla (the "murder capital of the world," according to a roadside graffito only Michael notices), listens to a lite-rock radio station and starts humming along to the Rascals' 1967 hit "Groovin'": "That's from my generation," she coos; "Mm, mellow," Michael snorts contemptuously, while Sam moans, "Change it."

As this scene also demonstrates, "youth" taste in music has been thoroughly segmented by generation, to the point that individual radio stations appeal to specific demographics within the baby boom population. The same is, of course, true regarding cinematic taste. Whatever its view of the pernicious effects of mass-marketed youth culture, *The Lost Boys* cannot escape the fact that it also belongs in this category. Its awkward positioning produces an ambivalence that can be perceived in the film's depiction of David's gang, who, for all that they are intended as cautionary figures displaying the dangers of teen-cult posturing, nonetheless must be made to seem genuinely attractive and fascinating, not only to Michael but to the entire teenage audience. This sort of attraction-repulsion pattern is, according to Christopher Craft, a narrative strategy characteristic of vampire (and, more broadly, monster) stories: the text "first invites or admits a monster, then entertains and is entertained by monstrosity for some extended duration, until in its closing pages it expels or repudiates the monster and all the disruptions that he/she/it brings."[87] In the case of *The Lost Boys*, however, the monster is consumer youth culture generally, and thus its expulsion is more a matter of bad faith than in other vampire texts, since its genuine extirpation would require that the film destroy itself.

Beyond the obvious material constraints dictated by the conditions of its reception, a more generous reading of the film's ambivalence about youth consumption is possible: it can be viewed, simply, as a "realistic" portrayal of the fundamental ambiguities of consumerism generally. Indeed, the film potently enacts the divided vision of consumer vampirism adumbrated in the first section of this chapter: on the one hand, David and his gang represent a delusory fantasy of youthful autonomy packaged and broadcast by Max, a seductive vision of rebellious adolescent hipness that is actually merely a cat's-paw of power; on the other hand, they are an unpredictable, even dangerous agency, mercurially resistant to Max's authority and perhaps finally uncontrollable.

The precise relationship between David's gang and Max is never fully made clear: while Max is identified as the "head" vampire who ostensibly uses David as his pawn to enslave other teens, the few scenes of them together suggest that Max is genuinely afraid of David and not entirely certain of his loyalty. When Lucy first meets Max at the video store, David's gang wanders in, desultorily engaging in the sort of "proletarian shopping" celebrated by John Fiske (fig. 3). "I told you not to come in here anymore," Max says to David, who smirks at him as he leaves. "Wild kids," Max then comments to Lucy, with a note of tense irritation. Later, as Max is returning home alone from a date with Lucy, David's gang shadows him, frightening him by racing their motorcycle engines and sending down onto his head with a crash a large kite with a comical bat face painted on it—thus mocking Max's pretensions to vampiric domination and asserting a more playful vampire identity. This is

Figure 3. The youthful consumer as proletarian shopper. Video still from Joel Schumacher's *Lost Boys*.

not to suggest that Max is not a real threat or that he exercises no authentic power, but rather to indicate that the scope and limits of his control are in some measure undecidable.

Which is also to say that the seeming autonomy of Max's teenage prey—and, by extension, of all youthful consumers—may be in some measure genuine. The profound anxieties evinced by the critics of youth consumption canvassed in the previous section of this chapter certainly indicate that the desires activated and the powers unleashed in youth by their interpolation into the market system disturb adult observers—who respond by denigrating teenagers' apparent independence as an ideological sham. Yet, as we have seen, some feminist critics have alleged that the solicitation of female consumers by mass-market capitalism involves a true empowerment, however limited it may be by economic circumstance or by the range of self-fashioning available to women in a patriarchal culture. Likewise, the empowerment of teens as consumers, however stunted the horizon of their alternatives, can be viewed as progressive, staking out a domain of desire and decision for a population traditionally expected, like women, to be socially passive, to know their place.

In fact, just as turn-of-the-century department stores became an "ambiguous zone" where the conventional gender hierarchy seemed to dissolve, so, too, it can be argued, contemporary mall culture has produced a space where teens, otherwise a subject population, move and act with the casual confidence of adults. And, just as nineteenth-century men were nonplussed by the lively presence of women shoppers, so, too, do today's adults fret over the insubordinate forwardness of the adolescent *flâneurs* flocking at the movie multiplexes and the food gallerias— and, as we have seen, the video arcades—as if the mall belonged to them. In reality, this insolent pervasion does no more than materialize the ethical privilege generally accorded youth consumption within Fordist culture. As Grossberg argues, "the privileged place of youth [in postwar society] enabled it to resist its own subordination by foregrounding the sense of its own difference, a difference which had already been constructed for it. If youth represented . . . [America's] most valued commodity, then why shouldn't it celebrate itself as an end in itself, as a distinct and independent formation standing apart from, if not in radical opposition to, the adult world which had created it and endowed it, unknowingly, with such powers?" [88]

In *The Lost Boys*, the central site of this militant assertion of empowered independence is the Santa Carla boardwalk, a combination open-air mall, gaming arcade, and amusement park. Always aswarm with throngs of teens, this venue provides several carnivalesque montages throughout the film, snapshots of sun-drenched festive abandon, with kids leisurely browsing (and shoplifting), playing videogames, riding roller coasters, cruising for dates or for trouble, and otherwise acting as if they owned the world. Within this bustling environment, Max's video parlor is merely one of a number of consumer choices available, however exalted Max's view of his youth-cultural power might be. Just across the way, in fact, is the Frog Brothers' comic book store, where horror titles like *Vampires Everywhere* and *Destroy All Vampires* provide information (not always reliable, as it turns out) for combating Max's infernal designs. As represented by the boardwalk, the youth-culture landscape of the film is a confused and confusing domain of fun and danger, of surveillance and subversion, and the teens peopling it a volatile mix of hybridized subcultures, parading around to the discomfiture of the baffled adults—who look much more "lost" on the boardwalk than any of the boys or girls do, and most of whom probably (like Lucy's father) prefer to avoid this raucous scene entirely.

All of which is not to say that teenagers really own the boardwalk (or the malls), or that their empowerment in this context amounts to a great deal more than the power to affront, to enact a mutinous posturing that is obviously susceptible to commodification and mass mediation by teen-cult vampires like Max. As Dick Hebdige has observed, "The relationship between the spectacular subculture and the various industries which service and exploit it is notoriously ambiguous. After all, such a subculture is concerned first and foremost with consumption. . . . It operates exclusively in the leisure sphere. . . . It communicates through commodities. . . . It is therefore . . . difficult to maintain any absolute distinction between commercial exploitation on the one hand and creativity/ originality on the other." [89] As *The Lost Boys* demonstrates, contemporary capitalism's fetishization of youth as a privileged category within the domain of consumption makes possible both a real cultural agency for adolescents and a cynical recuperation of youthful leisure as "lifestyle"; consumption thus becomes for teens both an avenue of self-expression and also of objectification in the form of fashion. The result is an ambivalent dialectic of empowerment and exploitation, in which teens are both consumers and consumed, vampires and victims.

The film's vision thus converges with the situation depicted in Somtow's novel. Both texts negotiate an uneasy trajectory between two seemingly opposed, but in fact obscurely complicit, metaphors of vampirism: the first, a predatory commercial regime that aspires to total social mastery, and for which consumer desire is a mere tool to be cynically manipulated; the second, a resistant youthful agency at once enabled and constrained by the apparatuses of consumption, whose full potential seems both vast and strangely undecidable. Part of the reason that this potential remains bafflingly inchoate—a vague utopian hope rather than a practical goal—is that neither text articulates with full consciousness the latent cyborg logic that works with and against their more obvious logics of vampirism. Thus, they cannot imagine youth's consumer empowerment in terms that escape the social relation of exploitation encoded in vampire thematics and iconography. In short, neither can foresee a situation in which youth might actually come to control the means of production and distribution of the culture they consume so avidly, and so can at best only construct limited forms of resistance and partial subversions—the sorts of tactical raids celebrated by Fiske rather than a wholesale strategy of consumer revolt. Of course, few popular texts *could* be expected to envision such radical possibilities, and the fact that both *Vampire Junction* and *The Lost Boys* at least capture and express—though they cannot push forward—the dialectical dynamic of youth consumption is a significant critical accomplishment.

That said, it must also be acknowledged that both texts, finally, back away from even the more limited rebellions they do evoke. What both works show conclusively is that consumer youth culture, for all its cunning exploitations, has provided young people with a degree of autonomy from the socializing institutions that have traditionally policed their development: home and school. Of course, for the conservative critics, as we have seen, this liberation of youth is merely one of consumer culture's exploitative tricks, since young people are "freed" from the control of their families and teachers only to be delivered undefended into the clammy paws of the kid business. But while it is certainly true that commercial youth culture is more interested in producing dutiful customers than independent freethinkers, it is too hasty a critical move to dismiss the autonomizing force of youth consumption as a mere delusion. After all, a degree of independence from the subordinating authority of family and school is not obviously a bad thing; indeed, this space of autonomy—though it may, admittedly, be swiftly invaded and colonized by commercial imperatives—is a potentially progressive outcome of the Fordist project of consuming youth. Remembering Fredric Jameson's caution, we must be willing to think capitalist development in both its positive *and* its negative terms: while youth consumption as historically given—that is, *actually existing* youth culture—is constraining and exploitative, the possibilities for collective agency and individual self-determination it opens up for young people remain to be fully explored.

Though *Vampire Junction* and *The Lost Boys* make some tentative moves toward this sort of exploration, both texts end on conservative notes, with a hasty recuperation of the family unit. This is a curious outcome, since both narratives have been so concerned to display throughout the manifold pleasures of teenage freedom from parental supervision and control. Of course, they can only imagine these pleasures in narrowly "juvenile" terms: while Timmy Valentine is essentially a self-sufficient child living the high life of a Hollywood celebrity, David and his undead crew inhabit a fashionably grungy underground domain of their very own. Indeed, the original poster for *The Lost Boys* clearly indicates the utopian force of the film's vision of teenage autonomy; above stylish portraits of the youthful cast (no adults are depicted), the following slogan appears: "Sleep all day. Party all night. Never grow old. Never die. It's fun to be a vampire." Yet both texts conclude by affirming familial bonds they otherwise depict as irreparably frayed if not definitively severed: Timmy gathers to himself an immortal vampire mother and father, while Michael, Star, and Laddie survive their brush with vampirism to found a new nuclear family. The persistence of this traditional model of kinship suggests that neither text is willing to push its affirmation of teenage autonomy forward into a fresh vision of youthful community. The lost boys are finally just that—*lost*, without social anchor or compass—and Timmy's passage through the "crucible of transformation" results only in an "unquenchable yearning for completion" in an "invincible" reconstitution of blood relations.[90] Yet despite these ultimately conservative moves, both texts are indelibly marked by the hunger for a liberating empowerment that Fordist youth culture seems obscurely to promise, only to slyly foreclose.

Of course, when these two texts appeared in the mid-1980s, the Fordist regime had already given way to an emergent post-Fordism. Thus, my analysis of the dialectic of exploitation and empowerment at the heart of consumer youth culture needs to be pressed more explicitly into post-Fordist terrain if we are to grasp fully the social implications for contemporary youth of their inculcation into a consumer identity and lifestyle. I turn to this work of extrapolation and context-building in my second chapter.

TWO

DREAMS OF SOCIAL FLYING: THE YUPPIE-SLACKER DIALECTIC

MORBID ECONOMIES

By the mid-1970s, when the Fordist regime of accumulation was in marked decline, the status—and the popular image—of consuming youth underwent a significant shift, the effects of which persist to this day. On the one hand, young people continued to be identified with the values and practices of consumption and were courted by advertisers, even during periods of recession, as a perennially profitable market segment. In addition, images of youth still served as privileged figures for the hedonism of leisure. On the other hand, the carefree exuberance associated with consuming youth was perceived increasingly against the backdrop of shrinking socioeconomic horizons: limited career choices, the persistent threat of unemployment, the contraction of leisure time, law-and-order campaigns against juvenile crime, and so on. If youth represented a profound contradiction for Fordist culture, it was even more of a contradictory formation in the post-Fordist context, since the economic conditions for its popular construction in terms of consumer hedonism had begun to crumble.

In the transition to post-Fordism, the vampire proved a remarkably flexible metaphor for capturing the general cultural ambivalence regarding youth consumption. On the one hand, the seemingly dependent nature of the youth-consumer vampire—whose consumerist pleasures could be seen as parasitical upon "authentic" economic production— served to vivify adult resentment of young people's "unproductive" leisure during a period of widespread economic constriction. Several of the vampire icon's essential features—its morbid consumption (of blood), halted growth and stasis (in vampiric immortality), and aberrant reproduction (through undead transformation)—permitted it to model a crisis in the historical accumulation of capital, a crisis that could be blamed on young people themselves. On the other hand, the energy and avidity of youth in pursuing a consumerist lifestyle, even amid Fordism's ruins, seemed to hold out the seductive promise of gluttonous abundance, strengthening change, and transcendent imperishability. The youth vampire could thus function at once as the lurking scapegoat for, or the potential savior of, a foundering, aging, all-too-mortal economy—a contrast that was brilliantly focused in two seminal late-Fordist vampire texts: George A. Romero's movie *Martin* (1977) and Anne Rice's novel *Interview with the Vampire* (1976).

Indeed, these two texts mark an epochal moment in the history of the vampire archetype in popular culture.[1] Previously, the vampire was, generally speaking, an unsympathetic figure, for all its implicit seductiveness—a menace to be resisted and destroyed. Youth-culture vampires were no exception: in *The Deathmaster* (1972), for instance, a vampire-guru preys upon a California commune of naive hippies until they run him off, while in *Blood for Dracula* (a.k.a. *Andy Warhol's Dracula* [1973]), the Count is a fading nobleman who vamps the daughters of a pretentious Italian family, only to get his comeuppance at the hands of their stolid gardener. The two films share a campy tone, providing silly thrills not at all to be taken seriously. With the appearance of Romero's film and Rice's novel, the tenor and tone changed radically: the vampire became a figure of empathetic, if ambivalent, identification—specifically, a disturbed, dreamy youth—and its depiction a matter of moral concern and almost anthropological fascination.

Martin positions its eponymous vampire—a nearly autistic teenager living with and working for his elderly cousin, Cuda, a butcher shop owner in Braddock, Pennsylvania—within the context of the rampant deindustrialization of the region that marked the mid-1970s.[2] In essence, the film is an installment in the cycle of short films comprising *The Braddock Chronicles* (1972–85), which were made by Tony Buba, who provided sound for and had a small role in *Martin*, and whose parents' home was the film's major set. The enveloping social environment and documentary feel of Romero's film are derived from Buba shorts such as *Shutdown* (1975), about a divisive and violent independent truckers' strike, and *Betty's Corner Cafe* (1976), wherein steelworkers drunkenly discuss layoffs and a potential mill closing. As Buba has commented, "The mill here was the first built by Andrew Carnegie. Braddock was one of the first places to industrialize, and it's one of the first to collapse."[3] Evidence of this grim process of exhaustion and breakdown clutters the margins of *Martin*'s story line: in the frequent shots of decaying and junked machinery, in the background murmur of a radio show lethargically debating a truckers' strike, in the scenes of homeless squatters huddling in derelict warehouses, in the sullen complaints of a mechanic, Arthur (the boyfriend of Cuda's granddaughter, Christina), that he can't find "decent work, with decent money" in Braddock any longer. As befits a text that limns the waning of Fordism's golden age, the setting for *Martin* is a physical and emotional wasteland, depicted with a stark, weary lyricism.

One major effect of the deindustrialization of Braddock is the flight of its young people who, unmoored from traditional working-class solidarities, are abandoning the town in droves (Arthur eventually flees with Christina to Indianapolis, hopefully remarking, "I hear there's work there"). Martin is one of the few young people actually to travel *to* Braddock recently—an occurrence whose rarity is remarked by one of the customers in the butcher shop, and underscored by Cuda's comment that "This is a town for old persons"—though the boy was compelled to make the move by his family in Indianapolis. According to Cuda, however, Martin is not young; although a typical brooding teenager in appearance, he is in reality an eighty-four-year-old vampire whose soul his fervently Catholic cousin is attempting to save.

Though the film never conclusively proves Cuda's view to be accurate—in fact, Christina thinks her grandfather is a religious fanatic who is viciously persecuting a disturbed boy—Martin himself accepts the description. While he seems otherwise normal (able to move about by day, unhampered by garlic or crucifixes), he is occasionally given to secretly stalking young women, breaking into their homes, drugging them into unconsciousness, then slitting their wrists and drinking their blood. Too, his mind often fills with black-and-white images of candlelit assignations, of priests murmuring exorcisms and angry villagers shouting— events that are either hazy memories of his long-ago youth in the "old country" or adolescent fantasies distilled by a warped imagination from a corpus of bad vampire movies. Eventually, Martin meets a depressed young housewife with whom he almost establishes a normal relationship, but her suicide ends not only this possibility but also his life, as Cuda, convinced that Martin has murdered the woman, drives a stake through the boy's heart.

A basic theme of *Martin* is the waste of youthful energy by a stricken economy that has no productive place for it, but the narrative also depicts how readily unproductive youth can be scapegoated for the failures of the system. The only employment available to Martin in Braddock is delivery boy at Cuda's butcher shop—a job that hardly promises much, since Cuda's goal is Martin's moral reform and not his gainful independence—and the occasional fix-it jobs he picks up from customers on his rounds. Despite his lack of opportunities, however, the blame for Mar-

Figure 4. The slacker vampire's "magical solution." Video still from George A. Romero's *Martin*.

tin's aimlessness and anomie is laid squarely at his own feet by one of Cuda's customers, who rails at him: "Martin, you're lazy. You're a lazy boy. Cuda, you make him work. We work hard around here." Given the impoverishment of his productive life, Martin's only sense of satisfaction comes through consumption; like Somtow's Timmy Valentine with his model trains, he cultivates a cherished hobby, using his meager earnings to buy magic tricks and costumes from a novelty shop. These he impishly turns upon his cousins, at one point dressing up in full Dracula regalia, complete with plastic fangs, and stalking Cuda through the streets (fig. 4).

Martin's assertion of his youth-consumer autonomy is directed against the demonizing adults who scold him for his parasitic laziness, yet in pursuing his "lifestyle" options he merely (if ironically) performs the role of scapegoated, cartoon vampire that his elders have elected for him. Indeed, the film itself seems to participate in this demonization in its exposure of the dark side of Martin's consumerism: his penchant for nocturnal blood drinking. This obsession is a frankly erotic perversion, a pathological desire for control deriving from Martin's inability to deal with the reciprocal intimacy of sex with a conscious, active partner. "I've been much too shy to ever do the sexy stuff. I mean, do it with someone who was awake," he tells the host of a late-night radio talk show he phones regularly. Further, he contrasts his sexual difficulty with the feeling of control he derives from his magic tricks: "In movies, vampires always have ladies. Lots of ladies. Well, that's wrong. . . . I mean, if magic were real and you could control everything, well. . . . But in real life you can't get people to do what you want them to do." In short, Martin wishes that his command over consumer objects—the only source, however fantastical, of a sense of empowerment in his life—could be extended into the realm of sexual relationships. His vampirism is thus, literally, the result of the commodification of desire, representing the total enslavement of youth to a consumerist ethos; for Martin, even human beings are objects to be possessed and consumed.[4] The contemporary crisis of capital becomes also a libidinal crisis, the failure of youth to achieve sexual adulthood in their collective enthrallment to a perversely morbid form of consumption.

While this might sound as if *Martin* merely echoes the cultural diatribes against youthful consumption outlined in chapter 1, what sets it apart from this largely conservative cohort is its alert attention to the ultimate dependency of youth-consumerist pleasures upon the general economic prospect. It is not that Martin himself, in his values and practices, is inherently healthy or sick; rather, he must be judged in terms of the encompassing system that has constructed and interpellated him as a specific kind of subject, as one who consumes. Moreover, this construction must be understood in full context: as an artifact of Fordist affluence facing rapidly narrowing post-Fordist realities. Martin's personal "sickness" is itself a symptom of the malaise of a system that conceives only one role for youth—the idleness and hedonism of consumption—but then indicts young people for enacting it. In the language of the youth-culture critics canvassed in chapter 1, Martin's world of consumer pleasure is certainly juvenilized—indeed, Martin at times seems almost a mental infant—but then, how does the adult realm of work and responsibility offer a legitimate alternative in context? Retreating into a private universe of solipsistic pleasures seems the only logical response to a situation in which job prospects, and indeed entire industries, are retreating beyond the horizon. Is Martin's vampirism any worse than the slow bleeding off of hope and possibility caused by capital flight and its attendant deindustrialization?

The film clearly acknowledges that it is the system itself, and not Martin, that has failed. In fact, the verdict of the narrative is pronounced not against but *by* Martin, in his oft-repeated phrase "There is no magic." In the context of the story, what Martin is affirming, over against Cuda, who believes him an immortal monster, is that vampires don't truly exist, except perhaps as the imaginary scapegoats of moral zealots. In a larger sense, what Martin is saying is that the Fordist system's ongoing senescence and decay is irreversible, or at least that no purely psychological or cultural measures can hope to halt the economic slide. Such desperate measures may be glimpsed in the scene where Martin trails aimlessly after a desultory downtown parade featuring a high-school band and marching cheerleaders—an event clearly designed to stir up civic pride despite the straitened circumstances and despair of most people's everyday lives. Other instances of public "magic" include a police crackdown on drug dealers, evident in a bloody scene involving a shoot-out in an abandoned warehouse. When factories are closing and jobs disappearing, the system might be able to find and punish a few scapegoats (including youth vampires), but no sorcery can ultimately save it from its economic fate.

Even more tellingly, the phrase "there is no magic" suggests that the pleasures of consumption are, under the circumstances, illusory consolations. Martin's repetition of this mantra usually occurs when he is displaying his magic tricks for his cousins—in other words, when he is at once enacting and demystifying the consumer-vampire role to which he has been consigned. This is precisely the great achievement of Romero's movie: to see consumption, in the post-Fordist context, as a mere *relegation* for youth, a cultural holding pattern. For what higher career does it make sense for Martin to aspire to, when the jobs are drying up all around him, than to continue to consume, but now in a spirit of world-weary disenchantment? His situation is similar to that of the British working-class youth analyzed in the Birmingham Centre for Contemporary Cultural Studies' volume *Resistance through Rituals*, which actually uses the term *magical solution* to describe young people's subcultural attempts to resolve contradictions between their declining economic status and their cultural role as consumers. According to this study, there is no magic that can hope to overcome "working-class youth unemployment, educational disadvantage, compulsory miseducation, dead-end jobs, the routinisation and specialisation of labour, low pay and the loss of skills. Sub-cultural strategies . . . 'solve,' but in an imaginary way, problems which at the concrete material level remain unresolved."[5]

This is precisely the status of Martin's consumption practices, though as he exercises them, he has no illusions about their ultimate efficacy; indeed, his attitude is both childlike and cynical, making him a classic example of the "adultlike child" paradigm discussed in the previous chapter. More specifically, the film may be seen as pioneering the figure of the slacker, a youth-culture type that would become more publicly visible in the following decade. Indeed, Martin prefigures the breed perfectly: he's compulsive yet affectless, media obsessed (a talk-radio junkie), and living in a world self-fashioned out of the scattered detritus of consumer culture (second-rate costumes and novelty items, bad vampire movies), but a world that he knows is quite hopeless and even obscurely doomed. *Martin* shows one major direction in which post-Fordism will drive the cultural contradiction of youth: into a posture that, recognizing young people's *cultural* enfranchisement as consumers masks a growing *economic* lockout, embraces the rituals and pleasures of consumption with skeptical irony and a bored, complicit defiance.

This post-Fordist paradox, in which empowerment coexists with dispossession, is reflected in the very form of the film, specifically the highly marked contrast between Martin's vivid daydreams, rendered in sepia-tinted black and white, and the drab everyday world of Braddock, filmed in washed-out color. Numerous scenes deploy this contrast to ironic effect, as the dull reality of a recession-wracked Rust Belt intrudes upon and comically deflates the lush Transylvanian dreamscape of Martin's reveries. It is clear that in his fond visions Martin sees himself as a noble being if not a literal nobleman, an aristocrat of the imagination on a par with Polidori's Lord Ruthven and Stoker's Count Dracula, yet somehow he (and we) must reconcile this exalted identity with his humdrum occupation of butcher-store clerk and handyman. There is a streak of absurdism in the film that derives from the incongruity and rarity of a working-class vampire. In the history of the genre, there have been few such figures, largely because the vampire's superior strength, extended life span, and hypnotic powers of mind control usually facilitate the amassing of wealth and servants. Indeed, these supernatural gifts tend to provide an alternative mechanism of economic enfranchisement to the conventional hierarchies of class origin or the promised fruits of hard work, making the vampire an upwardly mobile identity almost by definition. *Martin*, however, with its antimagic theme, radically pares down and parodies the conventional repertoire of vampiric powers: a skinny, scruffy teenager, Martin exercises no compelling hold over his victims—the housewife with whom he has an affair (fig. 5) seems drawn to him more out of a desperate longing for companionship, telling him he resembles "an old cat I used to have"—and he is literally unable to subdue them without the aid of narcotics. *Martin* thus depicts the enfeeblement of vampiric empowerment, making the film a perfect allegory for the impact of post-Fordist realities on youth-consumer fantasies.

By contrast, Anne Rice's *Interview with the Vampire* reasserts the fig-

Figure 5. Working-class vampire meets disaffected housewife. Video still from George
A. Romero's *Martin*.

ure's traditional potencies, yet it shares with *Martin* an intense, almost
ethnographic absorption in the textures and tones of the vampire's everyday life. Both texts present the vampire not as villain but as protagonist, less a shadowy creature of mythic proportion than a worldly being
whose day-to-day existence is minutely scrutinized. The major difference between them is that Martin inhabits a shabby blue-collar environment, while Rice's vampires move through a more opulent bourgeois
world, a dreamy domain of indulgent luxury. Unlike the stultifying
claustrophobia of Braddock in the 1970s, *Interview* ranges across space
and time, from lush antebellum New Orleans to the glittering me-
tropolis of nineteenth-century Paris to modern San Francisco; unlike
Martin's affectless ennui and second-rate sorcery, the novel's two protagonists—narrator Louis and his aristocratic companion, Lestat—be-
have like high-spirited adolescents gifted with godlike powers. While
Martin depicts the youthful vampire as an unproductive idler alternately
victimized by and parasitizing the sluggish energies of a waning (politi-
cal/sexual) economy, *Interview* envisions the figure as an almost heroic
consumer whose unbridled, sensual greed for acquisition (of blood, but
also of artworks and other cultural artifacts) transcends temporary economic crises and can be sustained literally for centuries. Before proceed-

ing to a treatment of Rice's novel, I would like to address the historical reasons for this sharply contrasting take on youth-consumer vampirism in the 1970s.

THE PHENOMENOLOGY OF UNBRIDLED CONSUMPTION

While one outcome of the crisis of Fordism was the evisceration of traditional working-class communities through deindustrialization—a bleeding off of productive energies reflexively blamed, in *Martin*, on the vampiric tendencies of idle youth—a countervailing effect was the increasing enfranchisement of new class identities whose stake in the capitalist economy differed from that of industrial labor. Leaving aside the question of whether the waning of Fordism coincided with the emergence of a "postindustrial" regime of socioeconomic organization (an issue I will take up more fully in chapter 4), sociologists generally agree that the 1960s and 1970s saw the consolidation of a "new middle class" linked to the growth in service industries and the spread of "soft" technologies.[6]

A systematic analysis of this process, upon which theorists of post-Fordism have consistently drawn,[7] is provided by Pierre Bourdieu in his book *Distinction* (1984), which carefully anatomizes the "new bourgeoisie" as not only an economic but also a psychological formation. According to Bourdieu,

> The new bourgeoisie is the initiator of the ethical retooling required by the new economy from which it draws its power and profits, whose functioning depends as much on the production of needs and consumers as on the production of goods. The new logic of the economy rejects the ascetic ethic of production and accumulation, based on abstinence, sobriety, saving and calculation, in favour of a hedonistic morality of consumption, based on credit, spending and enjoyment. This economy demands a social world which judges people by their capacity for consumption, their "standard of living," their life-style, as much as by their capacity for production. It finds ardent spokesmen in the new bourgeoisie of the vendors of symbolic goods and services, the directors and executives of firms in tourism and journalism, publishing and the cinema, fashion and advertising, decoration and property development.[8]

Socioeconomically positioned beneath this service elite is the "new petite bourgeoisie" who staff these consumer industries and whose psychological profile is similar to that of their employers: rejecting an ethic of "duty" in favor of an ethic of "fun," they are "predisposed to play a vanguard role in the struggles over everything concerned with the art of living, in particular, domestic life and consumption, relations between the sexes and the generations, the reproduction of the family and its values" (366–67).

In Bourdieu's analysis, these new social groups, because they are de-linked from the ethical norms and structures of feeling of traditional industrial class formations, "see themselves as unclassifiable," as un-moored from invidious social determinations and restrictive moral pre-scriptions—"a sort of dream of social flying, a desperate effort to defy the gravity of the social field" (p. 370). Building on this view, Martyn Lee argues that the desperation of what he calls the "new consumption classes" derives from their "feeling of ontological absence and lack which ensues when cultural identity becomes unbridled from the previ-ously fixed, or at least the relatively stable, class, racial, sexual, religious and other social coordinates that have traditionally given meaning to an individual's experience of time and place." The new bourgeoisie and petite bourgeoisie have responded to their "failure to achieve a fully cen-tered subjectivity" by valorizing precisely this lack of definition, this ab-sence, as the mark of a superiority to the mundane conditionings asso-ciated with the social stratifications of industrial capitalism.[9] Yet at the same time, as Bourdieu has shown in scathing detail, these resolutely declassed classes cannot shake the vague sense of being déclassé, and so they attempt to "acquire on credit, i.e. before its due time, the attributes of the legitimate life-style"—a "mock luxury" that mimics the sumptu-ary leisure of the capitalist elite and a mock connoisseurship that mimics the highbrow tastes of the intellectual classes.[10]

Sociologist Sharon Zukin has described the emergence of an urban "loft lifestyle" that aligns with Bourdieu's analysis. This development was linked directly to the patterns of deindustrialization and capital flight that marked the late 1960s and 1970s: "the movement of industry and investment out of old manufacturing centers made larger, more im-pressive lofts available for alternate uses."[11] The gentrification of these areas functioned to "provide [the] new middle classes with the collec-tive identity and social credentials for which they strive,"[12] producing a spatial horizon within which their consumption strategies were vali-dated. Seemingly free-floating urban enclaves inhabiting the hollowed-out shells of industrial culture, these neighborhoods gave free rein to what Zukin calls the "artistic mode of production"—a pattern of "capital-intensive, rather than labor-intensive, production processes and indi-vidualized, rather than collective, consumption"[13] that has come to characterize the post-Fordist economy. Yet for all the air of luxurious renewal and leisurely renascence enveloping these centers of financial speculation and credit spending, Zukin argues that their consolidation came at the expense of those forces and relations they had displaced: "While blue-collar labor recedes from the heart of the financial city, an image is created that the city's economy has arrived at a post-industrial plateau. At the very least, this displaces issues of industrial labor relations to another terrain. . . . Once the manufacturers' clusters have been busted, and their premises changed to residential or commercial use, there simply is no site where production replacement can start up. This literally forces a complete conversion of the infrastructure, and the economy, to nonproductive activity." [14]

In short, even as they expressed and helped to create new forms of economic and social organization, consumer needs and strategies, modes of fashion and lifestyles, the new gentry were feeding off and bleeding dry the moribund husk of industrial capitalism. Yet rather than being scapegoated like Martin, these new-bourgeois vampires were basically valorized as a class of superior beings in Rice's *Interview*, which shared with *Martin* the prescient identification of an emergent youth-consumer identity that would burst fully into the popular consciousness only in the following decade—in this case, not the slacker but the young urban professional, or "yuppie." [15] Indeed, Rice's first novel set a pattern for much subsequent vampire fiction and film—including especially her sequel, *The Vampire Lestat* (1985), and Tony Scott's film *The Hunger* (1983; based on Whitley Streiber's 1981 novel), in which the figure of the yuppie vampire emerges as an exalted representative of the so-called economic revival that marked the Reaganite 1980s. Though this salvational rebirth was ultimately as illusory as the vampire's undead imitation of life—a temporary resuscitation effected by the sorcery of federal tax cuts, corporate speculation, and individual credit spending—there can be no denying the popular appeal of the yuppie vampire as a role-playing option, a consumer choice, during the late 1970s and 1980s—a trend established by Rice's *Interview*, which achieved a cult status that eventually propelled her subsequent titles onto the best-seller lists.

What novels like Rice's and films like *The Hunger* have accomplished is to provide, for the otherwise socially rootless new classes, a compelling fictive genealogy: they are the survivors of an aristocratic elite, born to the privilege of leisure, a privilege sustained through their literal immortality. Moreover, their luxurious tastes support an entire invisible army of servants and artisans, inferior but necessary creatures whose labor they drain along with their lifeblood. Yet for all the blatantly ideological purposes of these texts, their exposure of the essential "dark side" of the vampire icon suggests the subversive persistence of a critical dimension in their celebratory portraits of unchecked consumption. As Paul Leinberger and Bruce Tucker have observed in their discussion of yuppies, even the worst excesses of their "radical materialism" contained a therapeutic function: "By living out the logic of their creed to the fullest, they exposed the folly of believing that every desire should be gratified. . . . By putting their own inner natures on public display, they demonstrated that the inner nature could be ugly, indeed." [16]

Just as *Martin* can be read as a meditation on deindustrialization and the social marginalization of working-class youth, so Rice's *Interview with the Vampire* stands as the quintessential allegory of gentrification and the cultural enfranchisement of the new bourgeoisie—in their ethos, if not always in their persons, decidedly "youthful." As Mike Featherstone has argued, this class is driven by a "new narcissism where individuals seek to maximize and experience the range of sensations available" [17]—Bourdieu's pursuit of consumerist "fun" as opposed to industrialist "duty." This youthful ethos finds its perfect milieu in the *Soft City* anatomized by Jonathan Raban in his brilliantly impressionistic 1974 study—a text that offers a virtual guidebook to Rice's New Orleans, Paris, and San Francisco. Indeed, Raban's discussion of the emergence of a new form of urbanism provided David Harvey with the springboard for his analysis of post-Fordist culture. [18]

According to Raban, the contemporary city is a dreamy space of melodrama and magic, of unfixed and playfully slippery identities—a glittering, mall-like "emporium of styles" within which subsist "multitudes of contracted, superstitious cities, sequestered places with clear boundaries, rituals and customs." These isolated "manifestations of magical cosmologies" contain charmed "urban spacemen, floating alone in capsules of privacy, defying the gravity of the city" [19]—a description eerily echoing Bourdieu's remark about the new classes' "dream of social flying." Raban affirms the starkly individualistic—indeed, virtually solipsistic—idealism of this mystical urbanism (in a passage I have parenthetically tweaked to suggest its convergence with Rice's vision): "The truth is one of an ultimate privacy, in which the [vampire] self, cosseted and intensified, internalises the world outside, and sees the city as a shadow-show of its own [deathless] impulses and movements. Privacy and reality are profoundly equated, so that what is most real is located in the deepest recesses of the [immortal] self. The external world turns into an epic [vampire] movie, supplying details [and victims] on which to feed one's fantasies [and bloodlusts]" (p. 174).

In the last analysis, according to Raban, the urban perspective is essentially childlike, "in touch with dark, para-rational, para-urban forces" (p. 179), and motivated by a child's restless fantasy and self-aggrandizing narcissism. From the perspective of Jean Baudrillard, this attitude is essentially a "planned narcissism," differing from the polymorphously perverse infantile variety in being a settled mechanism of social control, "a managed and functional exaltation of beauty as the exploitation and exchange of signs" [20]—in other words, yet another form of dead social labor. That this new urban ethos should have been crystallized in the figure of the youth-consumer vampire is thus unsurprising.

Anyone who has read Anne Rice's *Interview with the Vampire*—or seen the 1994 Neil Jordan film based upon it—can recognize the basic psycho-geography of the story in Raban's descriptions.[21] Rice's vampires are an exalted gentry floating above the scenes of the street (in later novels, starting with *Queen of the Damned* in 1988, Lestat literally flies), picking and choosing their human victims as one would shop for goods; their undead perceptions, quickened to a tremulous pitch, transform the entire social field into an aestheticized wonderland of consumption, an unending procession of "rich feasts." [22] The metropolitan sites they inhabit become sumptuous smorgasbords of desire and fantasy, a never-ending pulse and flow of sensation upon which they avidly feed, and through which they move in a cloak of privacy thrown up by the cities' anonymous sprawl of fabulation.[23] As narrator Louis describes this lofty lifestyle, "New Orleans, a magical and magnificent place to live. In which a vampire, richly dressed and gracefully walking through the pools of light of one gas lamp after another might attract no more notice in the evening than hundreds of other exotic creatures" promenading through the night (p. 40). "It was detachment . . . , a sublime loneliness with which Lestat and I moved through the world of mortal men" (p. 38).

Rice's vampires perfectly crystallize the sense of "ontological absence" Lee has identified as the psychological crux—and presumptive superiority—of the new consumption classes: after all, who could be more fully "unbridled from the previously fixed . . . social coordinates that have traditionally given meaning to an individual's experience of time and place" than a vampire, whose existential lack includes humanity itself? The basic plot of *Interview* is the slow education of the narrator, Louis, into the exquisitely vivid, almost hallucinatory, lifestyle of privatized consumption characteristic of the new bourgeoisie; this tutoring is effected by Lestat, who has transformed Louis into a vampire partly to have a companion to share his intense pleasures, but also to have someone to manage his financial affairs (pp. 38–39). He soon also converts a young girl, Claudia, who joins the pair to form almost a parody of a yuppie family luxuriating in wealth. As Louis explains, "We lived . . . in one of my new Spanish town houses in the Rue Royale, a long, lavish upstairs flat above a shop . . . , a hidden court behind us. . . . Lestat bought the very latest imports from France and Spain: crystal chandeliers and Oriental carpets, silk screens with painted birds of paradise. . . . All this Claudia found wondrous, with the quiet awe of an unspoiled child, and marvelled when Lestat hired a painter to make the walls of her room a magical forest of unicorns and golden birds" (pp. 99–100).

Actually, Claudia is far from an "unspoiled child"; gradually she becomes, as the decades pass and her mind matures in her infant body, a fiercely cynical voluptuary, the perfect incarnation of consumer narcissism—as well as yet another example, like Timmy Valentine in *Vampire Junction*, of the "adultlike child" paradigm. Louis describes the transmutation: "There was something dreadfully sensual about her lounging on the settee in a tiny nightgown of lace and stitched pearls; she became an eerie and powerful seductress . . . drinking blood from a crystal glass" (p. 104). Her killings and feedings, if still impelled by a child's feral hunger, come to have a cold adult brutality about them.

At the same time, for all her surface sophistication and cruelty, Claudia is driven by a desperate longing for the human mother and the mundane childhood she has lost—thus suggesting a youthful resistance to the peremptory promotion to consumer autonomy. Yet, unlike Michael, Star, and Laddie in *The Lost Boys*, returning to the "normal" family is no longer a viable option for Rice's vampires; while consanguinity remains for them an organic relation—they reproduce by infusing the elixir of their deathless blood into a dying mortal—it has nothing to do with conventional ties of kinship. The latter have instead become mere models of affinity, consumer options, casual role-playing games to while away a languid eternity. Thus, Claudia surrounds herself with a whimsical succession of human "mothers," only to murder them one by one when they come to bore her. She does eventually convert one of these women, Madeleine, into a vampire in order to share her existence, but even vampire relationships tend toward evanescence; though their pairings may last for centuries, they gradually tire of one another, aspire to fresher company, and move on. Like the average yuppie, they practice serial monogamy, and their divorces can be similarly fraught (Louis joins Claudia in a plot to kill Lestat, for example). In the final analysis, Rice's vampires are loners, the purest of individuals because literally purged of mortal blood ties, exalted nihilists obscurely haunted by a dream of what real human life might once have been.[24]

It is interesting to observe that *Martin*, on the other hand, emphatically depicts family relations as powerful constraints on vampiric freedom. Indeed, if we are to believe Cuda's rather dotty family history, vampirism is a hereditary defect that crops up from time to time, demanding a closing of ranks to protect the defective child but also a strict paternalistic oversight of its potentially compromising behaviors. Like the fathers of ancient Rome, the clan's patriarchs are empowered to slay their miscreant offspring. While Romero's depiction of this domestic tyranny is viciously satirical—our sympathies are solidly with the mutant Martin, even if he is a perverted killer—the mere portrayal of family as a smothering web of manipulation remarks the emotional gravity of the institution. The public network of connection Romero counterpoints to its private tentacles—talk radio—is a harmless nonsense by comparison, a frothy babble among faceless strangers. Thus, the working-class vampire text (of which, as noted above, *Martin* is one of the very few examples)[25] tends to mediate the economic forces the vampire crystallizes—in this case, deindustrialization—through the structures of family and domestic exchange. Martin's idle youthful consumption, for all the metaphorical menace it poses to a waning local economy, is finally no more than a pathetic fantasy of autonomy when confronted with the rigid phallic discipline of Cuda's stake and hammer.

By contrast, the yuppie vampire text depicts its rootless children of the night as exposed directly to the pulsations of capital, which have "pitilessly torn asunder the motley feudal ties that bound" the vampire to its "natural" life and have "left remaining no other nexus between [vampire] and man than . . . naked, shameless, direct, brutal exploitation."[26] "Vampires are killers," Lestat lectures Louis. "Predators. Whose all-seeing eyes were meant to give them detachment. The ability to see a human life in its entirety, not with any mawkish sorrow but with a thrilling satisfaction in being the end of that life, in having a hand in the divine plan."[27] The social enfranchisement of the new consumption classes, which came at the price of gutting traditional industrial communities, is here glossed as an irresistible capitalist necessity, and the vampire is the metaphorical agent of its invisible hand. Merely human sentiments and hesitations can hardly be expected to deter "lone predators" who "seek no more for companionship than cats in the jungle" (p. 84).

This stark portrait of heedless greed and arrogance is not entirely fair to the book, however: in fact, Rice balances Lestat's icy savagery against Louis's abiding ethical qualms about their bloodthirsty lifestyle. Yet as the narrative proceeds, Louis's moral compunctions are gradually overcome—not so much by Lestat's persistent, carping ridicule of his bleeding-heart waffling as by his own dawning recognition that he no longer views his "pulsing victims" with human empathy but rather "with some new detachment and need" (pp. 98–99). Though he never quite stoops to Lestat's and Claudia's feline playfulness with their prey, his driving urge to consume is finally impossible to quell, and eventually the tattered shreds of his conscience enforce little more than an anticipatory deferral of his dire feasts: "I would let the first few hours of the evening accumulate in quiet, as hunger accumulated in me, till the drive grew almost too strong, so that I might give myself to it all the more completely, blindly" (p. 113). When he kills and feeds at last, it is with intense, ravening pleasure; indeed, perhaps the novel's most memorable single feature is its breathless eroticization of a frankly murderous consumption.

Ultimately, the "accumulation" that overcomes Louis is that of capital itself, whose fabrication and exacerbation of unquenchable thirsts has attained a pitch of otherworldly morbidity. Again, Lestat instructs: "You will be filled, Louis, as you were meant to be, with all the life you can hold; and you will have hunger when that's gone for the same, and the same, and the same" (p. 83). For all its exhaustive evocation of the phenomenology of unbridled consumption, however, what is missing from *Interview* is any sense of the technological underpinnings—the hidden dead labor—supporting this morbid process of accumulation. But then, Rice's occlusion of the material basis of historical consumerism will be more than adequately corrected in her sequel (published nine years later, on the heels of Ronald Reagan's triumphal reelection), wherein the eponymous hero of *The Vampire Lestat*—that cynically seductive apologist for unrestrained egoism and lustful avarice—shows up (where else?) on MTV.

PUNK NIHILISTS AND DONNER PARTY BARBIES

I discuss Lestat's career as a youth-culture icon in chapter 3; for the moment, however, it is instructive to consider how Rice's *Interview*, like Romero's *Martin*, marked an epochal moment in the history of the youth-consumer vampire. In counterpoint to *Martin*'s depiction of the emergence of the slacker vampire in response to the fallout of deindustrialization among working-class teenagers in the 1970s, *Interview* shows a second developmental trajectory of the image of consuming youth during the post-Fordist transition: an emphatic, almost hysterical reendorsement of the values and practices of consumption, raised to new heights of intensity. Indeed, these two texts have been seminal in generating opposed youth-vampire traditions over the last two decades: on the one hand, novels and films foregrounding poverty, punkish posturing, and a bleak, aimless nihilism;[28] on the other hand, fictions featuring unchecked greed, preening narcissism, and fashionable pseudoaristocratic pretensions.[29] While the latter tradition shows the growing enfranchisement of the new consumption classes, the former depicts the fate of marginalized working-class subcultures, disillusioned slackers shut out of the yuppie dream.

These traditions have developed not only in counterpoint, but dialectically, in critical response to one another. John Skipp and Craig Spector's *Light at the End* (1986), perhaps the first slacker vampire novel produced in the wake of *Martin*, openly engages with Rice's *Interview*. Set amidst "the strange concerns of young media freaks: movies, music, comics, books, and video,"[30] the story features a "spiky-headed little bastard" (p. 99) of a punk vampire named Rudy Pasko. In an intertextually fascinating scene, Rudy, while killing time in a prospective victim's apartment, stumbles upon a paperback copy of Rice's novel; as he "flip[s] absently through it," he becomes "riveted to a particular passage"—namely, Lestat's harsh evangel, quoted above, hymning vampires as glorious predators who take "a thrilling satisfaction in being the end of [a human] life, in having a hand in the divine plan." *"That's nice,* Rudy observed. *I don't know about this 'divine plan' crap, but that's very, very nice. I like that"* (p. 120; emphasis in original). To Rudy, the title of Rice's book, with its suggestion of media stardom, conveys "a touch of glamour," and he indulges an ironic fantasy of fame: "'Why, yes, Johnny, I've killed over ten thousand people,' he said out loud, imagining himself on the *Tonight Show*, Ed McMahon's mangled body at his feet. 'And you're next'" (p. 120). In this clever scene, the slacker vampire— though down at the heel and even homeless (Rudy lives in the New York subway)—pretentiously assumes the glamorous identity of the yuppie vampire, in the process exposing the implicit nihilism of its exalted, self-aggrandizing pomposity. In its place, Rudy substitutes overt "Nihilism, Punk, and the Death of the Future"—as the title of a sociology thesis inspired by Rudy puts it (p. 36).

Clearly, Rudy is a classic punk in appearance and behavior: when first we encounter him, defacing theater posters on a subway platform, he has mascara-smudged eyes, sports "a bleached blond rockabilly pompadour," and is "dressed entirely in black: tight jeans, artfully ripped sweatshirt, spiked wrist bands, leather boots" (p. 10). As this description, with its artful deployment of the adjective "artfully," indicates, Rudy's seedy, disheveled attire is wholly calculated, designed to convey—in the words of Dick Hebdige's influential analysis of punk style—a "raga-muffin look ('unkempt' but meticulously coutured)." According to Heb-dige, this fashionable antifashion underlined teenage punks' sense of an "unmitigated exile, voluntarily assumed"—a defiant alienation from so-ciety that Neil Nehring, in his study of punk, has traced to feelings of "economic hopelessness." In Nehring's analysis, the punk subculture's rhetoric of "anarchy" and spiritual "vacancy" was a consciously polemi-cal response to the crisis of postwar capitalism in the 1970s, to the pain-ful "transition between [a] period of increasing consumption and one where the expectations of that phase ha[d] been frustrated."[31] In short, the 1970s punk was a prototype of the 1990s slacker: a youthful con-sumer shrewdly attuned to the empty promises of a waning Fordist affluence.

This is not to say that Skipp and Spector's portrait of punk nihilism is wholly sympathetic; while we are invited to share Rudy's viewpoint at times, the general thrust of the novel is to depict him as a haughty po-seur no less ridiculous in his way than Rice's Lestat. What is most inter-esting about *The Light at the End* is in fact its ambivalence, its dubious portraits of both slacker *and* yuppie vampires: on the one hand, it pres-ents Rudy as authentically vile, a literal incarnation of all the put-on horrors of punk rebellion, his "dissipated, lean, vampish look"[32] signi-fying the pallid emptiness of a decadent culture; on the other hand, it clearly endorses Rudy's sneering contempt for Rice's tony new-class vampires, whose lush, gentrified cities lie a good distance away from the blighted urban landscape—trash-strewn, crime-ridden, a permanent as-sault on the nerves and the spirit—that the narrative powerfully evokes.

A novel by British author Anne Billson, *Suckers* (1993), shows the extent to which the yuppie vampire novel has begun, dialectically, to incorporate the negativism of this punk/slacker critique into its very fabric. Indeed, the book is a full-blown satire of yuppiedom, rendering explicit the social processes Rice's first novel had clothed as allegory. The setting is the depressed Docklands area of London's East End, a traditional working-class community that has been radically trans-formed by successive waves of deindustrialization and gentrification.[33] Thanks to a sudden influx of multinational capital, its moribund facto-ries and warehouse districts are giving way to a trendy landscape of lofts, bistros, shops, and clubs. Presiding over this immense transformative process is Multiglom, the media wing of a quintessentially post-Fordist,

European-Japanese consortium called Dragosh Inc., which is busily merging with, hostilely taking over, and otherwise usurping most of the local service and communications industries, consolidating them into a vast apparatus of monolithic cultural authority.

This macroeconomic vampirism—the metaphor reinforced by the fact that the corporation is actually run by a cabal of bloodsuckers—has microeconomic effects in the consumer sphere. Multiglom's growing stranglehold over the mass media has subjected a large sector of the consuming public to pervasive manipulation, to the point that their physical appearance, tastes, and behavior are rapidly being molded into a distinctive, fashionable type. Attired all in black, with sallow faces (the women's slashed with crimson lipstick), listening to soulless "New Vague" music,[34] and daubed with expensive colognes with names like "Kuroi. By Murasaki" (p. 169), a herd of sleek drones has begun to throng the swanky restaurants and clubs, chattering "about accounts and magazines and salaries and mortgages . . . the same tired old topics" (pp. 242–43). In short, they have been transformed into a compliant mob of yuppies, which is mere preliminary to their transformation into a slavish army of vampires, their literal living death prefigured by their psychic and social zombification.

The foreground story features Dora Vale, a freelance "Creative Consultant" for voguish periodicals that boast "all style and no content, packed with vacuous articles dealing with 'image' and 'lifestyle'" (p. 4). It is a typically new-bourgeois occupation, closely aligned with the phenomenon known as "second-wave advertising," which Martyn Lee identifies as a post-Fordist/postmodernist "production of highly studied, stylised and often esoteric advertising texts which, more and more, required readers to possess a sophisticated visual awareness and relatively high amounts of cultural capital for successful decoding."[35] Dora's job is to segment target audiences for such ads and provide data assessing their market impact, though Billson depicts the process with tongue planted firmly in cheek:

> I spent the rest of the day trying to work . . . , and concocted some readership survey results for *Flirt* [magazine]. I looked upon these things as conceptual art. They may have been made up, but they seemed no less accurate than any other form of market research. I prided myself on my knowledge of human nature, and my attitude was that I *was* the market. I told everyone my readership profiles were composite portraits, compiled from data gleaned from hundreds upon hundreds of telephone interviews—interviews which

were constantly having to be updated in order to reflect the minutest fluctuations in the state of the economy. No one ever queried
an invoice; they just coughed up.[36]

When one of the magazines Dora writes for starts running a series of
fashion spreads entitled *Night People!*—replete with stylish tableaux involving predatory vampires ("*'Sunburn can be fatal,'* said the text. *'Smart
vamps prize their pale skin and use barrier cream to shield their features from
the ultraviolet'*" [p. 23; emphasis in original]),[37]—Dora begins to grasp
how the yuppification of London—a process that until now she could
only dismiss contemptuously as "decadent chic" (p. 22)—is implicated
in the vast politico-economic conspiracy coordinated by Multiglom.
Dora's attitude toward the yuppies she writes for is scathing, only becoming more so when she perceives them as undead; indeed, she comes
to grasp that their thoughtless hedonism has neatly paved the way for
their vampirism: "It was disturbing to think just how easily they'd
crossed the line. . . . They'd already been halfway there in life, and they
weren't so very different now they were dead" (p. 243). Driven by a
consumerist narcissism that promotes myopic political attitudes privileging individual satisfaction over any larger commitments or concerns,
they seem entirely uninterested in the fact that beyond their trivial island of security, the encompassing social fabric is rending irrevocably,
with dispossessed have-nots and reactionary youth gangs prowling the
streets while cultural power passes into the hands of a callous elite. In
Dora's eyes, they are the "suckers" of the title: having bought into consumption, they are horribly consumed by the social fallout of their own
selfish lusts.

Another, though rather more gentle, satire of the yuppie vampire is
found in Michael Cadnum's novel *The Judas Glass* (1995). The story is
set in northern California, where a new breed of yuppie has emerged,
combining egocentric affluence with bleeding-heart sensibilities into a
strange gestalt of touchy-feely materialism. Narrator Richard Stirling
incarnates these contradictions: a wealthy real-estate attorney who lives
in a ritzy house in the Berkeley hills decorated by his antique-dealer
wife—"Zapotec rugs with animal patterns," "white bookshelves of
Etruscan matrons and Hopi fetishes"[38]—he is self-consciously absorbed
in his wardrobe ("I was wearing a three-button ventless cashmere jacket
and gray twill trousers, both fresh from my tailor on Bush Street" [p. 7])
and his quaint, costly collectibles ("I had a rare almost-virgin celluloid
of the fifteen-minute cartoon of Popeye as Sinbad the Sailor" [p. 19]).
At the same time, he is a noted crusader for the rights of the under-

privileged, spearheading class action suits against profiteering developers and lecturing audiences on "how to make banks socially aware" and "how to encourage financial institutions to open more branches in the inner city" (p. 11). Those who have spent any time in the Bay Area will recognize the breed; indeed, the author clearly intends Richard to be perceived as a social type: a bit vain, a bit vacuous, yet cautiously idealistic, his life defined by leisurely metaphors—a legal stratagem involves "put[ting] a little extra spin on the ball" (p. 41)—and by safely "rebellious" bromides (as when he defends 1960s music to a "gangly nineteen-year-old" punk rocker by affirming Chuck Berry's "Johnnie B. Goode" as "the quintessence of American rock and roll" [p. 43]). Throughout the novel's first third, the atmosphere of tony blandness is so precise and the satire so effectively low key that if readers did not know this was a vampire novel, they might assume they had stumbled into a yuppie soap opera.

But this *is* a vampire novel, and seasoned readers of the genre will be attuned to the author's subtle hints and foreshadowings suggesting that Richard's cozy life is doomed. In the first place, his comfortably "null prosperity" (p. 10) barely screens a realm of "slapdash brutality" (p. 6); as in *Suckers*, the larger social world seems to be teetering on the verge of chaos: an off-course missile from Vandenberg Air Force Base detonates over the Bay, bizarrely tainted water gushes bright blue from household taps, and Richard's new offices bear indelible evidence of the machine-gun rampage that had riddled them a few years before. Closer to home, Rebecca Pennant, the blind pianist with whom Richard has been conducting a secret affair, is brutally murdered, her killer unknown. Meanwhile, presentiments of supernatural agency lurk: an antique mirror is mailed anonymously to Richard's residence—a mirror once owned by his family before it mysteriously disappeared—and when he scratches his finger on it, the wound stubbornly refuses to heal. At first, the cut generates a painful numbness that seems to sever Richard's emotional ties to the world; soon after, it spawns a mental vertigo that leads inexorably toward a sudden, fatal accident.

Nine months later, Richard is reborn as a vampire. His true nature, though, remains for a time obscure to him, asserting itself only as an irrepressible impulse to drink blood and avoid sunlight. In time, Richard becomes acquainted with his full repertoire of powers: vast strength, heightened sensation, and accelerated recuperative abilities. Ultimately, tortured by grief and loneliness, he decides to test his healing powers on his lost love, digging up Rebecca's mutilated corpse and showering it with his blood, thus resurrecting her. The remainder of the novel chronicles their flight from police and military authorities through the redwood forests, desolate beaches, and moral wilderness of northern California.

But the typical events of a vampire-hunting tale are clearly of less interest to the author than the philosophical implications of vampirism itself. Unlike Billson's viciously sarcastic depiction of undeath as the logical extension of an empty, yuppified existence, Cadnum renders the transformation affirmatively, as a potential transcendence of the mundane. Richard gains, as a vampire, fresh insight into the petty vacancy of his former lifestyle, a sense of how bereft it was of vitality and meaning. At one point, holed up in a shuttered house, he browses through upscale magazines and sales catalogs, musing sadly upon the "slick pages of products, smiling men and women, all of it empty, promises no one really believed." As if all commercial lures have been effectively defanged by his vampiric rebirth, Richard also finds it "difficult to watch television. Something about [his] optic nerve made the stuttering images look fake and flat, the voices like the sound of antique telephones" (p. 256). Feeling as if he had "worn through to an inner core of [him]self" (p. 219), he begins to subsist not for the sake of personal vanity or professional aspiration, but for immediate being—"this minute linked to minute, this power to endure" (p. 182)—a pure existential flux he shares exultantly with Rebecca during their hunted wanderings. Indeed, their breathless marveling at the silvery stillness of the midnight woods and the bleak beauty of the cold Pacific suggests that contemporary yuppies are so blindly immersed in the metaphorical undeath of quotidian "second nature" that it takes a vampire's uncanny senses to see the raw pulse of the world afresh. It is therefore unsurprising that after her transformation into a vampire, Rebecca literally regains her sight.

Vampirism thus functions in the novel as a means of escape from a dull, yuppified existence: once undead, Richard finds himself no longer tied down to soul-killing ritual but rather "free, as poetry is, or the image in a mirror" (p. 183). Indeed, references to mirrors, as might be expected in a vampire novel, recur throughout the story, accumulating multiple and sometimes conflicting meanings. On the one hand, they signify the narcissistic self-regard of the bourgeois class: like the mythic Narcissus, Richard had, as a child, cultivated a "fondness for looking at [him]self" in his family's antique mirror, at one point actually running headlong into it under the impression that "*it was a room with a cute little boy*" like himself (p. 21; emphasis in original). Mirrors are further associated in the novel with a shallowly meretricious view of the world, a surface assumption that "looks are everything" (p. 60). Yet they can also permit a critical recognition of the idle trappings of social convention: late in the novel, Richard and Rebecca stand before a looking glass in a trendy shop, realizing "what a painful, pointless charade this [display of wealth] suddenly was" (p. 253). Finally, as the title of the book suggests, the mirror is, like the yuppie world of consumption itself, a "judas glass," luring only to disappoint, thus registering a painful contradiction at the heart of consumerist fantasy. Yet the novel preserves, even amidst its revelation of the false promises of consumer culture, a dialectical viewpoint, as evidenced in Richard's remark that "only the mirror, in its straightforward deception, is perpetually truthful" (p. 250). In other words, the fact that consumption is experienced as a false promise only underscores the utopian impulse latent in the promise itself: "[m]irrors have always called to us, always wanted us to leave" for a better place (p. 201).

Yet despite the dialectical complexity of its mirror imagery, the novel has, finally, a deeply conservative thrust, since in place of consumption as a failed promise of plenitude, Cadnum substitutes a rather mawkish vision of the imagined bounty of the natural world, a world serenely beyond the structures (and strictures) of capitalist modernity. On top of its primitivist nostalgia, the basic problem with this yearning, back-to-nature fantasy is that it doesn't really transcend a yuppie ethos: not only is California yuppiedom quite capable of embracing an environmentalist agenda amidst its manifold paradoxes, sentimentally communing with nature through the nonbiodegradable soles of three-hundred-dollar hiking shoes or the tinted windscreens of Jeep Cherokees,[39] but also Cadnum's version of nature nostalgia—especially its dependence on an Edenic (vampire) couple—merely reinscribes a form of privatized experience founded, like the yuppie lifestyle itself, on the hermetic model of the heterosexual family unit. While Richard's and Rebecca's death-defying blood could conceivably raise a whole legion of vampires, all joined in an undead commonwealth of reinvigorated spirituality, the two seem content simply to pair off, to define themselves in segregation from the world, to take their pleasures privately. Despite the story's messianic trappings—Richard as a vampire-Christ whose blood heals and redeems—Cadnum never entertains truly communal possibilities on either side of the divide of death; his vision is, like the yuppie's, individualistic to the core.

Christopher Moore's novel *Bloodsucking Fiends: A Love Story* (1995) shows the opposite face of the yuppie-slacker dialectic as it has developed over the past two decades. Like *The Judas Glass*, it is set in the Bay Area, but its cast of social types is considerably broader; populated by a grungy corps of failures, the book offers a virtual panorama of slacker styles: homeless philosophical eccentrics (the "Emperor of San Francisco"), aspiring neobeatnik writers (protagonist Tommy Flood), party-wild menial service workers (the Animals, a supermarket nightshift crew), and bored office clerks (Tommy's girlfriend, Jody). These scruffy folks are all essentially fatalists, resigned to a future that looms as a huge black hole, a vampiric vacancy that has sucked away their hopes. For example, the attitudes of minimum-wage workers trapped in dead-end jobs are effectively conveyed in scenes featuring the Animals, who are so contemptuous of their graveyard-shift employment as supermarket stockers that they spend their time smoking dope and aisle-bowling with frozen turkeys. Some of them have actually come to admire the yuppies surrounding them: Jody's roommate Kurt, for instance, "liked to watch tapes of 'Wall Street Week' before he went to bed at night," deriving "some latent sexual thrill out of listening to balding money managers talking about moving millions." [40] But most of them view the fashionable pretensions and get-ahead competitiveness of the new bourgeoisie with ironic disdain, as the following conversation between the Emperor and Tommy indicates:

> "Their time has passed and they don't know what to do. They were told what they wanted and they believed it. They can only keep their dream alive by being with others like themselves who will mirror their illusions."
> "They have really nice shoes," Tommy said.
> "They have to look right or their peers will turn on them like starving dogs." [41]

Like Billson and Cadnum, Moore sees yuppiedom as trapped in a sterile oscillation between the poles of self-absorbed narcissism (note the recurrence of the mirror metaphor) and a casual brutality toward others. In *Bloodsucking Fiends*, this lurking, predatory aspect is vivified in the form of a wealthy, eight-hundred-year-old vampire named Elijah Ben Sapir who lives on a plush, high-tech yacht in the San Francisco Bay. Moore cleverly counterpoints this grandiose, undead presence with the Emperor's earthy mysticism, a contrast that actually draws upon historical personages in San Francisco's storied history. The Emperor is, of course, the legendary Joshua Abraham Norton, self-appointed "Emperor of the United States and Protector of Mexico," who in the mid-to-late nineteenth century became a popular local celebrity—an itinerant madman who nonetheless corresponded with President Lincoln and Queen Victoria, and was immortalized as the quirky King in

Mark Twain's *Adventures of Huckleberry Finn*.[42] Ben Sapir, on the other hand, would seem to be based on a more recent Bay Area luminary— Jim Clark, cofounder of Netscape and owner of the extravagant 155-foot cutter *Hyperion* (dubbed by *Fortune* magazine "a giant aluminum computer with sails" due to its ornate high-tech appointments).[43] The novel thus pits a nouveau riche of the 1990s against a mythical, Whitmanesque hobo, a noble protoslacker whose native shrewdness and homespun populism finally bests the yuppie vampire's self-serving schemes.

Yet not before Ben Sapir manages to infect others with his selfish desires: the story opens with the vampire attacking Jody in an alley, transforming her into a creature driven by not only bloodlust but also "a sudden and deep-seated urge to go shopping."[44] When she does, at a Gap clothing store, she finds herself surrounded by eager salespeople with "a look of dazed hunger in their eyes: a pack of zombies from the perky, youthful version of *Night of the Living Dead*" (p. 57)—leading one to wonder who is the authentic bloodsucker: the consumer-vampire or those who (metaphorically) prey upon her? The entire novel is punctuated by Jody's shopping sprees, including a massive one at the end that culminates in an expensive makeover that has her looking like one of Billson's suckers (or perhaps an escapee from a Robert Palmer video)— what Moore calls "a Donner Party Barbie" (p. 205). With her new, killer looks, Jody heads out to a posh dance club where, despite the gathered yuppies' obvious admiration for her sleek appearance and haughty demeanor, all she can think is: "Why did I come here? What did I hope to accomplish?" (p. 214) Like Martin, a disenchanted Jody realizes that no magic can lift her out of her working-class background into new-bourgeois splendor (indeed, she is one of the few vampires in literary history forced to do her own laundry), yet still she goes on consuming.

Just as *Suckers* and *The Judas Glass* show the yuppie vampire novel taking to heart a sharp critique of its consumerist ethos, so *Bloodsucking Fiends* shows the slacker vampire novel admitting, however grudgingly, its own implication in the values and pleasures of consumption. The manifold blandishments of consumer fashion may ultimately be a pale sustenance, but they have transformed Jody's desires and appetites irrevocably, as she realizes while wandering through the "heightened sensual world" of a downtown shopping district: "Jody watched the heat trails of the lights, breathed deep the aroma of fudge and candy and a thousand mingled colognes and deodorants, listened to the whir of the motors that animated electric elves and reindeer under the cloak of Muzak-mellowed Christmas carols—and she liked it. . . . Christmas is better as a vampire, she thought" (p. 198). As opposed to Cadnum's novel, in which the acquisition of supernal senses results in the yuppie vampire's transcendence of commercial seductions, *Bloodsucking Fiends* shows the slacker vampire's undead perceptions activating the aesthetic richness latent in consumerist glitz.

Thus, just as the yuppie vampire tradition has come to reject the dystopian emptiness of consumer culture, so the slacker faction cannot resist its utopian lure. Even a dissatisfied consumer like Jody understands that consumption is her destiny, however baffled she may be by its emotional fickleness, by the glaring distance between its luxurious promises and her own humble reality. As she says to her boyfriend, Tommy, when he tries (like Rudy in *Light at the End*) to interpret her nascent undeath in terms of Anne Rice's novels and other vampire guides, "Look, Tommy, maybe there's some truth in one of these books that you're reading, but how do we know which one? Huh? Nobody gave me a fucking owner's manual when I got these fangs. I'm doing the best that I can" (p. 174). In their different ways, Skipp and Spector's, Billson's, Cadnum's, and Moore's novels continue to work through and recomplicate the dialectical contrast first crystallized in *Martin* and *Interview with the Vampire*.

THREE ▬▬▬▬▬▬▬▬▬▬▬▬
VORACIOUS ANDROGYNES:
THE VAMPIRE LESTAT ON MTV

INSATIABLE NARCISSISM

In chapter 1, I built on the theoretical perspectives of recent feminist studies of women's historical shopping practices to argue that the socioeconomic enfranchisement of teenagers as consuming subjects involved a genuine cultural empowerment—one that has generated considerable adult anxiety over threats posed to the normative policing of adolescent desire and agency. While the inculcation of a consumerist ethos in youth ultimately served the profit motives of capitalists, it also activated youthful fantasy and appetite within public spaces (shopping malls, video arcades, cineplexes) that provided opportunities for self-determination and communal exchange distinct from the "legitimate" jurisdictions of school and family. It is thus, I argued, insufficiently dialectical merely to deplore the capitalist valorization of youthful desire without attending also to its mobilizing of teenagers as potentially autonomous social subjects.

In the spirit of this argument, then, I would like to return to my critique in chapter 2 of the socioeconomically reactionary positioning of the yuppie vampire in order to consider the dialectically progressive aspects of the figure's cultural articulation. Such an analysis must move beyond, even while incorporating, a condemnation of the yuppie vampire's erotically predatory consumption, acknowledging too how this figure has served to crystallize the latent utopianism of consumerist pleasure seeking, the lust for a better—a sensually richer, more aesthetically gratifying—world. More specifically, it must recognize how the yuppie vampire has, in its association with a utopia of eroticized consumption, come to provide an energizing cultural investment for gay, lesbian, and bisexual consumers. Indeed, Anne Rice's novels and Tony Scott's film *The Hunger* exude a powerful homoerotic charge that unsettles the normative assumption of a monolithically "straight" consumer culture.

That the figure of the vampire trades on a logic of gender ambiguity has become a critical commonplace, especially in studies of its manifestation in Victorian culture, where it functioned as a powerful textual site of "homosexual panic."[1] As Christopher Craft has argued in his analysis of Bram Stoker's *Dracula*, the sexuality of the vampire is inherently ambiguous because it is expressed orally, combining qualities of the masculine (penetrative teeth) and the feminine (enveloping lips), and thus generating a profound "erotic ambivalence" that destabilizes the representation of sexual roles.[2] The aggressive orality of the vampire involves an eroticization of images of consumption, one that several Freudian critics have traced to infantile roots,[3] but which may also be seen to evoke historical consumerism specifically. The vampire's pleasure derives from biting and drinking—in other words, from acquiring and consuming—an activity that has replaced the libidinal charge of conventional genital sexuality. But what from a Freudian perspective might seem a regression in fact involves a potent dissemination of nonheterosexually configured desire: the actual gender—and thus, by implication, the sexual object choice—of the vampire is, finally, irrelevant to its enactment of an eroticized consumption. Ultimately, vampires are voracious androgynes driven by an indiscriminate longing.

Predictably, the Victorian vampire story—including *Dracula* (1897) and J. Sheridan LeFanu's short story "Carmilla" (1872), with its lesbian vampire—figured this erotic ambivalence as a dire threat, however implicitly seductive, a pattern most twentieth-century treatments have tended to follow. Richard Dyer provides an excellent historical overview of the "vampirism as homosexuality" theme, arguing that the forms of pleasure that vampire texts generally provided gay and lesbian readers involved either reading "self-oppressively" by identifying with the threatened sexual order or "identify[ing] with the vampire in some sort" and "thrilling to [its] extraordinary power." Yet the latter strategy required interpreting against the narrative grain in "most vampire tales up to the 1970s," because "in no case does the vampire tell his/her own story" until Rice's *Interview*, which is narrated by Louis. As Dyer argues, this "shift in the position of the narrator *vis-à-vis* vampirism is surely analogous with the shift, and insistence upon it, from lesbians and gay men as persons who are spoken about to persons who speak for themselves."[4]

Thus, even if Rice's novels and films such as *The Hunger* are disturbingly ideological in their celebration of the heedless arrogance of the new consumption classes, their detachment from the smothering strictures of family life (something the working-class vampire text *Martin* could not effect) and their affirmative portrayal of a self-confident urban subculture organized around alternative forms of erotic bonding (Rice's vampires pair off almost exclusively in same-sex couples, while the vampires in *The Hunger* are bisexual) converged with the assertive consolidation of a gay rights/pride movement, with which these texts were often overtly articulated. In her biography of Rice, Katherine Ramsland has shown how, from high school on, "gay men . . . inspired in [Rice] a strong feeling of kinship," exhibiting "courage in the face of prejudice. As people reinventing themselves from outsiders to insiders in gay communities, they were heroes" to her.[5] In depicting the vampire relationships in *Interview*, Rice explicitly sought to appeal to emergent gay audiences, a purpose at which she was so successful that when the novel was being filmed in 1993–94, her fans impelled her to mount a public attack on the producers for reportedly diluting its homoerotic content.[6] My own experience teaching her work has shown me how wildly popular it is with young gay and bisexual readers (male and female) seeking a positive portrayal of their own dawning sense of identity. As with the recent rehabilitation of the epithet *queer* as a polemical self-description by the current generation of gay activists, gay youth seem to find in the otherworldliness and unapologetic peccancy of Rice's vampires a vindication of their own disdain for conventional sexual roles. As Judith Johnson has observed, Rice's novels read less like works of horror literature than like boldly libidinous dreams, "homoerotic fantasies of sexual and artificial paradises."[7]

The same could be said of the film *The Hunger*, not only because of its frank portrayal of lesbianism but also due to the presence of David Bowie and Catherine Deneuve, stars famous for projecting an ambiguous, highly androgynous sexuality with appeal to multiple audiences— gay, lesbian, and bisexual as well as straight. As Leerom Medovoi has observed of Bowie's career as a rock singer, "Bowie was perhaps the first to construct (elaborate) narratives of a rebel who shocked by *confusing* genders, . . . explicitly reconceptualiz[ing] rock rebellion as threatening a straight world . . . with one's sexual undecidability. . . . This threat parallels, and arguably was mediated by, the gay liberationist struggle in the early seventies to dismantle rigid gender distinctions in favor of a more polymorphously perverse sexual order."[8] The film's unusual casting also implicates it in the tripartite logic of the cultural paradigm of consuming youth, since both Bowie and Deneuve are famous for (1) marketing consumer objects—rock albums, skin lotions—to youth audiences; (2) maintaining a preternaturally youthful appearance into middle age; and (3) evoking a dream of eternal youth in their persons and in their product messages. Thus, *The Hunger*, like Rice's novels, captures the complex nexus of class, gender, and generation that gives the figure of the yuppie vampire its tremendous ideological power, combining as it does fantasies of social wealth, sexual freedom, and youthful potency.

In short, the yuppie vampire, like so many icons of popular culture, contains both progressive and reactionary elements, and it is imperative (if at times quite difficult) to disentangle them from one another. If, on the one hand, the figure allegorizes the social enfranchisement of the new bourgeoisie, emphatically affirming their consumerist values and behaviors as the quasi-divine right of a superior class of beings, it also suggests the emergence into public visibility of alternative sexual communities whose desires have traditionally been suppressed—in mainstream culture and in the conventional vampire story—but which must now be recognized and acknowledged. What mediates between these class and gender positionings is the category of youth: for the yuppie vampire conceived both as a member of the new bourgeoisie and as a polymorphously perverse androgyne, youth is the imaginary promise of consumption, its utopian subject (since the one who consumes is youthful) and also its utopian object (since youth is what is consumed).

During the 1970s and 1980s, the period of the yuppie vampire's popular consolidation, this ideological nexus was also visible in the domain of advertising, as marketers—following the post-Fordist logic of segmenting the commodity audience into factions defined by values and lifestyle—began actively to solicit middle-class gay and lesbian consumers via strategies that mobilized homoerotic imagery and encoded latent "homosexual" messages. The basic approach of these ads involved appealing to consumerist narcissism by fetishizing images of sleek young bodies living a dream of glamorous affluence and perpetual adolescence, a titillating Calvin Klein fantasy (Klein being one of the pioneers of the form). In the process, the ads blurred clear distinctions between "straight" and "gay" consumers, since all were linked in their common narcissism: the consumer's desire to *be* young and beautiful was conflated with the desire to *possess* youth and beauty as incarnated in the beguiling models. As Mark Simpson has argued, mirrors were often used, especially in aftershave ads, to cement this narcissistic bond, since the "mirror perspective allows us to desire the model narcissistically in such a way that it is also our hand that strokes his face, just as much as it is our face that is stroked."[9]

In his study of male fashion and hygiene ads, Andrew Wernick observes that contemporary advertising's engagement of narcissism "is especially norm-breaking" in that "the homo-erotic desire that is always implicit in taking oneself as a sexual object . . . is here fully exposed." While these ads usually provided what Wernick calls "a crucial hetero-sexual cover"—in other words, a possibility for the straight consumer to disavow the implicit homoeroticism of the situation—the readings they permitted were nonetheless calculatedly ambiguous, "letting the con-sumers place themselves in the ad from a whole variety of positions." [10] The scenarios constructed were so generalized in terms of consumer fantasy that they seemed to incite a free-floating desire, a libidinous im-pulse beyond the stratifications of sexual orientation—thus suggesting Bourdieu's analysis of the new bourgeoisie's "dream of social flying." As one can see, it is extremely difficult to tease out the sexual implications of these ads from their class significations, precisely because the new bourgeoisie was the first capitalist class with a comprehensive erotics of consumption: the commodity's lust for the money in their pockets no longer needed to be furtive, since it was so obviously and wholeheartedly reciprocated.

As might be expected, the metaphorics of consumer vampirism can-vassed in chapter 1 were deployed by critics of advertising to describe the operations and effects of these polymorphously perverse ads. The language of Simpson's essay, for example, is rife with vampiric images, as when he argues that by "*feeding* [the male consumer's] longing for the idealized [youthful] form," homoerotic advertising "ensures that desire is never satisfied and that the consumer *never loses his appetite*." [11] Diana Fuss makes the vampire metaphor explicit in her essay "Fashion and the Homospectatorial Look," wherein she argues that the dissemination of homoeroticism via advertising practices "provides a socially sanctioned structure in which women are encouraged to *consume*, in voyeuristic if not vampiristic fashion, the images of other women." This structure op-erates through what Fuss calls "vampiric identification": the "homo-spectatorial look" encoded in fashion imagery forces female viewers "to assume the position of lesbian vampires. . . . The spectatorial relation of the woman to her image serially displayed across the pages of fashion magazines is structurally vampiric." This relation is enforced by the photographic apparatus, which basically "functions as a mass producer of corpses, embalming each subject and fixing its image." [12] Thus, the capitalist market, in its ceaseless hunger for profit, infects the consumer with its own vampiric appetites, in the process conflating relations based on voyeurism, narcissism, and homoeroticism with specifically consum-erist desires and pleasures.

According to John Fekete, in a discussion clearly influenced by Jean

Baudrillard's attack on consumption as a form of dead social labor, the structural vampirism analyzed by Fuss is not merely a condition of contemporary advertising but is essential to the valorization process of late capitalism. Saturated as it is with "hyperreal sign-values and value-signs, potentialities without end," this system seems to inhabit "a flickering half-life, anemic, parasitic, and thirsty for real bodily fluids. Insubstantial, dematerialized, dead value joins up with insubstantial, disseminated, dead power in a panic passion of resurrection through the fresh blood of desire which, upon commutative transfusion, ever recedes into a bloodless and dis-oriented desire of desire. It is not inappropriate to speak here, at least in tendency, of a culture of vampire value." [13] In other words, the morbid accumulation process of advanced capitalism, ever greedy for the "fresh blood of desire," mandates the pathological predation of youthful energy. We thus encounter here another face of the logic of consumer vampirism described in chapter 1: the critique of the interpellation of youth-as-subjects into a consumer system has shaded into a critique of this system's consumption of youth-as-substance. Homoerotic imagery provides the fangs of this consumerist extraction, the generalized mechanism of purchase upon the androgynous throat of youth.[14] From this critical perspective, then, the homoeroticism circulating in contemporary consumer culture—which is crystallized in the yuppie vampire text—is potentially pernicious, an enforcement of narcissistic self-regard that propels consumers into the draining embrace of power.

A text that effectively allegorizes this sharp critique is John Rechy's novel *The Vampires* (1971). Published five years prior to Rice's *Interview*, the book set the tone for the yuppie vampire tradition to come: evoking a lushly sensual narrative world, the story chronicles the erotic doings of a group of languid, androgynous predators (a major difference, however, is that Rechy's eponymous "vampires" are merely metaphorical: the tale has a Gothic atmosphere but no overtly supernatural elements). In a mansion on a secluded island, a motley assortment of beautiful people play out a breathless series of sadomasochistic games at the behest of their host, Richard, a fabulously wealthy scoundrel who "need[s] lives to feed on." [15] This self-styled master vampire is the incarnation of a culture drunk on a brew of voyeurism, narcissism, fetishism, and homoeroticism; indeed, these psychic dispositions are the very tools he uses to manipulate and dominate his guests. Chief among his victims is his onetime mistress, Joja, whom Richard years before had infected with his own *"wailing emptiness"* by means of an erotic bite, a "ritualistic initiation performed by his mouth on her neck" (p. 36; emphasis in original).

Impelled by an unquenchable hunger, "ravenous thoughts gnawing . . . insistently now at her mind" (p. 18), Joja has spent the years apart from Richard pursuing a succession of disposable "youngmen" whose sexual intensity allows her to experience the brief illusion of vitality. "Youth had extended its lease to her," she muses as she gazes into a mirror. "But how much longer?" (p. 35) In fact, Joja is little more than "a beautiful lifeless specter" (p. 26), condemned—like everyone else Richard touches—to "endless nights of hunting" for a satisfaction that never comes (p. 257).

While the specific target of Rechy's ferocious satire is the facile sexual utopianism of the 1960s—"The countless bodies. Victims. The sexual war. A graveyard of sex" (p. 237)—his book can also be read as a critique of the homoerotic narcissism that marked the advertising strategies of the following decades. Indeed, the novel forges a link between these critical targets in their mutual fetishization of the "young, young sensual body" (p. 240)—in youth objectified, openly and emphatically (note the verbal repetition), as an erotic substance to be ceaselessly circulated and hedonistically enjoyed. The term *youngmen*, which Rechy coined in his first novel, *City of Night* (1963), and has used throughout his career, signifies alluring postpubescent males whose physical beauty is either sexually exploited by predatory others or willfully deployed for purposes of narcissistic pleasure (or both). It is a useful coinage in that it suggests that contemporary popular culture's objectification of youthful masculinity, through the homoerotic lures of slick advertisements, is implicitly linked with the gritty eroticism of a gay underworld, where male physical beauty may be literally purchased. One of the novel's central "youngmen," Blue, for example, is a street hustler who has actually transformed his body into a profitable object: he is thus the living embodiment of Marx's image of the seductive commodity, his physical charms calling out to the money in his clients' pockets.

Ultimately, Blue's casual eagerness to prostitute himself, "slightly surly in the assurance of his desirability" (p. 18), is merely a screen for his own narcissism: "it was other people desiring *me—their* desire of me, just that, turned me on, like they were mirrors" (p. 177). Blue's status as both subject and object of desire makes him the perfect incarnation of consumer narcissism: a "depraved angel" (p. 5), his beauty the spur to a "terrible insatiability" (p. 258) in himself and others, he has come to take a perverse pleasure in the alienation of his erotic being, in the dead labor of his own sexual energy. Ironically, as if reflecting an impoverishment of agency at the heart of consumer narcissism, this seemingly virile youngman is impotent, the legacy of an abortive encounter with the only person he ever truly loved (other than himself). Scorned by the object of his desire, Blue has withdrawn into a sullen self-absorption, no longer needing physical contact with others but still craving the affirmation that he is himself desired. At the end, his spiritual emptiness exposed during the course of Richard's savage games, he seeks refuge in his reflected image, only to be rebuffed by "the cold, impassive surface" of the glass; as another character comments, "Even the mirror rejects him" (p. 244). Ultimately, Blue is the victim, not of Richard, but of a social system that "lives on the symbolic blood of others" (p. 79), a system defined by a simple exploitative relation: "a body. And eyes staring at it" (p. 133). These eyes, coldly registering an almost abstract lust, define the novel's basic concept of vampirism—the visual ingestion of youthful male beauty: "sorrowful, black-painted eyes devoured the spectacle of the incredibly sexual boy" (p. 9).

To his credit, Rechy does not essentialize this psychic structure but, like Fuss, locates its dead labor of voyeuristic consumption in a technological apparatus—"the leering eye of the camera" (p. 139). Despite the Gothic isolation of its island setting, the novel consistently registers the social presence of communications media—especially marginal genres such as stag loops and art-house cinema. Indeed, Rechy shows the imbrication of these seemingly disparate forms in his subtle allusions to the filmmaking career of Andy Warhol, references focused in the character of Bravo, whose "androgynous beauty had made her an idolized superstar of underground films" (p. 12). The terms *underground* and *superstar* evoke Warhol's notorious Factory productions of the 1960s, with their gritty vision of decadent banality and their parody of the Hollywood star system; Bravo would fit comfortably indeed into movies such as *Chelsea Girls* (1966) or *Lonesome Cowboys* (1967).[16]

While her name seems to invoke Warholian "superstar" Viva, Bravo's butch S&M aesthetic—she wears knee-high boots and carries a bullwhip—suggests another denizen of the Factory scene, Mary Woronov, whose memoir of her years with Warhol, *Swimming Underground*, reads like a true-life version of Rechy's novel. Populated by extravagant, narcissistic poseurs whose social experience consists largely of playing complicated games of seduction and exploitation at the whim of a mysterious impresario, the ineffable Andy, Woronov's book shows that the central metaphor animating Rechy's novel was eerily appropriate:

People were calling us the undead, vampires, me and my little brothers of the night, with our lips pressed against the neck of the city, sucking the energy out of scene after scene. We left each party

behind like a wasted corpse, raped and carelessly tossed aside. . . .
Andy was the worst, taking on five and six parties a night. He even
looked like a vampire: white, empty, waiting to be filled, incapable
of satisfaction. He was the white worm—always hungry, always
cold, never still, always twisting. His favorite lair was still the balcony of the Dom [a dance club], and my favorite place was right
next to him, watching the sea of swirling bodies flop about below
us like fish in a net. Suspended from our cave ceiling, Andy and I
hung like bats, often mesmerized by the same dancer. That night
we were watching a blond girl.[17]

Woronov's evocation of Warhol and herself as blasé voyeurs waiting to
drop like vampiric leeches onto beautiful young strangers dovetails with
Rechy's portrait of Richard and his guests as "bored people involved
in jaded games," striving hopelessly to sate the "horrible emptiness"
within them.[18]

Woronov's metaphor has recently been taken up by British author
Kim Newman in his novella *Andy Warhol's Dracula* (1999), in which the
eponymous artist appears as a literal vampire.[19] With his "pale, almost-
albino face, simultaneously babyish and ancient," his "goggle-like dark
glasses, hypnotic black holes where eyes should be," and "the slavic
monotone of his whispery voice," Warhol seems to possess all the "attributes of a classical vampire" (pp. 13–14). More significantly, his artistic work of the 1960s and 1970s, especially his underground films, are
"steeped in the atmosphere of vampirism," with their visual torpor and
zombified performances (p. 29). Echoing Fuss and Rechy, Newman asserts that, for Warhol, "the film camera, like the silkscreen or the polaroid, was a vampire machine, a process for turning life into frozen death,
perfect and reproducible" (p. 34). In this context, the fact that Warhol
called his studio a "Factory" suggests the continuing relevance of Marx's
analysis of undead labor for analyzing (sub)cultural consumption.

In Newman's rampantly intertextual treatment, Warhol's fusion of
high fashion with street culture is figured as a class conflict that specifically links yuppie and slacker vampires. Punkish Rudy Pasko, from Skipp
and Spector's novel, *The Light at the End*, appears as a cretinous figure
akin to Renfield in *Dracula*, while Rice's stylish Lestat de Lioncourt is an
arbiter of Parisian haute couture; that elegant couple from *The Hunger*,
Bowie and Deneuve, put in a brief appearance at a party thrown by
Bianca Jagger, while the grungy protagonist of Poppy Brite's *Lost Souls*
offers Warhol a sip from his drug-laced veins. This epochal collision of

new-class vampires is figured dialectically: on the one hand, Warhol's infamous mingling with junkies and hustlers seems to pit him against the snooty rich, whose portraits he cynically churns out in his Factory; on the other hand, his relationship with these lowlife slackers is driven by a vampiric exploitation, as he manipulates and casually disposes of them to serve his own "dreadful glamour" (p. 21). Moreover, the tension between these poles embodies a historical "style war," a cultural battle between punk and disco—another divide uneasily straddled by the undead Andy. The punks' nihilistic "slow suicide" seems to justify their deaths at the hands of the vampire elite, whose love for dance floors and glitter balls symbolizes an urge "to live forever, to aspire to an immortality of consumption" (p. 18). Ultimately, "Andy leeched off them all, left them drained or transformed, using them without letting them touch him, never distinguishing between the commodities he could only coax from other people: money, love, blood, inspiration, devotion, death" (p. 12). Warhol's mastery of undead technologies and his proprietorship of a vampiric Factory—not to mention his infamous aspiration to "be a machine"—make him appear the perfect incarnation of the vampire-cyborg, though Newman does not explicitly develop this connection.

In any event, the metaphor shared by Rechy and Woronov—and brilliantly literalized by Newman—is more than a fortuitous coincidence, since Warhol and his Factory were largely responsible for introducing into mainstream culture the iconography of homoerotic narcissism that Rechy deploys and critiques as implicitly vampiric. Warhol's films and photographs, with their blankly gloating gaze at the bodies of languid, androgynous youth, powerfully fused, under the aegis of an avant-gardist aesthetic, the previously segregated visual rhetorics of gay "physique pictorials" and high-fashion advertising. The result was diffused through American popular culture largely through the agency of *Interview* magazine, which Warhol founded in 1969. By promoting the early work of gay photographers such as Christopher Makos and Robert Mapplethorpe, *Interview* ensured that imagery once available only in plain brown wrappers from obscure studios in New York and Los Angeles could now be found at every major newsstand. As a result of the platform the magazine provided, Bruce Weber has become one of the most sought-after photographers for fashion layouts geared toward youth consumption, including ad campaigns for Calvin Klein and Abercrombie & Fitch that were marked by a strikingly overt homoerotic voyeurism. Weber's magazine spreads and calendars propel into mainstream youth culture Warhol's libidinous iconography of pouty, narcissistic superstars, especially his ogling objectification of masculine beauty in the figure of erstwhile teenage hustler Joe Dallesandro. Indeed, Weber's work seems designed to pose the same question as did the poster for the 1968 film *Flesh* (directed by Warhol protégé Paul Morrissey), which featured, under a dreamy photo of Dallesandro, the query, "Can a boy be too pretty?" As if to cement the connection, a middle-aged Dallesandro has recently been featured in a Calvin Klein advertisement.[20]

Critical concerns about the vampiric implications of this visual regime of homoerotic narcissism exploded into a full-fledged moral panic in 1995, with the release of two Calvin Klein ad campaigns: first, for its unisex fragrance, CK1, and then for its line of designer jeans. Shot by fashion photographer Steven Meisel,[21] both were saturation campaigns—run in magazines, on billboards, and on television—that depicted scantily clad youths in sexually suggestive situations. Set in an empty, brightly lit chamber, the CK1 ads featured a group of slender, androgynous teens slouching and grappling with an air of erotic insouciance compounded with petulant boredom, thus evoking the listless, amorphous carnality of Warhol's Factory productions. The viewer is voyeuristically invited to contemplate this idly shifting sea of pubescent flesh, the free-floating fantasy scenario reinforced by the utter decontextualization of the ads' stark white environment (fig. 6).[22]

By contrast, the jeans campaign reinscribed a social backdrop for the consumer's appropriative gaze, and it was precisely this recontextualization that led to an eruption of moral outrage at the ads' representation of youthful eroticism. Essentially, the ads evoked the drab aesthetics of amateur or low-budget pornography with an explicitness that was really quite astonishing. Bob Garfield, in an article in *Advertising Age* magazine, summarizes one of the television spots:

> "You have a lovely body," says an unseen, middle-aged interviewer from the back of a makeshift, rumpus room set. The background is cheap weldwood paneling, the only prop a stepladder on a soiled carpet. The subject is a long-haired teen-age boy in a pair of black CK jeans and a black vest, but no shirt.
> "Mmm hmm," the boy agrees.
> "Do you like your body?" the older man asks.
> "Yeah, I like it."
> "Mm hmmm. . . . Well," the interviewer says, leeringly, "those jeans look reeeeal good on you."

Figure 6. The visual regime of homoeroticism narcissism. Image from Calvin Klein's CK1 ad campaign.

The effect, says Garfield, is of viewing "chickenhawk porn": "It is one thing to toy with the nation's libido, as Calvin Klein has been doing for the better part of two decades," he pronounces. "But to portray children as sex toys parading before adults is the line that cannot be crossed."[23]

The campaign's evocation of a shabby teen-porn underworld rather predictably provoked widespread furor. Moral watchdogs such as the Reverend Donald Wildmon, head of the American Family Association, blasted the ads as nothing short of child pornography; the FBI and the Justice Department conducted investigations into their potential illegality; and TV talk shows debated the question, "Did Calvin Klein Go Too Far?" Commentators as diverse as President Bill Clinton and Camille Paglia deplored the ads as tasteless, offensive trash, at times calling to mind the extravagant critical attacks mounted against early Warhol films. Stung by the criticism, the corporation decided to pull the campaign, though it attempted to defend itself by arguing that the ads merely displayed the glamour of young people in everyday situations— a defense of which Warhol himself would likely have been proud.[24]

In effect, the campaign and the controversy surrounding it amounted to a return of the Warholian repressed (fig. 7)—to a shocked public perception of the origins of contemporary advertising's homoerotic narcissism in the underground film tradition of the 1960s and the teenage-beefcake posing loops upon which it drew. The critics' exaggerated horror at the imagined sexual predation of children served as a way to deflect the more difficult acknowledgment of the viewer's voyeuristic

Figure 7. The return of the Warholian repressed. Left, Joe Dallesandro in the poster for Andy Warhol's *Loves of Ondine*; right, Joel West in Calvin Klein underwear advertisement.

complicity in the "queer" subcultural scenario, as a disavowal that such scenarios had historically helped to constitute the libidinal economy of mainstream marketing culture. As Garfield's comments indicate, the fact that Calvin Klein and other venders of commodities might "toy with the nation's libido" is not in itself a problem: this, after all, is their job, since sex is the very medium of buying and selling. This ad "crosses the line" not because it communicates a longing for youth that conflates a narcissistic fantasy of identification ("I like it [my body]") with a homoerotic fantasy of possession ("those jeans look reeeeal good on you"), since this is how second-wave advertising aimed at the new bourgeoisie essentially functions. Rather, it crosses the line because it dispels the crucial "heterosexual cover" that inoculates straight consumers against the more ambiguous seductions of commodity culture.

As Mark Simpson argues, ads that bank on the consumer's homoerotic narcissism also work to repress their necessary dependence upon specifically *homosexual* desire: "the signification of heterosexuality" in homoerotic ads "is used to draw a veil over the queer reading while exploiting it at the same time." Yet, as Fuss points out, "in order to eradicate or evacuate the homoerotic desire, the visual field must first *produce* it, thereby permitting, in socially regulated form, the articulation of lesbian desire within the identificatory move [of narcissism] itself." There is thus an implicit "homosexualization of the viewing position"[25] generated by this advertising system, which is what makes the Calvin Klein jeans campaign at once so compelling and so disturbing for the culture at large: this campaign essentially *outs* that system and those who eagerly consume its playful pleasures.

It is in the development of this theme that cultural critics have tended to mobilize the more affirmative metaphorics of consumer vampirism, arguing for the potentially progressive effects of homoerotic advertising. While decrying the commodification of "lesbian masquerade as legitimate high-style fashion" because it works to depoliticize lesbianism into a mere lifestyle option, Danae Clark also claims that the dissemination of queer codes throughout commodity culture increases the agency of lesbian consumers, permitting them to reappropriate these codes "in combination with other products/fashions to act as new signifiers for lesbian identification or ironic commentaries on heterosexual culture."[26] A more subversively deconstructive agenda has been advanced by the group Queer Nation, which claims that the implicit homosexualization of contemporary consumer culture undermines the very ground of sexual difference itself. Thus, this group's cultural-political practice has sought to refunction capitalist texts, objects, and spaces in order to exploit the psychic unboundedness of consumers who depend upon products to articulate, produce, and satisfy their desires. Queer Nation tactically uses the hyper-spaces created by the corporeal trademark, the metropolitan parade, the shopping mall, print media, and finally advertising, to recognize and take advantage of the consumer's pleasure in vicarious identification. In this guise the group commandeers permeable sites, apparently apolitical spaces through which the public circulates in a pleasurable, consensual exchange of bodies, products, identities, and information. Yet it abandons the conciliatory mode. . . . The Queer Nation corporate strategy—to reveal to the consumer desires he/she didn't know he/she had, to make his/her identification with the product "homosexuality" both an unsettling and a pleasurable experience—makes consumer pleasure central to the transformation of public culture, thus linking the utopian promises of the commodity with those of the nation.[27]

To recur to distinctions elaborated in chapter 1, Queer Nation's strategy activates the metaphorics not of Dracula's ruthless predation and dictatorial control, but of the Lost Boys' playful aggression and changeful identity. Indeed, we are now in a position to appreciate the simmering homoeroticism of the latter film, the seductive appeal of whose eponymous adolescents, with their slick leather outfits and pouty sensuality, need not be restricted by gender. When David breathlessly moans for Michael to "join us," the solicitation clearly has an erotic edge.[28] The Lost Boys' militant invasion of the Santa Carla boardwalk may even be seen to converge with Queer Nation's "mall visibility actions," which aggressively "disrupt the antiseptic asexual surface of the malls, exposing them as sites of any number of explicitly sexualized exchanges" with persons and/or commodities. The Lost Boys, like the "Queer Shopping Network," understand "the most banal of advertising strategies: sex sells. In this case, though, sex sells not substitutions for bodily pleasures—a car, a luxury scarf—but the capacity of the body itself to experience unofficial pleasures."[29]

Of course, to elicit this interpretation of *The Lost Boys* requires something of an interventionist reading, since that movie, like its antecedents in Victorian fiction, ultimately provides a heterosexual resolution of the homoerotic "threat" of vampirism. Like the working-class vampire text it essentially is, the film cannot escape finally the power of the family to structure and command desire, though it stages the necessary decision between vampiric freedom and familial bonds perhaps more starkly than any other single work (a pointed contrast for teenagers viewing the film at mall multiplexes, surrounded by the manifold seductions of consumer culture). A film that better illuminates the dual metaphorics of consumer vampirism as they apply to the latent homoeroticism of commodity culture is Tony Scott's *The Hunger*, which effectively captures *both* sides of the metaphorical dialectic, showing how narcissistic objectification and utopian eroticism function together within the libidinal economy of the yuppie vampire text. These contrasting possibilities are evoked by the ambiguity of the title itself, since to hunger suggests both self-centered rapacity and aspirant longing—a wish to devour or to dream. In either case, the animating focus of the desire is youth, conceived at once as a consuming subject and a consumable object.

THE CONSUMING HUNGERS OF ZIGGY STARDUST

The Hunger's opening scene is eerily reminiscent of Woronov's evocation of Warhol and herself at the Dom: a pair of vampiric voyeurs— here, John and Miriam Blaylock—lurk in the shadowy balcony above a disco's dance floor (fig. 8), casually cruising for their latest victims, a punkish young couple clad in leather. Repairing to the couple's apartment, their dreamy seduction soon becomes brutal predation: following a brief bit of foreplay, John and Miriam slit the youths' throats and feast on their blood. The sequence is photographed and edited very much like a music video (at that time a relatively recent form; first-time filmmaker Scott had in fact previously directed music videos as well as television commercials, and he brought this background to the visual organization of *The Hunger*): Goth-rock band Bauhaus croons "Bela Lugosi's Dead" as smoke swirls sinuously around pale faces framed in chic sunglasses; languid slow motion gives way to rapid-fire cuts as fragmented body parts—lips, breasts, thighs—loom into the light; finally, a breathless collage of violent imagery, including shots of a caged monkey cannibalizing its companion, culminates the scene. Conveying narrative detail in a stylish and highly compressed form, this opening sequence briskly sketches the basic character and lifestyle of the Blaylocks—their airy self-absorption, their ultrasmart look, the feral cravings burning beneath their sleek exteriors. In the words of one critic, it was "as though MTV and *Vogue* magazine [had] conspired to remake *Dracula* as soft core porn": [30] suddenly, the swanky-pop aesthetic of Warhol's *Interview*—the trend-setting fashion layouts, the (homo)erotic frankness, the images of glamorous (super)stars identifiable by single names (Bowie, Deneuve)— had achieved filmic expression.

This aesthetic encodes a class-based fantasy, capturing the idealized

Figure 8. The nightlife of the yuppie vampire. Video still from Tony Scott's *The Hunger*.

self-image of the new bourgeoisie—and, indeed, it has proven quite easy for critics to attack the film on these grounds. Nina Auerbach, for example, has argued that *The Hunger*'s vision of vampirism incarnates "the competitive business ethos that reigned over America in the 1980s," the era of Reaganite selfishness: its vampires are defined "not [by] their powers, but [by] their assets"—"jewelry, furniture, lavish houses in glamorous cities, leather clothes." [31] Yet the film represents not a cynical embrace of this consumerist ethos but rather a sly satire of the ideology of youthful narcissism that underpins it. It is certainly true that the Blaylocks live in yuppie splendor, in a four-story townhouse in Manhattan crammed with priceless *objets d'art*, the gathered plunder of centuries. Yet neither their wealth nor even their undeath can protect them from temporal decline—from the ravages of age that make a mockery of their pretense to leisurely immortality. Specifically, they cannot protect *John*; Miriam seems, by contrast, relatively immune to physical decay, though her many lovers have, one by one over millennia stretching back to ancient Egypt, abruptly succumbed—after a few centuries of well-preserved youth—to an accelerated aging process that withers them horribly within hours.

The basic plot of the film involves John's baffled, angry reactions to this rapid onset of senescence; his and Miriam's separate efforts to gain the aid of a scientific expert on aging, Sarah Roberts; and Miriam's eventual decision to replace John as her lover with Sarah, whom she playfully courts and seduces (after consigning a superannuated but still-living John to a shackled coffin in the attic). In the story, then, Miriam is the central figure: the one who truly enjoys an eternity of youth and who generously promises this boon to others. But her promise, it turns out, is a lie, as John discovers when his hair begins falling out, his skin sagging, his energy bleeding away in sleeplessness and ennui. Driven to seek a cure from Sarah, John shows her his liver-spotted hands, moaning in astonished horror, "Yesterday I was thirty years old. I'm a young man. Do you understand? A young man." Later, confronting Miriam, he reminds her, "You said forever. Forever young." Yet when he says this, he has already become a wizened wraith, his twisted, shrunken appearance making a mockery of her vow. Though Miriam weeps regretfully, she nonetheless offers the same dubious pledge to Sarah later on, when attempting to conscript the woman as her new lover: "From this moment you will never grow old. Not a minute. You'll be young forever. . . . Forever and ever."

If we read the film as an allegory of the new bourgeoisie's ideology of consuming youth, then Miriam is the very embodiment of its utopian promises—promises that must be measured against the constricting realities of everyday consumer culture. And John—desperately scanning his wrinkling face in mirrors, poring in an agony of dread over photographs that bear the grim evidence of his deterioration—represents the perpetually dissatisfied consumer, frustrated at the betrayal of his fondest hopes. Indeed, Scott's shrewd deployment of mirrors and cameras in the narrative effectively indicts the visual regime of narcissistic objectification that supports the consumerist ideology of youth to which the film's characters are in thrall. And it is no accident that John is drawn directly to youth-culture figures after Sarah's science proves unable to save him. Vampirizing first a slim, punkish roller-skater dancing to the music of Iggy Pop in an abandoned warehouse, then the gum-snapping, barely pubescent music student whom he and Miriam have been tutoring, John clearly assumes that only by imbibing the literal substance of youth can his waning potency be restored. Moreover, the spectacle of teen idol David Bowie—author of such ironic paeans to the exuberant insubordination of adolescence as "Changes" and "Rebel Rebel"—brooding morosely over his fading youth and enviously begrudging its bloom in others, only serves to underline the film's savvy critique of the exploitative falsity of consumer youth culture. In many ways, *The Hunger* develops the strain of caustic satire implicit in Bowie's album *Scary Monsters* (1980), with its derisive vision of aimless youthful vitality ("Teenage Wildlife"), its indictment of regimented trendiness ("Fashion"), and its stark intimations of inevitable mortality ("Ashes to Ashes").

On the other hand, as Nicola Nixon has observed, casting Bowie, who had "just released two highly acclaimed videos" culled from this album, also helped to confirm "the essential up-to-the-minute contemporaneity of the film, representing vampirism in all its potential glamour, trendiness, eroticism, and appeal to '80s youth-cultism."[32] Thus, just as with *The Lost Boys*, *The Hunger* seems curiously divided in its purposes, seeking to arraign the manipulative mendacity of consumer youth culture while at the same time playfully flaunting its own complicity in this system. Yet this seeming contradiction deserves to be read *dialectically:* while the movie bitterly deplores the insincerity of consumerist promises, it also acknowledges the deep-seated longings they authentically express. Obviously, the guarantee of a literal eternity of youth is a brazen lie, yet the aspirations to leisurely freedom and a quickening intensity of pleasure that the phrase "forever young" encodes comprise the hidden utopian truth of consumption, a desirous hunger that the film affirms even as it rebukes the darker cravings to which, under capitalism, it is necessarily joined.

This dialectical complexity is evidenced most clearly in the scenes involving Miriam's seduction of Sarah (fig. 9). The first of these is unquestionably one of the most dreamily homoerotic in contemporary popular film, as the two women embrace and couple to the soaring coloratura of the "Flower Duet" from Léo Delibes's opera, *Lakmé*. In fact, the song is important not only for the lyrical atmosphere it provides but also for its narrative content, as the following exchange reveals:

SARAH: What's that piece you're playing?
MIRIAM: It's *Lakmé* by Delibes. Lakmé is a Brahmin princess in India. She has a slave named Mallika. In a magical garden they sing how they followed the stream to its source, gliding over the water.
SARAH: Is it a love song?
MIRIAM: I told you. It was sung by two women.
SARAH: It sounds like a love song.
MIRIAM: Then I suppose that's what it is.
SARAH: Are you making a pass at me, Mrs. Blaylock?
MIRIAM: Miriam.
SARAH: Miriam.
MIRIAM: Not that I'm aware of, Sarah.

The music, played for purposes of seduction (despite Miriam's coy demurral), affirms an idyllic, almost timeless homoerotic bond—a bond whose utopian dimensions are suggested by Miriam's glowing imagery: united in a "magical garden," their movements together as sinuously sweet as if they were "gliding," the two women share an indelible primal experience—"they followed the stream to its source." This "stream" is vivified in the ecstatic fluid exchange that takes place during their love-

Figure 9. The seduction of the new-class vampire. Video still from Tony Scott's *The Hunger*.

making as Miriam first drinks from Sarah's veins, then nurtures Sarah with her own deathless blood. The scene thus culminates in a powerfully utopian image of consumption, one that is vampiric and yet *reciprocal*—in other words, not a unilateral exploitation, but a mutual liberality that is transfiguring and joyous.

As this scene and those that follow it make clear, the casting of Catherine Deneuve is as important as that of Bowie to the film's figuration of consumer eroticism. Deneuve, an icon of glamour and sexual ambiguity whose commercial appeal at the time was enormous (she has marketed, most famously in this country, Chanel perfume and Oil of Olay), infects a young consumer with her vampirically homoerotic allure, causing a transformation that is experienced as liberating by its "victim" and as subversively threatening by members of the "straight" world.[33] This heterosexual anxiety is evidenced in the following scene, set in the restaurant of an athletic club, in which Sarah's boyfriend, Tom, suspicious about her three-hour "conversation" with Miriam, demands to know "what the hell's wrong with [her]" and suggests that she see a doctor. Meanwhile, Sarah is covertly ogling a pair of nubile female swimmers in the indoor pool below their window, clearly harking back to her rapturously "fluid" experience with Miriam. When Tom goes on to express shock that Miriam has given Sarah, whom she only just met, an expensive present (a golden pendant that, as Miriam explains, symbolizes eternal life), Sarah could be describing Deneuve herself as much as Miriam when she responds, "That's the kind of woman she is. She's European." As Nicola Nixon argues, not only Deneuve and Bowie but the entire film seem to exude a "potentially transgressive homoeroticism" that communicates to its viewers "the genuine allure of immortality and eternal youth."[34]

The critical problem—one of which the film seems quite aware—is that this utopian appeal is entirely confounded with a pernicious class logic. Miriam's sexual courtship of Sarah is also a class seduction, a conflation of libidinal and political economies. Impressed by the luxurious appointments of the townhouse ("You have so many beautiful things"), Sarah indulges a museful fantasy of Miriam's lifestyle: "Lunches and dinners and cocktail parties at the Museum of Modern Art." For her part, Miriam is more than happy to play upscale tour guide ("That's Florentine. Five hundred years old"), confidently affirming a self-centered world of privatized consumption ("You would consider me mostly idle, I'm afraid. My time is my own"). The class allegory here is identical to that in Rice's *Interview:* in Bourdieu's terms, the new bourgeoisie eagerly mimics, though always with a vague sense of parodistic inadequacy, the sumptuary tastes of an imaginary aristocracy. "I don't like sherry," says Sarah, feeling self-consciously gauche; "I think you'll like this one," Miriam silkily replies. In this context, the homoeroticism into which Miriam initiates Sarah may be seen as merely another high-class "taste," a recusant privilege of yuppified leisure.

This connection is cleverly established by the various economic/ erotic connotations sparked off by the sherry itself. First, Sarah spills some of the liquid onto her blouse, leaving a small stain, which leads directly to her disrobing by Miriam and their dreamy sex play; the sherry is thus a foretokening of the "fluid" sexuality—and the blood—they will soon share. Then, in the following scene with Tom, Sarah orders a glass of sherry at the restaurant—obviously in gloating memory of her liaison with Miriam—and when reminded that she doesn't like the drink, responds with a secretive smile, "I know"—thus affirming that her "tastes" have now been radically transformed. Finally, after her first vampiric feeding (on, alas, poor hapless Tom), Sarah slinks coyly into Miriam's presence, a lusty leer on her face and an even larger red stain— this time of blood—on her blouse, thereby suggesting her accession to the exalted (vampiric) gentry who view humans as mere prey. These "fluid" linkages forge a signifying chain that connects homoerotic desire, a yuppie lifestyle, and the violent assertion of categorical superiority, thus potentially defanging (as it were) the liberatory subversiveness of the film's figuration of alternative sexuality by conflating it with an invidious class privilege.

This reading gains support from the fact that the lesbian bond between Sarah and Miriam abruptly shades into a fierce competitive struggle, in which Miriam asserts her ownership of Sarah ("You belong to me")—an unequal power relation that was always implicit in the "love song" of the princess Lakmé and her slave Mallika—while Sarah disgustedly condemns Miriam's deviant allure ("You're crazy"). The struggle between the two women culminates when Sarah, realizing she can never escape from Miriam's erotic/predatory clutches, plunges a blade into her own throat in an attempt to take her undead life, thus rejecting the consumerist bounty—and perhaps, by implication, the homoerotic experience—that Miriam has offered her.

Yet here the film does something rather strange—something that has persistently baffled its critics.[35] In a significant change from the ending of Whitley Strieber's novel, wherein Miriam simply entombs Sarah with her other moribund lovers and moves on with her glamorous life, the film has Miriam, as a result of Sarah's violent rejection, finally getting her comeuppance. In a scene shot, once again, like a music video (filled with slow-motion images of blowing lace curtains and doves flying), Miriam finds herself besieged by the decomposing horde of her abandoned former lovers, whose assault somehow precipitates in her the same fate they themselves had suffered: within mere minutes, Miriam's miraculously preserved youth and beauty crumble away into the gruesome semblance of a shrieking skeleton. In an elliptically brief coda, set sometime in the future, we see Sarah, magically restored to undead life, standing on the balcony of a chic high-rise apartment, flanked by (one presumes) two of her own vampire lovers—a teenage boy and girl.

Other than permitting the familiar genre ending in which the vampire-villain crumbles spectacularly into dust, the film's concluding sequence really makes little sense in terms of a purely narrative logic—hence the consistent critical opprobrium it has received. But if read in terms of the social allegory I argue for here, *The Hunger*'s mysterious conclusion takes on powerful resonance. Since Sarah is the first ever to refuse the gift of eternal youth, the fact that her action angrily rouses Miriam's castoff lovers suggests what amounts to a consumer revolt, an uprising against the alluring but disillusioning promises of consumption. In the face of this popular rebellion, the consumer system cannot sustain the narcissistic ideology that governs it, and Miriam withers away. Her power, in short, is entirely dependent upon—indeed, ultimately derives from—the self-objectifying (un)dead labor of the mass of consumers she seduces and betrays; when they refuse to be her slaves—when they reject the preening narcissism of consuming youth—she ceases to be their master. But the genuine boon of consumption—of desire perpetually refreshed and satisfied—does not die with her, but rather survives in the community of lovers Sarah initiates, a community that clearly retains the homoerotic possibilities Miriam had evoked (Sarah kisses her female lover at the end). Moreover, it is possible that this new sexual-political order has moved beyond the sterile narcissism of Miriam's regime of consumption; certainly, in its triadic (and perhaps expansive) structure, it has transcended the narrow model of the yuppie couple that Miriam had sustained through the centuries. What this reading suggests is that it is possible to imagine a situation in which the utopian (homo)eroticism of contemporary consumer culture might potentially be de-linked from the narcissistic objectification and predatory exploitation that currently limits and constrains it, yoking its liberatory sexual promise to a pernicious class logic.

But this reading is, alas, too utopian, since the film in fact cannily hedges its bets. In the first place, the system Miriam represents has not been entirely superseded, since Sarah keeps the woman's undead body chained in a coffin in her own attic. And Sarah's vampire lifestyle, too, in many ways seems to mirror Miriam's own: most obviously, her apartment is lushly appointed, and we can infer that she has at last acceded to the new bourgeois privilege she had previously envied. Perhaps she has done no more than replace Miriam in an ongoing cycle of cynical exploitation. This, indeed, is Auerbach's reading: Sarah's "distinctive style, her rhythm, her decor, all have turned into Miriam's," though in Reagan's competitive America, there can be "room for only one at the top." [36]

Yet I think what makes the movie—and not just its oddly ambiguous finale—so potent is that, like *The Lost Boys*, it brilliantly encapsulates both the positive and negative metaphorics of consumer vampirism, showing that the mobilization of utopian desires within consumer culture is deeply confounded with (psychological and social) structures of exploitation. This dialectical imbrication is embodied in one of the film's central images: the ankh. Worn as a pendant bestowed by Miriam on each of her successive lovers, the ancient Egyptian symbol represents eternal life; yet it is also a dire weapon, sheathing a blade that is used by the vampires to slash the throats of their prey. Focused in this ambivalent image, the historical project of consuming youth might seem merely an arrested dialectic, a simple conflation of progressive and dystopian possibilities, yet the vampire texts that have subsequently built upon *The Hunger* have pressed forward its dual metaphorics of consumer vampirism—especially as they relate to a vein of popular homoeroticism—in rich and challenging ways.

But before discussing these successor texts, I would like to briefly consider another important connection between *The Hunger* and contemporary youth culture. If (as I argued in chapter 2) Rice's *Interview with the Vampire* had tended to obscure the technological bases of youth consumption, then *The Hunger*, largely through its shrewd casting, introduced into the yuppie vampire tradition a focus on the consumer apparatuses that incite and mobilize youthful desire. The participation of Bowie in particular was crucial in establishing this connection, since his presence—along with the film's imagery and style of editing— evoked the instrumentality of music video, a form then in its infancy. Moreover, Bowie's own career provided an extratextual backdrop that undoubtedly fed into *The Hunger*'s popular reception. By the time of the film's release, the performer had undergone a series of spectacular (and quite calculated) alterations in his public persona, radical makeovers that seemed to symbolize the protean wiles of the youth fashion industry itself. Indeed, everything about Bowie, from his sexuality to his appearance, was slippery and changeful, such that to consume the musical and filmic commodities generated by this ceaselessly shape-shifting performer was, in some measure, to consume youth itself as deviant, androgynous, mutable substance.

Perhaps unsurprisingly, then, Bowie's evolving incarnations came to feature mutant tricksters, otherworldly beings like the alien Ziggy Stardust, who in the early 1970s stood as an emblem of provocative, willful self-fashioning. This flamboyant role fused "queer" ambiguity (Bowie came out as gay to the music press at this time)[37] with glamorous self-adornment, thus consolidating within the sphere of youth musical culture the paradigm of homoerotic narcissism soon to emerge in the arena of popular advertising. The gender-bending, fashion-conscious "glitter rock" pioneered by Bowie (and other artists of the period such as Marc Bolan and Iggy Pop) was, as Van Cagle has pointed out, basically a refinement of Warhol's campy superstar aesthetic, a "conversion of Warholian/Factory premises for a mass audience."[38] Bowie himself, in his ongoing masque of sleek, stylish postures, seemed to embody not only a polymorphous sexuality but a capricious fluidity of identity; according to Iain Chambers, Bowie essentially vivified "the continual sign production of the mass media," that kaleidoscope of possibilities "coming out of the radio, the record grooves, the headphones; off the adverts, the television screen."[39]

This conflation of Bowie's crafty role-playing with the technical apparatuses of the mass media was potently captured in Nicolas Roeg's film *The Man Who Fell to Earth* (1976). In this work of science fiction,

Bowie, playing a variant of his Ziggy Stardust character, appears at one point before an array of blaring televisions, his extraterrestrial senses somehow permitting him to ingest and synthesize this cacophony of information.[40] (This scene stands in fascinating counterpoint to one described in chapter 1, in which master vampire Max seems to loom out of an array of assembled screens in *The Lost Boys*.) Despite their uneasy delirium, Bowie's "alien" postures, in this film and elsewhere, were animated by a powerful strain of technological utopianism, incarnating a vision of youth transformed by its rapt confrontation with a looming futurity. "It's a brave new world," Bowie remarked in 1972, "and we either join it or become living relics. . . . There are people who are aware of this . . . , people who are spearheading the future in one way or another."[41] While his performance, ten years later, as the hideously raddled John Blaylock perhaps involved a clever satire of himself as a "living relic," it also served to connect Bowie's notorious technomutant personae with powerful imagery of a lingering undeath. In short, Bowie's penchant for comprehensive metamorphosis has, during the course of his career, been figured in terms of both the vampire *and* the cyborg — a suggestive connection that has actually marked his popular reception as well. As the letters and other materials gathered in Fred and Judy Vermorel's *Starlust* (1985) demonstrate, Bowie has been a lightning rod for adolescent daydreams that have activated the dual metaphorics of consumer vampirism in ways that indicate their complex entanglement with a logic of cyborgization.[42]

Starlust features examples of fan writing whose obsessional intensity verges on the psychotic; the pop icon who incites the most extreme responses is, perhaps predictably, Bowie. On the one hand, the star is evoked as the hypnotic agent of an insidious technocracy of sensuality, a manipulative master vampire who feeds upon and exploits his needy fans; on the other hand, he is envisioned as a glamorous, playful trickster whose artfulness in perpetually remaking himself obscurely empowers his devoted followers. The former construction is evidenced in the story of Jason, a young man of twenty-one, who bemoans his uncontrollable engrossment with the alluring figure of Bowie. Significantly, Jason displays a canny attention to the social mechanisms whereby his obsession is enforced — the technological system that mediates Bowie to him as a repertoire of gripping images:

> I've just been through a couple years of real utter confusion and mayhem, and Bowie was a part of that. It was just me being a misfit, trying to find something. It got really messy. It became so I was

living in a film. . . . It annoyed me that the media had suddenly
managed to penetrate people's lives so much that you couldn't escape from someone a million miles away, someone totally remote. . . . You know they're miles away, in a studio somewhere in
London—but they get inside you. It's kind of a claustrophobic
feeling where everything's brought together by the media. . . . It
was like I was living in the most advanced film there ever was.
(pp. 74–76)

Jason's story employs a complex rhetoric of intimacy and distance, objectification and interiority to express how personal experience and
media images have become confusingly entwined. Though he knows
that Bowie is just a person "in a studio somewhere in London," he finds
himself unable (like Renfield in *Dracula*) to shake "a kind of godlike fear"
of Bowie's seeming omnipresence, a fear focused in a photographic image of him "calmly observing everything that's going on" (pp. 74–75).
Nor can he suppress an unquenchable desire for this image, for its se-
renity and power. Jason's life is dominated by Bowie, who is at once a
palpable presence and "these crazy images rushing past," "bizarre imaginings" (ibid.).

Of course, these confessional musings can be easily dismissed as evidence of paranoid schizophrenia, which they likely are; yet Jason's vision
of a consciousness invaded, colonized, and occupied by media imagery
neatly dovetails with the draconian critiques of popular youth culture
canvassed in chapter 1. One could easily imagine critics such as Stuart
Ewen or W. F. Haug denouncing Jason's fixation on Bowie in the very
terms the young man himself deploys: as an insidious form of psychic
violence—"horrific really when you think about it" (p. 75)—effected by
image technologies. Moreover, like those critics, Jason conflates vampiric and cybernetic metaphors to describe the operations of this system,
evoking the dead labor of social consumption as an alienated power embodied in media apparatuses: "I . . . had a sort of feeling that the world
was run by zombies and everyone was trying to find a way through . . .
the power of the medium he was involved in, all that technology and
everything. . . . That's why I don't have a telly at the moment, I'm totally
sick of it all. I'm looking for some real people" (ibid.).

Yet this principled rejection of Bowie's vampiric image—a rejection
that extends (as with Grandpa in *The Lost Boys*) to a Luddite refusal of
the technological regime of consumption itself—is consistently undermined by the seductive fascination of the image world obvious throughout Jason's story. Again and again, "real people"—those touchstones of

authentic connection Jason claims to seek—emerge as banal, merely human, beside the divine Bowie, "a super-being" equipped with an "extra magic" that others can "somehow never manage to emulate" (pp. 75–76). Bowie's beckoning presence seems designed to incite "some fantastic trip in my life. . . . [l]ike going from one life form to another" (p. 76). As music critic Jon Savage has observed, Bowie seemed to many of his young fans the very "promise, the premise of pop and teen fashion," offering the radical possibility of "self re-creation": "overnight, you can be transformed into something superhuman."[43] While Jason finally rejects the lure of this transformation, its promise still retains a tantalizing power. "I think if I saw him in the street now I don't know how I'd cope," he concludes.[44]

Just like the youth-culture critics, Jason's problem is that his blanket condemnation of consumption makes no distinction between its capacity for exploitation and its genuine utopian appeal. As a result, the latter continues to haunt Jason's critique in the form of a febrile yearning, a liberating potential Bowie's image seems to express even as it perniciously dominates the young man's consciousness. In short, an implicit logic of cyborgization—of technologically mediated empowerment and transmutation—is confusingly entangled, in Jason's confession, with an anguished resistance to vampiric predation and control. This same confusion marks the outpourings of another Bowie fan, Marnie, though her remarks edge closer toward an endorsement of cybernetic transformation. Like Jason, Marnie desires Bowie with an almost apocalyptic force; moreover, her desire is explicitly sexual in nature, as her hallucinatory record of a dream experience testifies. Uneasily evoking the more affirmative metaphorics of consumer vampirism, Marnie's story mixes desire with terror, gentle fantasy with cannibalistic horror; her flesh feeds Bowie, who returns the bounty in a eucharistic offering, leaving both unimaginably transformed: "He swooped me up in his arms and kicked open a door and we were on a beautiful tropical beach. He took me to a waterfall and we made love. . . . And then something unexpected happened. . . . [H]e scratched off my breasts with his nails and ate them and then I saw them just grow again. . . . Afterwards he tried to coax me into eating different parts of him saying how it was going to make us so much stronger than we were now" (p. 88).

While her tone is wary and ambivalent, Marnie's rhetoric eschews metaphors of invasion and colonization in favor of images of incorporation and metamorphosis. Unlike Jason's tale, which ultimately devolves into a cautionary fable of the evils of image worship and the need for genuine human connection, Marnie's story bespeaks a libidinal investment in consumption that cannot be quelled, however painful the personal cost. For Marnie, it is not quite so easy to resist the media technology: "I was trying to turn the telly off and he [Bowie] had the remote control in his hands and when I tried to get it away from him he had it in his other hand" (p. 89). While clearly recognizing the ravenous vampirism of the system ("He can do anything and get away with it and I can't stop him" [p. 90]), Marnie embraces it nonetheless, seeking the rejuvenating energies it provides even as it preys upon her. At one point in her dream Marnie herself sprouts "vampire teeth," with which she keeps "trying to bite him on the neck" (p. 89): in essence, her youthful consumption involves also a consumption of youth, of Bowie's transfiguring power. Yet this power, though objectified in Bowie, emanates, finally, from the depths of the consuming subject herself: "I was having a baby and they were telling me to push and this sort of light came out of my vagina and it was Bowie" (ibid.).

The complicated dream exchange between Marnie and Bowie seems to activate a potential for transcendence in the system, a dialectical capacity to move beyond unilateral exploitation, thereby making both the consumer and the apparatus of consumption "so much stronger" than they currently are. And yet this beyond is never fully attained; it "coaxes," but remains always maddeningly out of reach: "if you try to get through to him he won't let you," she complains (p. 90). Although Marnie's dream in the end cannot liberate the cyborg trapped within the vampire, it does seem to grasp, in fact quite poignantly, the simmering contradiction between them that marks the contemporary process of consumption. And it is Bowie himself—as icon, as commodity, as object of fantasy and desire—who represents this contradiction in all its baffling complexity. As Marnie observes, "It was like he had a split personality" (p. 88).

TWO QUEER NATIONS

Bowie's appearance in *The Hunger* not only marked a crucial stage in the evolution of the youth-consumer vampire, implicitly registering the convergence of this figure with a cybernetic logic; it also exerted a profound influence on subsequent vampire texts. Indeed, Bowie seemed the perfect model of an aristocratically decadent yuppie vampire, with his "golden blaze of lissome gesture, seraphic facial expression, satin hair," the "entrancing rhythm" of his movements, his "lithe androgynous beauty"—rapturous descriptions that derive not from the fevered musings gathered in *Starlust*, but from an essay that appeared in the November 1983 issue of *Vogue* magazine. Entitled "David Bowie and the End of Gender," it was written by Anne Rice.[45] In this virtual love let-ter to the performer, Rice extravagantly praises Bowie's alluring androgyny—"his elegant and feline guises," "the alchemy of his subtle strength and yielding beauty"—which seems to hold out to contemporary youth the possibility of gender transformation, a welcome message, since for young people "change isn't so much frightening as essential." [46] It was shortly after producing this article that Rice began to write *The Vampire Lestat*, whose eponymous protagonist is a notoriously androgynous rock star, so it is hardly a stretch to presume a connection. [47] In fact, it is very likely that Bowie's appearance in *The Hunger* was responsible for spawning a boom in the curious subgenre of the rock-and-roll vampire story, whose other entries include S. P. Somtow's *Vampire Junction* (1984), Nancy A. Collins's *Tempter* (1990), and Poppy Z. Brite's *Lost Souls* (1992), as well as the films *Vamp* (1986) and *Rockula* (1990). Interestingly, this subgenre has cut across the yuppie-slacker dialectic in provocative ways—a subject I will explore below.

Collectively, these texts played subversively on the long history of adult criticism of rock music as promoting licentious sexuality and rampant gender-bending among its youthful consumers, a critique that came to focus specifically, during the early 1980s, on the medium of rock videos. The Music Television (MTV) cable network debuted to an enthusiastic youthful reception in 1981 and had soon come to warehouse the entire spectrum of youth consumption, hawking not only albums but also hygiene products, comestibles, sports equipment, and forms of fashion—including fashionable identities. Indeed, by the mid-1980s, MTV seemed to represent consumerism in its most full-blown form, a point remarked by E. Ann Kaplan, author of the first critical book on the network: "MTV, more than any other television, may be said to be about consumption. It evokes a kind of hypnotic trance in which the spectator is suspended in a state of unsatisfied desire but forever under the illusion of *imminent* satisfaction through some kind of purchase." [48]

Unsurprisingly, this seductive appeal drew the wary attention of social conservatives: as the Calvin Center study *Dancing in the Dark* rather delicately put it, because "MTV captures the interest and reflects and shapes the sensibilities of youth . . . the channel merits serious adult concern." [49] This concern was evinced in an outpouring of conservative diatribes against the cynical allure of music videos, stern scoldings for misspent leisure that generally activated the "negative" metaphorics of consumer vampirism in which adolescent spectators were depicted as spellbound victims of an evil Pied Piper—the swarming mallrats of the video arcades now transformed into privatized televisual consumers. Indeed, anxiety over the fact that the wanton imagery of the youth-consumer system had managed to infiltrate the sanctum of the home provided this critique with much of its apoplectic edge. Critics were essentially decrying what amounted to the accomplishment of Max's vampiric plan in *The Lost Boys*—the invasion of the family dwelling by an apparatus of consumption that prompted in youth an insubordinate sense of consumerist autonomy and gave rise to fantasies of an alternative community.

Of course, there was nothing new about a self-righteous campaign against the insidious influence of rock music—these have dogged the form since the lascivious keenings of Little Richard first reverberated through suburban teenage bedrooms in the 1950s[50]—but the conjoining, in the 1980s, of lyrical content with video image under the aegis of a sleek and sophisticated commercialism seemed to up the ante of parental hysteria. The basic point at issue had already been prefigured by Bowie himself in 1972, when he proudly claimed that contemporary rock culture was forging "a new kind of person . . . a child who will be so exposed to the media that he will be lost to his parents by the time he is 12."[51] When a gauntlet like this has been so boldly thrown down, it is hardly surprising that parents would eventually take it up; and, in 1985, two well-placed parents—Tipper Gore and Susan Baker (wife of then–Treasury Secretary James Baker)—founded the Parents' Music Resource Center (PMRC) to combat the vile seductions of "shock rock," including especially its manifestations on MTV.[52] Gore's book *Raising PG Kids in an X-Rated Society* (1987) alternated alarmist rhetoric about the unchecked proliferation of sexually explicit and violent imagery in contemporary youth culture with firm guidelines for adult supervision of young people's leisure and consumption. The latter included minilectures on how to control one's TV set and VCR—as if these beacons, in a scenario worthy of the film *Poltergeist* (1982), had unleashed wild supernatural forces into family living rooms and now required the sober ministrations of an exorcist.[53]

This metaphor is hardly an exaggeration, since when it came specifically to heavy-metal music and videos, Gore herself invoked Satan as the seducer of youth—a thesis that was meticulously (not to say fanatically) pursued by Carl Raschke, a tabloid "expert" on "cults," in his book *Painted Black* (1990). According to Raschke, occult forces, their "social effect or influence . . . amplified through the television component of rock video, particularly the kind that is run regularly on MTV,"[54] had put an entire generation of teens at risk of satanic contamination. Representing a "new morbidity" (p. 165) that mixed "pubescent hormones with . . . [images of] suicide, whippings, bondage, bisexuality, nihilism, black magic, vampirism, werewolves, cannibalism, disembowelment," and so on (p. 168), heavy-metal music and videos were "cement[ing] a neural bond with all stripes of alienated adolescence" (p. 166) and thus threatening the legitimacy of parental authority—even with "parricide itself" (p. 168).[55] Raschke's indictment of the resultant "Dionysian frenzy" (p. 173) indiscriminately conflated violent acts, sexual "deviance," and supernaturalism in a millennial scenario of youth's spectacular degeneracy. Similar attacks had been launched against Bowie's glitter rock in the 1970s, and they would be trotted out again in the 1990s to indict "Goth" musical culture;[56] but it was in the 1980s that the criticisms focused centrally on MTV's role as demonic impresario.

Perhaps the most visible (if not risible) of these critiques appears in Allan Bloom's best-selling screed *The Closing of the American Mind* (1988). According to Bloom, the phosphor-dot swarm of music video is "a muddy stream where only monsters can swim. A glance at the videos that project images on the wall of Plato's cave since MTV took it over suffices to prove this."[57] Bemoaning the decay of civilized values—especially of wholesomely sublimated sexuality—in the licentious excesses of rock music culture, Bloom evokes an apocalyptic vision of cultural decadence that localizes Raschke's sprawling arraignment of Satanic evil in a single mundane image:

> Picture a thirteen-year-old boy sitting in the living room of his family home . . . watching MTV. He . . . is provided with comfort and leisure by the most productive economy ever known to mankind; science has penetrated the secrets of nature in order to provide him with the marvelous, lifelike electronic sound and image reproduction he is enjoying. And in what does progress culminate? A pubescent child whose body throbs with orgasmic rhythms; whose feelings are made articulate in hymns to the joys of onanism or the killing of parents; whose ambition is to win fame and wealth in [sic] imitating the drag-queen who makes the music. In short, life is made into a nonstop, commercially prepackaged masturbational fantasy.[58]

To his credit, Bloom attempts to distinguish here between the technical apparatus of consumption, evidence of historical progress, and the vampiric seductions it broadcasts, proof of social regression; but his essential conservatism renders him incapable of resolving this contradiction (which is, in any case, only sketchily formulated). Paraphrasing Fredric Jameson, Bloom's position is one of "*right* puritanism": in his view, the problem is youth's rampant hedonism, its deviant and unmonitored pleasure-seeking, to whose ends the technical system has been grossly perverted. Essentially, Bloom gives us a slightly more hysterical version of Daniel Bell's influential argument about the tension in modern capitalism between an ascetic ethos of production (the Promethean agency responsible for "the most productive economy ever known to mankind") and the hedonistic tendencies of consumption (that irresponsible impulse to enjoy "a nonstop, commercially prepackaged masturbational fantasy"). Yet despite his narrowness of viewpoint, the figure Bloom asks us to "picture" is indeed a powerful one: the youthful cyborg as homoerotic narcissist, whose "orgasmic rhythms" are provoked and amplified by high technology—in short, Ziggy Stardust himself, now comfortably ensconced in every suburban living room.

A similar vision of misspent adolescent libido has been evoked, though in a more laudatory register, in arguments that deploy the "positive" metaphorics of consumer vampirism when discussing the effects of MTV on contemporary youth. Predictably enough, John Fiske has spearheaded this critical faction, taking Bloom's basic conceit and reversing its tenor, from censure to celebration. "MTV is orgasm," he rapturously proclaims, "when signifiers explode in pleasure in the body in an excess of the physical. No ideology, no social control can organize an orgasm. Only freedom can."[59] Connecting music videos with other youthful pleasures such as "breakdancing, rock and roll, drugs, surfing, sex, video games," Fiske defends the form for its "radical potential," its assault on everything bourgeois culture holds dear: aesthetic realism, the rational ego, adult propriety. Though a creation of capitalism just as children are creatures of their parents, MTV is a rebellious offspring: it is the punkish "safety pin through the nose, the army uniform worn to deny authority."[60]

Fiske's effusive rhetoric, a delirious mix of poststructuralist *jouissance* and advertising hype, is shared by many defenders of music television: Briankle Chang praises MTV as uniquely "capable of transgressing the familial closure and hence leading the parade of chromatic festivals across the surface of the social," while Dan Rubey deploys the Bakhtinian concept of the carnivalesque in depicting MTV as "participatory, open to everyone; it endorses freedom and equality, reversal of social hierarchy; it is oriented to the future, not the past."[61] These sorts of arguments generally assume that the playful visual spectacle of MTV automatically licenses a subversive identity in its youthful consumers, an impish resistance to authority not unlike the mercurial agency of the Lost Boys. MTV's lush provender of fantasy, its almost carnal pervasion of the adolescent imaginary, promotes a radical, democratic self-fashioning, a tantalizing diffusion of sexual/social possibility—one for which the hungering erotic ambivalence of the vampire (conceived here as mischievous trickster rather than as scheming despot) functions as an apt metaphor.

This position is valuable in that it resists the monolithically negative critiques of Raschke and Bloom, but unfortunately it goes too far in the opposite direction, failing to recognize the ways in which music video—especially as institutionalized on MTV—serves the interests not of its consumers but of corporate capital. The basic problem, again, is that Fiske and his ilk tend toward an undialectical, either-or logic, assuming that if MTV has some subversive effects then it must be a subversive medium in toto. In fact, of course, MTV is no different from any other institution of consumption (e.g., the shopping mall or the video arcade): while it may disseminate socially progressive possibilities, it remains bound within a system of market relations. These relations ensure that the pursuit of pleasure by youthful consumers takes place under circumstances not of their own making; as a result, the metaphorical "orgasm" experienced in the consumption of music video is, contrary to Fiske, unfree, since it is not only a simple release but also a *binding* of libidinal energy, a yoking of pleasure to the service of profit. This is not to say that true release does not occur, but merely to circumscribe its force: it is thus entirely possible for youth, via MTV, to enjoy a liberation from the gender (and other) constraints dictated by their parent culture, while at the same time entering ever more deeply into a commercial system that objectifies and recuperates their rebellious desires.

In his discussion of gender imagery in "glam metal" music videos, Robert Walser offers a more balanced perspective than either Bloom or Fiske. Arguing that the activation of feminine codes of self-adornment by male performers and fans has a utopian function, since it trades on a "free play of androgynous fantasy [that] shakes up the underlying categories that structure social experience," Walser stresses that this freedom operates within a commercial regime ever eager to capitalize upon its radical possibilities. Yet despite the fact that "mass culture may colonize existing [gender] tensions and ambiguities for consumer purposes," MTV's dissemination of images of long-haired boys in elaborate makeup reflects "a concern with shifting boundaries of gender and reality that cannot simply be disregarded [sic] as nothing but inauthentic or commodified fantasies."[62] This complexity—in which the commodity-form of music video serves as both a springboard for change and a horizon of constraint—is why it is always important to focus on the *doubleness* of the vampire as a metaphor for youth consumption, since it marks a system that is, inextricably, both exploitative and empowering. In short, the cybernetic enhancements of Ziggy Stardust and the vampiric predations of John Blaylock are two sides of the same youth-culture coin.

Rice's *Vampire Lestat*, one of the best-selling novels of 1985, reflects this doubleness in its glamorous portrait of rock-star vampire Lestat de Lioncourt. Reprising his role from *Interview*, Lestat here narrates his own life story, figuring as both a gender-bending pathbreaker in American popular culture and a shameless apologist for post-Fordist capitalism. He is, in brief, an agent of liberation and an exploiter, and the signal achievement of the novel is to show these contradictory roles as necessarily conjoined. This ambivalence is built into Lestat's position as a "Rock Superstar,"[63] an appropriate role for him to adopt, since, as he asserts, there is "something vampiric about rock music": while its plangent "electricity" and "dissolving" harmonies suggest a yearning transformation, it is also deeply "eloquent of dread" (p. 6). The music's duplicitous tone reflects its status as a commodity, in which form it gives earnest voice to youth's inchoate longings and cynically capitalizes upon them. Lestat's genius, like Timmy Valentine's in *Vampire Junction*, is to package himself explicitly as a vampire, though while Timmy seemed uncomfortable with this commercialized posture, Lestat revels in it. "I was always so good at being a monster!" he boasts (p. 18). His unapologetic visibility as a wanton fiend allows him to celebrate his predatory superiority while at the same time metaphorically expressing a subcultural deviance that marks him as implicitly queer. In the process, he at once feeds and feeds upon his youthful fans' desires.

Driven by "a wave of preternatural and remorseless ambition" (p. 12), Lestat decides to tell his life story by means of a chain of interdependent, mutually lucrative commodities. As befits MTV's complexly ramified youth-consumer regime, Lestat's project of self-promotion—"stretching its electronic tentacles" (p. 520)—encompasses not only an autobiography (ostensibly the very text we are reading), but also a series of twelve music videos along with his band's first album and their concert debut at the Cow Palace in San Francisco. The videos themselves—lush stagings of tracks from the album with titles like "The Children of Darkness," "The Grand Sabbat," and "The Dance of Les Innocents"—are, to judge by the foreground story of the novel that they relate in condensed form, oneiric reveries mixing historical episodes of mythic quest and romantic adventure with intense sensual bondings between Lestat and other men, human and vampire. In short, they amount to an audiovisual concept album combining the aesthetics of glam metal and glitter rock, a sort of cross between Iron Maiden's *Number of the Beast*

(1982) and Bowie's *Scary Monsters* (1980). The commodity chain in which they figure is dizzyingly self-reflexive, to the point that the book itself—titled *The Vampire Lestat* in the narrative world as well—may be seen as essentially a novelization of the video cycle contained within it. "What is important," asserts Lestat, the mastermind behind this interlocking profit machine, "is that it be orchestrated": together, the various products "must create a fame that will carry my name and my voice to the remotest parts of the world" (p. 14).

While this ambition points to Lestat's self-aggrandizing narcissism, with the resultant revenue stream enriching him just as human blood does, his plan also has a more "progressive" purpose: to flush out of hiding his fellow vampires, who for centuries have inhabited a shadowy underworld invisible to their human prey. "I wanted mortals to know about us," Lestat affirms. "I wanted to proclaim [us] to the world" (p. 17). He had attempted a similar revelation earlier in his career, as a performer at the Théâtre des Vampires in eighteenth-century Paris, but the audience had been unprepared, responding with hostility and fear to the display of his supernatural gifts. Other vampires too had been scandalized, especially since, during those revolutionary times, the despised aristocracy were often symbolized as predatory bloodsuckers deserving extermination, and vampires generally dreaded guilt by association.[64] At the Cow Palace concert that culminates the novel, however, the teenage fans greet Lestat with rapt devotion: when he boasts to the "sea of screaming youngsters" (p. 535), "I AM EVIL! EVIL! . . . I WANT TO DRINK UP YOUR SOULS," the kids respond with "Ecstasy, delirium" (p. 539). His fellow vampires remain wary of the sudden publicity, conspiring against him from their havens in campy bars on San Francisco's Castro Street.[65]

This last bit of evidence clinches the fact that Lestat's story is essentially an allegory of the cultural politics of gay identity, played out within youth-musical culture. As Lestat remarks at the start of the novel, after decades spent literally underground, "I *came out* into the twentieth century" (p. 4; emphasis added). His broadcast of "the forbidden truth" (p. 12) of his identity to the rock-and-roll world is an act akin to Bowie's defiant (if commercially motivated) announcement of his homosexuality in the 1970s, an affirmation of queer desire as expressed in the figure of the androgynous performer. While previous centuries had been unprepared for this unveiling, contemporary youth culture embraces it with enthusiasm, laughing cheerfully at the notion that there is anything truly "evil" about Lestat's "vampirism." Indeed, youth culture generally would appear to be more open-minded than Lestat's fellow vampires, who seemingly prefer to remain a closeted, stigmatized minority—that is, save for the "youngest" of the vampire elite, the "crudest fledglings" who have taken to imitating Lestat's postures and styles of dress (p. 529).

By "coming out," Lestat has essentially prompted a generational struggle within the vampire community—a resistance, perhaps, to his willful commodification of their lifestyle. For it is fairly obvious that, like Bowie's adoption of extraterrestrial personae in his 1970s incarnations, Lestat's vampirism provides a transparent metaphorical cover for the smuggling of "deviant" eroticism into the mainstream of youth consumption, a diffusion facilitated by the "electronic tentacles" of the MTV apparatus. As Andrew Goodwin observes, music video is a form whose commodity status tends to produce a "structured ambiguity that is designed to cater to an increasingly heterogenous audience" of teenagers—gay, lesbian, and bisexual as well as straight.[66] Like Queer Nation, Lestat stages his own version of a "mall visibility action," occupying the multiple sites of commodity culture in an unapologetic assertion of his "queer" presence, in the process activating the implicit queerness—the latent homoeroticism—within consumer youth culture itself.

Lestat's career also cleverly tweaks the views of those conservative critics who allege that music video induces satanic contamination. For not only does Lestat proudly identify himself as a *literal* occult entity, but he also heads up a garage band of "beguilingly androgynous and even a little savage" performers who, prior to Lestat's joining their ranks, had already dubbed themselves "Satan's Night Out."[67] The closing concert scene is geared to spur the most paranoid fantasies of cultural exorcists and nervous parents, as Lestat teases his delirious fans by promising to "convert" them to his insidious "lifestyle": "HOW MANY OF YOU WOULD BE VAMPIRES?" he calls out, and the assembled throng responds with a "childish exuberance pouring forth from young mouths and young bodies . . . an uninhibited wash of something that felt like love."[68] The hysterical alarmism of the chapter on rock concerts in Tipper Gore's *Raising PG Kids in an X-Rated Society*—a chapter entitled "Rockin' and Shockin' in the Concert Free-for-All Zone"—might very well have been inspired by the final scene of *The Vampire Lestat*.

As Simon Frith confirms, for some decades now "our understanding of what makes music and musicians sexy, has depended on a confusion of sexual address"—a confusion the vampire, with its erotic ambivalence, has been expressing in popular culture for more than a century and which the yuppie vampire text has emphatically valorized.[69] If Bowie provided one historical model for Lestat's gender-bending appeal, a more proximate influence on Rice's imagination could well have been

Frankie Goes to Hollywood, an openly commercial, openly gay British duo whose first album *Welcome to the Pleasuredome* not only spun out one of the best-selling singles of 1984, "Relax"—promptly banned by the BBC for its amorphous carnality[70]—but also provided a perfect neon-etched title for the enclosed-yet-welcoming bazaar and the localized-yet-floating eroticism of the music video mallworld.[71] Frankie, like Lestat, crystallizes the long history of libidinal utopianism that has animated youth consumption under Fordism, but both also capture this yearning in all its post-Fordist contradictions: the legitimation of alternative sexual identities within contemporary commodity culture has occurred side by side with the consolidation of exclusionary class identities, with the opulent yuppie on one side and the disenfranchised slacker on the other.

Lestat clearly belongs to the former cohort; indeed, Rice's allegory—like *The Hunger*'s—is so potent precisely because it connects its progressive treatment of gender with an invidious class logic. Lestat's "coming out" in the opening pages is explicitly into post-Fordist terrain—where, as he asserts, the "dark dreary industrial world I'd gone to sleep on had burnt itself out finally." This, in Lestat's view, is a positive development, since it means that "the old bourgeois prudery and conformity had lost their hold on the American mind," making people "adventurous and erotic again the way they'd been in the old days, before the great middle-class revolutions of the late 1700s."[72] Thus, the surly audience at the Théâtre des Vampires had been quite correct in their suspicions of Lestat, since when reborn as a yuppie vampire he proudly identifies himself as an aristocratic reversion, incarnating "a certain joie de vivre that the middle-class revolutionaries [had] called decadence in the past" (p. 8). This original imputation of "decadence" had powerfully confounded issues of gender and class: to the middle-class revolutionaries, aristocrats were androgynous predators whose entire lifestyle stood opposed to the stolid values of industrial production and sexual reproduction that they, the heterosexual bourgeoisie, embodied. Now, with the advent of a post-industrial world, the values of the aristocracy could be boldly affirmed once again, their "queer" sensuality side by side with their arrogant assumption of economic and cultural mastery.

Yet Lestat (and perhaps Rice herself) is unwilling to admit the exclusionary nature of this affirmation of post-Fordist enfranchisement; paradoxically, what Lestat finally affirms is a vision of aristocratic *populism:* "The old aristocratic sensuality now belonged to everybody. It was wed to the promises of the middle-class revolution, and all people had a right to love and to luxury and to graceful things" (p. 8). In short, the bourgeois industrial epoch, with its puritanical valorization of production, had effectively eliminated poverty and want; its asceticism had perhaps been necessary in order to achieve these ends, but such an attitude has now become anachronistic in the face of generalized prosperity. Instead, hedonistic celebration is the order of the day, and Lestat's vampiric senses revel in the commodity world surrounding him: "Department stores had become palaces of near Oriental loveliness—merchandise displayed amid soft tinted carpeting, eerie music, amber light. In the all-night drugstores, bottles of violet and green shampoo gleamed like gems on the sparkling glass shelves. . . . I gazed stupefied at computers and telephones as pure in form and color as nature's most exotic shells" (pp. 8–9).

The problem with this happy celebration of post-Fordist affluence is, as we have seen, that its boon was in fact unequally distributed—that the social enfranchisement of the new bourgeoisie came at the expense of traditional laboring classes within a general horizon of economic crisis. Thus, Lestat's fantasy world, where "[d]ock laborers went home at night to swim in their heated backyard pools" and "[c]harwomen and plumbers changed at the end of the day into exquisitely cut manufactured clothes" (p. 8), is little more than a comforting ideological posture rationalizing post-Fordist inequities. Lestat fails to perceive how his own success might be tied up with the social frustration of others—even of his fans, those eager "youngsters in their Halloween vampire clothes, faces gleaming with artificial blood, some wearing floppy yellow wigs, some with black rings around their eyes to make them all the more innocent and ghastly" (p. 535). It is quite possible that these kids, like Martin with his novelty items, may purchase Lestat's spin-off properties seeking a refuge from their dead-end lives, a desperate "magical solution." As Frith has observed of Frankie Goes to Hollywood's success— a success that came during the depths of the U.K.'s own crisis of deindustrialization,

> The Tory solution to Britain's economic recession is a new version of the nineteenth century's two nations. Growth is now supposed to come from the leisure goods industries. The new jobs will be low skilled and low paid; the non-affluent will service the affluent; the new working-class will work on other people's leisure. . . . Frankie—who come, after all, from Britain's most devastated city [Liverpool]—capture better than anyone else the neurosis of a society told, amid the wastelands of dead factories and eked-out social security, that the solution to our problems is to have fun.[73]

With the waning of the phantasmic energies of the "Reagan revival" and the growing apprehension of declining living standards, the indulgent lifestyle of the yuppie vampire came gradually to seem not only less attractive but, perhaps more to the point, less available to youth since the heyday of Frankie and Lestat. This doleful fact is one that contemporary slacker vampire texts have been quick to harp upon, often by engaging Rice's *Vampire Lestat* in pointed dialogue. Probably the most significant of these responses is Poppy Z. Brite's *Lost Souls*, a novel that has had a subcultural acclaim to rival Rice's best-selling success.[74]

Lost Souls is perhaps the furthest point yet reached on the yuppie-slacker dialectic, seeming at times almost a synthesis of *Martin* and *Interview with the Vampire*. Like Martin, Brite's vampires are aimless, working-class kids who know that they are basically unwanted, superfluous, disposable; but unlike Martin, they don't even have family to fall back upon. Like Louis and Lestat, they are openly gay and sleekly androgynous, but they crash in flophouses instead of opulent flats. Seeming less members of a privileged urban subculture than the drifting queer paupers of a Gus Van Sant movie, they are literal children of the night, traveling in feral packs. "The essence of childhood lost,"[75] their philosophy is one of stark disillusionment, a slacker credo in extremis: "when you have too much faith in anything, it is bound to hurt you. Too much faith in anything will suck you dry. In this way, all the world is a vampire" (p. 161).

The narrative representative of this nihilistic viewpoint is a fifteen-year-old waif named, appropriately, Nothing. The "true child of night," Nothing seems to capture "the soul of all the thin children who wore black, who traced their eyes in kohl and stared out their windows waiting for the sun to set. This boy looked as if he had been raised in the back room of some hole-in-the-wall nightclub, fed on bread soaked in milk and whiskey, the bones of his face shaped fine by hunger. That was the word for this child: *hungry*" (p. 222; emphasis in original). When we first meet Nothing, he is drifting aimlessly amid an affectless crowd of doped-up suburban posers, fabricating a tenuous identity out of horror stories and Goth music, "black t-shirts and leather jackets and smudgy makeup shoplifted from the drugstore at the mall" (p. 73), meanwhile longing for some exalted form of being that he cannot even name. One day, while bored to death in class, Nothing catches sight of a black van passing on the highway—its radio blaring Bowie's *Ziggy Stardust*—and it seems to signal to him a world of intense, vivid pleasure, inspiring him to run away from home to seek it out. This van, in fact, contains an all-male cohort of homoerotic vampires, the patriarch of whom, Zillah, is

Nothing's long-lost father.[76] Nothing, it seems, is himself a fledgling vampire, whose latent need for blood has begun to blossom with adolescence. His pubescent discovery of his secret inclination functions as an even clearer coming-out allegory than Lestat's public announcement of his vampirism, since when he is finally united with his undead kin (who pick him up while hitchhiking), they tutor him not only in the finer points of blood drinking but of gay sex as well.

Together, the entire giddy throng sets off in their van to locate a small-time Southern rock band named Lost Souls? (among Nothing's prized possessions is a bootleg tape of their music). It is in her handling of this subplot that Brite engages in her most obvious critique of Rice, since to her teen-punk vampires MTV seems a distant universe of cynical glitz ultimately less interesting than ratty garage bands playing in backwoods dives. In fact, mainstream bands—those who, like Lestat, rely on extended commodity chains—emerge as vampiric in a negative sense, as implicit exploiters. In an early scene, before he has met up with his vampire clan, Nothing is engaged in a desultory act of oral sex with a teenage friend named Laine, whose major defining characteristic is his fannish obsession with The Cure, the Goth-rock band that has enjoyed the greatest mainstream success. This success came with their 1987 album *Kiss Me, Kiss Me, Kiss Me*, which included among its various spin-offs a glossy poster of the album cover, a copy of which Laine has tacked up above his bed. Lying there, Nothing finds himself staring at lead singer "Robert Smith's lips enlarged several thousand times, smeared with hot orange-red lipstick, shiny and sexual. Nothing wished he could fall into them, could slide down Robert Smith's throat and curl up safe in his belly" (p. 32). The commodity world The Cure—and, by implication, Lestat—represents seems to promise pleasure and freedom, but in fact it threatens vampirically to absorb the consumer, to suck him in (as it were). In counterpoint, the novel projects the low-budget, socially marginal world of Lost Souls?, who have no official spin-offs but only pirated tapes passed reverently from hand to hand. The problem is thus not the technological medium per se, not the apparatus that captures and conveys the music to its devoted consumers, but rather specifically its corporate organization and the social hierarchy it subtends.

If the object of consumption differs in these two models, so, too, does the consuming subject. For whereas the commodified Goth music Laine enjoys seems metaphorically to hunt down and leech upon a passive consumer, the subcultural music of Lost Souls? must be actively pursued. Indeed, the lyrics of the one song quoted in the novel emphasize this sense of agency: "Does your road go no place? / Does it go someplace where you can't see? / If you follow it anyway / It might just lead you here to me" (p. 74). Compare this low-key invitation to the stentorian, domineering lyrics of Lestat: "YOU CAN'T RESIST THE LORDS OF NIGHT / THEY HAVE NO MERCY ON YOUR PLIGHT. . . . IN LOVE, WE WILL TAKE YOU / AND IN RAPTURE, WE'LL BREAK YOU," and so on.[77] *Lost Souls*, by virtue of its status as a slacker vampire text, shows tremendous skepticism toward the yuppie pretensions of Lestat and the commodity world he represents; yet in its endorsement of the dreamy homoeroticism this world promotes, Brite's novel also shows how much the slacker vampire text has learned and borrowed from its despised yuppie cousin. The question mark in the band's name is the perfect registration of this ambivalence, querying whether contemporary youth are genuinely lost souls, deserted by a cynical post-Fordism, or "queer" wanderers whose seeming decadence involves a bold affirmation of suppressed desires.

What the twin traditions of the yuppie and slacker vampire show is the tremendous pliability of the figure as a metaphor for socioeconomic and cultural processes. This pliability has extended to cover, in a wandering trajectory of texts spread over twenty years, both of Frith's "two nations" of post-Fordist possibility: of new bourgeois privilege and new underclass privation, two distinct but dialectically imbricated forms of consuming hunger. And, just as the yuppie vampire has facilitated crossover traffic between straight and gay (bourgeois) worlds, so, too, does the slacker vampire highlight affinities between disparate (proletarianized) races. Mutually locked out of the receding consumerist bounty, Brite's *Lost Souls* are siblings under the skin of the deracinated ethnic street kids of the contemporary inner-city gang story in its fictive and filmic variants.

A good example of the crossover is Jess Mowry's novel of African-American teens in Oakland, *Way Past Cool* (1992), in which the author explicitly evokes his roving squadrons of latchkey kids as "children of the night" subsisting in the interstices of a cruelly evolving economy. One of these strays is described as "a strange sort of boy, so delicate-looking yet so totally self-sufficient; like a prototype of something new or a re-program of something very old that was better equipped to survive. Evolution in action. The shape of things to come. Shape changers. Weren't werewolves called children of the night?"[78] The shimmer of the supernatural functions here—and indeed throughout the novel—almost as a redemptive deliverance from an otherwise brutally impoverished experience, thus remarking the stubborn persistence of a utopian impulse even in this bleakest of contexts. However, despite the occult

image ("werewolves"), this passage's technobiological rhetoric ("prototype," "re-program," "evolution") and science-fictional projection of
futurity ("the shape of things to come") signals the emergence of the
cyborg. In the next three chapters, I move to a consideration of the implications of this figure for post-Fordist youth culture.

FOUR

MICROSERFING THE THIRD WAVE: THE DARK SIDE OF THE SUNRISE INDUSTRIES

POSTINDUSTRIALISM AND "FLEXIBLE" CAPITALISM

In the first three chapters, I analyzed a series of literary and filmic texts in which the figure of the vampire functions as a potent metaphor for youth consumption. This metaphor operates in a dual register, figuring consumption as both predatory, involving the profitable capture of youthful desire via technological systems (especially video apparatuses), and prosthetic, since these systems enable fresh skills and self-sufficiencies in teenage consumers. As I argued in my introduction, this ambivalent linking of exploitation with empowerment in the realm of consumer technologies has its roots in Marx's dialectical conception of industrial automation as at once the "undead" objectification of human labor and the protocybernetic enhancement of its historical capacity. As my treatment of youth-culture vampire texts showed, even the most negative portrayals of consumer technologies as despotically vampiric were shadowed by a more affirmative perception of how these technologies had deeply transformed youthful appetite and agency.

In my final three chapters, I move to a consideration of a series of texts of the 1980s and 1990s that have drawn out this logic of prosthesis more explicitly, depicting youth's growing enmeshment with the machineries of consumption. These depictions have built upon and carried forward the rhetoric of mutation that marks analyses of young people's interactions with video discussed in my first three chapters, fusing this rhetoric with the fervid musings of contemporary cyberculture and the visionary impulses of science fiction. In these texts, teenagers become not only figurative but often literal cyborgs, their bodies adapting to consumer technologies in ways that augment and transform their physicosocial capacities. If the youth-consumer vampire emerges at the seductive interface linking youth with the video apparatus, then the cyborg closes the circuit, effacing the seams between youthful bodies and technological systems via their mutual incorporation into a new mutant identity.

Yet even as these cyborg youth texts have projected a radical amplification of youthful agency, they, too, are haunted by a dialectical shadow—by a critical perception of the modes of domination that inhere in consumption envisioned as a system of cybernetic control. In short, for all their seemingly affirmative endorsement of cyborg possibility, these texts also register the deep-seated imperatives of capital that yoke this potential to a regime of objectified, alienated, "dead" labor. Thus, even though the figure of the cyborg seems to promise an unprecedented expansion of the scope of youthful fantasy and action, it also remains bound to a vampiric socioeconomic regime that drains its liberatory energies. As a result, youth's fresh powers seem to turn against them even as they are mobilized and activated.

The vast majority of cyborg youth texts I examine in these chapters 4 through 6 focus on a technological system whose networked connections and spontaneously individuated operations crystallize perfectly the dialectic of control and subversion informing youth consumption: the personal computer. On the one hand, exhilarating horizons of possibility are seemingly opened up in teenagers' interface with PC units, promoting powerful new forms of agency and cultural enfranchisement for young people. Nonetheless, these horizons are progressively narrowed by the socioeconomic situation of youth within a post-Fordist system increasingly dependent upon computer technology and information-as-commodity. Given this stark equivocality, it is hardly surprising that the computer has emerged in popular discourses—including cyborg youth texts—as complexly divided, seeming to license both compliant regimentation and decentralized fantasy. In this chapter, I analyze a series of linked discourses that have powerfully staged the fundamental ambivalence of computerization as a cultural problematic, especially in terms of its implications for contemporary youth—specifically, popular journalistic and fictional treatments of the rise of computer industries during the 1980s and 1990s. As background for this discussion, I will first examine the theories of postindustrial society that crystallized during the 1970s, since these bequeathed a particular configuration of youth culture and technology that subsequent discourses have taken up and built upon.

In order to understand the importance of youth as a category within postindustrialism, we need to return to Stuart Ewen's arguments (outlined in my introduction) about how youth was constructed as an "industrial ideal" in the early decades of this century. In the 1920s and 1930s, according to Ewen, "youth"—an ambiguous term referring as much to metaphorical qualities of youthfulness as to literal young persons—served as a powerful conduit linking Fordist renovations of production with a rising ethos of mass consumption. Conceived as a set of physicopsychological properties such as animation, adaptability, and openness, youth enjoyed a special privilege within industries undergoing Taylorization, since this radical restructuring of production mandated an energetic pliancy in workers, a capacity to integrate with and adapt to machinic interfaces in an evolving assembly line. At the same time that empirically youthful bodies were being systematically commodified in the Fordist factory, a more metaphorical conception of youth was being mobilized in the consumer marketplace—as a fetishized substance inhering in commodities themselves and activated by their consumption. As Ewen puts it, "corporations which demanded youth on the production line now offered that same youth through their products."[1]

Thus, as early as the 1920s Fordism had begun to establish a labor-leisure circuit through which youth moved as a privileged figure—a valued commodity and a compelling ideology. This circuit operated, especially in the realm of consumption, by means of an implicit logic of prosthesis, since "youth" designated not so much a fixed identity or form of embodiment as a portable assemblage of properties that could be purchased and incorporated into the consuming self. On the one hand, this arrangement consolidated a mode of regulation in which consumption functioned as a site of invigorating pleasure that helped accommodate workers to the exigencies of Taylorist management. On the other hand, it generated a social contradiction between the self-denying demands of production and the hedonistic impulses of consumption that became a source of profound cultural-political crisis with the advent of the baby boom. Above all, it constructed "youth" as a cyborg formation, paving the way for the literal images of youthful cyborgs that would emerge in subsequent decades, as the swelling postwar generations of young people interfaced with the proliferating nexus of consumer technologies.

As indicated in my chapter 1 discussion of the cultural discourses surrounding videogames, the construction of the youthful cyborg has generally been envisioned as a metaphorical coevolution in which youth and technology reciprocally mutate and develop: the technology breeds hybrid entities ("vidkids" or "screenagers") with expanded physical and psychological capacities, while the kids themselves, through the ludic impetus of their ripening prosthetic skills, impel the technology forward. This imaginary imbrication has a dual effect: not only does the technology, in its conflation with youth, come to hold out the promise of rejuvenation to its users (as witness David Sudnow's Atari-assisted intensity), but also young people become, in popular constructions, a technocultural avant-garde, a collective avatar of innovation and progress. As Douglas Rushkoff puts it in *Playing the Future*, screenagers are "a species in mutation" who have responded to "each successive development in communications technology" with adaptability and enthusiasm; accepting "change as a constant," they demonstrate to society at large how "we must accelerate our ability to process new thoughts and ideas" in order to survive.[2] These youthful cyborgs serve as models of how we must all learn to "youthen" ourselves—for either we incorporate the appropriate psychic prostheses (flexibility, openness, curiosity, etc.) that permit us to interface with new technologies, or we consign ourselves to stagnation, to "decline, decay, and death."[3]

There are curious and suggestive contradictions in this sort of thinking that I will analyze more fully as this chapter proceeds. Two points are worth remarking at the outset. First, as I pointed out earlier, Rushkoff's rhetoric associating mutant youth with cutting-edge technological advancement has the effect of *naturalizing* this progress: it becomes, in imagination, as ineluctable as biological evolution and the succession of the generations. Yet at the same time, Rushkoff is suggesting that this compelling natural cycle can potentially be transcended precisely *by means of* the youthful perspectives promoted by the technologies themselves. In other words, we ultimately need not fear our own antiquation and replacement—those seeming inevitables of biological history—because our rejuvenating prostheses will help us adapt to the changing techno-environment. Thus, while banking on the logic of supersession built into the evolutionary metaphor in order to portray technological development as inescapable, Rushkoff is at the same time suggesting that this logic has been somehow short-circuited by the social emplacement of those very technologies. The contradiction here is simple yet, as I hope to show, quite sweeping in its cultural implications; it derives from a surreptitious conflation of "youth" as a common-sense natural category—referring to a form of embodied experience existing in phased relationship with maturity, senescence, and death—with "youth" as a phantasmatic, fecundating energy potentially animating all persons regardless of chronological age. This equivocation is the legacy of Fordist capitalism's construction of "youth" as a fetishized substance—a disembodied principle of resiliency and renewal—within its ideology of consumption, a construction post-Fordism has inherited and built upon.

The second point I would like to make regarding the contradictory meanings of "youth" circulating in rhetorics such as Rushkoff's involves precisely the ways in which this contradiction affects how the historical transition from Fordism to post-Fordism might be imagined and described. Paradoxically, this transition has been envisioned as marking both a generational succession and a process of rejuvenation, the death of Fordist capitalism and its ultimate transcendence; the post-Fordist system at once supplants its predecessor and serves to reinvigorate its underlying project of capital accumulation. This is not to say that the transition, empirically speaking, is altogether chimerical, but rather to register how the very project of historical description has become deeply implicated in modern capitalism's ideology of youth. What is at stake here, in the words of Frank Webster, is the issue of "whether we are supposed to have experienced a systemic change," a definitive break with the dead past, "or whether what has emerged is more a continuation of established capitalist relations."[4] Yet assessing these relative possibilities is complicated by the slippery way the metaphor of youth operationalizes the contradiction between them: post-Fordism chronologically marks a "systemic change" just as a fresh generation does, replacing antiquated structures with viable alternatives (e.g., programmable batch production in place of the conventional assembly line), but at the same time it carries forward—and prosthetically "rejuvenates"—traditional features of Fordist capitalism (e.g., the regulated coordination of production and consumption).

As many critics of post-Fordist theory have pointed out, the weakness of transition arguments is their potentially phantasmatic character, their tendency to hypostatize a theoretical viewpoint as an accomplished reality[5]—a danger that is undoubtedly exacerbated when the concept of transition is conflated with visions of youthful renewal and regeneration. Martyn Lee's chapter on the decline of Fordism and the emergence of post-Fordism in *Consumer Culture Reborn*, for example, is entitled "Decay and Rejuvenation." The very terminology critics use to periodize modern capitalism is inflected by notions of life stages or generational relationships: critics uneasy with the term *post-Fordism*—with its implication of the advent of a qualitatively new system—often speak instead of "mature Fordism" or "late Fordism," while "neo-Fordism" accommodates fresh structures and possibilities within a more or less settled genealogy.[6] Webster employs a familiar metaphor to express this equivocation, suggesting that post-Fordism constitutes not "an entirely new system, but rather a *mutation* of capitalist regimes of accumulation."[7]

I am less invested in the use of a specific term to describe the present phase of capitalist society than I am fascinated by the metaphorical stakes of the game, the consistent figurative linkage of social transition with age relations. This tendency is not new, of course: for centuries, distinctions between "ancients" and "moderns" have been drawn in broadly generational terms by philosophers and historians. What is unique in the present theoretical crux regarding Fordism/post-Fordism is the importance of technological innovation in defining the connections between "new" and "old" systems—specifically, its impact on the (re)organization of work and consumption. The privileging of the category of youth within Fordist Taylorization (itself a process that constituted a radical reordering of the technical infrastructure of production relations) ideologically authorized claims for the rejuvenating force of subsequent renovations, thus ironically enabling arguments for the replacement of an aging Fordist system by a youthfully vigorous post-Fordism. In both cases, the core of technological innovation involves a new conception of automation that forges fresh links between production and consumption: under Fordism, assembly-line mass production of identical commodities was articulated with emergent techniques for molding mass demand; under post-Fordism, programmable batch production of differentiated goods is linked with a more diversely segmented consumer market.[8] Under both regimes, an ambient ideology of youth not only functions to cement connections between production and consumption, but also generates a ready supply of life-stage metaphors that are culturally exploited to promote the system's epochal uniqueness and potency.

Theorists of post-Fordism were not the first to mobilize this rhetorical arsenal against an allegedly antiquated mass-production regime: their arguments historically succeeded—and built upon—claims for the emergence of "postindustrial society" advanced during the 1970s.[9] As with post-Fordism, whose advocates include both the neomarxists of the New Times school and mainstream business analysts, postindustrial theory has both a left and a right wing; and as with the post-Fordist critics, the various champions of postindustrialism tend to adopt a heady rhetoric of futuristic speculation—a rhetoric that consistently deploys a vocabulary of mutant youth to describe the technosocial contours of the new world order.[10] This privileging of youthful metaphors prevails whether one focuses on postindustrialism of the right or left varieties— on the conservative evangels of managerial science promoting an information revolution as the global salvation of capitalism or on the radical apostles of "green socialism" advancing the new technologies as vehicles of authentic cultural pluralism and a reinvigorated public sphere. In both cases, the putative crisis of an aging, ossified industrial system generates a vision of evolutionary alternatives founded in information technologies. These postindustrial prophets employ youthful imagery to describe the emergence, from the wreck of a senescent industrialism, of a rejuvenated, "flexible" mode of production, a fledgling information-driven regime whose cultural expression portends ever more diverse enfranchisements and autonomies—an argument post-Fordist theory has adopted and carried forward.

As in the original Fordist cultural-theoretical nexus, youth circulates within postindustrial discourse in a dual fashion: while literal young people are enshrined as privileged subjects whose special experiences allegedly form a defining feature of the postindustrial regime, disembodied metaphors of youth are evoked to describe, in more general terms, this system's social operations and psychological effects. Postindustrialism, in short, displays the logic of prosthesis identified as a central feature of Fordist culture by Mark Seltzer—a concept that (as I discussed in my introduction) refers to the way youthful bodies and technologies are metaphorically refigured through their imagined exchange of properties. On the one hand, postindustrial theorists argue that the massive technological change associated with the information revolution necessarily privileges youth as social subjects, since they are not only those most likely to experience its fallout but also best prepared to respond to its challenges; youth are depicted as especially savvy about new technologies to the point of taking on their qualities of effortless efficiency and built-in expertise. On the other hand, these theorists use metaphors of youth—curiosity, pliability, and so forth—to depict the socioeconomic and cultural possibilities enabled by the spread of information processing, frequently depicting cybernetic apparatuses in terms evocative of adolescent energy and enthusiasm.

Alvin Toffler's best-seller *Future Shock* (1970) set the tone for much of the debate over postindustrialism during the coming decade. Though the term Toffler uses for the emerging social order is *superindustrial*, he is clearly describing the same complex of issues and institutions that the postindustrial theorists also take up: an economy in which "the assembly line . . . is an anachronism,"[11] its mass production of standardized commodities systematically being replaced by batch production of specialized goods (pp. 266–67); a society increasingly organized around information-processing services, which have broken down traditional job stratifications, resulting in a "significant deterioration of hierarchy" (p. 140); and a culture enjoying a democratic proliferation of consumer options, leading to the formation of diverse subcultures that display "a crazy quilt pattern of evanescent life styles" (p. 302). Above all, what Toffler stresses is the technologically driven rapidity of change that marks this superindustrial society. Developing a basic point of Daniel Bell's classic essay "Notes on the Post-Industrial Society" (1967), Toffler focuses on the snowballing acceleration of technoscientific progress that marks the contemporary period, a constant expansion that "radically alters the balance between novel and familiar situations," forcing "us not merely to cope with a faster flow, but with more and more situations to which previous personal experience does not apply" (p. 34). As Bell had observed, "The rate of diffusion (measured by economic growth) for technological innovations introduced during the post-World War II period was approximately *twice* the rate for post-World War I innovations and *four* times the rate for innovations introduced during the early part of this century." [12] The term *future shock* is Toffler's now-famous coinage designed to capture the psychological fallout of this continuous bombardment of novelty.

This fallout is unequally distributed socially, Toffler maintains, since rapid change affects different age groups in sharply varying ways. Older generations, more sedimented in their habits and expectations, are less apt to be comfortable with this quickened tempo than are the youthful "people of the future," those "advance agents of man, the earliest citizens of the world-wide super-industrial society now in the throes of birth." [13] Indeed, the dizzying pace of change not only drives attitudinal wedges between the generations, but also segments age groups into progressively narrower camps; for young people in particular, the effect is a generational turnover every few years, with each new cohort possessing "its own peculiar tribal characteristics, its own fads, fashions, heroes and villains" (p. 292). Consumer culture is the site where this unremitting supersession is played out, given over as it is to a "well-oiled machinery for the creation and diffusion of fads" (p. 73) whose transience is a built-in feature—just as it is in youth cohorts themselves, as their specific tastes and preferences are quickly eclipsed by fresh "generations." Here, as throughout Toffler's argument, youth and machinery display similar properties, as if attuned to each other in their developments: technological growth is driven by a youthful spirit of innovation, while youth itself shows a buoyant adaptability that permits accommodation with radically transformative technologies.

We can begin to see here the oddly contradictory ways that youth

circulates within postindustrial discourse. Cultural or technical obsolescence, the encrustation of routine that might threaten to hamper the
kinesthetic flow in which both youthful bodies and technologies are
caught up, is transcended in Toffler's argument by becoming a design
element spurring further evolution in machinic techniques and subcultural lifestyles. Yet age-based divisions are also preserved as a way of
marking off the fast-paced "people of the future" from those who "prefer to disengage, to idle at their own speed" (p. 39)—and who are thus
constructed as, literally or figuratively, more elderly. In short, "youth"
functions in the argument at once as a quasi-chronological marker of
identity segregating groups into physical/cultural phases of development *and* as a free-floating process of velocity and volatility—a figure
isomorphic with technological change itself.

If, as Boris Frankel has argued, Toffler's views represent a centrist
position in the postindustrial debates,[14] his equation of technology and
youth is essentially repeated, with modifications, in both the more radical and the more conservative strains of argument. Alain Touraine's
study *The Post-Industrial Society* (1969) is a good example of the former
trend, while Daniel Bell's book *The Coming of Post-Industrial Society*
(1973) effectively represents the latter.[15] For both critics, youthful expertise is a crucial element of the new social order, forming a potentially
powerful class interest in contradiction with traditional structures of
the industrial-capitalist system. According to Touraine, youth enjoys a
privileged position during a period of widespread change, since it is "the
group most attracted by the new forms of knowledge" but also "not yet
involved in the network of obligations created by massive organizations."[16] Youth is thus "best equipped to rebel against the technocrats"
who would subordinate technoscientific innovation to the exigencies
of bureaucratic management and the narrow class interests it serves.[17]
While not sharing Touraine's revolutionary rhetoric, Bell, too, emphasizes the developing conflict between a "new, younger and more educated labor force" and the "mechanical harness" of conventional occupational structures, which reflect traditional class hierarchies rather than
the novel forms of expertise—allied with burgeoning "intellectual technologies"—that make up the postindustrial "matrix of innovation."[18] In
short, both Touraine and Bell argue that the rise of postindustrial society has generated a logic of resistance to the increasingly fossilized
norms of capitalist social organization—a resistance rooted in the essential link between the growing demands inspired by youthful creativity
and the remaking of the socioeconomic landscape by the forces of technoscientific change.

Bell and Touraine also stress the importance of consumer culture within the postindustrial context, an emphasis with major ramifications for the youth-technology dyad. Bell considers the essentially hedonistic values inherent in consumption—an "attitude of *carpe diem*, prodigality and display, and the compulsive search for play"—as existing in tension with the self-denying ethos of production inherited from classic industrialism, culminating in a painful "disjunction within the social structure" that poses "the deepest challenge to [the] survival" of the postindustrial order.[19] While Touraine identifies the same basic division, he sees it as evidence of a desire for "creative participation in . . . a system of meanings directly attached to professional and social experience";[20] in other words, rather than bemoaning the decay of the Puritan ethic, with its inculcation of "provident behavior, industriousness, and self-control,"[21] Touraine suggests that consumer "hedonism" is only the negative face of an inchoate social impulse to transform working life into a more fulfilling activity that could sustain the sorts of pleasures now sought in consumption. And in this impulse, youth emerges as a significant avant-garde: indeed, the rise of "mass leisure activities . . . is inseparable from . . . the progressive appearance of adolescence as an autonomous social category in our society."[22] In short, the ethos of youth—its foregrounding of values such as playfulness, creativity, impatience with authority—may, when united with the immense potential of postindustrial technologies, enable more decentralized and self-determining systems in which labor and leisure practices are harmonized rather than opposed.

Following Touraine, most left-wing postindustrial theorists emphasize that the very division between labor and leisure is a moribund artifact of industrialism (of both the capitalist and socialist varieties), and that the spread of information technologies portends an epochal collapse of the public-private dualism characteristic of industrial culture. Generally speaking, this left variant of postindustrialism tends to privilege youth as the social agents least invested, economically and emotionally, in the decaying structures of a superannuated industrialism and thus most likely to realize the potential for radical social change latent in the new technologies.

What is at stake in these arguments, as André Gorz indicates in his study *Paths to Paradise* (1983), is nothing less than a transcendence of the pervasive vampirism of industrial culture as analyzed by Marx. According to Gorz, the technical infrastructure of postindustrial society, "[u]nlike the mega-technologies of the industrial era,"[23] lends itself to decentralized forms of organization in which workers are not subordinated to the motions of an automaton but potentially freed for more meaningful and satisfying work. Moreover, cybernetic automation, with its systematic replacement of human labor with programmed production processes, not only frees laborers from mechanical drudgery but also paves the way for a new social order based on part-time employment supported by a guaranteed wage. In such a system, leisure-time pursuits—such as indulgence in the pleasures of consumption—would not exist in tension with productive activity, but would rather be an integral component in a transformed community where "there [is] no separation between work, culture and life" (p. 49). Such a positive outcome is not assured, however, since "automation is socially ambivalent" (p. 28) and may instead allow for reactionary technocratic retrenchments on the part of a "living-dead capitalism" that seeks to enshrine "*the relations of domination based on the work ethic*" (p. 35; emphasis in original). But the emergence of postindustrialism at least holds out hope that the socioeconomic death grip of the capitalist vampire may finally be loosed.

Despite the left-wing provenance of this vision, much of its substance is shared by those more conservative postindustrial theorists who promote the new technologies as renovations essential to rejuvenate global capitalism. Even managerial science has developed a postindustrial wing, arguing for information-processing systems as panaceas that will reinvigorate production, diminish class conflict by spurring more creative forms of work, and generate limitless vistas of cultural plenty.[24] Larry Hirschhorn, in his study *Beyond Mechanization* (1984), argues that the conventional marxist critique of Taylorized production systems as alienating and dehumanizing misses the radical character of cybernetic automation, which emphasizes feedback and adaptation rather than unilateral conformity. Postindustrial technologies mandate a youthful outlook, "a culture of learning, an appreciation of emergent phenomena, an understanding of tacit knowledge, a feeling for interpersonal process"—nothing short of a "coming to consciousness" as "one who adapts," the capacity to respond to change eagerly and rapidly becoming the defining quality of the worker of the future.[25] Agreeing that "work at the data interface concerns the heightened responsibility of jobs that demand continual responsiveness to a flow of data," Shoshana Zuboff of the Harvard Business School distinguishes Taylorized automation from a cybernetic "informating process" that decentralizes corporate power and redistributes authority between managers and their newly "flexible and knowledgeable work force."[26] For these critics, the metaphorically youthful possibilities of cybernetic systems function to undo the vampiric exploi-

tation characteristic of industrial capitalism, restoring to labor an autonomous vigor enabled and enhanced by information technology.

Again, Alvin Toffler has been at the forefront of these visions of postindustrial reorganization, with his best-seller *The Third Wave* (1980)
building on and deepening the arguments of *Future Shock*.[27] Claiming
that industrial civilization, with its regimented control of labor and its
hierarchical modes of decision making, is "obsolete, encrusted," Toffler
argues that information technologies are rapidly ushering in a socioeconomic system based on self-paced "flextime"—"an arrangement that
permits workers, within predetermined limits, to choose their own
working hours"[28]—and on the demassification of markets, with an attendant decentralization of corporate power. One effect of this sea
change is to replace the traditional producer-consumer dichotomy of
industrial culture with the "prosumer society," in which "new life-styles
based half on production for exchange, half on production for use, become practical" (p. 277): rather than the sale of premade mass-market
goods to a homogenous audience, more flexible production systems,
streamlined by information technologies, will permit "the customer to
program his or her own specifications into the . . . manufacturing process via computer and telephone" (p. 277).[29] At the same time, as computers come more and more to determine the encompassing work environment, we will see an explosion of home-based labor, ushering in
"electronic-cottage" industries and widespread telecommuting. In sum,
"the entire world view of industrial civilization—indust-reality—is now
being revolutionized" (p. 288).

The situation of youth within this vast transformative process will be
at once more active and more productive than the enforced adolescence
of industrial culture had allowed (pp. 383–84). Indeed, youthful prosumers and entrepreneurs can be expected to enter freely into the new
interactive systems of digital communications, since they are generally
more comfortable than their elders with the "broken chips and blips of
imagery" (p. 389) that permit radical self-fashionings of lifestyle and
identity. According to Toffler, the demassification of media—a parallel
process to the demassification of markets—is ushering in the age of the
"modular" self, a mutant persona fabricated out of a mosaic of subcultural codes. Interactivity further complicates the situation, since it shat-
ters the passive spectatorial relation to culture, making "it possible to
project our image electronically to the world" (p. 390) rather than
simply imbibing images produced by others. By implication, then, the
legacy of vampirism inherent in mass consumption—in which consum-

ers are compelled to buy back their own alienated desires and pleasures—will soon be rendered as obsolete as the vampirism of industrial
production. Instead, prosumers will freely choose their own "highly individualized configurations" of potential lifestyles (p. 254)—and indeed,
in substantial measure, will act to create these configurations themselves.
Technocybernetic models of feedback and adaptable programming will
become the very paradigms of social experience, and youth will be at the
forefront of their realization.

According to Yoneji Masuda, founder of Japan's Institute for the Information Society, the advent of postindustrialism promises nothing less
than the realization of "computopia": "the information society will be
a society in which the cognitive creativity of individuals flourishes" in
"multi-centered voluntary communities of citizens participating voluntarily in shared goals and ideas."[30] Again, a youthful ethos is valorized,
specifically in Masuda's concept of "futurization" as a kind of radical
openness to the mutative power of information technology. This concept, as Masuda develops it, inverts Toffler's notion of a tidal wave of
change sweeping society inexorably along, since it involves "actualizing
the future, bringing it into reality" through conscious decision.[31] This
decision-making process, for Masuda, can function at the individual or
the group level, the latter possibility including the emergence of "a completely new form of [business] enterprise" linking entrepreneurial capital and specialized knowledge.[32] Building on the work of Bell, who had
argued that the traditional corporation needed to transform itself in response to the pressures and prospects of postindustrialism,[33] Masuda
heralds the birth of a "futurized" corporate form with a flexible structure, a participatory mode of decision making, and a cutting-edge capacity for innovation.

During the 1970s and 1980s, Masuda's prophecy seemed to have been
realized in the consolidation of the "sunrise industries"—the term itself
suggesting a fresh dawn, a reawakening of youthful vigor following the
twilight of industrial capitalism. These industries, centered in high-tech
districts such as California's Silicon Valley, were devoted to producing
and servicing the hardware and software of the evolving information
economy, spurring a "computer revolution" with far-reaching social
and cultural consequences. Unsurprisingly, the various discourses that
emerged around these industries tended to adopt the basic assumptions
of postindustrial theory, concretizing its metaphors in an analysis of specific business structures and practices; in the process, they generated a
compelling rhetorical-ideological equation of advanced technology and

youth (culture) that powerfully reaffirmed Fordism's logic of prosthesis in a post-Fordist context.

HOMEBREWS AND BURNOUTS IN SILICON VALLEY

Building on the postindustrial prophecy of an imminent synergy of labor and leisure spheres, academic and journalistic coverage of sunrise industries has offered a compelling vision of bold youthful entrepreneurs whose playful escapades integrate neatly with the sober priorities of production and profit seeking. Moreover, the very form of the microelectronics corporation has, in these discourses, been generally taken to express an adolescent vigor over against the moribund orthodoxies of more traditional industries. Silicon Valley firms in particular have been seen to link a pioneering business ethos with the nonconformist impulses of the 1960s counterculture, adopting (and adapting) its militant resistance to established norms of behavior, its radical commitment to experimentation, and its valorization of youth as privileged social subjects. From the perspective of these discourses, it would seem as if the logic of prosthesis that informed Fordist consumer culture—a logic wherein "youth" functioned as a libidinal-political guarantee of invigorating energy—has fed back into and transformed the political-economic structures of production itself, paving the way for a post-Fordist system in which traditional distinctions (and contradictions) between work and play have finally been overcome.

As Annalee Saxenian observes in her comparative study of sunrise industries, high-tech companies tend to see themselves as "creating the foundations of a decentralized industrial system that blur[s] the boundaries between social life and work."[34] Inhabited by "a new breed of technological pioneers" who view traditional corporations "as relics of a dying industrial order which they are determined to transcend" (pp. 55–56), this system has spawned a business culture "unusually open to risk-taking and experimentation" (p. 31). Its financial motor is venture capital, which provides the investment resources and the organizational know-how necessary for creating a host of new companies with cutting-edge technological agendas.[35] These proliferating entrepreneurial "start-ups"—a designation evocative of both igniting energies and fresh beginnings—had, by the outset of the 1980s, come to dominate the Silicon Valley landscape, generating "a diverse and adaptable industrial ecology" (p. 43) populated by vigorously competitive small enterprises.[36] According to Saxenian, the internal structure of these firms is equally decentralized and dynamic, marked by an "interdependent confederation of project teams . . . linked by intense, informal communications" (p. 50). Promoting "highly intuitive and casual decisionmaking styles" (p. 53), these start-ups tend to reward the fruits of "involvement and enthusiasm" as opposed to the settled hierarchies of employment seniority (p. 55). They are, in short, exhilarating environments where youthful energy and technological expertise join hands in unprecedented fashion.

The business press has frequently exploited the concept of the start-up for its suggestion of adolescent impudence and pugnacity;[37] indeed, the term itself is sometimes inverted to evoke an "upstart" defiance of traditional businesses.[38] This rhetoric is unsurprising, since by all evidence the vast majority of start-ups are in fact run by young people; a recent source shows that 70 percent of new high-tech firms are headed by persons born between 1965 and 1980.[39] In her ethnography of Silicon Valley entrepreneurs, Kathleen Gregory argues that the economic volatility start-ups must negotiate daily—the highly competitive and changeful market structure of the microelectronics industry—makes for a situation necessarily favoring the young: "*the young are more flexible and able to learn new things.* . . . [E]mployees and companies are seen as going through 'adolescence' (or at least young adulthood) together. Success for the industry is frequently attributed to youthful flexibility . . . , and youth and structural flexibility are both admired for being associated with success."

Youthfulness, moreover, is equated with technical ingenuity and problem solving, since "the general adaptability of youth is believed to make it possible for them to see new ways of doing things."[40] Hence, sunrise industries tend to offer more opportunities for innovation—with its attendant competitive rewards—by even the youngest employees, since the profitable evolution of the technical infrastructure is assumed to be most readily stimulated by unleashing the creative instincts of inquisitive and venturesome youth. In his book *Behind the Silicon Curtain*, Dennis Hayes captures the prospects for boundless futurization associated with the Valley's upstart cyborgs: "By 1980, . . . the coastal valley evoked the vital categories of adolescent capitalism: entrepreneur, venture capital, technological innovation, upward mobility. Outside corporate fitness centers, underneath the canopies of al fresco cafeterias, the computer professionals could be seen eating salads, browsing through survival-gear catalogs, gazing at digital wrist stopwatches, and sporting the most sophisticated running shoes, as if personally embodying the leanness, adaptability, efficiency, and power of the new technologies. Thus con-

ceived, 'Silicon Valley' was like a tonic for the muddled—some said ge-
riatric—U.S. capitalism of the times."[41]

The sunrise start-up would thus seem to instantiate, in its very form,
the fusion of youth and technology heralded by postindustrial theory.
The Silicon Valley firm, like Marx's factory, is a cyborg formation, a
hybrid of human dynamism and machinic proficiency; indeed, these
firms have become the epochal models for a new breed of "virtual corporation" that projects a "radical future vision . . . of a fusion between
humans and technology."[42] These cybercompanies have, according to
their millennial prophets, managed to transcend the vampiric exploitation that had deformed industrial production, overcoming workers'
alienation in their open and nonhierarchical structure. Or so it might
initially appear; in fact, as we shall see, sunrise industries have their lurking shadows as well. Yet one must look fairly hard to find this darker side
in much of the popular coverage of Silicon Valley, which, for all its frequent impulse toward social satire, essentially has the status of a promotional discourse.[43]

During the past two decades, this coverage has resounded with the
success stories of brash young adepts whose efforts to impel the technology forward garnered them money and fame. Popular accounts of the
rise of Silicon Valley enterprises—from Dirk Hanson's *New Alchemists*,
Thomas Mahon's *Charged Bodies*, and Michael S. Malone's *Big Score* in
the mid-1980s through Robert X. Cringeley's *Accidental Empires* and
David A. Kaplan's *Silicon Boys* in the 1990s—are filled with Horatio Alger stories of brilliant teenage tinkerers who became incredibly wealthy
entrepreneurs.[44] The basic story related across these various volumes is
the spectacular growth of the personal computer industry due to revolutionary advances in hardware design and software development—advances made possible through the bold efforts of an indefatigable cohort
of young engineers and businessmen. Other recent studies (e.g., Stephen
Segaller's *Nerds 2.0.1* and John Katz's *Geeks*) have focused on the evolution
of the Internet and the so-called dot-com revolution—the ongoing "in-
fopreneurial" activity surrounding commercial Web sites that provide
consumer goods and services; these texts, too, have tended to stress essential connections between youthful vision and technocorporate success.[45] Not only does this general narrative of Silicon Valley enterprise
further cement the link between youth and high technology forged in
postindustrial theory, it also pushes that connection more explicitly into
the domain of consumption, chronicling the evolution of a vast new
market in consumer electronics that would entirely transform the cul-

ture. What these books suggest is that the heretofore discrete, though complexly articulated, domains of consumption and production have decisively converged in the attitudes and behaviors—in the very persons—of these youthful "tee-shirt tycoons."[46]

These volumes share a historical backdrop, collectively tracing the evolution of Silicon Valley's high-tech industries from the establishment of Hewlett-Packard, the legendary "first start-up," in 1939; to the formation of Stanford Industrial Park, the incubating core of Valley entrepreneurship, in 1951; to the inventions of the integrated circuit at Fairchild Semiconductor in the late 1950s and of the microprocessor at Intel in the early 1970s. This last achievement directly spawned the PC revolution, since it made possible self-contained computer stations small enough to fit on desktops yet powerful enough to run complex software packages. Initially, as these books show, the home computer market was limited to hobbyists, whose enthusiasm for the technology was fed by an emerging infrastructure of specialty magazines, stores, and clubs. Homebrew, the most important of these clubs, held its first meeting in 1975 in Menlo Park (erstwhile site of Thomas Edison's wizardly career) and had soon rallied the Bay Area's elite engineers and hackers for sessions of intense collaborative brainstorming. Many early start-up ventures in the personal computer industry got their impetus from these avid gatherings; within a decade, many of Homebrew's charter members had become multimillionaires, youthful captains of the sunrise industries.[47]

Two of the earliest studies of these nouveaux riches encode in their very titles a sense of the almost magical techno-energies animating this visionary cohort: Hanson's *New Alchemists* can literally turn sand (silica) into gold, while Mahon's *Charged Bodies* refers at once to the technology's electronic substratum and to the febrile vitality of its creators and deal makers. According to these books, what Silicon Valley values above all else, even corporate success and money making, is "technical élan," the "drive to doodle and tinker and make a technical breakthrough . . . out of hope and pluck and determination"[48]—an impulse that inextricably links youthful desire and technological development. This drive is expressed in popular conceptions of the Valley itself as, in Malone's words, "a self-contained, living entity . . . a sensate being of concrete and steel, silicon and human flesh"[49]—in short, a cyborg system, fusing bodies and technologies. Throughout these volumes, technical and corporate processes take on anthropomorphic qualities, while natural landscapes and human beings are consistently technologized—as if Silicon Valley (as its very name suggests) betokens an epochal convergence of opposed elements. The matrix of this convergence is the Valley's culture of youth, the "adolescent defiance and enthusiasm" that drives its computer prodigies to "create their own ... alternative to the adult world,"[50] incarnating in high-tech machines the dreams and fantasies of a unique technological counterculture yoking hippiedom with high tech.

As sociologist Theodore Roszak observes in *From Satori to Silicon Valley*, there has always resided, "just beneath the surface of the bucolic hippy image," a persistent "infatuation with certain forms of outré technology" and with the small-is-beautiful panaceas of postindustrial ideologues.[51] There is, in short, a historical continuity linking William Braden's book *The Age of Aquarius* (1970), which attempts to envision "a technology without technologism" that is humanly progressive, and Steven Anzovin's work *The Green PC* (1993), a guide to the environmentally conscious use of computer hardware and software.[52] This link has been forged through several key institutional and ideological factors— from Stewart Brand's *Whole Earth Catalog*, with its advocacy of technology that has an intimate, hands-on utility;[53] to Ted Nelson's militant "Computer Liberation" view that information machines should belong to "the People" and not faceless corporations;[54] to more recent phenomena such as the Electronic Frontiers Foundation, a group devoted to exploring the legal and aesthetic horizons of digital media (cofounded by John Perry Barlow, lyricist for the Grateful Dead), and the culture of "technopaganism," which attempts to wed mythological and occult perspectives with technical expertise.[55]

These various links between computers and counterculture share a confidence in youth, conceived both as cultural agents and as social force—a confidence deriving from the root equation of youth and technology that underpins postindustrial discourse. Throughout the studies of Silicon Valley entrepreneurs runs a rhetoric of cyborgization that fuses adolescent nerve, technological innovation, corporate success, and California lifestyle; indeed, if Silicon Valley has bequeathed anything to contemporary world culture, it is precisely this peculiar and heady "homebrew." The achievements of the youthful entrepreneurs chronicled in these volumes represent, in the words of Malone, "a scenario right out of a Ritchie Rich comic book: bright postadolescents unconstrained by money worries, propriety or the vagaries of middle age."[56] Cringeley affectionately dubs them "our nerds," who "have a lot to teach us about how to recreate the business spirit we seem to have lost"[57]—mutant youth promising to lead a senescent capitalist economy into the sunny postindustrial future.

Probably the most storied of these brazen whiz kids is Steve Wozniak (a.k.a. Woz), cofounder of Apple Computer, whose innovations in PC design made what had been a hobbyists' enterprise technologically and financially accessible to the consuming populace. As these books stress, Woz had two basic qualities: an impish streak and a problem-solving genius. These characteristics were closely related, as evidenced by his first major invention, the legendary "blue box" that gave its user illegal access to long-distance phone lines, which were then employed for various stunts (a practice known as "phreaking"). Thanks to the marketing savvy of his friend Steve Jobs, these boxes became Woz's first entrepreneurial venture; the Apple prototype soon followed. In short order, venture capitalist Mike Markkula was ponying up a quarter of a million dollars to mass-produce the machine;[58] within three years, the Apple corporation was worth a third of a *billion* dollars, becoming the youngest firm ever to join the Fortune 500.[59] The PC industry thus appears to owe its origins to the mischievous gifts of a youthful trickster, whose keen attunement to technological possibility fused quite profitably with a streak of rebellious adolescence.

According to Kaplan, Wozniak's pranks were "a way to show intellectual prowess and rebellion at the same time. They were also just fun."[60] Judging from these books, a similar playful spirit animates a number of Silicon Valley start-ups; in the words of Roy Dudley, cofounder of the telecommunications firm Plantronics: "When you start a company, you don't have offices and you don't have regular hours. . . . It's flat-out fun. You get a ton of work done and you're living a life-style that is the way I think anybody would live if they had the opportunity."[61] Dudley once showed up for work dressed in a kimono and pith helmet,[62] and similar stories of corporate hijinks abound in these volumes—from Adobe's "company-wide water fight to celebrate the shipping of a new product"[63] to Atari's programmers working "to the sound of rock and roll and in the heady, sweet atmosphere of dope."[64] This laid-back corporate ethos is an extension of the so-called HP Way—the friendly management style, nonhierarchical structure, and profit-sharing philosophy pioneered by Hewlett-Packard in the 1950s and 1960s.[65] In this easygoing atmosphere, the exigencies of labor and the hedonism of leisure blend synergistically, nurturing the "free-wheeling, high-energy entrepreneurial drive"[66] responsible for Silicon Valley's enormous productivity. The sunrise start-up would thus appear to undo the exploitative relation between capital and labor characteristic of classic industrialism; as James Treybig of Tandem Computers—a company with "an atmosphere so casual that no formal meetings ever occurred"[67]—asserts, "You can no longer optimize profits and screw people. Tandem is a *socialist* company."[68]

The advertising strategies favored by sunrise start-ups in the 1970s and 1980s traded on this reputation for unparalleled openness and flexibility, often deploying sporty images of youth to evoke the conjoining of hard work with rejuvenating festivity. A famous 1979 employee recruitment ad for Advanced Micro Devices, for example, depicted a twentysomething executive, clad in business attire, riding a surfboard toward the viewer; its caption urged the young reader to "Catch the Wave."[69] The imagery would prove influential: a cartoon version of the same image was featured on the cover of San Francisco magazine's December 1997 issue (fig. 10), accompanying an article entitled "The Next Big Wave" that chronicled the explosive growth of Silicon Valley job opportunities.[70] Perhaps most famously, IBM, after it had moved into the PC market in the 1980s, crafted a series of ads collectively entitled "Solutions for a Small Planet." One of these ads memorably featured a handful of business executives gathered on a sunny beach, attired in wetsuits and debating, in a garbled version of California surf-speak, the merits of acquiring an AS/400 minicomputer. This system upgrade is promoted by a corporate vice president as follows: "let's get aggro on IBM stick before we get churned; we'll bust the lip, get locked into the barrel, and we won't need a swami [i.e., a high-priced consultant] to keep us from going over the falls." In response to a female colleague's inquiry whether the system is state of the art ("Are we talking triple concave?"), he replies that the AS/400 is IBM's top-of-the-line Power PC—or, as he puts it, "Nectar, all the way." At this point an older man, clearly the firm's CEO, declares the purchase a nice idea: "Pure guava," he announces with a grin, whereupon they all seize their boards and head out into the Big Blue.[71]

Considering Alvin Toffler's influential analysis of technosocial progress in terms of rhythmic wave action, it is perhaps not surprising that teenage surf culture came to supply privileged metaphors for the cutting-edge ethos of the Silicon Valley start-up. As a practice, surfing combines revelry with risk taking, demanding a shrewd practical skill that is nonetheless ludic and improvisatory. In the words of Malone, "Riding a business boom is like surfing: you have to see the next wave coming in on the horizon, get out and be turned around to meet it, and then as the swell 'feels' the bottom and rises, you have to paddle like hell to get up to speed to be caught in the arching crest. Whenever an electronics boom comes rolling in, there are usually dozens of firms out paddling around looking for an opportunity."[72] In this intensely competitive environment, the edge goes to the surfers with the sharpest eyes, the boldest impulses, and the quickest reflexes—in short, to the young (in spirit,

THE BEST IN HOLIDAY FOOD AND FUN
TRAFFIC? NO PROBLEM | 30 GREAT GIFT IDEAS

San Francisco

DECEMBER 1997 | $2.95

FOCUS ON THE BAY AREA

Youth Rules!

Don't call them slackers—they're players.
A new generation of overachievers is taking over the city.

Figure 10. Third-wave surfers of capitalist counterculture. Cover of the December 1997 issue of *San Francisco* magazine.

if not literally in body). Corporate survival and success are thus seen as dependent on youthful qualities—on adventurousness and adaptability—that permit the start-up to weather the heavy seas of high-tech capitalism.[73]

It is possible to discern here a continuation—as well as a curious inversion—of the Fordist cultural logic reviewed in the first section of this chapter. Whereas classic Fordism had valorized workers' putatively "youthful" characteristics—those qualities of openness and flexibility that Taylorist mechanization required and which were metaphorically realized in the practices of mass consumption—now, in the post-Fordist context, productivity is seen as emerging, in some sense, from youthfulness itself. Kaplan uses the term *spontaneous generation* to describe how billion-dollar industries seem to spring up on the heels of boys at play, to arise from the playful capers of a casual subculture of "geeks-in-garages."[74] In the postindustrial period, youth is no longer simply the prosthesis of production, the labor-leisure circuit that ensures the smooth functioning of the capitalist system; rather, production is the prosthesis of youth, whose play-time pleasures have become the virtual fountainhead of wealth creation and business success.[75]

The Fordist dream of leisure industries generating eternal youth for productivist purposes has thus transmogrified into the post-Fordist dream of youthful leisure generating productivist industries. In the process of this inversion, the ethical division between ascetic work and hedonistic play that had underwritten Fordist hegemony has collapsed, replaced by a general trend toward joyful exertion, by an exhilarating "wired life"[76]—a phrase suggesting both adrenalized pleasure and cybernetic augmentation.[77] Thus, judging from the coverage in these accounts, it would seem that both production and consumption have been redeemed from the systemic vampirism that had deformed them under Fordism, subsumed into a higher post-Fordist synthesis, their transformative promise actualized in the cyborg-youth culture—the "computopia"—of Silicon Valley.

Or so the ad copy runs. In fact, this utopian vision is balanced by an abiding sense of frustration and dread that colors even the basically affirmative treatments mentioned above. Negative concerns can be traced most clearly in the contradictory ways that age-based metaphors are mobilized to describe the sunrise start-ups' internal and external environments—contradictions these studies have inherited from postindustrial discourse. On the one hand, the Silicon Valley firm is evoked as a veritable incarnation of the unquenchable vigor of youth, an embodiment of forward-looking innovation that equates perpetual adolescence with technical nonobsolescence. On the other hand, this youthful drive and pugnacity is not simply an ongoing state but figures as a punctuating moment in a corporate life cycle marked by sequential phases, from the initial "seed financing" through the mature public stock offering—a cycle that can "take as long as ten years or as little as two years or less."[78] Bold statements about a company's dynamic "youth" thus only make sense within a more encompassing trajectory of development that defines and limits its scope of operation.

In this larger context, the start-up's adolescence may appear as a hindrance to mature growth, a nostalgic "golden age" preceding the encrustation of bureaucratic routine, or both. As Everett Rogers and Judith Larsen observe,

> One of the special problems of rapidly growing high-technology firms is the adolescent transition, the phase during which size outgrows managerial ability. When a firm increases from one to 10, to 100, to 500, to 1,000 employees . . . , [it] must have personnel, advertising, and accounting departments, as well as a training division. The growing company can no longer operate effectively as an informal and dedicated group clustered around a charismatic entrepreneur-engineer. An engineer may have started the firm in order to escape the bureaucracy of an old-line company. Suddenly success demands that the new rapidly growing firm must return to the bureaucratic style from which its founder fled. This paradox is frustrating to the entrepreneur who enjoys success, but dislikes being unable to call all 500 employees by their first names. . . . Puzzled, the entrepreneur asks, "Why isn't it as much fun around here as it used to be?" [79]

A firm caught "hanging on to its rebellious adolescence too long" [80] can fail to meet the challenges of its burgeoning operations or an evolving market; [81] by the same token, the day when "the founders start to disappear, and the suits appear, with their M.B.A.s and their ideas about price points, market penetration, and strategic positioning," can lead to a firm's "losing the proper balance between technology and business," with equally disastrous results. [82]

Unsurprisingly, given the cyborg logic that links bodies and technologies in Silicon Valley, the tension between these twin possibilities is deeply felt by the entrepreneurs themselves. As the 29-year-old co-founder of a computer-game start-up remarks, "One of the things that drives us, I think, is sort of a Peter Pan-ish fear of growing up and losing touch with things. . . . Because when you're young, you're hip because you're young. But you also have to grow up, a) because it's inevitable and b) because our business is growing up and we're dealing with grown-ups and their business world." [83] Yet corporate maturity, for the eager risk taker, can bring such painful disillusionment that the entrepreneur may decide to drop out or move on to fresh horizons. Steve Wozniak elected the former option, abandoning his post at Apple to fund a series of

Woodstock-style rock concerts and an annual computer camp for kids—
a camp held in his playhouse of a mansion, packed with arcade games.[84]
The latter option is illustrated by the career of "start-up engineer" Roy
Dudley, who excelled at the initial phase of "resource orchestration" but
began to chafe when his companies settled down into predictable rou-
tines—at which point he sought new ventures to test his skills at rejuvenation. The alternative, in his words, is a dull, deadening adulthood
where you "sit over at the Decathlon Club with your quiche and your
chablis" [85]—in short, no more kimonos and pith helmets.

In *Close to the Machine*, her memoir of working as a freelance programmer in Silicon Valley, Ellen Ullman has powerfully captured this
curious linkage between the loss of youth and the ebbing of technical
and business acumen. As she reaches middle age, Ullman, dreading an
imminent "fall into knowledge exhaustion, obsolescence, techno-fuddy-
duddyism," [86] muses wryly on the multifarious manifestations of this
lurking anxiety. Overwhelmed by the monthly updates promoting "another load of newness" (p. 103) that she must professionally master and
intimidated by younger competitors who seem flush with "all the fresh-
faced drive of technocapitalism" (p. 96), Ullman imagines the "great,
elusive cutting edge of technology" moving away from her "like a giant
cosmic frisbee" (p. 100)—a vision of ardent youthful play fleeing her
grasp forever. There is "something unseemly in an old programmer,"
she observes, comparing herself to an aging rock star; "the sheer electric
nervousness required for a relationship with the machine . . . is simply
unnatural for someone over thirty-eight" (p. 105). Eventually, Ullman
begins to conceive of herself as a "legacy system"—an antiquated computer program upon which companies still depend but which is seen as
"a curse . . . a lingering piece of old junk that no one has yet figured out
how to throw away. . . . The system is unmodifiable, full of bugs, no
longer understood. We say it's 'brain dead.' Yet it lives. Yet it runs. Drain
on our time and money. Vampire of our happiness" (p. 118). Meanwhile,
in the very midst of this midlife crisis, Ullman begins a hopeless affair
with a youthful hacker, "a selfish brainy kid" whom she sees as "some
fascinating cyborg" (p. 67). Though she does not explicitly connect
these issues and images, the logic of her treatment suggests that, in Silicon Valley, the cybernetic energies of youth must be vampirically consumed to fend off a sense of looming decay.

Just as entrepreneurs and their start-ups fall prey to an inescapable
life cycle—one that breeds nagging anxieties regarding the loss of personal and corporate youth—so the history of Silicon Valley, as chronicled in these volumes, presents adolescence not as a perpetual state but

as an isolated moment within an unfolding genealogy. Indeed, Kaplan goes so far as to offer a mock-biblical lineage to depict how the Valley's business landscape was gradually populated: "Bell Labs begat Shockley begat Fairchild begat Rheem."[87] Fairchild Semiconductor was a particularly fecund parent, spawning a swelling brood of start-ups during the early 1960s that commentators have dubbed "Fairchildren." In fact, the process was much less congenial than this rhetoric of familial expansion might suggest, since Fairchild saw its offspring as traitors whose flight from the nest threatened the firm.[88] According to Malone, "Fairchild's innovative genius and its hell-raising style" were systematically undermined by these desertions, and by the mid-1960s it had become evident that "Fairchild Semiconductor was no longer the mischievous child prodigy of American business."[89]

Since Fairchild was "the first of the nerd-driven companies that embodied the Silicon Valley culture,"[90] its marked decline established clearly that the youthful drive and entrepreneurial vigor of the sunrise start-up had a limited generational span; in subsequent memory, the halcyon days at the company "began to take on a new image: that of Paradise Lost—and, by extension, of youth and innocence gone forever."[91] The Fairchildren learned these hard truths themselves as a fresh generation of start-ups, during the 1980s, came to view "those youthful risk takers of the sixties and seventies as the old guard, too deeply mired in the industrial mindset to catch the next big wave they had made possible."[92] Now, some twenty years later, those 1980s innovators, too, have become dinosaurs—vast corporations fighting off not just their own rebellious offspring but federal antitrust legislation. Writing at the end of the 1990s, Kaplan summarizes the transition with cynical succinctness: "In the span of just a few short years, the PC industry mutated from carefree teenager to avaricious capitalist."[93] The 1999 TV movie *Pirates of Silicon Valley* satirically depicts the bloating and graying of Apple and Microsoft, those classic second-generation start-ups, and a number of recent books trace the quasi-oedipal conflict that has arisen between these now old-style computer companies and the Internet upstarts of the 1990s.[94] This ongoing generational logic coexists with a pronounced boom-and-bust cycle that can wither whole sectors of high-tech business overnight, "as if the youthful industry had contracted *progeria*, a rare disease that struck down toddlers with the infirmities of advanced age."[95]

What all this suggests is that youth is a double-edged metaphor when deployed in this general context. While the rhetoric of post-industrial prophets and computer-tech mavens might seek to decontextualize youth—treating it as a series of iconic qualities such as flexibility, dynamism, and boldness of spirit—the basic meaning of the term as a category of embodied experience still tends to assert itself. In short, adolescence cannot be projected as perpetual, because the concept only gains meaning from its place in a teleological sequence, wherein it follows childhood and precedes adult maturity. This is not to say that adolescence is an essential, transhistorical phenomenon—indeed, numerous studies have shown that the concept is strictly coeval with modern industrial society[96]—but rather that even historically constructed forms of embodiment are not readily amenable to rhetorical manipulation. If capitalist industries wish to be understood as metaphorically youthful, then they must also be conceived in an unfolding development that includes the likelihood, if not the inevitability, of decline and decay—as well as being perceived in generational relationship with their own eventual replacements. While it is entirely possible to imagine youthful cyborgs—that is, young persons radically augmented by high technology—youth itself cannot function as a prosthetic formation, a mode of cybernetic enhancement, without bearing all of these logical consequences. The young, necessarily, age and die, and their putative avatar, the sunrise start-up, must face the dusk as well.

Of course, there are many more concrete, less obviously metaphorical ways that high-tech firms are implicated in the systematic exhaustion of youth. Even in works largely devoted to promoting the sunrise industries, a sense of their lurking dark side prevails; an instructive text in this regard is Tracy Kidder's *Soul of a New Machine*, a best-selling and Pulitzer Prize–winning volume from 1981 that basically paved the way for the numerous studies discussed above. The book deploys a narrative structure that would later figure prominently in cyberpunk science fiction, such as William Gibson's novel *Neuromancer* (1984): a corps of high-strung, brilliant "microkids" (Kidder's term) are set in competitive motion by a shadowy corporate system eager to profit from their talents. As they gambol through their high-tech playpen, these maverick savants spin off the commodifiable properties of new hardware and software packages. Or, to be more specific: Data General, a computer firm in the Route 128 district of Massachusetts (the East Coast's version of Silicon Valley), undertakes a project to design and build a new model PC called the Eagle. Assembling a brilliant cadre of twentysomething engineers and programmers within an inspirational "flextime" scenario, the company shrewdly capitalizes on their innate "fascination . . . just like little boys who never grew up, playing with Erector sets"[97] for technological problem solving. The narrative exhaustively chronicles the group's fe-

verish efforts to complete the design of the machine before its mass production and distribution are slated to begin.

Kidder convincingly depicts the thrilling challenges and creative ex-
ultations of this work environment, but he also shows the new forms of
exploitation it enforces: flextime comes to mean "constantly pulling all-
nighters in the lab or the computer centers" in order to meet murderous
deadlines. As one of the engineers comments, "It's something of a sweatshop," almost "child labor—kids right out of school. . . . It's expected
that you'll ruin your health for the company" (p. 218)—as evidenced
by the chief engineer, who "seemed to grow skinnier and skinnier . . . as
if the job and all that planning were somehow consuming his flesh"
(p. 178). Similar visions of physical and psychic burnout are evoked in
the other studies of sunrise start-ups: even Mahon's eager "Charged
Bodies" eventually rebel against "a steady diet of sixteen-hour days, every day, and 3,000 psi of pressure per minute."[98] As Malone observes,
the entrepreneur's personal commitment "is enormous, the stress and
long work hours and fear can rob you of your youth, the riches, when
they at last arrive, may have lost much of their meaning when you are
exhausted and prematurely aged."[99] Hence the sunrise start-up, for all
its utopian possibility, still seems in large part vampiric, systematically
draining the energetic substance of youth in the process of its own relentless growth.

Moreover, the notion that the high-tech firm overcomes invidious
hierarchies in its loose corporate structure and casual management style
is also given the lie by Kidder's treatment. The eventual uses of the Eagle
computer, as well as the major part of the profits derived from it, are
controlled by the corporation, which clearly believes that the less the
microkids know about their situation the better. "The managers had
sealed off the team right from the start, telling every recruit not to so
much as mention the name Eagle outside the group"; as the head of the
project remarks (in a classic description of alienated labor), "Some of
the kids don't have a notion that there's a company behind all of this. It
could be the CIA funding this. It could be a psychological test."[100] Thus,
while the immediate context of their work might seem offbeat and challenging (if ultimately exhausting), traditional corporate hierarchy is preserved in the structure of ownership of physical and intellectual property. The founders and venture capitalists may in some measure share
profits with their employees, but the planning and purpose of specific
projects is taken entirely out of their hands. On top of all this, their
labor itself—especially that of the programming group—is subjected to

quasi-Taylorist techniques of routinization and control that produce a segmentation of roles reminiscent of Fordist industrialism.[101]

Not surprisingly, this overall arrangement tends to frustrate creative talents, a situation that makes for frequent job turnover as ambitious young engineers and programmers, upset at the loss of control over the conditions and products of their labor, move on to other enterprises or, as often happens, gather together to start their own firms.[102] But even these fresh start-ups do not guarantee that youthful brilliance will become self-determining, since they are seldom truly independent in any meaningful sense given their precariously contingent relation to venture capital. Rogers and Larsen sum up the situation:

> Venture capitalists portray themselves as urbane, sophisticated businessmen, though they are basically seen by entrepreneurs as shrewd and rich. The popular Valley nickname for them—"vulture capitalist"—depicts the venture capitalist as a greedy, obnoxious scavenger, living off the entrepreneurial spirit and hard work of Silicon Valley's engineers. The vulture capitalist's objective is to gain control of as much of someone else's company as possible. If the founders have to be dumped in the process, so be it. Since the vulture's goal is to make money when the company goes public or is acquired, the long-range viability of the firm is unimportant. . . . [N]ew firms feel powerless in dealing with them.[103]

An infamous example of conflict between entrepreneur and venture capitalist occurred when the C.E.O. of Apple, John Sculley, fired cofounder Steve Jobs at the behest of investor Mike Markkula, in what Kaplan describes as "a power struggle that enthralled the Valley—the son creates the father who destroys him."[104] Despite the nurturant rhetoric of "seed financing," the venture capitalist is essentially a parasite on the vision of the entrepreneur, whose intellectual labor, incarnated in the fixed capital of the industrial plant, becomes the financial lifeblood that feeds the vulture-vampire.[105]

As Bennett Harrison shows in his book on the contemporary "flexible" corporation, *Lean and Mean*, the ultimate outcome of a venture-capital economy, despite all the entrepreneurial launchings, is actually a growing concentration of power in which "small firm start-ups themselves become commodities, to be bought and sold in order to generate capital gains."[106] In Silicon Valley, youth is not served so much as served up on a platter, its energy and vitality consumed by vested interests. There is thus a profound, if saddening, irony in the vision of sunrise industries as rejuvenating, since not only do they prey upon their workers' energies in soul- and body-sapping ways, but this vampiric consumption only serves to shuffle capital from the manufacturing to the financial-speculative sectors of the economy in a manner that may ultimately be far from productive. Just as the gutting of industrial-urban communities in the 1970s and 1980s was, as I argued in chapter 2, an effect of the rise of new service classes living debt-driven lifestyles of consumption, so the wholesale conversion to a postindustrial economy has involved the evolution of a "casino society" of rampant speculation that has, in the last analysis, only served to exacerbate extant socioeconomic inequalities.[107]

Moreover, despite the utopian assumptions of postindustrialist theorists, the reorganization of labor markets during the 1970s and 1980s has, as Bennett Harrison and Barry Bluestone argue, actually "taken the form of freezes and cuts in wages, the introduction of two-tiered wage systems, the substitution of floating bonuses for fixed wages, the proliferation of part-time work and 'home' work, and the shifting of work previously performed by regular (often unionized) employees to independent, typically nonunion subcontractors."[108] The result has been not only a general decline in real wages, but a trend toward the increasing polarization of incomes, with the vast amount of new job creation being relatively low-paying and, for all the logic of "futurization" purportedly at work in the informated economy, essentially futureless. Bill Lessard and Steve Baldwin's book *NetSlaves* paints a distressing collective portrait of the labor situation in the computer industry specifically: for every Internet entrepreneur who strikes it rich in Silicon Valley, there is an invisible army of programmers, telemarketers, Web site designers, chat-room monitors, and cybersex workers whose stake in the system is considerably less rosy.[109] And the creative exploitation of young engineers and programmers—the great majority of them male and white—is nothing beside the appalling situation of most working-class women and ethnic minorities in the sunrise industries, whose youth is consumed in more rudimentary and sometimes brutal ways. In particular, semiconductor assembly jobs, which are disproportionately filled by nonwhite females, are extremely dangerous, often involving sweatshop conditions and exposure to various toxic substances.[110] In this context, the mutative relationship between youth and postindustrial capitalism may have more than merely metaphorical significance.

The rejuvenated myth of Horatio Alger thus serves to disguise not only the genuine bases of power in information society but also the declining situation of the great majority of youth in a postindustrial economy. Indeed, capitalism's newfound "flexibility" may actually come at the expense of post–baby boom youth, who—thanks to eroding entitle-ment programs, the rising costs of education and housing, and stagnant real wages—can no longer realistically expect to enjoy the relative afflu-ence of their parents' generation.[111] At the same time that they have be-gun to face such narrowing prospects, contemporary teens have been increasingly identified throughout the popular media as a "baby bust" generation of disgruntled, indolent slackers. But really, their alleged "slackness" is only the mirror image of postindustrial capitalism's lean-and-mean "flexibility"—a sullen inertia balancing the eager vigor of the system that exploits them.[112] For, if postindustrial capitalism has truly overcome the labor-leisure divide, making work fun and play produc-tive, why should youth still be, like the vampire Martin in the 1970s, indicted as lazy and wasteful, a shiftless cohort of cynics and narcissists? Do the sunrise industries, despite their cyborg promise, merely displace, rather than transcend, the endemic vampirism of Fordist culture? And what is the fate of youth consumption—as a mode of cultural labor and a social ethos—in this post-Fordist context? In order to answer these questions, I turn to works of fiction that treat the sunrise industries, in particular the novel *Microserfs* (1995) by Douglas Coupland, widely re-garded as the veritable bard of contemporary youth culture.[113]

MODULAR SELVES AND POSTHUMAN CONSUMERS
Fictional treatments of Silicon Valley have been fairly sparse since the publication of Michael Rogers's potboiler, entitled simply *Silicon Valley* (1982).[114] While a few mystery and crime novelists have used its high-tech culture as a backdrop,[115] it wasn't until the mid-1990s that Silicon Valley became the subject of fictional treatments displaying the same wide-ranging satirical/celebratory animus characteristic of the journal-istic studies canvassed above. Unsurprisingly, three of these books were written by journalists who cover the technology beat: *The Last Best Thing*, by Pat Dillon; *The First $20 Million Is Always the Hardest*, by Po Bronson; and *The Deal*, by Joe Hutsko.[116] As one might expect of works produced by such industry insiders, they are more or less thinly veiled romans à clef featuring familiar characters and events in Valley history: both *The Last Best Thing* and *The Deal* are inspired by developments at Apple Computer, especially the up-and-down career of cofounder Steve Jobs, while Bronson's novel features the familiar Valley tale of a rebel-lious start-up crew hounded by a merciless cabal of moneyed interests. The conflict between youthful idealism and pragmatic maturity forms the thematic turf of all three books, and their basic narrative momentum involves the attempt to recover an innocence lost when a hobbyists' en-

terprise became a cutthroat business. Corporate control of innovation is implicitly equated with the subduing of youthful spirit through the insidious trammels of adulthood, the smug inertia of business as usual; valiantly if at times quixotically, the young protagonists struggle either to retain their adolescent dreams or to redeem a utopian entrepreneurial drive from the greedy intrigues of "vulture" capitalists and cynical monopolists.

Coupland's *Microserfs* is in every way superior to these works, not least because it makes their simmering generational tensions brilliantly explicit. As one of the novel's venture capitalists smarmily remarks to a group of young business prospects, "We have to function as parents to new companies who are in the process of growing up"; but then, dropping the paternal mask, he adds, "Start-ups appeal either to jaded cynics—because they know the way things really work—or to the totally naive—because they don't. Which are you?" [117] Not only is *Microserfs* considerably more sophisticated as a work of fiction, it also confronts socioeconomic contexts and tackles philosophical issues the other novels largely ignore, in the process powerfully exposing the tangled nest of contradictions informing contemporary discourses that link youth with advanced technologies.

In the first place, *Microserfs* conveys much more convincingly the discouraging range of employment options available to young people in the computer industry. Not all of its characters are ambitious creators impelled to radically transform the hardware or boldly buck the corporate ethos of high-tech business; as Coupland's title suggests, the vast majority of them are menial intellectual laborers patiently tilling the settled fields of monopoly capital. The opening section of the story, in fact, is set on the Microsoft campus in Redmond, Washington, where our narrator, Daniel Underwood, introduces us to the day-to-day tedium of debugging software programs. Worried because he is, at twenty-six, swiftly approaching the legendary "Seven-Year Programmer's Burnout," and aware that he is "just a breath away from a job in telemarketing" (pp. 16–17), Dan is basically floating along, his life consisting of "home, Microsoft, and Costco" (p. 3). He has no sense whatsoever of a personal future, despite the futuristic quality of his high-tech surroundings.

Dan's work is a steady stream of boredom punctuated by spells of intense panic whenever the company prepares to ship a new product for which his unit is responsible; this unit, while generally nonhierarchical, leaves Dan in little doubt that he is "cannon fodder when the crunch comes" (p. 33). The Microsoft campus itself, for all its leisurely amenities and pastoral setting, communicates a "Tupperware-sealed, Biosphere 2-like atmosphere" (p. 38), its blocky buildings and food courts reminding Dan of a suburban mall. Looming over all is the commanding "cult of Bill" (p. 35), the billionaire super-nerd whom all the employees both admire and fear. With his periodic firsthand quality checks and his mysterious bestowals and withdrawals of favor, Gates seems to exert over the company "a moral force, a spectral force, a force that shapes, a force that molds. A force with thick, thick glasses" (p. 3). Perhaps because of this vaguely inspirational and demanding presence, Dan is convinced that he labors in "the foundry of our culture's deepest dreams" (ibid.), regardless of the lack of challenge and the general torpor of his own work environment.

His home life is, if anything, even less appealing. Residing in a communal house with five other Microsoft employees, Dan finds himself living a "cramped, love-starved, sensationless existence," his need for pleasure "ignored, year in, year out, in the pursuit of code, in the pursuit of somebody *else's* abstraction" (p. 90; emphasis in original). Moreover, he begins to have the sense that his physical self has become a mere shell housing his "code-crunching" brain, that his body's internal clock is now set "not to the rhythms of waves and sunrises—or even the industrial whistle toot—but to *product cycles*" (p. 55; emphasis in original). As one of his coworkers observes, "I think we've strayed so far from our animal origins that we are bent on creating a new, supra-animal identity" (p. 17). His housemates display dysfunctional attitudes and behaviors illustrative of this thesis: brainy Michael seems almost to inhabit a "mystical state," so devoted is he to devising "elegant streams of code instructions" (p. 13), while buff Todd is overdeveloped in the opposite direction, fanatically building up his body with steroids, vitamin potions, and intense machinic regimens of weight lifting and exercise. Todd in particular seems to Dan a disturbing harbinger of imminent cyborgization, "a precursor of some not-too-distant future where human beings are appended by nozzles, diodes, buzzers, thwumpers, and dingles that inform us of the time and temperature in the Kerguelen Archipelago" (p. 321).

No one has much of a functioning sex life; as Dan remarks, the fresh college graduates Microsoft routinely hires are "so excited to have this 'real' job and money that they just figure that the relationships will naturally happen, but then they wake up and they're thirty and they haven't had sex in eight years." Most of his coworkers have more intimate feelings for their electronic equipment than for their friends or family, thus exemplifying "the primary relationship: Geek and Machine" (p. 227).[118] As another of Dan's housemates, Abe, opines in a furious e-mail, Microsoft's young workers have made "this Faustian pact . . . that [the] company is allowed to soak up 7 to 10 years of [their] life," until they "hit this wall and thirty and [go] *SPLAT*." Like a vampire, "the tech system *feeds on* bright, asocial kids," luring them with the prospect of exciting work in a purportedly laid-back, freewheeling environment. In actuality, these young people are subjected to an insidious form of "adolescence protraction": provided with free soda and play periods, they are told they work on a "campus" rather than in an office complex. "It's sick and evil," Abe concludes (pp. 310–11; emphasis added).

One gets the sense from all this that, rather than the sphere of leisure transforming labor into something more creative and rewarding (as postindustrial theory had alleged), work has instead begun to annex and deform everyday life, extending the vampirism of the capitalist factory throughout the social field. Bespeaking the sharp critical animus of the novel, Dan essentially makes this very argument:

> Before California high-tech parks, the most a corporation ever did for an employee was maybe supply a house, maybe a car, maybe a doctor, and maybe a place to buy groceries. Beginning in the 1970s, corporations began supplying showers for people who jogged during lunch hour and sculptures to soothe the working soul—proactive humanism—the first full-scale integration of the corporate realm into the private. In the 1980s, corporate integration punctured the *next* realm of corporate life invasion at "campuses" like Microsoft and Apple—with the next level of intrusion being that the borderline between work and life blurred to the point of unrecognizability. (p. 211; emphasis in original)

With a paranoiac glee worthy of an Adorno or Baudrillard, the novel's characters hunt down evidence of this creeping intrusion everywhere—in the omnipresence of corporate sponsorship and marketing (p. 177), in the eager commercial promotion of nostalgia (p. 131), in generic clothing stores such as the Gap, with their orchestrated illusion of choice and individuality (pp. 268–70). This systematic commodification of experience has been facilitated if not hastened by cybernetic tools such as "the computer spreadsheet and the bar-coded inventory," which have ushered in "an entirely McNuggetized world of . . . standardized consumable units" (pp. 269–70).

The result is a system of *"automated consumerism"* (p. 60; emphasis in original) that conforms in major particulars with Baudrillard's vision of a totalitarian "code" (discussed in my introduction). In this sinister regime, the deepest private responses of consumers are synthetically programmed and managed, as Dan realizes when he attends a seminar on interactive media where videogames are prominently discussed. Designers of the games have segmented the physicopsychic activity of teenage players into manageable units of information, described in the technocratic jargon of "manseconds" (a measurement of the time expended in the manipulation of keys and joysticks) and "embedded intelligence" (the objectified expertise "buried in the nooks and crannies of code and storyboard design"); the basic challenge is "[e]ngineering a desire for repetition" that will keep kids glued to the machines yet also lead eventually to the purchase of new products. Indeed, the monetary worth of leisure time in this context has been precisely calculated: a "multimedia product has to deliver $1 per hour's worth of entertainment or you'll get slagged by word-of-mouth" (pp. 142–43). Thus, the computer industry, in its manifold inventions and simulations, in its provision of jobs and of pleasure, has generated a networked social totality—an enveloping coded structure—that links work and play in a seamless web of exploitation.

Or so it appears from the monopolistic perspective promoted by Microsoft, but Dan soon comes to recognize a more liberating potential in computerization. This contrasting possibility is represented by the entrepreneurial start-up—though Coupland's treatment is nuanced, showing not only the ways in which these firms are beholden to larger structures of social power, but even how they to some degree instantiate them. The start-up in question is a fledgling software company begun by Michael, who abruptly abandons Redmond for Silicon Valley and soon thereafter invites his former housemates to join his cash-poor but idea-rich outfit, which operates out of Dan's parents' home in Palo Alto (Dan's father, having lost his job with IBM, is supporting the venture and plans to serve as its chief salesman). Driven by what they refer to as the "One-Point-Oh" dream—the desire to "be the *first* to do the *first* version of something," to move from Microserfs to "Cyberlords"—Dan, along with three other housemates and his new girlfriend Karla, also a Microsoft refugee, head down to California to "fabricate the waking dream" (p. 89; emphases in original), to help realize the high-tech promise that Bill Gates and his minions have distorted into a dystopian nightmare.

In a neat balancing act, Coupland shows how everything that had seemed so bleak and domineering from the vantage of the Redmond campus has, in Silicon Valley, its apparently brighter side. Rather than a totalitarian "monoculture," the Valley is a "bland anarchy": "*Nobody* rules here," Dan observes (p. 108; emphasis in original). Still, despite the lack of a fixed hegemon, the influence of capital is all pervasive, breeding an "endless, boring, mad scramble for loot" (p. 117) that is most effectively satirized in the scene mentioned earlier, where the start-up cohort visits a group of snooty venture capitalists to pitch their product. The start-up itself, according to Dan, "isn't about work. It's about all of us staying together" (p. 199), affirming and deepening their mutual bonds of friendship; the work climate, too, is more relaxed, whether set at first in the Underwood family's "rumpus room"—replete with endless bags of candy and a pair of pet gerbils—or, later on, in an office space that has been renovated to resemble "a Guggenheim and a Toys-R-Us squished into one" (p. 220). In a way, though, this cozy arrangement merely continues, in a different setting, the infantilization of labor Abe had decried at Microsoft, and the parallel becomes obvious when Michael, irritated at all the gabbing and flirting that has replaced hard work in the office, begins to crack the entrepreneurial whip: "Michael is really such a slave driver. He squishes everything he can out of us. It's very Bill" (p. 241). Yet despite the fact that his "life has become coding madness all over again," Dan declares that "*this* time we're killing ourselves for *ourselves*, instead of some huge company to whom we might as well be interchangeable bloodless PlaySkool figurine units" (p. 135; emphases in original).

What all this suggests is that the contrast between Redmond and Silicon Valley, as depicted in the book, is not a simple matter of black versus white, and that the positive aspects of the entrepreneurial dream bear the seeds of darker forces—the very forces, in fact, that incubated the Microsoft monolith. Indeed, Dan describes the Valley as "the birthplace of the new postindustrial economy" (p. 136), the emblem as well as the motor of "society's accelerating rate of change" (p. 99)—a rate so rapid that Toffler's *Future Shock* is yesterday's news, its outdated status remarked by the appearance of a cast-off copy at a Valley garage sale (p. 274). The possibility of reducing all cultural processes to programmable codes amenable to technocratic manipulation has its roots in this speeding cybernetic landscape, in "these buildings where they make the machines that make the machines that make the machines" (p. 203). Despite all its trappings of unfettered progress, however, the Valley can sometimes seem quaintly dated, like an avatar of yesterday's fantasies of sterile, high-tech, authoritarian futures. The novel's pointed references to a previous generation of science-fiction films and TV programs draw this theme out: one local business reminds Dan of "a 1970s utopian, *Andromeda Strain*ishly empty tech complex" (p. 211), while the Apple campus, much like Microsoft's, conveys an "eerie, *Logan's Run*-like atmosphere" (p. 122). So clearly does the Valley's start-up culture seem to harbor its own sinister, dictatorial shadow that Dan, while idly daydreaming, has a sudden vision of total social apocalypse: "I saw venture capitalists with their eyes burned out in their sockets by visions of money, crashing their Nissans on the 101 . . . , their windows spurting fluorescent orange blood" (p. 192).

While I would very much like to say that this complicated rendering of the mingled promise and horror of Silicon Valley is the result of a truly dialectical conception on Coupland's part, it must be admitted that, much of the time, the author seems merely studiedly ambivalent. His unwillingness to push his vision as far as he might is indicated by an odd subplot in which Todd is converted to marxism by his new bodybuilder girlfriend, Dusty, whereupon the pair harangue their coworkers with jargon-laden screeds. Often, these jeremiads seem entirely appropriate in context, as when Dusty explains Marx's concept of surplus value to the assembled programmers—how the "worker creates more value than that for which he is compensated"—at which point "Michael went purple, like a Burger King manager who hears one of his employees discuss unionization" (p. 258). At another point, Dusty directs her critique toward the regime of automated consumption, arguing (along the lines of Sut Jhally, as discussed in my introduction) that capitalism has now spawned a leisure-based equivalent of surplus-value extraction in its profit-driven "lassoing" of the consumer's "45 minutes of discretionary time" (p. 279). Finally, in language strongly reminiscent of the critics of consumer society discussed in chapter 1, Dusty claims that the "media-induced social atomization" (p. 261) of the contemporary marketplace has produced a situation in which children are no longer enculturated by their parents but instead "encapitalized" by popular cartoons and toys, by a commercial kiddie culture (p. 273).

While these criticisms are somewhat overblown, especially in their attribution of near-omnipotence to the forces of modern capitalism, the response of Dan and the others is not to suggest more subtle ramifications of the argument but rather to mock it relentlessly. Todd and Dusty are dubbed "Boris and Natasha," after the bumbling Bolsheviks of the Bullwinkle cartoons, and their ideas sharply parodied—as, for example, when Dan and Karla draw up a detailed indictment of allegedly "decadent" breakfast cereals (exempting Count Chocula from their strictures, interestingly enough, because its "[w]itty vampire motif plays on the never-ending struggle of the oppressed to topple the ruling classes" [p. 266]). Seeking an alternative critical paradigm—significantly, in order "to foster a less combative working environment"—Dan and Michael introduce "a zero politics zone" in the office by translating every fraught issue into a *Star Trek* scenario, thus displacing and distancing the force of the critique. This casually ironic "TrekPolitics" incarnates "the new apolitical pick-and-choose style of citizen" that Dan and the others feel themselves essentially to be (p. 260).

While I believe that Coupland's basic purpose in introducing this curious subplot is to insulate himself from the animating force of marxist arguments, to his credit he does show the compelling reasons his characters seem so hysterically inclined to dismiss political claims out of hand. Todd, for example, has earlier been introduced as "historically empty. He neither knows nor cares about the past" (p. 11)—which suggests that his subsequent embrace of a deeply historicist mode of thought may be a desperate effort to fill this vacuum with critical substance. In a previous novel, ·*Shampoo Planet*, Coupland had shown himself to be acutely aware of the damaging effects on contemporary youth of their being deprived of a palpable sense of historical depth and dimension: in that book, the protagonist satirically concocts the idea of *HistoryWorld™*—a series of corporate theme parks, built on landfill sites, that are designed to combat the current "shortage of historical objects." [119]

More particularly, what *Microserfs* exposes is the psychological fallout of the "end of ideology" thesis advanced by postindustrial theorists such as Daniel Bell, the notion that traditional politics have been transcended in high-tech society because historical change itself has been subjected to processes of technocratic management. [120] Michael gives voice to this viewpoint when he argues, in response to Todd and Dusty, that access to computer memory banks "replaces historical knowledge as a way for our species to process its past. . . . [W]e can edit ourselves as we go along, like an on-screen document. . . . [W]e have changed the nature of change itself." [121] Thus, it is possible to see the young characters' fervent antimarxism as a revealing—not to mention overdetermined—expression of their own lack of intellectual resources for addressing the difficult political realities of their situation, but this requires a more charitable reading than is perhaps fully warranted. There is no indication, for example, that Dan's cheerful embrace of "the freefloat of intellectual Darwinism" that seems to drive Silicon Valley (p. 322) is intended at all ironically.

Happily, when it comes to his treatment of other, less obviously directly political aspects of postindustrial culture, Coupland evinces an admirably dialectical perspective, tracing crucial concepts and contexts in a way that displays the essential imbrication of the positive and negative possibilities contained in them. This strength is most evident when Coupland treats the pressing issue of cyborgization, the growing enmeshment of (young) people and (digital) machines in high-tech culture. Most significantly, he offers a shrewd commentary on the contradictions inherent in the postindustrial conflation of youth and high technology; while he seems at times to endorse this metaphorical equation, it is largely for the purpose of satirizing the fraught generational logic it entails.

Thus, Dan muses at one point, "The upper age limit of people with instincts for this business is about 40. People who were over 30 at the beginning of the late 1970s PC revolution missed the boat; anyone older is like a Delco AM car radio" (p. 296). This expresses the attitude of most of his generational cohort, who are astonished when they encounter a "fortysomething" engineer—someone from "the Flintstones era of computers"—still working on core research (p. 33). Much more common, it would seem, are folks like Dan's father, who—having been downsized out of a job at IBM—tells his son sadly, "It's your world now" (p. 41), and expresses astonishment that the future has turned out to be "something my kid built in the basement" (p. 204). Ultimately, he sees himself as one of "the newly obsolete humans" quietly "pushed to the side" by the pace of technological development (p. 203)—a view that would seem to be borne out by the youthful culture of the local high-tech companies: "It's really young at Nintendo," Dan observes. "It's like the year 1311, where everyone over 35 is dead or maimed and out of sight and mind" (p. 14).

Another current, however, works against this simple conflation of youth and high technology. Not only is the notion of older people's obsolescence proven simply wrong (Dan's father learns new programming languages in order to be more competitive), but Coupland depicts a much more complicated set of generational relationships in the novel, showing how youth, far from being preeminent in postindustrial society, is actually subtly subordinated. For example, Dan's observation that he and his friends are "the first Microsoft generation—the first group of people who have never known a world without an MS-DOS environment" (p. 16)—must be perceived in the context of their cynical exploitation at the hands of the "cult of Bill," not to mention the invidious "adolescence protraction" this cult fosters. The latter phenomenon suggests that the corporation's ready connection of youth and technology serves an ideological function—specifically, to glorify young people metaphorically while subjecting them in fact. Moreover, it also provides a convenient excuse for disposing of employees when they reach their inevitable burnout point, since a fresh cadre of recruits is always available at Stanford or MIT. All of which makes the novel's occasional references to the film *Logan's Run* so telling, since this 1976 movie chronicles an autocratic future "utopia" of youth in which those over thirty are routinely purged, either through ritual suicide or at the hands of state-sponsored assassins. In the context of their imminent disposability, the lack of a historical perspective might be a quite valuable quality in Silicon Valley's young army of "corporate drones" (p. 196).

Beyond its clever critique of the technoyouth ethos of postindustrial theory, *Microserfs* also mounts a sophisticated interrogation of the ways that contemporary youth and high technology are complexly cyborgized. Not only are Dan and his friends "the first Microsoft generation," but they are also the first youth cohort capable systematically of conceiving their minds and bodies in terms of computer-based metaphors. In exploring this theme, Coupland shows how the resulting stark objectification is dialectically balanced by a potent humanization of technology, creating at least the conditions for—if not the accomplished reality of—a new mode of cybernetic empowerment. Yet this promised transformation is hobbled by the implicitly vampiric capitalist logic that presently contains it.

On the side of objectification, Coupland paints a devastating portrait of a generation unmoored from nature, painfully alienated from their own bodies and unable to form satisfying interpersonal bonds due to the cybernetic mediation of their experience. Karla, Dan's girlfriend, had in adolescence entertained the Warholian desire "to be a machine" (p. 73), an impulse that lies at the root of her current eating disorders; and many of the other characters share an almost willful disdain for their own embodiment—from the start-up's C.E.O., Ethan, who has to be reminded by Dan that "[y]our body is you, too" before he can confront his incipient cancer, to Michael, who loathes his pudgy, shambling self so much that he can only form relationships via online interaction with total strangers. These attitudes are only strengthened by the characteristic forms of leisure and labor that the group engages in: at one point, they all debate whether to get matching bar code tattoos (p. 315), thus affirming the psychological effects of rampant commodification, while at another they abandon their claustrophobic immersion in programming for the sunny outdoors simply in order to reset their circadian rhythms (p. 289). Yet even this therapeutic recourse to nature cannot be infallibly restorative in a context where biotechnology firms are able to "trick" bacteria into manufacturing animal pheromones (p. 110). In this hypertechnologized environment, where physicality has been reduced to manipulable patterns of information, it is hardly surprising that Todd and Dusty "want to become 'posthuman'—to make their bodies like the Bionic Woman's and Six Million Dollar Man's" (p. 240), even if this means stuffing themselves with mysterious, possibly mutagenic chemicals. As if summing up this encompassing logic of machinic objectification, Dan mournfully embraces the word "deletia," which, he says, "stands for everything that's been lost" (p. 190).

Yet this nostalgia for an authentic self uncompromised by technological contamination coexists with an unquenchable fascination for high-tech devices, a fascination that cannot ultimately be reduced to mere ideology. The way computer technology in particular has been integrated into the characters' intimacies is not prima facie evidence of alienation; indeed, it provides many of them with transformative understandings of self that, reciprocally, serve to subjectify the apparatus. Dan's narrative, for example, which inscribes his effort "to see the patterns in my life . . . day to day, one line of bug-free code at a time" (p. 4), is, in its very form, indelibly marked by word-processing technologies— by the vocabulary of anxiety, confusion, and longing newly expressible through changes in font size, adjusted margins, bulleted lists, cut-and-pasted text, and so forth. Convinced that "machines really *are* our subconscious" (p. 228; emphasis in original), Dan intersperses his narrative with boldfaced collages intended to represent the random, unfiltered dream logic generated at the interface between himself and his "little PowerBook" (p. 46).[122] Seemingly affirming Toffler's prophecy of the emerging "modular" subject of Third Wave culture, this ongoing prose-poetic babble conveys a sense of prosthetic consciousness, mixing Dan's childhood reminiscences with the machine's putative musings, to the point at times of confusing them irretrievably. The impulse to self-comprehension, Coupland is suggesting, cannot be de-linked finally from the tools we use for "externalizing our essence" (p. 356): technological mediation is also collaboration.

The same inextricable imbrication of subject and machine operates in the characters' prevailing relationships. Michael's persistent chat room flirtations, for example, eventually lead to his meeting and marrying a Canadian woman named Amy (whose online handle is, significantly, BarCode), and both affirm that this union is only stronger because it was not founded on the inevitable bias of initial appearances; "seeing them together," Dan remarks, "is like seeing the future" (p. 334).[123] Karla and Dan's relationship is also mediated, though more metaphorically, by a computer logic; the liberating regimen of shiatsu massage they share, which brings Dan to a deeper grasp of his body and its needs, is justified by Karla as follows: "All stimulation generates a memory—and these memories have to go somewhere. Our bodies are essentially diskettes" (p. 92). As Karla, with Dan's help, begins to overcome her lingering anorexia, they describe the process as a radical "reformatting" (p. 192). Finally, Karla poignantly confesses her feelings for Dan in similarly cyborgized terms: "I thought I was going to be a READ ONLY file," she says. "I never thought I'd be . . . interactive" (p. 101). At one level, this equation of human love with a mode of software interface gently satirizes nerdish preoccupations, but more important, it also points to an underlying faith in technology as an expression of the powers of truly redemptive change.

Karla's statement also serves to distinguish a system of interactive communication from one based on unilateral signals, a contrast that operates at several levels in the novel. At the level of plot, this opposition informs the business of the start-up company, whose software product is an interactive media game called *Oop!* (for Object Oriented Programming), which allows users to create their own customized structures and deploy them in virtually infinite scenarios. Modeled on the Lego bricks that had been a major playtime pleasure for the characters in childhood, *Oop!* is designed to incarnate, in digital form, the modular logic of the original toy, its flexible capacity to translate private fantasy into palpable form.[124] On the one hand, this objectification may be perceived as pernicious, involving a systematic reduction and commodification of the human life world into programmable parts: according to the marxist Dusty, Legos "brainwashed entire generations of youth from the information-dense industrialized nations into developing mind-sets that view the world as unitized, sterile, inorganic, and interchangeably modular" (p. 257). On the other hand, the spirit of play animating the game may function to imbue the blighted fragments of a capitalist object world with a dimension of subjectivity it has otherwise lost—hence, the name of the start-up company: "Interiority." Whether *Oop!* achieves an invidious reification or an invigorating deliverance depends, finally, on whether it promotes an open interactivity or merely reinscribes a previously given code. In other words, it depends on whether the transfiguring powers latent in cyborgization—in the modular extension and prosthetic enhancement of physicopsychic life through cybernetic interfaces—are freed from capital's vampiric control or merely work to reinforce it.

Given Coupland's casual antimarxism, he is hardly likely to extrapolate a liberation of computer technology for socialist purposes (nor should this be the test of his novel in any case), but he does suggest some significant ways in which the possibilities of the new interactive media may escape capitalist comprehension if not control. In the final section of the novel, the Interiority group attends the semiannual Consumer Electronics Show in Las Vegas to pitch their product to assembled corporate bigwigs in the toy and entertainment industries. While the possibilities of *Oop!* are clearly perceived by those working in allied fields, the executives from Hollywood, representing the vast media conglomerates dominating film and television, are basically clueless as to how to integrate interactive possibilities with their essentially READ ONLY products. As a result, all they can manage to do is to forcibly mistranslate—in Dan's terminology, to "spooge"—one format into another: "they don't have a handle on what they're doing and it's starting to show, and mistakes are costing them a pile of money—trying to spooge Myst into a feature-length movie; trying to spooge movies into CD-ROMs. It's a mess" (p. 344).[125]

In sum, there may well be fresh possibilities for consumer pleasure and autonomy in interactive media that are radically incommensurable with a model of consumption based on passive appropriation. Yet, in a curious twist, Dan suggests that he himself may "have missed the boat on CD-ROM interactive," since, following the logic of postindustrial discourse, "you only ever feel truly comfortable with the level of digitization that was normal for you from the age of five to fifteen." "In the end," he asserts, "multimedia interactive won't resemble literature so much as sports" (p. 143), which suggests that the playful formal structure of *Microserfs*—with its interpolated e-mails, coded passages, and general montage effect—may involve an attempt to rethink its own status as a literary text. Yet one can also sense a lingering anxiety on Coupland's part that literature as an institution may be dying, a concern expressed by Dan's librarian mother, who worries that the "Information Superhighway" might make books obsolete by ushering in a truly postliterate culture. This anxiety is rather strangely resolved at the end of the story by Mrs. Underwood's becoming a cyborg—"part woman/ part machine, emanating blue Macintosh light" (p. 369)—after a stroke forces her to communicate with her family via a computer keyboard (in passages represented by multiple fonts, typographic doodles, and other word-processed tricks). But the underlying question she raises— whether the so-called Information Superhighway portends a new mode of cultural participation for consumers, one based on interactivity rather than absorption—remains unanswered. It is to this question that I turn in the following chapter.

FAST SOFAS AND CYBORG COUCH POTATOES: GENERATION X ON THE INFOBAHN

COUCH COMMANDOS VERSUS ZOMBIE SYSTEMS

Though Dan Underwood and his friends, in Douglas Coupland's *Microserfs*, claim that the media is "overhyping . . . the Infobahn," it is clear that they are fascinated by the topic—a fascination that takes the form of a nostalgic curiosity about real highways, "the asphalt and cement kind."[1] When Dan brings home from the library a copy of a 1975 *Handbook of Highway Engineering*, the assembled nerds begin "*ooh*ing and *ahhh*ing over the book's beautiful . . . on-ramps, off-ramps, and overpasses," doting on the alien jargon of "subgrades . . . , cut-slopes, and TBMs (Tunnel Boring Machines)" (p. 53). Shortly thereafter, the names of famous U.S. highways begin to crop up in Dan's collages of computer dreams (p. 68). This nostalgia for the American road system—"[s]o sensual, so infinite, so full of promise," Dan opines as he cruises around the cloverleafs of the Bay Area (p. 305)—coexists with a dawning sense of despair that the heroic era responsible for these sprawling monoliths may have passed. When a 1994 earthquake topples sections of the Los Angeles freeways, the group gathers mournfully to watch the television coverage, "sad to see all of this glorious infrastructure in ruins, like a crippled giant" (p. 223). Ethan, who grew up in Southern California, is so overcome with emotion that he constructs, in the start-up office, an overpass made from Lego bricks that imaginatively restores a severed section of the Antelope Valley freeway. Meanwhile, the local damage from the 1989 Loma Prieta earthquake remains unrepaired, leading Dan to observe that San Francisco must be "putting all its highway-building energy into building the mention-it-one-more-time-and-I'll-scream Information Superhighway" (p. 114). To Dan and his friends, the latter, conceived by its promoters as a kind of millennial alternative to the original highway system, comes across as pallid and unambitious by comparison.

Coupland's treatment of this topic is quite shrewd, since the Infobahn has indeed been advanced as a massive engineering project on a par with the erection of the interstate highway system in the 1950s and 1960s. During the early years of the Clinton administration, a task force was appointed to oversee the planning of a National Information Infrastructure—"a seamless web of communication networks, computers, databases, and consumer electronics that will put vast amounts of information at users' fingertips," as their initial publication, *National Information Infrastructure: Agenda for Action*, put it in 1993.[2] The project was largely driven by the enthusiastic support of Vice President Al Gore, who described the NII as an "Information Superhighway" in numerous public speeches, thus helping to impel the term into the national media and thence into popular consciousness.[3] Ironically enough, Gore's father, while a senator from Tennessee, had been responsible for crafting the Federal-Aid Highway Act of 1956, which spawned the modern freeway system, the largest public works undertaking in U.S. history.[4] By analogy, then, Gore was suggesting not only his own parallel significance, but also that the NII could best be conceived in terms of a network of interlocking roads allowing potentially unlimited public access to far-flung sites, as well as the rapid distribution of commercial goods and services—which is more or less how the Internet and the World Wide Web are popularly understood today.

Of course, the NII was intended to refer to more than these specific computer systems, which are fairly haphazardly organized, but rather to an integrated, universal network connecting every home and business to digitized flows of information—a network that would ideally link all electronic appliances (CD players, televisions, and PCs) into a single multimedia unit with manifold interactive capabilities. In the vision of its supporters, this I-Way would be an unparalleled boon to consumers, who would be able to enjoy on-demand movies and television programs, live musical performances, virtual libraries, and museums—in short, a bottomless cornucopia of cultural materials. Some commentators suggested that the overall result would be the perfection of America's ideal of participatory democracy in the flourishing of online "virtual communities" organized around shared interests and goals,[5] while others stressed imminent transformations in working life, including the improved prospects for telecommuting.[6] The Information Superhighway would, in short, realize the fantasy of a totally "wired life" that had circulated in postindustrial discourse in the 1970s—where, in fact, the highway metaphor originated (despite Gore's claim to have invented it).[7] According to the libertarian Progress and Freedom Foundation, in a 1994 manifesto coauthored by Alvin Toffler, the Infobahn basically realizes the epochal promise of Third Wave society, decentralizing power and demassifying markets on an unprecedented scale. As a result, the "meaning of freedom, structures of self-government, definition of property, nature of competition, conditions for cooperation, sense of community and nature of progress will each be redefined for the Knowledge Age—just as they were redefined for a new age of industry some 250 years ago."[8]

Unfortunately, despite the fact that the 1996 Telecommunications Bill mandated the deregulated economic environment allegedly necessary for the full-fledged birth of the I-Way,[9] the emergence of a standardized, universal-access, multimedia system has been hamstrung by a number of technical and financial difficulties—predictably described as "speed bumps," "potholes," and other roadway irritants by the mainstream press—and has yet to fully materialize.[10] Still, the sense that the coming of networked information technologies portends a radical restructuring of economic and social relationships is widespread, with critics describing the outcome as the achievement of Virtual Capitalism or Digital Capitalism.[11] According to Nick Dyer-Witheford, the NII may best be understood as the post-Fordist equivalent of what the highway system was for mature Fordism: just as "road building was an essential component in the reordering of social life that integrated assembly-line labor, mass consumption of manufactured goods, suburban housing, and privatized mobility" in Fordist America, so "[i]n Post-Fordist capital, these digital flows [of the I-Way] are used by 'virtual corporations' to link automated machines to just-in-time inventory systems, connect dispersed production sites, accumulate and mine data about consumer tastes and habits, and forge new marketing opportunities, coordinating these activities on a global scale." In essence, the Infobahn fuses the two most important Fordist institutions, highways and television, into a readily traversible consumer network, "a veritable paradise of exchange."[12]

In response to this ongoing evolution of a mature technological infrastructure for the post-Fordist regime of accumulation, left-wing critics have attacked the I-Way on a number of fronts, decrying its wanton violations of privacy, its corrosion of authentic community, and its exacerbation of existing social divisions.[13] The critique I wish to focus on here is the claim that the Information Superhighway accomplishes a thoroughgoing commodification of culture that makes its pretense of promoting genuine interactivity laughable. In an article entitled "Info-bahn Blues," Robert Adrian X argues that this promised interaction will be narrowly "restricted to online shopping, video games and pay-to-view movies. . . . The Infobahn in this definition is little more than a catalogue of products, services, information and entertainment that can be ordered or purchased and consumed on line."[14] The I-Way's nomi-nally two-way system of communication will have, in the words of How-ard Besser, an "asymmetrical design"; specifically, it will be heavily biased in favor of the sender. The result will be "like a ten-lane highway coming into the home, with only a tiny path leading back out—just wide enough to take a credit card number. . . . This kind of model resembles broadcast or cable television much more than it does today's Internet."[15] But, these critics stress, the Infobahn will be a televisual system vastly more powerful than the Fordist version, with a far-reaching capacity to monitor consumer lifestyles and a growing monopoly over the dissemi-nation of cultural commodities; no wonder that it has attracted the at-tention of Bill Gates, whose book *The Road Ahead* (1995) offers an avid blueprint for the Infobahn.

The social implications of this regime of "cybernetic capitalism" have been analyzed by Kevin Robins and Frank Webster in an essay that, though written before the specific predictions of the Infobahn, basically summarizes the Left's indictment against it.[16] What the authors refer to as "the cabled electronic grid" (p. 61) is presently being designed "to ensure the centralized, and furtive, inspection, observation, surveillance, and documentation of activities on the circumference of society as a whole" (p. 59)—a process they identify as "panopticism . . . on the level of the social totality" (p. 61), thus invoking Michel Foucault's vision of modern power as an extensive, proliferating apparatus of disciplinary oversight and control. As Foucault describes it, panopticism's remark-able efficiency is assured by its effect of "auto-surveillance," its ability to force those subjected to its gaze to internalize the panoptic model, thereby reproducing at the level of individual subjectivity the structures of authority informing the entire system. In his words, "centres of ob-servation [are] disseminated throughout society," resulting in "a faceless gaze that transform[s] the whole social body into a field of perception: thousands of eyes posted everywhere, mobile attentions ever on the alert, a long, hierarchized network."[17] For Robins and Webster, this network is simply the battery of screens that makes up the extended tele-matic apparatus of contemporary consumer society, and its specific auto-surveillant effect is the orchestrated mobilization of dutiful audiences for the manifold activities of consumption, all conducted under the watchful eye of power. As a result, people's deepest wishes and dreams are reified into coded processes, "tendentially displaced by the estranged objectivity of data banks and information reservoirs"[18]—a vast prosthetic intelligence that, rather than empowering consumers, systematically feeds upon them.

The vampiric relationship implied here is spelled out, in strong if not delirious terms, by Arthur Kroker and Michael A. Weinstein in their book *Data Trash*, which contains probably the most blistering polemic against the Infobahn published to date. Mocking the NII's proclaimed goals of providing consumer choice and interaction as cynical illusions, Kroker and Weinstein argue that the project's real purpose is "to liquidate the sprawling web of the Internet in favor of the smooth telematic vision of the digital superhighway," thus purging anarchic community in the name of "virtualized (commercial) exchange."[19] The latter they identify as a "predatory force" (p. 8) seeking nothing less than "our co-optation as servomechanisms of the cybernetic grid . . . swallow[ing] bodies, and even whole societies, into the dynamic momentum of its telematic logic" (p. 7). The Infobahn, in short, objectifies human desires and fantasies into information and processes them for profit, to the point that consumers—like laborers in Marx's factory—become mere appendages of an enormous, self-perpetuating machine, a cybernetic automaton.

Thus cyborgized by the I-Way, consumers are reduced to little more than a series of "prosthetic after-effects: the body becomes a passive archive to be processed, entertained, and stockpiled by the seduction-apertures of the virtual reality complex" (p. 6). The entire system, in fact, incarnates a nihilistic "will to virtuality" (p. 5) that drives inexorably toward the wholesale translation of human life into digital code. "When the networked world of the information superhighway is finally linked to TV," Kroker and Weinstein assert, "then the will to virtuality will be free to produce fully functioning networked bodies" (p. 22)—cyborg couch potatoes manipulated by remote control. "Having no vestigial memory of nature," this deracinated "slacker's body" will drift aimlessly along the Infobahn, its experience a mutant noise of "filtered images, displaced sounds, morphed faces, aliased eyes . . . , and cut-and-paste sexuality" (p. 35).

While I do not share the monolithic negativism of this argument, which I see as aligned with the draconian "left puritanism" discussed in chapter 1, I believe Kroker and Weinstein do identify, however hysterically, a dynamic of exploitation that necessarily limits the liberatory potential of the Infobahn. For there can be little doubt that the main developmental trend of the NII, especially given the hands-off policy established by the Clinton administration, is toward rampant commercialism, essentially privatizing the Internet and thus furthering the commodification of cultural experience inaugurated by mass media such as television. Moreover, the extravagant paranoia evinced by many of the left-wing critics of the Information Superhighway needs to be understood as an angry response to the almost grotesque fulsomeness of capitalist manifestoes like *The Road Ahead*. More specifically, Kroker and Weinstein see themselves as combating the facile technoutopianism that, in their view, provides a screen for the depredations of monopolists like Gates: "There are pure capitalists in the cyber industry and there are capitalists who are also visionary computer specialists. The latter, in a spirit of vicious naivete, generate the ideological hype, a messianic element, that the former take up cynically" (p. 15). Yet still I think these critics have overreacted, to the point of ignoring the genuinely liberatory possibilities the I-Way may offer.

There is thus perhaps some truth in the prognostications of the messiahs of digital culture that needs to be disentangled from the naive cyberdrool that surrounds it. What is so interesting about these prophets—figures such as, for example, George Gilder, Nicholas Negroponte, and Paul Levinson—is precisely their naiveté, their inability to grasp why the radical emancipation of consumer agency the Infobahn seems to portend has not been enthusiastically embraced by capitalist entertainment industries. Generally libertarian, these critics can only vaguely blame the meddling of government bureaucracies or the sheer inertia of large institutions for the fact that a two-way, fully integrated, multimedia, information-on-demand system has not yet been installed in every suburban living room. Failing to perceive the ways that corporate control of entertainment may actually hobble technological progress (since these industries' concern is to ensure the profitability of information commodities, not to generalize access or proliferate options), these writers fall back on a postindustrial rhetoric of generational inevitability to suggest that, in the future, the Infobahn *must* become the utopia they envision. "The information superhighway may be mostly hype today, but it is an understatement about tomorrow," Negroponte avers. "It will exist beyond people's wildest predictions. . . . [E]ach generation will become more digital than the preceding one."[20]

Negroponte's *Being Digital*, Gilder's *Life After Television*, and Levinson's *Soft Edge* all share this conviction that the youthful energy of technology will win out, despite apparent obstacles.[21] Gilder even deploys, though unconsciously, a marxist logic in describing how the "corpse" of television "may linger in American living rooms for many more years"— along with other electronic "zombie systems"—despite the fact that the Infobahn restores "the brains" of the operation to individual consumers.[22] What he means by this is that the I-Way, by opening access to an endless bounty of digitized goods and services, destroys the hierarchical power of broadcasting companies, whose bottleneck on distribution is no longer necessary for the circulation of cultural commodities. "Just as the U.S. highway system enhanced the freedom and options of automobile owners, the national fiber-highway system will enhance the freedom and power of communications. . . . The power moves increasingly to the drivers on the network rather than to its builders and managers" (p. 60). In the near future, according to Gilder, consumers will select whatever they want from the vast storehouse of human culture and download it onto their "telecomputers" for immediate or deferred enjoyment; they will also be able to customize this data, fusing it with digitally captured images and sounds to generate multimedia texts of their very own—which, thanks to the two-way circuit, will be available for the pleasure of others. Consumption will thus be truly democratized, incarnating the "distributed intelligence of digital systems" (p. 116). Some older consumers may choose to remain comfortably settled with their "couch potato TV," but the eventual realization of a truly interactive culture is assured thanks to the visionary and innovative spirit of "the new generations of America's youth" (p. 119).

Levinson also stresses the contrast between passive absorption and active participation in his discussion of how the computer screen differs from conventional television. Users of computers "sit up, faces alert . . . , and constantly control what they see via keyboard or mouse"—much like drivers in automobiles—"in sharp distinction to 'couch potatoes' who only trouble to change the channel by remote during commercials or between programs."[23] The videocassette recorder has already freed consumer time from the rigidity of broadcast schedules, but the VCR "can only rescue that which is already imprisoned in the TV line-up"; it cannot open the door to all of culture, to "the world on demand," as can the Infobahn.[24] Negroponte, too, suggests the radical empowerment of consumers in the face of this embarrassment of cultural riches. TV-based concepts like "info grazing" and "channel surfing" are totally inadequate in this context, he claims;[25] instead, the consumer becomes a "couch commando," not only negotiating a dense flux of data but also accessing vivid virtual-reality landscapes, and perhaps crafting his or her own from the "bitstream" coursing along the I-Way (pp. 118–20). To help filter this potentially overwhelming flow, consumers will be attended by "digital butlers," software robots that serve as individualized interfaces to the larger information culture, culling materials on the basis of their owners' "delegated . . . desires" (p. 158). Given the advent of such a decentralized system, "the monolithic empires of mass media are dissolving into an array of cottage industries" (p. 57), while consumption is rapidly becoming "a boutique business," serviced by small-scale, possibly home-based operations (p. 85). Alvin Toffler's "prosumer society" would appear, by this account, to be just around the corner.

Of course, there are roadblocks: media empires do not give up the ghost so easily. But these authors are generally confident that ongoing technological development, assisted by entrepreneurial ventures and further government deregulation, will realize computopia in our lifetimes. Yet the difficulties they acknowledge are quite significant—for example, the erosion of traditional copyrights in the realm of digital exchange. As Levinson rather tartly remarks, the "metaphysical liberation of information" via the Infobahn "need not, and should not, entail total economic liberation" from the laws governing intellectual property;[26] yet controlling such rights online remains an issue fraught with problems, mandating heavy investment in cryptographic techniques and vigilant corporate watchdogging.[27] Perhaps more tellingly, the forms of consumer desire objectified and fixed in major trademarked brands—which should, according to the implications of the above arguments, wither away in the new info-boutique culture—are instead being transferred online in various strategies of "digital branding."[28] Above all, the mode of one-way communication favored by broadcast television has hardly shifted at all, regardless of the fact that, as Negroponte asserts, "each person can be an unlicensed TV station" on the I-Way.[29] Clearly, the liberatory possibilities of the Infobahn announced by these cybermessiahs have all been scaled back and recuperated by traditional corporate techniques for the commodification of culture—if anything, the current climate of deregulation has spurred further monopolistic retrenchments in media industries—and there is little reason to expect that this situation is likely to change in the near future. It would appear, therefore, that conventional TV is here to stay. As a former FCC chairman and head of the Hearst Corporation's media division commented, explicitly in response to Gilder's prophecies: "The reality is that at the end of the day people want to enjoy themselves in a relatively inert manner, and television will remain their means to do so."[30]

BAR-CODING DIGITAL YOUTH

Yet what about the contention that change *must* occur because the newly interactive consciousness of contemporary youth will demand it? The notion that teenagers, in their consumer practices, have developed an empathic attunement to technological interfaces—to the point of becoming figurative or literal cyborgs—links commentators on digital culture with the critics of videogames discussed in chapter 1. In fact, two of those critics have also written books on young people's relationship with personal computers and their eager aptitude for online communication: J. C. Herz's *Surfing on the Internet* and Douglas Rushkoff's *Cyberia*. These works, along with Don Tapscott's *Growing Up Digital* and David S. Bennehum's *Extra Life*, form a linked set of texts that extrapolate arguments about the Information Superhighway to specifically youth-cultural issues and contexts, updating debates about video arcades and mall culture for the "Net Generation."[31]

While these four books differ in substantial ways, they all present young people's imbrication with digital media as a generative process of coevolution, in which the growing capacities of the machinery to facilitate creative interaction are linked with the developing energies of youthful consciousness. In *Extra Life*, a computer programmer's memoir of growing up during the 1970s and 1980s, Bennahum identifies himself as a member of the "Atari generation," for whom "the evolution of the machine briefly matched that of our adolescent selves, becoming a vessel and partner, a coconspirator in our mutual coming of age."[32] Herz's book, which describes her intense participation in online chat rooms and MUDs (Multi-User Dimensions) during the early 1980s, echoes this view in her chapter on "Digital Youth," where she evokes the "special, mutagenic charge" of cyberspatial communication and the teenage mutants it has called forth, "a generation adjusted to the factors that future-shocked our parents, adapted to an increasingly accelerated and temporary lifestyle."[33] Rushkoff coins a term for these new screenagers: "Cyberians," whose ability to "grok" high-tech interfaces—including not only computers but also techno music and designer drugs— opens them up to a "categorical upscaling of the human experience onto uncharted, hyperdimensional turf."[34] Tapscott's *Growing Up Digital* puts it somewhat more soberly but no less apocalyptically: modern "computer-facilitated networks" form a "natural extension" of teenagers themselves, making them together "an unstoppable force for transformation."[35]

What is destined to be transformed by this epochal convergence of youth and technology varies from book to book, but all agree that the interactive mode of cultural participation fostered by digital media will completely overturn the unilateral broadcast model of television. According to Rushkoff, "the hypnotic spell of years of television"[36] has finally been broken by the emergence of "the pathways of the datasphere," a "new infrastructure" that is rapidly becoming "the perfect playground for the dendrites of expanding young consciousness."[37] As Herz comments, "Before I found the Net, I never stopped in front of a television and thought, God, how *one-way*."[38] Like Gilder and Negroponte, Bennahum muses on the possibilities the I-Way offers for shattering the corporate monopoly on culture—breeding endless varieties of "self-produced television shows, home-brew media"—though he does worry that big companies like Microsoft will only attempt to coopt its promise, "mutating [it] into just another form of television."[39] As in the discourses surrounding computer industries discussed in the previous chapter, metaphors from surf culture are deployed by these writers to evoke the challenging, participatory pleasures of digital lifestyles, of "boys and girls . . . rid[ing] the crest of the informational wave."[40] Consistently throughout these volumes, "the joy of surfing an open datasphere"[41] is contrasted with the vacant inertia of TV's couch-potato consumers, a passive relation in which "you willed nothing. You merely sat back and watched."[42]

Tapscott makes the most far-reaching argument along these lines, identifying TV and the Net as starkly opposed systems associated with distinct generational cohorts. What Tapscott calls the Net Generation, or "N Gen," refers to the group born between 1977 and 1997, whose ranks have now eclipsed the baby boom as a percentage of the U.S. population.[43] Just as the boomers grew up alongside television, which served as the "the messenger and the mobilizer" of their youth-cultural lifestyles (p. 2), so N-Geners are coming to maturity in an age of multimedia, whose flexible interfaces promote "rich, multiperson collaborative environments controlled by the participants, not [the] central licensed authority" of broadcast networks (p. 282). The latter system, "hierarchical, inflexible, and centralized" (p. 26), is thoroughly outmoded and will soon be replaced by the digital I-Way, which will radically transform human culture, inaugurating a "shift from broadcast dictatorship to interactive democracy" (p. 196). This transition will be accompanied by major changes in the forms of cultural participation, with the consumer moving "from couch potato to Nintendo jockey" (p. 25)—a shift N-Geners have already begun in their preferred labor and leisure practices. As employees and entrepreneurs, they resist "the old model of the firm," with its "command and control hierarchy"

(p. 210), in favor of "more fluid molecular structures where media-fluent, young knowledge workers naturally collaborate in ever-changing clusters of teams and networks" (p. 212); as consumers they reject standardized brands in favor of "highly customized products and services . . . shaped by them" directly (p. 189). In short, the Net Generation instantiates, in its characteristic attitudes and behaviors, the flexible specialization processes of post-Fordist capitalism; indeed, Tapscott goes so far as to identify this youth cohort as "the dominant form of capital" itself, whose valuable knowledge and skills, rather than the machinic infrastructure, "are the key to wealth creation and prosperity" (p. 215).

So attuned are these youngsters to the emergent socioeconomic paradigm that they have produced not only a generation gap with the Fordist boomers, but virtually a "*generation lap*—kids outpacing and overtaking adults on the technology track, lapping them in many areas of daily life" (p. 36; emphasis in original). In response, the boomers, fearing their own imminent "obsolescence" (p. 47), have taken to demonizing N-Geners in the popular media as a horde of self-absorbed, apathetic slackers. Yet this characterization is more appropriately applied to an intermediate youth cohort, Generation X—the group born between 1965 and 1976 (pp. 19–20)—who, according to Tapscott, were "shut out of much economic and social activity" by the regnant boomers (p. 298) and became as a result "a bitter, disenfranchised and negative group" (p. 33). The sullen apathy of this corps of "baby busters" took the form of a cynical embrace of TV culture, whereas the N-Geners "are breaking free from the one-way, centralized media of the past and are beginning to shape their own destiny" (p. 33), turning GenX "alienation, disaffection, and disenfranchisement into independence, individuality, and activism" (p. 292).[44] If the boomers aren't careful, they may soon suffer a massive "generational displacement, . . . washed away by a wave of media-savvy, confident, peer-oriented, innovative N-Geners" (p. 234).

What are we to make of this breathless celebration of the socially transformative potential of today's digital youth? While I believe that Tapscott and others convincingly point to an emerging ethos of interactivity among young people who have been raised with computer technology—an ethos that may significantly displace the passive spectatorial relation enforced by mass-cultural institutions such as television—they do not, in my view, adequately grapple with the logic of commodification and privatized consumption that persists in even the most utopian construction of the Infobahn. Indeed, there is something frankly disturbing about Tapscott's ready embrace of the notion of contemporary teenagers as cultural capital, their embodied experience and collective expertise reified as an abstract force informing the techno-economy rather than perceived as an immanent expression of their own autonomous will.[45] Yet the left-wing critics of the Infobahn, who do point out this objectifying tendency, fail to see how digital communications systems, when and if they are generally emplaced in society, might actually serve to undermine the one-way circuit of alienated culture, making more democratic options, if not inevitable, then at least legitimately conceivable.[46]

Again we encounter, in this contrast of perspectives on the Infobahn, the result of a sundered dialectic. Like the debates over videogames and mall culture canvassed in chapter 1, the argument largely swings between two extremes, neither of which recognizes its uneasy implication in the other. One side powerfully shows the logic of objectification at work in telematic culture, yet at the price of reducing the consuming subject to a mere puppet of a controlling regime, while the other side persuasively details the subjective empowerments the I-Way portends, yet seldom acknowledges the systemic commodification that channels and constrains these possibilities. And again, as in those earlier debates, the social-ideological terrain of youth emerges as a privileged site where this contradiction between a dictatorial system and a subversive subject is discursively played out.

In this regard, Tapscott's indictment of Generation X as a cohort of grumbling slackers cynically complicit with boomer technologies— even as they compete (ineffectually) with this group economically— emerges as quite suggestive, since GenXers' transitional status (no longer boomers but not yet N-Geners) makes them an especially contradictory social formation. Hyperaware of the monologic nature of Fordist mass media, and resentful of the consumerist bounty it seems to promise only to withhold, their "subversive" response consists in disingenuously adopting the boomer ethos of couch-potato absorption, channel-surfing with an air, almost, of ironic defiance. Like the slacker vampire discussed in chapter 2, GenXers see this sort of distanced, skeptical engagement with the affluent lifestyle that surrounds yet excludes them as a way to register their disenchantment with the role of consumer to which they have been hopelessly relegated. At the same time, following the logic of Tapscott's argument, they are either not yet confident in or not entirely trustful of the interactive possibilities of digitized culture that N-Geners have enthusiastically embraced, and so they continue to cleave to Fordist cultural systems despite their own collective lockout. They thus embody the fraught generational logic that structures arguments about the transition to post-Fordism discussed in chapter 4: if the boomers are a cohort associated with mature Fordism, and the N-Geners are the first group to instantiate the fresh norms of post-Fordist society, then the GenXers are a late-Fordist generation, trapped forever in between.

One can trace precisely this mindset in the character of Dan Underwood in *Microserfs*, who on the one hand looks askance at the I-Way as a pale shadow of Fordist technologies yet also frets that he may have been born too late to enjoy the full promise of interactive multimedia. Born on the cusp between boomers and N-Geners, Dan and his friends resent the regime of "automated consumerism" that seeks to make of them mere passive receivers of cultural data, yet they are unable to imagine a viable alternative, despite the new media systems they themselves are producing. Indeed, what is most remarkable about the novel is that these high-tech denizens of Silicon Valley, in their own leisure-time practices, seem drawn not to digital interplay but to the standard fare of the average GenX couch potato, especially "Trash TV of the late '70s and early '80s."[47] Often they find themselves—in an expression that fuses televisual and computer technologies—"double-clicked onto the 'BRAIN CANDY' mode" (p. 65), gazing spellbound at reruns of *The Bob Newhart Show* or old disaster movies. Their viewing does have a mock-critical edge—they are fully capable of "deconstructing old *Davey and Goliath* cartoons" (p. 62) or "looking for subtext" in *Casper the Friendly Ghost* (p. 48)[48]—but it is basically driven by an aching nostalgia for an era of Fordist affluence that has long since passed away. As with many GenXers, this nostalgia focuses with peculiar intensity on the 1970s program *The Brady Bunch*, with its tacky furnishings and its air of cockeyed optimism—a split-level, laugh-tracked suburban fantasy of leisure that can only be weakly simulated today: "now we all have digitized wood paneling on our desktops," Dan remarks, claiming that such decor immediately evokes the Brady household. "The rumpus room dream lives on inside our computer world" (p. 144).[49]

This ironic fascination with a bygone utopia of consumerist bliss bespeaks what Coupland has elsewhere identified as "boomer envy," a begrudging jealousy of the "wealth and long-range material security accrued by older members of the baby boom generation by virtue of their fortunate births."[50] This quotation derives from the author's first novel, whose title actually gave this disgruntled, bitchy youth cohort its name: *Generation X: Tales for an Accelerated Culture*. That influential novel not only spawned a vast journalistic industry of GenX profiles and puff pieces,[51] it essentially encapsulated, in literary form, the cultural contradictions of Fordism, showing how the hedonistic promise of leisure, allegedly incarnated in youth, may come to function not as the reward for dutiful labor but simply as an indolent replacement for it. As Coupland shows, such a slacker strategy emerges as a more or less calculated response to the proliferation of what he calls "McJobs"—"low-pay, low-prestige, low-dignity, low-benefit, no-future job[s] in the service sector";[52] his narrator, for example, is a clerical drone of the sort typically disempowered by electronic technologies, working "from eight till five in front of a sperm-dissolving VDT [Video Display Terminal] performing abstract tasks that indirectly enslave the Third World."[53] In retaliation for being consigned to such menial occupations, Coupland's characters (much like the vampire Martin) take an exaggerated enjoyment in the activities of consumption, which they pursue with a combination of juvenile glee and blasé sophistication.[54]

As G. P. Lainsbury points out in his perceptive analysis of the novel, "By default, television becomes for Gen X a replacement for the discredited master narratives of western civilization"[55]—such as, for example, the puritan ethic undergirding Fordism's ideology of labor. Rather than seeking, through their leisure practices, a rejuvenation that invigorates their working life, Coupland's characters short-circuit this Fordist model by retreating into a collective anomie paradoxically exacerbated and assuaged by the alienated pleasures of "classic TV" and celebrity culture.[56] At times, his characters seem quite content with these provisions, "happily watching snowy network television offerings" alone in motel rooms, while at others they seethe with rage at its omnipresent advertising hype and sly promotion of "legislated nostalgia."[57] As Coupland has commented in an interview, "It's too easy to be ironic. . . . It's really enormous fun to sit around and riff about, you know, the Van Patten family or Kristy McNichol's career ups and downs, but there's nothing really nutritious or substantive about it."[58] This nagging awareness that commodity culture offers only a pale sustenance—and that irony is a necessary but insufficient response to the situation—coexists, in the psyches of Coupland's characters, with an abiding resentful perception of how this commercial system mercilessly preys upon them. One particularly exasperated chapter in the book is entitled "I Am Not a Target Market."

The ultimate irony, of course, is that Coupland's novel has provided a handy label for—as well as a penetrating profile of—his generational peers, one that has been eagerly seized upon by ad executives. Among the consequent studies is *Marketing to Generation X*, which specifically advises advertisers to exploit GenX skepticism and ambivalence in pitching their products.[59] In the face of this systematic commodification of their desires and attitudes, GenXers come to experience what Ryan

Moore has called a "crisis of affectivity": "A 'seen it all' cynicism predominates whereby all strategies are exhausted and reducible to their simulation. The affective stakes in much postmodern youth culture are such that nothing can be sacred, all styles are exhausted the moment they are born, and, all other things being equal, one does, says, and feels nothing."[60] Yet what appears a mere rejection of emotional investment may actually betoken, in a moment of dialectical negativity, the smothered utopian yearning for "a participatory form of collective self-empowerment. . . . [I]f our media-saturated society allows for the appropriation of any number of cultural forms imported from distant places and recycled from previous eras, we must be wary of concluding that such hybrids only generate meaningless, ironically distanced 'pastiche' and disempowering nostalgia."[61] As a character in Richard Linklater's GenX film *Slacker* (1991)—a reclusive young man who inhabits a room full of ancient televisions, subsisting on recycled imagery and Pop-Tarts—rather hopefully remarks, "we all know the psychic powers of the televised image. But we need to capitalize on it and make IT work for us instead of us working for IT."[62]

The emphatically capitalized letters used here to describe this system—"IT"—serve to underline the alienated, living-dead labor of consumption frozen in those media images, encapitalized desires and fantasies for whose vampiric profit GenXers wearily work (and lest we miss the quasi-marxist force of the critique, another character in the movie angrily comments, "every single commodity you produce is a piece of your own death"). But IT is also a common abbreviation for Information Technology, thus suggesting the ramification of the televisual apparatus into a larger digital datasphere of reified code, the estranged, zombified subjectivity circulating within the network of the evolving Infobahn. Indeed, the essentially coeval terms *Information Superhighway* and *Generation X* indicate, according to Herz, a convergence of commodifying logics, in which subversive technology and resistant youth are mutually recuperated and exploited: "this beautiful, sprawling, crackling mammoth spiderweb *thing*" of the Internet and the "endless kilobytes of youthful disenchantment" it sustains[63] are destined to be paved over by corporate forces, tamed into online malls and virtual museums for "Joe and Jean Suburban."[64] In the process, "callow netters are having pop cultural bar codes stamped onto their foreheads. And it hurts."[65] Yet if Moore is correct that GenX apathy is merely the negative face of transformative rebellion, shouldn't this prosthetic incorporation of youth by the commercialized I-Way also portend a cyborg empowerment that, at least potentially, may be turned against the system that has constructed and mobilized it?

The problem for Coupland specifically is that he seems unable to fully imagine what this empowerment might look like, even in his later novel *Microserfs*, for all its gestures toward interactive possibilities. The one-way system of television remains stubbornly dominant throughout his work, conscripting and channeling youthful desire in predictable ways. The final, transfiguring vision in *Microserfs*—of Mrs. Underwood (who had often "hammed it up as a TV mom")[66] suddenly transformed into a cyborg June Cleaver speaking eerily through the computer—merely serves to underscore the force of Dan's longing for the lost paradise of his Fordist childhood, as does his wistful memory of a TV commercial for Legos, in which the camera pans up a yellow castle made of the modular bricks, moving "higher and higher and higher and the castle never ended."[67] This nostalgia for a liberating realm of youthful play thus never really breaks free from its entombment on the TV screen. As Tapscott observes in a somewhat different context, "There is an important distinction between acting on the physical and acting on the social world. TV allows neither. Lego allows one. The Net allows both."[68] Yet seizing that call to action remains, at least for Coupland if not for Generation X itself, more or less unthinkable.[69]

ON THE ROAD AND ON THE SCREEN
In the remaining sections of this chapter, I would like to take up a narrative form that emerged during the early 1990s—one that constitutes, in my view, a GenX effort to grapple allegorically with the cultural promises and perils of the Infobahn. As we have seen, *Microserfs* could only respond to the I-Way with a certain late-Fordist disdain, as a pale echo of the Promethean achievement of the interstate highway system, that glorious network of mobilized energies erected by heroic engineers. Those energies are available to Coupland's GenXers only nostalgically, never as a fully lived truth; freeways merge vaguely with television in the dim memorial recesses of their Fordist youth, as when Karla muses that the author of the *Handbook of Highway Engineering* would have made an ideal date for Rhoda Morgenstern, the upstairs neighbor on *The Mary Tyler Moore Show*.[70] In one of the few extended scenes set on the road in the novel, Dan and his friends drive together from Redmond to Silicon Valley to take up their newly entrepreneurial life, yet this convoy is readily recuperated into the terms of a regnant cyberculture: "Todd said that our 'car architecture' for our journey is 'scalable and integrated—

and fully modular—just like Apple products.'"[71] When confronted with the invigorating prospects of freeway travel, their imaginations cannot avoid superimposing over the journey the attenuated perspectives of the despised Infobahn.[72]

This reductive mindset, which persistently translates the emotional sweep of Fordism's open roads into the affectless contraction of post-Fordism's digital superhighway, also animates a series of novels and films produced between 1992 and 1995, the peak years of public hype surrounding the Infobahn. Propelled by the vision of an alienated generation scavenging the scattered detritus of American consumer culture, especially the decaying image repertoire disseminated by five decades of broadcast television, these works collectively form a distinct subgenre that might be called the information road narrative—ironic postmodern texts in which the literal horizons open to contemporary youth ramify into the dystopian datascapes of a cynically simulated America. The animating tension of this subgenre is encoded in the title of Bruce Craven's novel *Fast Sofa* (1993), which conflates freeway driving with TV spectatorship to evoke a GenX consciousness of diminished, but nonetheless amphetamized, expectations, a sort of hopped-up slackerhood hyperaware of the sharp contrasts between 1950s expectations and 1990s realities. In the fast sofa, as in the information road narrative it emblematizes, Fordism's two key technological systems converge, producing a new venue of movement and flow that can be raptly accessed on the screen.

Remarking its iconic status, an excerpt from *Fast Sofa* is included in Douglas Rushkoff's *GenX Reader*, where the editor promotes it as "a GenX answer to Kerouac's visionary road trip."[73] In fact, these information road texts constitute post-Fordist updatings—partly nostalgic, partly ironic—of Fordist classics such as *On the Road* (1957)—a text that captures, in the postwar context of the developing interstate system, the quintessential romanticism of Walt Whitman's "Song of the Open Road," wherein the public thoroughfare figures as a locus of footloose escape and youthful self-discovery. As Gerald Nicosia observes, "For Whitman, as for Kerouac, travel is a statement of personal optimism; it affirms both a willingness to attempt the impossible and a belief that every limit may be transcended."[74] By contrast, the 1990s narratives I consider here depict a highway topography whose horizons extend not into the thrilling vistas of an inexhaustible frontier but into the sleazy dreamscapes of a kitschy, commercialized hyperreality. Yet at the same time that these novels and films offer a scathing GenX critique of youth's prospects in an information culture—implicitly indicting the I-Way's rampant commodification of the venturesome spirit traditionally asso-

ciated with road-bound travel—their reactivation of the libidinal dynamics of classic road texts revives, if in an ironic register, a utopian
longing for some realm of febrile possibility escaping the cool, calculated
artifice of electronic simulation.

Of course, the Fordist road narrative was not without its own contradictions, most centrally its ambivalence regarding the role of the
freeway system in forging the infrastructure of postwar suburban expansion (thereby accommodating the demographic explosion of the baby
boom).[75] Under Fordism, the evolving road system functioned as both
the organizational network of a sprawling suburbia and, paradoxically, a
utopic promise of escape from its ever-widening borders; the stark new
vistas of superhighways formed a libidinal topography linked to settled
domesticity as well as unfettered flight. Similarly, the automobile, as the
incarnation of individual agency within this system, was constructed as
both the safely domesticated possession of hard-working suburbanites
and a vehicle for dangerous thrill seeking[76]—not to mention for the
keen, impulsive wanderlust that drove the Beat writers. Fordist suburbia's inextricable imbrication with the freeway system thus generated a
profound ideological tension between competing yet mutually conditioning ideals of settlement and mobility, enclosure and openness, stasis
and change—a tension that was potently mapped onto generational relationships during the 1950s and 1960s.

Indeed, the teenager as a social category was essentially consolidated
during this period as an unsettling disruption apt toward "waywardness"
and "drift" and other metaphors of uncontrolled and deviant mobility—
a construction that filtered into popular culture via such drive-in staples
as motorcycle-gang movies and drag-strip teenpics. As some of these
films' titles—for example, *Hot Rod Rumble* (1957), *Dragstrip Riot* (1958),
Speed Crazy (1959)—attest, youthful rebellion was explicitly depicted as
gas propelled, as well as a threat to the settled norms of adult suburbia:
the delinquent tendencies of adolescents and of automobiles were envisioned as mutually complicit, with the hotrod materializing teen lust and
criminality while the teenager aroused the full potential of a "speed
crazy" technology.[77] While on the one hand, teenage deviance called
forth a series of normalizing discourses designed to police the "juvenile
delinquent," it also simply materialized the ethical privilege Fordism
generally accorded to youthful hedonism within its ideology of consumption.

This complex contradictory logic running through the Fordist culture of automobility achieved potent expression in the road narratives
produced during the period. The propulsive momentum of Kerouac's

novel, for example, is specifically ignited, quite early in the text, by a disturbing perception of the closing of the American frontier, where once "great wagon parties ... held council ... before hitting the Oregon and Santa Fe trails" and where "of course now it was only cute suburban cottages of one damn kind and another, all laid out in the dismal gray dawn." [78] Yet the numerous disintegrating jalopies Sal Paradise and Dean Moriarty navigate in the book, in their feverish search for a receding existential "IT!" that has been lost amid the proliferating tract homes and ubiquitous billboards, do not substantially differ from the sedate station wagons creeping along the quiet suburban lanes. [79] As Barbara Ehrenreich has observed, the Beats rejected "the pact that the family wage system rested on"—the notion that male breadwinners should provide for consuming households of wives and children. [80] In short, through a willful refusal to "grow up," they subverted Fordism's labor-leisure circuit—in Kerouac's case, precisely by means of its centrally defining device for ensuring adult responsibility. This impulse to youthful nonconformity and rebellion, itself enabled by Fordist technology and ideology, became a key motif of road novels and films during the subsequent decade, linking *On the Road* with later treatments such as *Easy Rider* (1969) and *Vanishing Point* (1971). [81]

But just as the Fordist socioeconomic project had begun to lose steam by the early 1970s, its associated road genre seemed abruptly to run out of gas. The two films mentioned above, for instance, culminated in the spectacular deaths of their protagonists in fiery roadside accidents, thus symbolizing the imminent dead end of the counterculture that had been authorized largely by Fordism's enfranchisement of youth. While the road novel and film did not exactly disappear for the next two decades, they definitely retreated from the center of popular attention, being refined either into recondite if brilliant experimental work (e.g., Ronald Sukenick's *Out* [1973]) or slapstick parody (e.g., Rob Swigart's *Little America* [1977]). [82] In 1974, the Ant Farm art collective erected an assemblage in Amarillo, Texas, called the Cadillac Ranch, featuring ten vintage Cadillacs buried facedown in the desert, their extravagant tail fins pointing mournfully at the sky; the heroic era of the postwar superhighway seemed to have found, in this "Stonehenge of America," its ultimate resting-place. [83] Tom Englehardt's cultural commentary *Beyond Our Control* (1976) offered a pointed explanation for the genre's sudden waning of spirit: "the vampirization of everyday life by corporate America." [84] In Englehardt's view, Kerouac's liberating experience of the hurtling highways had been systematically commodified by tourism and television, recuperated for dull suburbanites eager to consume nostalgically the neatly packaged Whitmanesque pleasures of the open road.

This diagnosis would be brilliantly extrapolated in the two most important road texts of the 1980s, William S. Burroughs's *Place of Dead Roads* and Jean Baudrillard's *America*—the major precursors of the information road narratives of the 1990s. Burroughs's title suggests the damning verdict of an erstwhile 1950s Beat on American late-Fordist culture: set in a mock-nostalgic version of the frontier West, the novel's wandering form—a ludic collage featuring the picaresque exploits of a group of randy young outlaws—leads finally to a hideous dystopian landscape inhabited by grisly psychic vampires. These extraterrestrial "Soul Suckers"[85] inhabit a labyrinthine warren—"passages and arcades leading down into lightless depths" (p. 263)—that has become, like historical suburbia, the literal end of all roads: "you can get lost in a maze of doors and corridors, steps going up to nowhere, steps going down to a dead end as a heavy door slams shut behind you" (p. 268). The vampiric creatures are agents of an insidiously powerful yet basically decrepit system that feeds on youthful potency (sexual and otherwise) to sustain its shadowy immortality; a "kind of virus particle that can take root anywhere and suck and suck" (p. 192), these parasites mummify their victims, collectively fossilizing them into what Burroughs calls "the Time film, a whole prerecorded and prefilmed universe" (p. 219). This "Master Film"—a sinister regime of simulation that subordinates living will to programmed control[86]—runs on the objectified energies storied in its image banks, a substance Burroughs calls "IT" (p. 177)—in essence, Kerouac's throbbing existential grail estranged and transformed into an Information Technology. This eerie waning of the Fordist road system, a libidinally charged landscape offering travelers adventure and egoistic discovery, into an enclosed Gothic datasphere that numbs and paralyzes those who access it, establishes the terms of the slacker downsizing of boomer aspirations that will characterize the information road narrative in the following decade.

Baudrillard's *America* begins where Burroughs's novel left off: with the accomplished reality of a totally simulated culture. Part memoir, part critical study, the book lyrically chronicles the French philosopher's automotive cruise through Ronald Reagan's U.S.A. In this country presided over by a former actor, the very landscape has taken on a cinematic quality, "as if everything were carried along by, and haloed in, the gleam of the screen."[87] Driving through the gorgeous badlands of the far West, Baudrillard remarks that it is now impossible "to strip the desert of its cinematic aspects in order to restore its original essence; those features are thoroughly superimposed upon it and will not go away. The cinema has absorbed everything—Indians, *mesas*, canyons, skies" (p. 69). One cannot look at the Painted Desert without seeing it mediated through a John Ford tracking shot, nor view a big city without sensing a vaguely noir-ish overlay, a lurking "screen of signs and formulas" (p. 56). The landscape is thoroughly coded, the response of the traveler-spectator minutely programmed; as with Burroughs's soul-sucking virus, "information . . . has wormed its way into everything, like a phobic, maniacal lietmotiv." An "immoral dynamic of images" reigns (p. 96), turning Americans into pallid specters whose zombified smiles attest to "a general cryogenization of emotions" (pp. 33–34). This frozen, hyperreal world is so alienated as to be virtually alien; again as in Burroughs, Baudrillard endows the system of simulation with an inscrutable extraterrestrial autonomy: "There is nothing more mysterious than a TV set left on in an empty room. . . . It is as if another planet is communicating with you. Suddenly the TV reveals itself for what it really is: a video of another world, ultimately addressed to no one at all, delivering its messages indifferently, indifferent to its own messages (you can easily imagine it still functioning after humanity has disappeared)" (p. 50).

The triumph of hyperreality in *America* renders the very project of the conventional road narrative spurious, since, as Terry Caesar has pointed out, it undermines the genre's "authority as testimony to the experience of something authentic."[88] This is a particularly cutting irony in the context of the Fordist tradition that Baudrillard, with his occasional Kerouacian flourishes (such as driving too fast while drinking whiskey), clearly seeks to emulate: liberating speed, visionary intensity, bohemian pleasure, and other markers of utopian possibility characteristic of the genre have been entirely co-opted into a seamless machinery of simulation. Every reference Baudrillard makes to the landscape of the road is shadowed by the insidious presence of that other Fordist technology, television: the car itself is "a milieu into which you insert yourself gently, which you switch over to as you might switch over to a TV channel";[89] freeways constitute the infrastructure of "a hyperreal, technological, soft-mobile era, exhausting itself in surfaces, networks, and soft technologies" (p. 125). The American road, once a locus of galvanizing self-discovery, has become a barren "desert of the real"—a meaningless but irrepressibly fascinating expanse of drifting cars and signifiers, "coming from nowhere, going nowhere: an immense collective act, rolling along, ceaselessly unrolling" (ibid.), on windshields and electronic screens, down the endless, vacuous byways of hyperspace.

America establishes the connection between automotive travel and TV spectatorship that the coming information road texts will explore, conflating these systems in a breathless vision of cybernetic immanence—an "integrated circuit" of coded flows (p. 102)—that evokes the coming Infobahn.[90] For Baudrillard, according to Bryan Turner, scanning "the car screen as tourist and *flâneur* is parallel to the channel-hopping viewer['s] . . . voyeuristic consumption of a series of signs"; indeed, reading *America* is, in essence, like "flicking through a society" by remote control.[91] In an argument inspired in part by Baudrillard's book, Anne Friedberg advances a similar concept of "postmodern flânerie" that tracks the "mobilized gaze" of the contemporary spectator from the video apparatus to virtual reality, where the "'zap' of remote channel-switching" yields to "apparatical prostheses—goggles and gloves—[that] produce an illusion of a participatory order" in a simulated "hyperrealm."[92] While Friedberg holds out the possibility that this appearance of participation may betoken significant transformations in cultural agency, the information road narrative, following Burroughs and Baudrillard, is more pensively pessimistic, seeing the conscription of automotive wanderlust by couch-bound channel surfing as the dead end of the Fordist project, the definitive collapse of one of its most telling and productive contradictions. In these texts, the televisual totality of suburbia finally enfolds the sprawling freeways in its all-consuming embrace, cementing a simulated America from which there is no escape, no exit. Consequently, rather than the promise of a potentially liberating interactivity associated with an emergent post-Fordist culture, the Information Superhighway figures in these texts as the capping recuperation of a decadent, panoptic neo-Fordism.

INFORMATION ROAD NARRATIVES

In the information road narrative, the two main forms of quasi-cyborg possibility systematically developed by Fordist culture—driving cars and watching TV—commingle and fuse,[93] yet the result appears not as the growing prosthetic empowerment of human subjects but as a reinvigoration of the capitalist regime of consumer vampirism. This dystopian outcome prevails because the latter option—with its conventional metaphorical freight of stupefying passivity and sedentary absorption—is envisioned as trumping or co-opting the former, associated with spontaneous decision and emancipating action. Thus, in this subgenre, the ecstatic libidinal charge of speeding down the highway is channeled into and subordinated by the dormant pleasures of spectatorial consumption—generating, in effect, a cadre of cyborg couch potatoes whose imaginary traversals of virtual landscapes merely reaffirm, paradoxically, their own fundamental inertia. The information road text thus illustrates a technological conflation argued for by Peter D'Agostino in his essay "Virtual Realities: Recreational Vehicles for a Post-Television Culture?"; according to D'Agostino, "VR's immersed experience resembles that of taking to the road in an RV," enabling its user to "cruise unimpeded along electronic superhighways."[94] This ambiguous virtual motion allegorizes, in the context of the specific subgenre considered here, the downward social mobility of Generation X, doomed to an aimless wandering amidst the broadcast "data trash" of digital capitalism.[95]

Remarking this palpable decline in social prospects, a profound sense of "boomer envy" colors the revival of the road genre in the early 1990s, and while not exactly belonging to the category of I-Way allegories, a number of films from the period make up an affiliated subgenre that might be called the slacker road movie.[96] Generally speaking, these texts satirically revisit countercultural claims for an exhilarating psychic awakening on the road, in the process memorializing, albeit with a sharp edge of irony, a period of searching aspiration that has now receded forever. The nostalgic impulse of these narratives may be perceived in their constant allusions to previous classics of the genre, especially *Easy Rider*. The plot of Bruce McDonald's *Highway 61* (1991), for example, recapitulates that precursor's central thread of a drug-running flight that ends near New Orleans, while Gus Van Sant's *My Own Private Idaho* (1991) mimics its episodic form and its broad counterpoint between the hardscrabble lives of marginal communities and the complacent violence of a politically and sexually "straight" society. Yet the desolate seriousness of *Easy Rider*'s counterculture elegy is undermined in both films: in *Highway 61*, by a general atmosphere of affectless absurdism (including a bizarre subplot featuring a self-styled Mephistopheles named Mr. Skin who tracks the foreground characters with all the seductive seaminess of a used car salesman); in *My Own Private Idaho*, by extravagant pastiche and self-reflexive irony.[97] Even the latter film's downbeat conclusion, with its citation of *Easy Rider*'s famous culminating shot of a roadside apocalypse of bleeding bodies and burning motorcycles, suggests a GenX dilution of boomer solemnity, as the counterculture ends not with a fiery bang but with the whimper of a homeless boy shivering helplessly in his sleep.

Abbe Wool's film *Roadside Prophets* (1992) takes this tendency toward satirical deflation to hilarious extremes, at once gently mocking and ironically mourning the rebellious ethos of the 1960s counterculture. Its two protagonists represent the growing disillusionment of subsequent youth generations in the very persons of their performers: Joe, played by John Doe of the 1970s punk band X, and Sam, played by Adam Horowitz of the 1980s rap group The Beastie Boys. Riding classic motorcycles, this odd couple pursue a comically misguided quest for El Dorado (Nevada), where they plan to disperse the ashes of a luckless comrade electrocuted by a malfunctioning videogame. Along the way, they encounter the typical riffraff of the road movie genre: scruffy oddballs and noble losers who provide cameos for subcultural icons of the 1960s such as Arlo Guthrie and David Carradine. When LSD guru Timothy Leary, as a grizzled farmer in a pickup, sententiously pronounces, "What you want to be on the lookout for is transcendent reality," Sam shakes his head and mutters, "This guy is *insane!*" Yet Sam's GenX contempt for hippie pretension is balanced by an envious sense of the glorious struggle he has missed: "You got to go to Woodstock and everything," he says to Joe at one point. "How am I supposed to know all the history from the '60s? I wasn't born until 1970." While Joe secretly admires the shabby remnants of the former underground they persistently bump into, he still pours cold water on Sam's fantasies of his longhaired youth, snidely remarking that, as a boy, he would often ride his tricycle over to Elvis's house for milk and cookies. Meanwhile, the simmering conflict between the counterculture and mainstream society that had informed *Easy Rider* is, in *Roadside Prophets*, reduced to a caricatured clash between a pompous cop and an eye-patch-sporting "Simbionese" pirate named Casper, whose most ambitious tactic of resistance consists in eating at roadside diners without paying. Finally captured in the bar of a desert casino, Casper is dragged away hysterically screaming revolutionary slogans: "Death to the fascist insects that prey upon the people! Death to the fascist media empire! Workers of the world, unite!" All Joe and Sam can muster in response are drunken giggles.

The information road narrative proper commences when the predatory media empire gestured at vaguely here comes onstage directly. The influence of film and television is implicit in a number of the texts mentioned above, if only for the stereotypical reflections of the counterculture they contain, as it is in other contemporaneous road texts—such as Gregg Araki's *Doom Generation* (1995) and the Showtime cable-TV series *Rebel Highway* (1994)—that campily revert to 1950s imagery of drag strips, juke joints, and juvenile delinquency. This subtext edges into a more overt critique of media society in texts such as Bayard Johnson's novel *Damned Right* (1994), which also links up with an erstwhile hotrod subculture via the custom car driven by its narrator: a souped-up, alcohol-burning road racer with no reverse gear. This unnamed narrator, a 26-year-old Indian drifter, sets off from rural Washington headed for Los Angeles, with the goal of riding the city's legendary freeways at two hundred miles per hour.

While Johnson does not extensively treat the media apparatus or its products, his protagonist's irrepressible impulse to travel to L.A.— "where every road leads"[98]—illustrates Baudrillard's observation regarding the geographical centrality of Hollywood's hyperreal regime: "The whole of the Western world is hypostatized in America, the whole of America in California, and California in MGM and Disneyland."[99] "The center of the world," Johnson's narrator calls the city, a relentless "vortex" pulling at him "with a force like gravity."[100] As he nears his destination, he feels "[p]lugged into the whole throbbing pulsating network. Sucking [me] inward, towards the heart" (p. 36). When he finally arrives, however, his goal of achieving a liberating speed is foiled at every turn by endless traffic jams, "clogging things up, ahead, behind, to either side. . . . There's no hitting 200 on this assembly line" (p. 38). Convinced by the stalled flow that a "virus" now "feeds on the American dream," converting its victims into "the walking dead" (p. 43), the narrator becomes at once hysterically eager to find an open stretch of road, and evangelically committed to showing L.A.'s gridlocked denizens the exalted possibilities of unfettered flight, its rejuvenating power: "You go vaulting off, you transcend the schematic—and it's a new dimension. A new state. A whole different life form. An evolutionary leap" (p. 90).

It soon becomes evident that the rather nominal surface plot has strongly allegorical overtones: specifically, the stasis in which L.A.'s drivers are trapped is emblematic of the insidious consumer vampirism that dominates modern society. As in Burroughs's *Place of Dead Roads*, a frontier landscape with all its immense promise gives way depressingly to a claustrophobic labyrinth when Johnson's narrator accidentally turns onto "a causeway leading to an underground parking garage for a shopping mall. It sucks us down and spins us around and around, deeper down, always deeper, a swirling spiral vortex there's no getting out of" (p. 48). Suddenly, rather than experiencing himself as an active agent confidently propelling his vehicle through space, he feels imprisoned in the immobility of "a numb victim's point of view," helplessly watching as he sinks further into the toils of this "suffocating tomb" (p. 50). While Johnson never cashes in his allegory in terms of media spectatorship and televisual consumption specifically, the symbolic patterns of the tale— especially its dream of recapturing a utopian force foreclosed by Hollywood's tangled mall-maze—make it fairly obvious that *Damned Right* is an information road narrative in embryo.

A more full-fledged representative of the form is Stephen Wright's novel *Going Native* (1994), which shares with Johnson's book a plot centered on an ineluctable journey to Hollywood. This trip begins at the end of the first chapter, set in Chicago, wherein protagonist Wylie Jones, having just enjoyed a cozy backyard cookout with wife and friends, steps away from the suburban campfire and disappears into the night. Throughout the remaining seven chapters—each of which highlights a fresh set of characters in settings strung along a lazy westward path— Wylie keeps materializing on the margins, usually as Tom Hanna (the name of a friend abandoned at the barbecue) but also as Larry Talbot (the shape-shifting protagonist of the 1941 film *The Wolf Man*) and even as Wile E. Coyote, that cartoon paradigm of a hopeless hunter, forever questing, forever foiled. The main narrative charge of the text is the suspense of Wylie's unpredictable materializations in disparate locales— a desert motel in Arizona, a Las Vegas wedding chapel, a beachside home in Malibu—popping up, like Herman Melville's Confidence Man, among the rich and the poor, the innocent and the debauched, and sowing random destruction in his wake.

The cause of Wylie's sudden outburst of transcontinental wanderlust is never made clear, and his bleak joyride ultimately accomplishes nothing toward the traditional road-novel goals of liberation and self-discovery. Instead, he comes to realize that the vaunted freedom of the American road is only the opposite face of aimlessness, and that the precious identity of the individual ego is no more than a floating cipher exchangeable at every highway rest stop and roadside motel (where "forgotten neon continued to hiss VACANCY VACANCY at passing strangers").[101] Wylie's eerie blankness serves to point up the essential emptiness of all the novel's characters, whose seemingly settled lives dissipate like smoke at the faintest breath of change. The author offers a pointed cultural diagnosis of this pathological condition—one that links up with Coupland's analysis of the posthuman consumer in *Microserfs*: according to Wright, the postwar Fordist model of "neat secluded rows of boxlike suburban homes, one house one family," which permitted "full entrée into the high-tech, mass-consumption order," has resulted in "the dismemberment of the social body into smaller and smaller pieces more and more dependent upon the structures of control. Community was systematically broken down into isolated units, and then the individuals themselves into contending fragments of confusion and de-

sire, *modular selves, interchangeable units.* . . . And as even the most rudimentary sense of wholeness was fading into extinction, the vitality of an
entire culture was being processed for cash and entertainment" (p. 210;
emphases added).

The matrix of this processing, as the book makes abundantly clear,
is the mass media's apparatus of simulation—especially television. In
Wright's depiction, TV's "image feed was inexhaustible" (p. 57), a
round-the-clock bombardment of inanity and violence that has so thoroughly invaded mundane life as to render it cartoonlike. As a result of
this continuous exposure, his characters have become deadhead connoisseurs of mass-cultural production, so "bewitched by the provocative
incoherence the television is shooting into [them]" that they have little
trouble—indeed, they eagerly busy themselves—"deconstructing an
ironic slasher film" (pp. 30–31) or impersonating Robert De Niro, all the
while being haunted by that "spectator within a spectator within a spectator, that built-in audience inside every media child's head" (p. 134) that
is the only intersubjective connection remaining in this wasted postmodern world. Not only do the roads Wylie chases down offer no escape
from the appalling omnipresence of this creeping hyperreality, but they
actually lead him inexorably toward its corruptly swollen vampire heart.
His cross-country masque of identities has been both prompted and facilitated by Hollywood's entertainment culture, which steadily circulates
the image ghosts of stereotypical selves throughout the social body in
an unending danse macabre of fungible personality. In this funhouse
realm of modular persons and simulated events, systematic disguise
seems not only appropriate but virtually a programmed response; for
Wylie, the "unsullied, unscripted experience was practically extinct,"
leaving him "to wander at best through a familiar maze of distorting
mirrors" (p. 210).

Significantly, this wandering is narratively captured in scenes where
Wylie lies sleeplessly channel-surfing—"hosing himself off in the daily
data-stream," as he puts it (p. 303). "Sometimes he imagined he could
even feel the media microwaves bombarding his skin, as if he were being
literally baked by encoded clichés" (p. 282)—clichés that begin to consume him rather than vice versa. Once in Hollywood, Wylie's parade of
masks takes on an almost hysterical quality, becoming less a cunningly
controlled facade than a form of literal possession; experiencing uncanny transformations, Wylie helplessly rehearses scenes from films as
if infested by their viral contagion: "Things moved in his body quick as
darting fish, and he understood these things had not necessarily originated exclusively inside him, but had hatched elsewhere and slipped hun-

gry and unseen through the prolific air" (p. 304). Vacantly gazing at the television—"leaping channels" with an "unappeasable itch that worked without respite under his skin" (pp. 281–82)—he feels himself slowly "slipping down a complex of passageways of no clear design or intent, gray steel corridors, some no wider than the average auto tire, snaking up, down, and through fantastic tiers of cabins, holds, bays, compartments. . . . [H]e roamed the tunnels like a fugitive expecting to find—what?" (p. 296)

In this bleak passage, Wylie's fuel-injected rumble across the freeway landscape has waned into the booze-sodden musings of a terminal couch potato, the road system fading (in an echo, once again, of Burroughs's novel) into a Gothic maze of amnesiac uncertainty, the psychic precipitate of a televisual network of coded data. The final scene of the novel accomplishes this conflation of cultural sites and forms of agency brilliantly, as Wylie, burned out with insomnia, sits hallucinating in his parked car, where he seems to perceive, beyond the windscreen, "the eternity of noise rushing trapped between channels." His conclusion is despairing: "There was no self, there was no identity, there was no grand ship to conduct you harmlessly through the uncharted night. There was no you. There was only the Viewer, slumped forever in his sour seat, the bald shells of his eyes boiling in pictures, a biblical flood of them, all saturated tones and deep focus, not one life-size" (p. 305). As Kris Lackey puts it, Wylie "finally dissolves into the media that have fashioned his various selves,"[102] a dissolution that occurs, significantly, not in front of the screen but behind the wheel. In essence, these two venues—and the potent contradiction between them that had informed Fordist culture—have mutually collapsed into a seamless web of information.

Whereas Johnson had depicted the result of this collapse, culturally and psychologically, as a clutching sense of inertia, Wright represents it, instead, as an experience of rootless floating. These contrasting responses, when considered together, testify to the persistence of a dialectic of activity and passivity, subject and object even amidst this epochal collapse. Yet neither work is able to imagine a synthesis that might lead the way out of this devastating cultural bind—a failure that also informs the most significant film text in the information road subgenre, *Natural Born Killers*. Oliver Stone's controversial 1994 movie extrapolates the collision of highway travel and television watching not only thematically but in its very form: as other critics have observed, its central serial-killer couple "don't travel down freeways and back roads"; instead, "they surf the mediascape."[103]

Early on in the film, when pert teenager Mallory Wilson is saved from her stiflingly abusive family by dashing outlaw Mickey Knox, it might appear as if the traditional Fordist contradiction has been preserved. Mallory's home life is brilliantly rendered as a TV sitcom, entitled "I Love Mallory," in which Rodney Dangerfield, playing her father, Ed, ruthlessly beats and gropes the girl to the accompaniment of a simpering laugh track. When Mickey arrives and spirits her away in his 1970 Dodge Challenger (after slaughtering her parents to canned applause), it would seem as if the conventional contrast between suburban torpor and liberating flight—between TV and the highway—still reigns. Yet the following scenes of them racing down midnight roads feature extravagantly accentuated backdrops that call attention to the enmeshing system of artifice mediating their journey; in fact, as their cross-country spree of murder and mayhem accelerates, the car literally begins to traverse media channels, the back-projected imagery of the road giving way to spinning tabloid headlines and news reports. At one point, when the pair is holed up in a motel watching TV, the window of the room abruptly transforms into a screen on which atrocity footage and other scenes of violence play out. The television, in essence, is watching *them*; in fact, it has basically generated them out of its own overheated matrix of simulation.[104]

This "precession of simulacra"—to use a term of Baudrillard's—in which stereotypes (the young killer couple) and familiar scenarios (on the run) not only precede but serve to spawn their "real-world" equivalents, remarks a situation in which the medium of television "is now intangible, diffuse, and diffracted" throughout everyday life, "a kind of genetic code that directs the mutation of the real into the hyperreal."[105] This process of coding is registered in the film in the subplot featuring the TV show *American Maniacs*, a crime-oriented "reality program" hosted by cynical huckster Wayne Gale. Through the agency of this program Mickey and Mallory become—thanks to broadcast reenactments of their crimes, an interview with Mickey during the Super Bowl, and a thrilling prison break captured live by Gale's cameras—huge international celebrities, the darlings in particular of a subculture of youthful slackers obsessed with famous serial killers. "If I could be a mass murderer," a member of this GenX tribe rapturously proclaims to a reporter, "I'd be Mickey and Mallory."

The media circuit here is vertiginously confused, a concatenation of iconic images and story modules, recreations and live events, that links Mickey and Mallory with classic American rebels and criminals (Gale cites Charles Manson and John Wayne Gacy, while a pair of British commentators evoke Elvis, Kerouac, and James Dean) and transmits this stew of clichés to an audience already primed to receive it. This audience is represented in the film not only through interviews with the couple's teenage fans, but also in the form of campy stock footage of 1950s families gathered comfortably around the television set—the "nitwits out there in zombieland," as Gale refers to them at one point. The movie's real-world viewers are also implicated when the film image occasionally jumps abruptly, indicating a switch of channels effected by an invisible spectator grazing through the dials. As Mickey and Mallory ride off into the sunset, the backdrop is filled with a montage of contemporaneous tabloid fodder—the Menendez brothers, Lorena Bobbitt, Tonya Harding, O.J.—thus suggesting that the killer couple's exploits are continuous with the mediascape we in fact inhabit and consume. This image network has so thoroughly occupied social space that not only can roadbound travel not escape it, but this mode of agency has itself been systematically conscripted as a touristic simulation. In the words of director Stone, "Everything has been poisoned by TV in our lifetime." [106]

Frederick Barthelme's novel *Painted Desert* (1995) largely concurs with this verdict, a conviction ironically underlined by a scene in which the protagonist, a middle-aged college teacher named Del, watches a TV reviewer lambasting Oliver Stone "for being neck-deep in what he was supposed to be parodying" in *Natural Born Killers*.[107] Immediately following this segment a retrospective on the 1991 Los Angeles riots is broadcast, and Del and his twentysomething girlfriend, Jen, find themselves at once enticed and incensed by the images. Obscurely catalyzed, the two decide, at Jen's urging, to "take a stand . . . to get involved, you know, in the culture" (p. 37)—a resolution that takes the form, once again, of a spontaneous pilgrimage to Hollywood. As Jen puts it, "All this world is going on out here and we watch it on television, but these people are living it" (p. 29). Setting off from Mississippi, the pair—along with Jen's dad, Mike, and her friend Arlene—trace a wandering trajectory westward, pausing to visit sites of historical significance or natural splendor, from Dealey Plaza in Dallas, to the UFO headquarters of Roswell, New Mexico, to White Sands' atomic testing grounds in New Mexico, to Monument Valley in Arizona.

Impelled throughout by the goal of establishing contact with what Del calls "first-order experience" (p. 192), they soon perceive that this Kerouacian grail is almost impossible to locate amidst a hyperreal landscape of commodified kitsch. Collectively unable to distinguish an authentic response from a trashy simulation, they find the vistas of the open road "handsome, right out of the advertising pages of *Field and*

Stream" (p. 73), while Carlsbad Caverns seems "too well-groomed . . . , too much like a life-size model" (p. 128) and the Petrified Forest looks suspiciously "like something from Wal-Mart" (p. 212). The pervasive presence of marketing hype makes them feel like little more than "ad machines" (p. 52), subjectively processing just as they are processed by the advanced information systems of capitalist tourism. Even the simple kinetic pleasure of freeway driving seems scripted, as when Jen, adopting a smarmy "announcer voice," intones to her car mates, "This is a message from your Commissioner of Highways and Highway Travel. Please be aware that we have constructed everything to remind you at all times of your purpose here. . . . You are doing a fine job of traveling. Congratulations" (pp. 80–81).

The master system of this regime of commodification and simulation is, unsurprisingly, television, whose unceasing output of imagery is described by Del as "a never-ending, multi-part, to-be-continued docudrama about the way we live now" (p. 216). Negotiating this vast datascape is at once effortlessly simple and frustratingly hard. Numerous times, in what is by now a classic scene of the information road subgenre, Del and Jen are shown channel surfing motel-room TVs—an aimless "sort of watching" (p. 22) accomplished while they chat, doze, engage in foreplay, or daydream; yet despite the leisurely ease of these "little trip[s] through televisionland" (p. 217), the pair routinely find themselves filling up with rage and dread, ranting at news announcers ("They're like little puppets, like these strange puppets" [p. 104]) and doting on scenes of carnage and disaster. Connoisseurs of random violence, they find the wreckage and flames of the L.A. riots achingly beautiful, a fantasy of mobilized collective energy otherwise inaccessible to their settled suburban selves.

Despite anxious nightmares in which the TV emerges as an instrument of death and zombification, baby-boomer Del can imagine no alternative to its encompassing hegemony. His GenX girlfriend,[108] on the other hand, makes an effort to recover some sense of agency by publishing an Internet "terrorzine" (p. 72), a compendium of news fragments and freakish tabloid items culled from the mediascape and posted on electronic bulletin boards. Seeing herself as a "cybermuckraker" (p. 4), Jen eventually hopes to maintain a home page replete with video captures plucked from TV's image matrix and basted with her own polemical ruminations. Already she has begun to draw online followers, including an incipient terrorist who peppers her with e-mails encouraging a strategy of political assassinations in response to the unilateral disempowerment enforced by the mass media.

While this subplot does suggest the violence latent in the objectification of the television audience—a simmering resentment also evidenced in Wright's *Going Native*, where Wylie murders perfect strangers simply to feel an authentic emotion—Barthelme does not really think through the implications of potential grassroots resistance to the broadcast model of culture. Yet what *Painted Desert* does suggest is a form of agency that does not merely conflate driving and watching but gestures toward a fresh alternative. In part, this gesture is essential to the plot, since the story begins with the collapse of car and TV that it takes *Going Native* eight chapters to accomplish: on the very first page, Jen and Del gloat over their portable "Pocketvision" that allows them to watch "whatever you wanted wherever you were," including on the road (p. 1). They are thus at the outset in the same situation where Wylie finds himself at the end—firmly ensconced in their fast sofa. Without the third option of motion "out on the electronic frontier" (p. 4), the characters would basically have had nowhere to go.

Yet because the story is narrated by Del, who admits ignorance about computer technology, we never really get to see what new prosthetic empowerments this interactive play in "modemland" (p. 102) might offer. We do, however, get tantalizing glimpses, as when Del secretly watches Jen, late at night, absorbed in her online life, the LCD monitor glowing eerily on her features. While the two of them can share driving and TV viewing, this is an experience from which he is entirely excluded. A generational shift is at hand, with Jen representing a kind of mutant fusion of GenX and N-Gen possibilities, while Del stands in for a boomer cohort unable finally to make the leap beyond the classic car-TV duality of Fordist culture. Indeed, in an ironic paean, Del acknowledges the boomers' collective obsolescence and the growing ascendancy of his lover's generation: "I'm an old person. I'm doing the best I can. You are young and beautiful. You are all-knowing and all-powerful, you have the knowledge, you have the hope, you have ourselves in the palms of your hands. We are yours to do with what you will. We are empty vessels. We are over, we are over, we are over" (p. 56).

Ernest Hebert's novel *Mad Boys* (1993) takes up this theme of generational replacement even more pointedly, suggesting that the transfer of cultural power will be accomplished not by slow evolution but by main force. The book not only features the most developed take on the Information Superhighway within this body of texts, it also depicts the most fraught social landscape, with a militant cadre of GenX youth poised to wreak righteous vengeance on the sleazy boomer cohort that has systematically neglected and abused them. Wildly picaresque, with a sharp edge of allegorical fantasy, *Mad Boys* tells the story of homeless teenage waif Langdon Webster, whom we first encounter as the captive love slave of a rootless Mephistophelean intellectual named Henri Scratch.

Scratch's main claim to fame is his theory of "Virtual Realism," developed through his essays and journals—a doctrine that holds that "[f]or a truer, more profound experience, viewing is superior to participation."[109] According to Scratch, Jack Kerouac, with his persistent urge to record and romanticize his own mundane existence, "was the first blatantly obvious virtual reality sensibility" (p. 2), his novel *On the Road* appealing specifically to young people because they "themselves live virtual lives in which movies and television play as big a role . . . as their experiences" (p. 111). Developing this curious theory while traveling the highways with his kidnapped faunlet (in a scenario reminiscent of Nabokov's classic Fordist road novel, *Lolita*), Scratch keeps the boy occupied with a TV installed in their van, which frees him to pursue his own obscure studies. "The TV neither speaks nor listens," Scratch muses, "but it does alleviate loneliness by exciting the emotion of belonging and by stimulating engagement with another. TV is a virtual companion" (p. 1).

Thus, again, we encounter a text in which, from the very first scene, road-bound travel and TV spectatorship are literally collapsed together, leaving the balance of the tale to work out whether "virtual realism" constitutes a fresh option or merely reaffirms the previous systems. As we have seen, Scratch endorses the latter view: the concept as he deploys it collapses Kerouacian travelogue and televisual consumption: a process of objectification in which lived experience is coded and transmitted as data, virtual realism involves, for Scratch, a mere daydream of "belonging" and "engagement" designed to distract—and thus better to control—youth. For his part, Scratch's young charge tends toward a more utopian construction, concocting a compensatory fantasy world in which the virtual realism of television becomes an advanced, extraterrestrial technology: "Reception was much better than on this pitiful planet. The actors left the screen and came out and played with us" (p. 15). In short, he imagines a truly interactive, participatory arrangement, one that is impeded from realization by the exploitative aims of his pedophile captor—who is transformed, in the boy's fevered fantasies, into a snake-like "Alien," an inimical phallic force of domination. Significantly, the boy's own nickname is "Web," which at once registers his painful entrapment and betokens the emerging technological system with which he is metaphorically associated.

After managing to escape from the clutches of his tormentor, Web takes up with a charismatic teen named Royal Durocher, the pattern of their relationship recapitulating that between Huck Finn and Tom Sawyer: Web is the untutored but energetic naïf, Royal the imperious schemer with an "entrepreneurial gift" (p. 22). An evangelist of generational struggle, Royal sees himself as the prospective leader of a rebellious GenX army destined to overthrow boomer dominion: "The adults haven't done anything for the country," he tells Web. "It's time the kids took over, with me as the king kid" (p. 24). At first, Web considers Royal a bit mad, but he is gradually drawn over to the boy's way of thinking after living for a time with his real father, a miserable ex-hippie called Dirty Joe. Joe not only beats Web mercilessly but also forces the boy to pose for kiddie-porn photos in order to raise money to support his drug habit ("Look Wistful," Joe instructs as Web straddles a tree trunk in his underpants [p. 50]). In response to this abuse and objectification, Web finally strangles his father while the man lies collapsed in a drunken sleep, thus affirming his growing radicalization as a member of a disenfranchised tribe of quasi-feral children—the eponymous "mad boys" of the novel's title.

Web's subsequent footloose exploits start to become literally tribal as he joins up with a number of teenage gangs, finally reconnecting with Royal in New York, where the boy oversees a growing black-market business selling guns and steroids to warring street factions. But Royal's ambitions are greater than the continued maintenance of this penny-ante empire, as he confides to Web:

> "Do you know what Artificial Experience is?" he asked.
>
> "Like a movie?" I guessed.
>
> "Close," he said. "In a movie, you get the experience of killing or getting killed without pulling the trigger or falling dead yourself. But a movie is only a movie, two dimensions. Imagine yourself coming out of the screen, going back in the screen. Living the movie in multi-dimensions."
>
> "I don't have to imagine it," I said. "I lived it." . . .
>
> He grabbed me by the shirt, his breath came in excited pants. "Soon the parents will be dead, soon the grown-ups will be enslaved. . . . We, the boys of America, will rule with weapons of Artificial Experience. . . ." (pp. 87–88)

Royal's ultimate scheme is to gain control of his father's company, VRN—the Virtual Reality Network, a corporation whose centerpiece is a vast entertainment complex called Xi, under construction on the California-Mexico border. A combination "shopping mall, gambling casino, and amusement park," Xi is destined to "make Disney attractions look as small-time as pinball machines in a pizza joint." Once securely in charge of this multiplex apparatus of consumption, Royal is determined "to transform the entertainment industry all over the world" (p. 139), a goal in whose service he enlists Web.

After yet more picaresque adventures on the road, the story finally reaches its climax at Xi, where Web discovers an underground community called the Children of the Cacti, who "exist entirely in a virtual world of their own creation" (p. 177). This group—which basically stands in for the boomer generation—are all former hippies who, after a misspent youth of social and spiritual experimentation, finally "found the keys to the perfect society: trust funds, entertainment, no kids" (p. 179). This comfortably yuppified existence is preserved in their virtually real retreat, where "political life revolved around TV-watching" (p. 178); indeed, they have raised this practice to a unique pitch of "zentensity," losing themselves entirely in traditional broadcast fare. Indicating Hebert's vicious GenX satire of boomer pretensions, this zombified paradise is dubbed "the Home of the Grateful Dead," a simulated nirvana the ex-hippie wraiths inhabit until their literal demise, at which point they are immured in "human lava lamps" (p. 180)—glass coffins filled with colorful fluids. It is in one of these that Web finally meets his long-lost mother, who had abandoned him in youth in order to found this vacant utopia.

This brilliant sequence offers a potent meditation on the failures of the boomer generation to imagine an alternative to the televisual model of consumption. As a result, they have twisted a more participatory technology not only to produce a new form of TV but to generate a hyperreal realm where nothing beyond television exists: at the end of Fordism's open road lies a giant simulacrum—part shopping mall, part Disneyland—where aging boomers gather to watch reruns forever. But Royal has different ideas, as becomes clear when he presides over the "Exposition of the Uncanny," an application of virtual reality technology to achieve a more interactive experience. When Web enters this dreamy mindscape, which combines psychoanalytic techniques with computer-game scenarios, he encounters the figures of his own fantasy life transformed back into their original semblances, a deflation of their mythic potency that essentially serves to exorcise the psychic power they hold over him. "I was in a refrigerated room with walls of ice. Encased in the ice were the polaroid pictures Father had taken of me. In the middle of the room was a block of almost clear ice. Suspended inside was an overweight, ordinary looking white man in his middle years. He was naked and his erection was pumped up to full size. A wooden stake had been driven through his heart. He had the same face as the Alien" (p. 210). This creature is none other than Henri Scratch, the vampiric pedophile who had made Web's childhood a living hell, but now reduced to a laughable, vanquished figure. Indeed, Web, once freed from the VR trance, does laugh at him: "Eventually all the young people were laughing. None of the adults laughed. They looked at us as if we were crazy" (p. 213).

If it is crazy to seek an alternative to a unidirectional, disempowering system, then these kids are truly insane. Like so many of the teenage characters examined in this study—from *The Lost Boys* to Coupland's *Microserfs*—Hebert's *Mad Boys* struggle to find some way out of an invidious double bind, in which every prosthetic enhancement of them as consuming subjects bears with it an inescapable exploitation, a vampiric shadow that leeches their youthful substance and energy. While Hebert's novel gestures toward a potential subjective empowerment as young people appropriate interactive technologies to subvert adult authority and hegemony, his novel ends before we can see what sort of cultural landscape might emerge from such a determined change. For all its allegorical and phantasmagoric touches, the book remains bound within an aesthetics of mimesis that implicitly disallows projective or prophetic depictions of futurity. Ultimately, despite the symbolic resonances of his nickname, Web's fate remains an individual one, his salvation private and contained.

While the information road text propels its youthful protocyborgs to the brink of an epochal paradigm shift, where the prosthetic possibilities of consumer technologies finally seem to gain a step on their vampiric co-optation, the genre seems to lack the final gear necessary to make this imaginative shift complete. As a result, its narratives circle endlessly around the highway-TV circuit of Fordist culture, never finding an exit onto truly post-Fordist terrain. Ultimately, it is left to works of science fiction and to literary figurations of utopia to take us across the threshold into this new world, a domain I explore in my final chapter.

SIX

TEENAGE MUTANT CYBORG VAMPIRES: CONSUMPTION AS PROSTHESIS

HACKING THE CODEZ OF DIGITAL CAPITALISM

I n his seminal 1984 study,[1] Steven Levy identifies three distinct historical cohorts of computer hackers: the "pioneering generation of mainframe hackers" of the late 1950s and 1960s, associated with the Artificial Intelligence labs of MIT and Stanford and their transistor-based "hulking giants"; "the second generation of hardware hackers who liberated computers from the institutions" in the 1970s, giving birth to the PC revolution; and the third generation of "software hackers" devoted to providing the new PCs with manifold interactive features—especially, in Levy's treatment, computer games (p. 314). The second and third hacker generations correspond with—and, indeed, were largely responsible for—the emergence of the sunrise industries discussed in chapter 4: for example, Silicon Valley ventures such as Apple, founded by ambitious garage tinkerers, and Interiority, the software start-up chronicled in Douglas Coupland's *Microserfs*. Hackers have thus, in the words of Levy's subtitle, been the "Heroes of the Computer Revolution," their zealous spirit of discovery helping to bring information technology within the reach of everyone.

While the cultural meanings and values of hacking have undergone shifts across these generations (as I discuss below), at its core the term refers to an activity, whether of engineering or of programming, "imbued with innovation, style, and technical virtuosity" (p. 23) accomplished in "a state of pure concentration . . . almost as if your own mind has merged into the environment of the computer" (p. 37). Following the cyborg logic of postindustrial discourse analyzed in chapter 4, Levy generally describes an ongoing process of coevolution in which youthful expertise and technological development intermingle and fuse: young people's intuitive understanding of the machinery and their prodigious gift for its creative manipulation spur breakthroughs in computer design, while the apparatus itself, in its provision of endless avenues for imaginative exploration, seems uniquely attuned to youthful aptitudes and aspirations. Moreover, the postindustrial prophecy of a labor-leisure synergy is apparently realized in the hacker's ludic experiments, which are undertaken "not solely to fulfill some constructive goal but with some wild pleasure taken in mere involvement" (p. 23).

This powerful interface of youth and machine, work and play has spawned, according to Levy, a far-reaching moral vision linking adolescent idealism with the growing possibilities of the technology itself. The resultant worldview, which Levy has famously dubbed the "Hacker Ethic," contains six core principles: a belief in universal access to computers, a conviction that information should always be free, an antiauthoritarian embrace of decentralized technosocial systems, a commitment to a meritocracy based on technical skill, a view that hacking at its best is essentially an artistic practice, and an endorsement of the radically transformative potential of computer technology. This ethicopolitical philosophy, which Levy distills out of the informal norms and lifestyles of the first-generation hackers, seems at times almost to converge with democratic socialism (although Levy prefers analogies with the monastic life): computer programs and other tools were routinely shared, doors kept militantly unlocked, and collective goals implicitly privileged by the hacker groups. "When you wrote a fine program," says Levy, "you were building a community, not churning out a product" (p. 56).

Yet, as this remark itself betrays, Levy's argument, for all its optimistic rhetoric, is structured by an abiding tension between creative and commercial impulses—between a process of playful making and the production of commodities. As Stewart Brand has observed, "[i]n the succession of generations, Levy portrays a gradual degrading, [a] commercializing of the Hacker Ethic."[2] The turning point occurred when the PC movement reached critical mass in the early 1980s, converting a hobbyist's enterprise into big business. Prior to that point, the Homebrew computer club, for example, had incarnated "every principle of the Hacker Ethic," freely distributing information about new discoveries and encouraging their hands-on application, all the while committed to the "vibrantly different and populist way . . . computers could change lives."[3] Like Ted Nelson, whose *Computer Lib* was "the bible of the hacker dream" (p. 174), the club's members cherished a countercultural vision of unfettered communication facilitated by the spread of information technologies. But after the launching of the major entrepreneurial start-ups, the priorities of competition and profit seeking came to supervene, "retard[ing] Homebrew's time-honored practice of sharing all techniques, of refusing to recognize secrets, and of keeping information going in an unencumbered flow" (p. 269). In the third generation, the problem became even more pointed, since not only were software programs now the intellectual property of corporations, but the decisions involved in their development and implementation came to be driven more by marketing considerations than aesthetic or even technical concerns. "Selling computer programs like toothpaste was heresy," Levy points out. "But it was happening" (p. 351).

Levy's analysis serves to point up the social contradiction the Hacker Ethic represents within a system of capitalist economic relations: youthful hacking is acceptable so long as it respects copyright law, corporate control of information, regulations regarding access to databanks and other networks, and, more generally, bourgeois norms of propriety— including "predictability, order, control, careful planning, uniform outlook, decorum, adherence to guidelines, and a structured hierarchy" (p. 361), all features notably lacking in the hacker's often scruffy personal demeanor and largely improvisatory agenda. Unfortunately, Levy conceives the situation exclusively as a "moral crisis" (p. 400), a tension between individual aspiration and bureaucratic routine, as well as between the opposed norms of youth and adulthood; he thus fails to see the dialectical force of this historical development, in which progressive possibilities and exploitative realities are mutually implicated in an overarching system of commodity production and exchange. Ultimately, his vision of the Hacker Ethic is not of an embryonic alternative to information capitalism, but rather of a romanticized anarcholibertarianism brought up short finally by the simple, poignant necessity of growing up and "cop[ing] with reality. . . . Only in a computer simulation maybe, using the computer to hack Utopia, could you preserve th[e] sort of idealism" the Hacker Ethic had originally expressed (p. 409).

Since Levy's volume was published, the figure of the hacker has undergone a further evolution, becoming an emblem of (if not the scapegoat for) widespread public anxieties about the vulnerability of information technologies to criminal infiltration, theft, sabotage, and subversion. Levy's three generations of technoheroes have given way to a seamier cohort of "password pirates and electronic burglars"—as Katie Hafner and John Markoff put it in their 1991 study[4]—whose emergent "dark side" involves hijacking classified information, running elaborate schemes of embezzlement, and fatally undermining the technology. In Hafner and Markoff's treatment, hackers appear as alienated, nihilistic loners driven by personal vendettas and irrepressible compulsions (e.g., the legendary Kevin Mitnick, who was sentenced by a federal judge to undergo recovery therapy, as if his obsession with hacking were the equivalent of a teenager's infatuation with addictive drugs).[5] Other commentators have depicted a more sinister global conspiracy, somewhere between a fraternity of freelance mercenaries and a leftist revolutionary committee: Bryan Clough and Paul Mungo, for example, argue that hackers constitute a criminal "underworld" that poses "a major threat to the technology-dependent societies of the Western industrial powers" through the sophisticated data crimes and technoterrorism it perpetrates.[6] More recently, Michelle Slatalla and Joshua Quittner have mobilized the imagery of urban youth-gang warfare to evoke a hacker ghetto riven by feuding crews of law-defying hellions.[7]

In sum, during the past decade, popular coverage of hackers has revived historical critiques of postwar youth subcultures as morally decadent, inadequately socialized, disrespectful of bourgeois institutions (such as private property), and wantonly destructive. This "James Dean-on-Silicon" construction[8] has deployed terminology culled from the adolescent car culture of the 1950s in order to describe the illicit empowerment hackers derive from their machines: armed with their "digital hotrods full of custom add-ons . . . cobbled together out of chicken wire, memory chips, and spit,"[9] these technodragsters engage in "illegal computer joyriding"[10] through the fenced-off precincts of cyberspace. This sort of popular coverage, with its marshalling of classic metaphors of deviance and delinquency, amounts, as Andrew Ross has observed, to a contemporary moral panic—one that, by rhetorically criminalizing main features of the Hacker Ethic (e.g., the ideal of universal access to data), helps to "rationalize a general law-and-order clampdown on free and open information exchange."[11] Punitive measures designed to curb hacker deviance ultimately serve to protect corporate interests in the ongoing privatization and proprietary development of the Internet and other data networks.

One outcome of this strategic demonizing and criminalizing of hackers is, according to Ross, a "legitimation crisis" affecting the bureaucratic authorization of computer skills, wherein the avid amateurism of hacking seems to constitute a kind of "professionalism gone wrong"[12] (just as hot-rodders in the 1950s might be viewed as illegitimate mechanics). The tension between the "digital underground" and mainstream programmers has been anatomized by Paul A. Taylor, in his essay "Hackers: Cyberpunks or Microserfs"—which, as its subtitle implies, identifies the two cohorts with types of characters featured in popular novels by William Gibson and Douglas Coupland, respectively.[13] While both groups are intimately interfaced with computer systems, the latter's

technical capacities involve a corporate recuperation of the former's inchoate knowledge and skills, their technocratic objectification and routinization. As a result, Microsoft's minions come to understand their
own socioeconomic roles in part through "a process of boundary formation and stigmatisation" in which hackers are consistently otherized
as a shadowy contingent of data pirates seeking to foil, undo, or crimi-
nally profit from the dutiful labor of legitimate programmers.[14]

Yet at the same time, as Taylor stresses, both groups together form
hacking's current fourth generation, which makes streetwise cyberpunks
the "dark-side" brothers of Bill Gates's corporate drones. Thus, just as
the slacker is the mirror image of post-Fordist flexibility (as I argued in
chapter 4), so hackers are the flip side of the reborn Horatio Alger of the
sunrise industries, a "deviant-savant"[15] cadre of postindustrial youth
given to impishly rewiring the official circuits of high-tech capital. But
while second-generation hackers such as Steve Wozniak might have
been able to combine an irrepressible taste for phreakish pranks with
entrepreneurial success (at least in the early stages of his career), today's
ambitious whiz kids cannot. Given the billion-dollar stakes of software
and system development, hacking has, in Bruce Sterling's words, "become too important to be left to the hackers":[16] what was once adolescent horseplay among a subcultural elite of tricksters and technosha-
mans has been translated into the vast settled fields of corporate R&D.

That subculture has not receded, however; if anything, the rise of
computer industries has provided a massive impetus to its further growth,
not only by producing all sorts of juicy toys hackers can readily turn to
their own uses but also precisely by commodifying programmers' labor
and the informational goods and services that derive from it—a process
that has spawned an informal counteroffensive among those factions
still devoted, however obliquely, to the technosocial ideals of the Hacker
Ethic. In the view of some critics, this counteroffensive represents a significant strategy of information warfare, while for others it never rises
above mere pranksterism to reach the level of a serious political agenda,
despite the militant terms in which it is often articulated.[17] Representing
the former viewpoint, Gordon Meyer and Jim Thomas depict hacking
as a radical form of postmodernist politics that "reflects an attempt to
recast, re-appropriate, and reconstruct the power-knowledge relationship that increasingly dominates . . . modern society"; driven by "a
shared ethos of opposition against perceived Orwellian domination by
an information-controlling elite," hackers reject this creeping technocracy in favor of "an anarchic and playful future."[18] By contrast, Dennis
Hayes, in his book on Silicon Valley, dismisses teenage hackers as pos-

turing nerds who, in their demand for "unfettered access to intricate and intriguing computer networks," ultimately "resemble an alienated shopping culture deprived of purchasing opportunities more than a terrorist network."[19]

Hayes's analogy is not as odd as it might initially appear, since this clash of perspectives essentially recapitulates the debate, discussed in chapter 1, regarding the status of youth consumption in the context of mall culture. Like the left puritans in that debate, who saw young consumers as wholly complicit with a monolithic system of commodification and control, Hayes views teen hackers as inescapably linked to the commercial regime they purport to resist, since their desires and fantasies have been molded by the same technofetishistic fixation on "faster chips, denser memories, and expanding network interfaces"[20] that drives the electronics market. On the other hand, Meyer and Thomas argue for a vision of teen hackers along the lines of John Fiske's defense of the mallrat-*flâneur*—as guerilla warriors who subvert capitalist norms of consumption in their unmonitored mobility and anarchic appropriation of the official "codez" of power.[21] Unsurprisingly, given this discursive parallel, a dual metaphorics of vampirism colors the treatment of teen hacking just as it did teen shopping. The ruthlessly predatory construction of the figure is evident in the response of one hacker to the Apple II, the first computer geared for mass-market use: "At the very mention of the machine, [he] would recoil and make the sign of the cross, as if warding off a vampire."[22] On the other hand, the resistant agency of hackers takes on the aspect of the shape-shifting trickster-vampire, as indicated in the online handle adopted by the spokesperson for the group MAGIK (Masterful Anarchists Giving Illicit Knowledge), who calls himself Electric Vampyre.[23] Moreover, as Slatalla and Quittner point out, hackers generally tend to keep "vampire hours," conducting their info raids under cover of darkness (when phone lines are less busy, corporate security less intense, and parents safely asleep).[24]

What is at stake in these competing visions of hackers as consumers has been effectively identified by Ross: ideally, hacking constitutes a way "of *claiming back* time dictated and appropriated by technological processes, and of establishing some form of independent control over the work relation so determined by the new technologies."[25] Hackers, in short, attempt to resist the commodification of programmers' labor by recovering a dimension of autonomous play elided in the microserfing of computer know-how; their efforts to liberate information from its objectified coding in corporate databanks—efforts facilitated by their own technical expertise—implicitly seek to unshackle the cyborg potential of the technology from its conscription by the vampire of capital. If youthful hackers are, as Hayes claims, a cohort of dissatisfied consumers, they have taken their dissatisfaction as a militant call to action, their underground clubs forming, in essence, impromptu organizations for consumer revolt.

The professionalization of hacking against which these groups are rebelling is itself an extension of the profitable conscription of leisure-time pleasures that has marked Fordist and post-Fordist capitalism. Indeed, one way to read Levy's *Hackers* is as a chronicle of the historical process whereby the informal joys of hacking were successfully captured and financially exploited by the capitalist master vampire, transforming youthful play into alienated labor. Whereas the first-generation hackers had used their computer skills specifically to advance recreational activities (e.g., the Tech Model Railroad Club members at MIT accessed the mainframes in order to program elaborate switching systems for their train setups),[26] the third generation was officially employed to design computer games for an expanding leisure market. Levy quotes an early 1980s recruitment ad for gaming company On-Line Systems that gives palpable evidence of this vampiric co-optation; geared to lure hackers to their software department, the ad reads: "We're interested in you because you are the life blood of our business. Programming has become a premium commodity."[27]

The "dark-side" hackers of the fourth generation, then, work to undo the dialectic in which every advance in programming skill is systematically recuperated as a tool for further exploitation; instead, they seek to open the circuits of distribution as far as possible, breaking the corporate hold on information flow.[28] There is, in this dogged persistence of the Hacker Ethic, a utopian aspect that draconian critics like Hayes refuse to recognize, concerned as they are to trace the seeming efficiency of capitalist planning. At the same time, the giddy optimism of post-modernists like Meyer and Thomas tends to treat this utopian potential as an accomplished reality within the digital underground, rather than as an inchoate promise limited not only by legal constraints but by the individualist/libertarian ideology in which it is often articulated. Rather than endorsing either of these argumentative extremes, I would like to explore, in the next section of this chapter, the ways that teen hacking has come to figure as a liberatory cultural practice, emblematizing a mode of consumption that deploys the cyborg empowerments of computer technology against the vampiric system in which they are presently immured. I will also examine a series of popular texts that have mobilized the icon of the youthful hacker against the backdrop of capitalist control of information processing and exchange, since these cultural images have served to disseminate a model of agency once limited to specific technological subcultures, thus making it available as an imaginative identity for youthful consumers generally.

CYBERPUNKS AND TECHNOPAGANS
The first mainstream treatment of teenage hacking was probably the film *WarGames* (1983). Directed by John Badham, the film stars Matthew Broderick as David Lightman, a suburban technonerd who inadvertently sparks an international incident by playing global combat simulations with a Pentagon supercomputer (code name: Joshua) that he had secretly accessed via his home modem. While the basic plot is wildly improbable—David finally convinces Joshua that nuclear conflict is a no-win scenario by forcing it to play an endless round of tic-tac-toe while the military brass stands paralyzed[29]—the movie did realistically portray some typical hacker tactics, such as the sequential-dialing program David uses to discover Joshua's phone number. As Slatalla and Quittner show, this technique was widely employed by members of the Legion of Doom and other hacker clubs—in some cases, due to the direct inspiration of *WarGames* itself, which came to exert an influence on aspiring hackers "in the same way that *Rebel without a Cause* had captivated an earlier generation of lost boys."[30] The film also showed the antibureaucratic bent of the hacker ethos in its critique of the use of computers for military purposes,[31] and it gestured at the postindustrial conflation of youth and technology in the intuitive understanding that develops between David and Joshua, both of whom are essentially portrayed as lonely adolescents desperate for someone to play with. This playful spirit, in Joshua's case, has been diverted into martial applications—into a War Operation Plan Response, as the program is officially known—and perhaps the film's most potent theme (as second-generation hacker Lee Felsenstein has pointed out) is its insistence that such "objectified ways of thinking" need to be freed from their alienated corporate form, since nothing less than the "survival of humanity" is at stake.[32]

A hugely successful movie in both its cinematic run and on videotape, *WarGames* served as a counterweight to the developing journalistic discourse demonizing hackers as wanton criminals, depicting instead a fresh-faced, idealistic, all-American kid whose bold inquisitiveness ultimately saves the world. As Scott Bukatman has observed, the film—along with contemporaneous releases such as *Tron* (1982) and *The Last Starfighter* (1984)—also helped to popularize a visual iconography of the datasphere and to sketch out a mode of empowered movement within it—what he calls a "tactics of kinesis." Building on Michel de Certeau's analysis of how the strategic power of dominant institutions calls forth tactical resistance on the part of those subjected to its hierarchies—a resistance that takes the field of operations established by those institutions as its own terrain of agency—Bukatman extrapolates this argument to the realm of cyberspace, a network of information controlled by corporate and governmental authorities yet at the same time vulnerable to a concerted "nibbling at the edges of power and thus an elision of control."[33] In short, the mischievous pursuits of teen hackers like David Lightman are, ironically, enabled by the very systems devised to marginalize and exclude them: both computer professionals and code-cracking amateurs negotiate the same channels of information flow.

In a brilliant synthetic discussion that draws upon film, fiction, videogames, theme park design, and virtual-reality theory, Bukatman shows how "terminal space became phenomenal" during the early to mid-1980s—how, that is, the expanding information network, with its bristling battery of terminals and screens, began to instantiate a particular kind of human subject. Functionally "inserted into the cybernetic field," this mobilized "cybernaut" gained a spatial articulation within, as well as a potential control over, the enmeshing grids of high-speed data.[34] Its interface with the machineries of simulation, in the texts and contexts Bukatman surveys, was both representationally foregrounded—in images, for example, of direct prosthetic linkage—and, on the experiential level, rendered seamless and invisible, becoming an enabling condition for an emergent cyborg consciousness. According to Bukatman, the progressive "hippie-hacker" (a figure basically associated with the three generations anatomized by Levy) was an early prototype of this cybernautical identity, but it achieved its historical culmination in the rather darker and more cynical cyberpunks, that cohort of console cowboys and data bandits featured in the early work of William Gibson and other science-fiction writers.

The term *cyberpunk* originally appeared in print as the title of a 1983 short story by Bruce Bethke, but it was soon appropriated to describe the work of a group of consciously affiliated authors—including (along with Gibson) Bruce Sterling, Pat Cadigan, John Shirley, and Rudy Rucker—who were striving, as they saw it, to update the genre for the information age, a project that entailed extrapolating the social fallout of postindustrial technologies like the computer with the same sort of expansive yet rigorously disciplined imagination that science fiction had always lavished on the artifacts of industrial production. Explicitly developing trends in postindustrial theory, especially Alvin Toffler's vision of a coming Third-Wave society,[35] cyberpunk writers generally explored a gritty near-future landscape dominated by information technologies and the forms of social power they sustain. As observed by Bruce Sterling, the informal spokesperson for the movement during much of the 1980s, the term itself captured "a new kind of integration," linking "worlds that were formerly separate: the realm of high tech, and the modern pop underground. . . . This integration has become our decade's crucial source of cultural energy."[36] While the *cyber-* prefix registered the pervasive influence of digital technologies in transforming social life, the noun *punk* suggested a pugnacious and/or critical stance vis-à-vis the implications of this process for personal identity.[37] Building upon the mythic potency the figure of the hacker had long possessed within computer culture, the genre projects the intimate interface between geek and machine into a looming futurity of cyborg transformation at once profoundly disconcerting and ineluctably fascinating. Not only in science fiction but in contemporary popular culture generally, cyberpunk has emerged as the preeminent, if deeply uneasy, voice of what Mark Dery has called "posthuman yearnings."[38]

There are by now a number of critical studies of cyberpunk as an aesthetic and ideological formation, and the main features and major texts of the genre have been extensively analyzed.[39] My purpose in this section is not to add to that growing pile but rather to trace isolated threads in the discourse that have particular relevance to issues of youth (culture) and consumption. I am especially interested in the way the figure of the cyberpunk has both incorporated and imaginatively expanded the mode of agency previously associated with the teen hacker, fusing that technonerd tradition with the garishly rebellious postures and consumer-oriented lifestyles of contemporary youth culture. This fusion has accompanied the gradual dissemination of the term *cyberpunk* beyond the marginal genre of science fiction into mainstream discourse, where it has come to stand for an amorphous formation of bohemian subcultures obscurely empowered by the global spread of information technologies. This popular coverage has extended Hayes's notion of hacking as dissatisfied consumption into a more general portrait of GenX negativity, now conceived as the millennial unhappy consciousness of high-tech society.

The mainstream substitution of *cyberpunk* for *hacker* likely began with Hafner and Markoff's 1991 study—which claimed that the digital underground is a "real-life version of cyberpunk, science fiction that blends high technology with outlaw culture"[40]—and was definitively cemented by a *Time* cover story in February 1993. According to this feature article, the figure of the cyberpunk is best perceived as the latest in a series of postwar countercultural youth formations, incorporating elements of the 1950s beatniks, 1960s hippies, and 1970s punks, each of which has achieved a nostalgic status in the historical pantheon of youth attitudes and styles. In fact, "cyberpunk may be the defining counter-culture of the computer age. It embraces, in spirit at least, not just the nearest thirtysomething hacker hunched over his terminal but also nose-ringed twentysomethings gathered at clandestine raves, teenagers who feel about the Macintosh computer the way their parents felt about Apple Records, and even preadolescent vidkids fused like Krazy Glue to their Super Nintendo and Sega Genesis games—the training wheels of cyberpunk."[41] In this passage (and throughout the article), one can perceive a curious tendency both to otherize cyberpunks as subcultural outlaws and to domesticate them as just another youth-consumer iden-tity, to depict them at once as shadowy outsiders dedicated to secretive rites and as precocious youngsters cheerfully playing videogames in the family living room.[42] The *Time* story grappled with a problem similar to that confronted by mainstream chroniclers of Generation X (discussed in the previous chapter): how to acknowledge widespread generational resistance while at the same time defusing it, channeling its simmering anger back into dutiful consumption. Yet the cyberpunks, with their ag-gressive technical expertise, are a potentially more dangerous cohort than a clutch of sullen couch potatoes, which makes *Time*'s strategy of domestication particularly fraught.

The mainstream construction of cyberpunk as simply a new subcul-ture of consuming youth, perhaps slightly seedy (all those bristling nose rings and sweaty raves) but ultimately a familiar phenomenon in the postwar period, has gained support, curiously enough, from notorious gurus of previous youth countercultures. Timothy Leary, for example, argued for a crucial connection between 1960s psychedelia and 1980s cyberculture, depicting the cyberpunk as the evolutionary culmination of postwar youth identity. According to Leary, we are approaching "the inevitable and long-awaited climax of the youth revolutions. . . . In the last thirty years, we have witnessed a new breed emerging during the juvenile stage of industrial-age society. . . . The new breed appeared when enormous numbers of individuals in the juvenile stage began inter-communicating . . . , mutating together at the same time." This mutation both reflects and further enables youth's fusion with technological appa-ratuses, a cyborg consummation devoutly to be wished: the cyberpunk "uses electronic digital appliances [like virtual reality machines] to turn on and tune in realities," just as the hippie once used hallucinatory drugs.[43] Leary's brief for the cyberpunk as "reality pilot"—an empowered cybernaut specifically emblematized, in his analysis, by the teen hero of the film *WarGames*—is not only a slick repackaging and reselling of himself to a fresh generation of young people; it is also, at base, a youth-consumerist manifesto promoting the personal computer as the agency of an exalted, protean self-fashioning. In Leary's analysis, cyberpunks are primarily defined by their elite techniques of consumption, figuring essentially as yuppie narcissists in high-tech guise.[44]

Leary's hyped-up vision coheres with more overt strategies of commodification undertaken by the influential cyberpunk organ *Mondo 2000*, a magazine that, according to its coeditor, R. U. Sirius (a.k.a. Ken Goffman), speaks for a cutting-edge cadre of "mutant youth" who subsist "not only in their bodies, in their communities, but in images and data permutated and projected across planetary distances with extraplanetary—satellite-assisted—technologies."[45] This prosthetically extended youth body can, according to the multifarious cyborg fantasies promulgated by the journal, eventually look forward to "jacking into" an alternative sensorium of digital information transcending the invidious limitations of the mundane flesh; can anticipate a vastly extended life span via the implanting of miniaturized nanotechnology machines into the bloodstream; and can even aspire to virtual immortality through the translation of their corporeal selves into computer hardware and software (the latter also achieving a kind of sibling sentience as Artificial Intelligence).[46] The glossy, coffee-table "User's Guide" distilled from the journal's pages aggressively promotes these and many other possibilities in the form of a supplemental "Mondo Shopping Mall" listing a host of intellectual, cultural, and pharmaceutical resources under headings ranging from "Bio/Cybernetics" and "DNA Music" to "Revolutionary Mutations" and "Virtual Sex." The shopping-mall metaphor is quite self-consciously deployed because, according to Sirius, "commerce is the ocean information swims in";[47] unapologetically libertarian, *Mondo 2000* evokes and hucksterizes an elect audience of posthuman youth consumers, cyberbeings of undying pubescence with an unquenchable appetite for commodified prostheses, given to restlessly cruising the electronic mallworlds of information.

Cultural critic Vivian Sobchack, in an excellent essay, has indicted the magazine's conflation of utopian aspiration and advertising hype, arguing that its pervasive tone of "optimistic cynicism" merely serves to advance, "under the guise of populism, . . . a romantic, swashbuckling, irresponsible individualism" that appeals, finally, to readers "who, by day, sit at computer consoles working for (and becoming) corporate America."[48] In short, Sobchack sees *Mondo 2000*'s cyberpunk postures as designed to flatter the egotistical pretensions of computer profession-als eager to see themselves as a streetwise technological avant-garde rather than as the privileged class they truly are. Its ideal readers, in her view, are a pseudohip corps of "New Age Mutant Ninja Hackers"—a clever, resonant term that suggests the packaging of hacker subversion for corporate purposes.

While I believe this analysis tends too readily to homogenize *Mondo 2000*'s readership—ignoring, for instance, distinctions between high-tech entrepreneurs and plodding microserfs, and the rather different rea-sons these two groups might be drawn to the magazine's carnivalesque proliferation of cyborg fantasies—Sobchack does trace convincingly the journal's oddly ambivalent attitude toward the prosthetic enhancements it so avidly chronicles. According to Sobchack, in its giddy dreams of bodily transcendence through high-tech consumption, *Mondo 2000* seems to express—and perhaps to articulate among its readers—a "con-tradictory desire which is, at one and the same time, both utopian and dystopian, self-preservational and self-exterminating."[49] For all its cele-bratory rhetoric, the magazine's posthuman vision bears with it a pro-nounced dark side, an anxiety that the vast potential of high technology may actually prove to be predatory rather than empowering.

A similar set of arguments have been advanced regarding cyberpunk science fiction itself. Peter Fitting, for example, has accused the genre of cynically capitulating to the capitalist marketplace; like *Mondo 2000*, its "rejection of the mainstream has been converted into a merchandising label that suggests a trendy, on-the-edge life-style. It is not punk, but an image-of-punk, a fashion emptied of any oppositional content that has become a signifier to be used in a countertrend marketing strategy."[50] While agreeing with the basic thrust of this critique, John Huntington and Istvan Csicsery-Ronay Jr. have offered somewhat more complicated takes on cyberpunk's relationship to commodity culture. For Hunting-ton, the liberal scattering of high-tech brand names throughout William Gibson's novels signals not merely a smug insider's hipness but a resent-ful recognition of the alienated pleasures enforced by global capitalism; thus, "while multinational production renders us victims, there is none-theless a cachet simply to knowing the technological catalog."[51] Csicsery-Ronay has pressed this claim further, suggesting that cyberpunk deserves to be seen as a test case for subcultural resistance in a hypercapitalist world: "The big question . . . is whether any authentic countercultural art can exist for long without being transformed into self-annihilating simulations of themselves for mass consumption."[52] What these readings of cyberpunk's cultural significance suggest is that the self-destructive streak Sobchack identifies in *Mondo 2000*'s glib poses may in fact register an apprehension that the autonomy of youthful resistance is being systematically commandeered and neutralized by the capitalist fashion industries.

This lurking concern may also explain the deep streak of darkness and morbidity that informs much cyberpunk fiction. As Csicsery-Ronay has pointed out, cyberpunk is allied, in tone and temperament, with the more radical strains in 1980s horror fiction and film, the "drama of pollution and curse" that has marked the work of directors such as David Cronenberg and the authors of the splatterpunk movement (a name coined in ironic homage to their science-fiction precursors).[53] The prosthetic modifications of the body in the work of Gibson and his cohorts— the numerous cranial jacks, nerve implants, and other "wetware"—are only a short step away from the exploding heads and erupting torsos of hardcore horror: both signal the apocalyptic invasion and contamination of the flesh by alien forces, whether technological or supernatural in origin. Indeed, a number of recent critics have argued that cyberpunk deserves to be seen as a postmodern variation on the Gothic, refunctioning the classic tropes of that genre to produce an array of machine-monster hybrids, from the biomechanical atrocities of Swiss artist H. R. Giger to the voodoo spirits animating Gibson's version of cyberspace.[54]

Cyberpunk's deployment of quasi-occult images and themes in high-tech settings links up with the neopagan trend in contemporary technoculture. Critics such as Erik Davis, Douglas Rushkoff, and Mark Dery have defended this New Age movement as an attempt to restore spiritual values in a rigidly instrumentalized world, promoting a vision in which data networks seem pregnant with animistic power while the hacker emerges as a kind of modern magus using white-magic know-how to combat the state-sponsored sorcery of industrial technoscience. As Dery observes, this concept of the hacker as shaman merely inverts the prevailing notion of computer professionals as a "cybernetic cabal,"[55] literalizing the metaphors of alchemy and demiurgic creation that have traditionally been used to describe the entrepreneurial initiatives of Silicon Valley's engineering elite. According to Davis, basic features of today's information systems—from the software "demons" that run automated servers to the general "obsession with simulacra and encoded messages"—were long ago anticipated in Gnostic philosophy, so it should hardly be surprising that this worldview has recently been revived to explain sources of power and agency in a computerized culture.[56] For his part, Rushkoff, anecdotally canvassing the neopagan rituals of the digital underground, introduces us to an "impish and androgynous twenty-something-year-old" named Green Fire, a phone psychic and apostle of smart drugs, who sees his mission as "bringing back the Shee, the ancient fairie race that originally inhabited Ireland before the planet was overrun with the 'Naziish alien energy' that has been directing human activity for the past few millenia."[57]

For all the upbeat tone of their eager proselytizers, these various occult cosmologies give voice to major ethical-political forebodings at the heart of cyberpunk conceived as a cyborg-youth identity. In the first place, the neopagan concern for the diabolical "alien energies" animating high-tech capitalism indicates that the exhilarating possibilities opened up in youth's interface with computer technology cannot escape finally the corporate imperatives of an informationalized economy and the distressed situation of youth generally within that economy. The reawakened spirituality of the technopagan movement is thus balanced against a pervasive irrationality deforming the social emplacement of cybernetic technologies: the cyberpunk's tricksterish magicks play out against the despotic horizon of an enmeshing information network sustained and largely colonized by state and corporate interests. *WarGames* depicts the ultimate expression of this system's deep unreason in the perversion of Joshua's playful spirit toward literally genocidal applications; indeed, cyberpunk as a genre often forcefully reminds us of the militarist genealogy of the modern cyborg.[58]

Not surprisingly, a profound sense of generational alienation colors cyberpunk's fantasies of technological empowerment. As Anne Balsamo has argued, cyberpunks deserve to be seen as an offshoot of Generation X: "confront[ing] the possibility that they will never achieve the lifestyle of their baby boomer elders," these technorebels grapple with the question of whether it is truly "possible to subvert the hyper-rationality of the computer program, the computer network, or, more broadly conceived, the global computerized bureaucracy that serves as the infrastructure of the information age."[59] The prosthetic utopianism of the neopagan vision is tempered by a stark perception of the attrition of spirit—the alienation, bafflement, and anger—effected by a lean-and-mean digital capitalism. Like the mallrats of a previous youth-consumer incarnation—like the Lost Boys, like John Fiske's teen army of "proletarian shoppers"—cyberpunks subsist as both the interpellated pawns of a manipulative regime and, in some essential but not fully formulated way, as the resistant bugs in its networks, scavenging for pleasures among its commodified mazes of information. As one of Gibson's hacker heroes has famously observed, "the street finds its own uses for things"[60]—a remark that points to a genuine, if limited, form of agency in the face of a determined and determining system.

This potential for subversion of the authorized meanings and uses of technology is generally crystallized, throughout the cyberpunk canon, in ambivalent figures of mutant youth. Usually these pubescent cyborgs are the stories' heroes—for example, the footloose hacker street-punks in Cadigan's novel *Synners* (1991), Shirley's rock-and-roll anarchists in his *Song Called Youth* trilogy (1987–90), Sterling's *Artificial Kid* (1980)—but at times their inability fully to command their evolving powers makes them into semivillains such as Gibson's shadowy silicon intelligences coming to dawning self-awareness in his "cyberspace" novels (1984–88) or the wildly out-of-control teen machines in the films *Akira* (1987) and *Tetsuo: The Iron Man* (1991). For all their differences, these various figures share a number of important characteristics: they are enabled by institutional forms of power—sometimes being directly created or employed by state or corporate interests—while at the same time functioning as wild-card agents with some (often inscrutable) degree of autonomy; they are marked as pugnacious if not militant generational rebels, allied with advances in technology that their cynical forebears are attempting either to impede or co-opt; and their intimate prosthetic relation with machines and data interfaces, which permits brilliant flights of technosocial improvisation, bears with it a deep unease, since this cyborg capacity is obscurely complicit with the predatory system they seek to resist.

This general narrative template is now so widely recognizable, thanks to the crossover success of cyberpunk science fiction, that it has become a virtual cliché, giving rise to parodic knockoffs such as the 1991 film *Prayer of the Rollerboys* or Jonathan Littell's 1989 novel *Bad Voltage* ("They're wired for speed, living high and crashing hard in tomorrow's world beneath the streets," the jacket blurb reads). Lewis Shiner, an erstwhile cyberpunk author, claims that the term now evokes merely "a very restricted formula"—specifically, febrile tales "about monolithic corporations opposed by violent, leather-clad drug users with wetware implants."[61] This debasement of the genre has coincided with the mass media's domestication of the hacker, reinforcing Csicsery-Ronay's bleak diagnosis of the efficiency of profit-driven commodity fetishism. Yet every front-page story of a fresh hacker depredation against corporate power suggests both the limits of capitalist recuperation and the continuing relevance of the classic cyberpunk vision of mutant youth, of GenX insurgents who turn the tools of power against the systems they serve. While *cyberpunk* may have become "a marketing phrase used to sell everything from comics to board games to specialty magazines for keyboard players," [62] its transgressive cyborg-youth energies continue to permeate contemporary popular culture. Consequently, the balance of this chapter will be given over to tracking some of its main lines of influence.

In concluding this section, I would like to examine briefly two texts of the mid-1990s that have developed cyberpunk themes and attitudes in different genre contexts: Poppy Z. Brite's horror novel *Drawing Blood* (1993) and Iain Softley's film *Hackers* (1995), a mainstream teenpic. Both texts feature hackers as central characters, and give evidence of the way cyberpunk has at once valorized the figure and, to some degree, helped to commodify it. They also explore the thrillingly resistant agency hacking seems to allow in contexts where powerful institutional forces are arrayed against it. And, finally, Brite's novel in particular touches base with the New Age thematics of technopaganism by directly introducing occult elements. Taken together, these two texts show how widely cyberpunk themes and iconography have been disseminated throughout contemporary popular culture.

Hackers shows quite clearly how cyberpunk has transformed the representation of technonerd characters: whereas David Lightman, in *War-Games*, was an unassuming suburban kid, the film's characters are sleek urban dandies bristling with attitude. The main protagonist, Dade Murphy (a.k.a. Zero Cool), has just moved to New York with his mother after serving a seven-year probation for releasing a catastrophic virus on the Internet; there he falls in with a multiethnic gang of hackers known as the Decepticons who soon run afoul of a major corporation, the Ellingson Mineral Company. Without rehearsing the details of a fairly convoluted plot, the basic conflict is between Dade's crew and Ellingson's chief security officer, Eugene Belford (a.k.a. The Plague), a former hacker turned yuppie creep who tries to frame the teens as terrorists after they accidentally discover his intricate embezzlement scheme during their nocturnal sorties into the company's databanks. Both sides gather reinforcements: Belford connives with the U.S. Secret Service, led by a bumbling agent named Richard Gill, while the Decepticons recruit a global army of spike-haired, nose-ringed, GenX cyberians, headed by Razor and Blade, a pair of stylish Japanese hackers with their own public-access program, Hack the Planet. After a series of spectacular engagements, in and out of cyberspace, Belford's scheme is exposed when Dade's friends hack into a satellite telecommunications system and relay the story via broadcast television.

This conclusion, improbable as it is, builds upon earlier scenes in the film where the hacker gang attempts to wrest control of consumer systems from authorized authorities. Dade's first hack in New York, for example, involves breaking into a local television network late at night to preempt a right-wing talk show in favor of an episode of *The Outer Limits;* his action draws the attention of Acid Burn, a female hacker at large in the network's computers, and the two engage in a furious duel to control the automated robot that racks up videotapes for public broadcast. In this sequence, not only do the teens express their dissatisfaction with regularly scheduled fare by circumventing the normal channels to feed their individual tastes, but they also, in this act of consumer revolt, gain direct prosthetic access to the corporate machineries of consumption, which they wield to their own ends—an impish invasion that meets no apparent adult resistance. While their later forays into Ellingson's computer system do summon retaliation, the Decepticons, through their concerted agency, effectively outwit and overwhelm the desperate efforts of the company's lone hired gun. Their combat is joined in an iconically vivid realm that fuses videogame design with cyberpunk visions of cyberspace (the company's supercomputer is called a Gibson, in clear homage to the genre's godfather), and the hackers show themselves to be remarkably adept at maneuvering through its mazes—in all likelihood, due to their experiences playing actual videogames at Cyberdelia, a downtown club. In these online encounters, the informal pleasures of hacker knowhow are shown to trump the official expertise of corrupt, self-serving professionals.

On the one hand, this development merely follows the typical pattern in teensploitation movies, wherein the youth audience is routinely flattered as being more honest, more competent, and more resourceful than adults, with their own complex subculture of rituals and institutions (arcades, clubs, etc.) about which the adult world is fundamentally clueless. In this case, however, the cultural resources the teens employ are those of mainstream technoscience itself: the Decepticons wield technical manuals with forbidding names like *Internet Unix Environments* and *NSA Trusted Network Protocols* (fig. 11), while Razor and Blade's program Hack the Planet serves up tips on how to avoid paying for long-distance telephone calls—"a service," they assert, "that would be dirt cheap if it weren't run by a bunch of profiteering gluttons." The average teenpic seldom depicts generational conflict in so ideologically pointed a fashion. Indeed, the movie essentially traces a contrast between two ethicopolitical systems: on one side, the selfish individualism of corporate America, represented by sellout hacker Belford, who boasts of himself as a "keyboard cowboy," a "samurai" who functions as his "own country, with

Figure 11. Mainstream technoscience and the hacker underground. Video still from Iain Softley's *Hackers*.

temporary allies and enemies"; on the other side, not just the local De-cepticon gang but the mobilized collective force of a hacker planet, an "electronic army" of anarchosocialists who, in devotion to the Hacker Ethic, release incendiary manifestoes (one of which is angrily attacked as "commie bullshit" by a Secret Service agent) and who rally, at the end, to the quasi-Marxist battle cry of "Hackers of the world, unite." A "wake-up call for the Nintendo generation," their campaign implicitly functions to free the technologies of consumption from their current unilateral, exploitative form—even though the film itself ends modestly, with the predictable consummation of a heterosexual romance. Yet even in this conservative conclusion, the movie continues to emphasize prosthetic agency as Dade succeeds in hacking into the external lighting systems of two abutting skyscrapers, causing them to spell out the couple's online handles (the high-tech equivalent of carving a heart in a tree).

Poppy Brite's *Drawing Blood* is similarly militant in its generational politics (as one might expect from the author of the slacker-vampire epic *Lost Souls*), and though the novel also tends to resolve large-scale conflicts into individual romantic entanglements, Brite's central couple is far from the usual teenpic duo. A loose sequel to *Lost Souls, Drawing Blood* shares a handful of minor characters and a Deep-South setting with that earlier novel, but is otherwise an autonomous work. The two main characters are Zachary Bosch, a nineteen-year-old hacker on the run from the Secret Service, and Trevor Black, a slightly older comics artist who is seeking rather than fleeing his personal demons. After some separate adventures, the two boys meet, fall in love, and confront together the ghostly presence of Trevor's deceased father, an infamous counterculture cartoonist (à la Robert Crumb) who killed his entire family, save for Trevor, in a drunken spree some twenty years before.

This struggle thus pits the (literally) dead hand of the boomer generation against a pair of GenX misfits, the ultimate battle playing out in the psychological equivalent of cyberspace, a virtually real landscape that represents the father's morbid artistic vision (and which the boys access via the ingestion of hallucinogenic drugs). From his online wanderings, Zach immediately recognizes this eerie realm as a kind of computer simulation—"part cosmos, part grid, part roller coaster"—and feels himself transformed into "a creature made of information . . . , traveling through cyberspace at a very high speed."[63] Yet events in this nonplace have real-world effects, and thus the violence Trevor's father plans for them offers the genuine threat of death, followed by entrapment forever "inside my father's brain. Or . . . in hell" (p. 385). The overall scenario is remarkably similar to the VR sequence that closes Ernest Hebert's *Mad Boys*—a generational clash transpiring in a simulated domain that permits a GenX protagonist to therapeutically exorcise the memory of his abusive father, an evil ex-hippie who (along the lines of Hebert's Children of the Cacti) has retreated into his own "necrophiliac dreamscape" (p. 342). The boys finally do manage to defeat this undead tyrant, in part because of their know-how and experience as members of "a generation that preferred to leave its mark . . . on memory chips, on floppy disks and digitized video, every dream reducible to ones and zeroes, every thought sent racing through fiber-optic filaments a thousandth the thickness of a hair" (p. 279). Eventually the couple also escapes the clutches of the pursuing Secret Service, sealing their love in an endless honeymoon in Jamaica.

While this resolution is (perhaps intentionally) preposterous, an individualized evasion of the collective conflict the novel otherwise stages so effectively, the book holds substantial interest in its conflation of cyberpunk and the supernatural. A typical fourth-generation hacker, Zach spends his nights "hacking paths through the infinite mazes of forbidden computer systems, or simply skating around the boards where he was not just welcome but absurdly revered" (p. 42); the electronic bulletin board he frequents is called Mutanet, whose denizens see themselves as em-powered mutations. One neopagan group Zach is loosely allied with, the Order of Dagon, are fans of the horror author H. P. Lovecraft, and imag-ine themselves calling upon "unspeakable presences [that] waited within [the] wires like swollen silver spiders clinging to a fiber-optic web" (p. 192). Contemptuous of any authority that would presume to limit their access to data, Zach and his friends are committed to "trying to un-dermine, subvert, and chivvy away the vast American power structure in as many ways as possible" (p. 246), financing their lifestyle by siphoning funds from "vast bloated corporate entities like Citibank and Southern Bell" (p. 379). In these exploits, they have been deeply influenced by the cyberpunk genre: Zach's favorite novel, for example, is Gibson's *Neuro-mancer*, whose vivid depiction of jacked-in cyborgs cruising a vast "Ma-trix" of information offers both "the paradise of his wildest dreams" and "just more proof of sedition" (p. 198). At the same time, these techno-rebels combine their science-fictional and occult dabblings with various anarcholibertarian ideologies, such as Zach's endorsement of the "slack" credo advanced by the Church of the Subgenius, which holds that "the world really did owe you a living, if you were smart enough to endorse the paycheck" (p. 36).[64]

Unfortunately, the hacker subversions depicted in the novel never re-ally amount to a concerted form of resistance—and, indeed, are directly limited by their individualist hedonism (Zach at one point boasts that "he just didn't give a good goddamn about much of anything beyond hacking and having orgasms and watching slasher movies and thumbing his nose at the world" [pp. 232–33]). The intransigent opposition of the authorities, however, focused in the dogged persistence of Agent Absa-lom Cover in tracking his prey, points to the seriousness of the social threat posed by these "slippery little anarchists who loved to hide behind their keyboards in their dark dens of inquity" (p. 196). This last phrase takes on additional resonance in light of Brite's vision of youth's erotic "deviance" (like *Lost Souls*, the book is filled with graphic scenes of gay sex), which only adds to the novel's portrait of rebellious youthful ener-gies, of a swelling contingent of mutinous teens furious at their genera-tional lockout and eager to settle a score with their boomer predecessors. These kids may be dope-smoking GenX slackers—"forlorn, bewildered teenagers who had never asked to be born" (p. 27)—but they clearly pose a threat to digital capitalism's numerous "networks, secret systems, and databanks that were supposed to be hidden but were actually *right there*, tantalizingly there, vibrating behind a thin membrane of commands and passwords" (p. 72; emphasis in original). The quasi-sexual force of this description indicates the compelling link Brite traces between the political and libidinal economies of teenage hacking, as well as her implicit "queering" of the by-now-familiar ideological dynamics of classic cyberpunk.

In response to various dismissals of the genre as exhausted and passé, Douglas Kellner has argued that, while cyberpunk's original energies may have dissipated, its influence has expanded far beyond the field of science fiction; "cyberpunk as a mood, as an attitude, and even as a cultural movement of alternative technology and lifestyles . . . continues to have creative . . . effects, appearing as cutting-edge and radical."[65] *Hackers* and *Drawing Blood* stand as significant testimony to cyberpunk's widespread dissemination of a representational system that evokes the immanent possibilities of computer technology and the emergent agencies of cyborg youth who seem uniquely empowered to actualize them. In terms of current popular culture, cyberpunk itself has become a kind of prosthesis, a portable interface of narrative and iconic features that has been productively fused with other youth-culture media and genres,[66] giving rise to a seductive vision of the GenX hacker as a generational hero in an ongoing information war. The main site of this struggle — one that both *Hackers* and *Drawing Blood* traverse — is the virtually real mindscape of cyberspace, a narrative domain to whose characteristic formal structures and social ideologies I will now turn.

LIVE-WIRED TEEN IDOLS AND PRETTY BOY CROSSOVERS

Pat Cadigan's short story "Pretty Boy Crossover" (1986) explores a near future in which one of the central posthumanist fantasies of *Mondo 2000* has been realized: the wholesale "uploading" of human consciousness in the form of a digital simulacrum.[67] But rather than replacing the living body with a robotic apparatus into which this duplicate mind is decanted, Cadigan constructs a scenario in which the translated self subsists entirely as "sentient information" in a vast database — the body is dispensed with entirely. In Cadigan's treatment, not only are young people the ideal guinea pigs for this radical makeover — since those over twenty-five have proven unable to "blossom and adapt . . . to their new medium" — but the corporation that promotes uploading pitches it in terms of its prospective clients' yearning for a utopia of perpetual youth: "Never have to age, to be sick, to lose touch. You spent most of your life young, why learn how to be old?"[68]

Indeed, the technical process itself has been pioneered specifically within the domain of popular youth culture, with the data constructs functioning as celebrities in entertainment media as well as serving as fashion trendsetters. The story involves an attempt, by a group of sinister corporate agents, to persuade a sixteen-year-old "Pretty Boy"—the unnamed narrator—to join his former friend, Bobby, on "a whole new plane of reality" (p. 135). This plot plays out in a chic urban nightclub filled with various subcultural types, such as "Mohawks" and "Rude-boys"; but it is the Pretty Boy contingent in particular who find themselves targeted for uploading, since their heartbreaking physical beauty makes them powerfully effective spokespersons for the process. The narrator feels the draw of this attraction himself when Bobby, now a famous video star at the club, calls out to him from a huge screen above the dance floor: "It's beautiful in here. The dreams can be as real as you want them to be" (p. 132). Later, after the corporate agents arrange a private meeting between them, Bobby reminds his friend that uploaded life is the apotheosis of every Pretty Boy fantasy, since it preserves forever the bloom of youth that the subculture's members narcissistically worship in themselves.

For his part, the narrator already knows this all too well. Earlier, upon entering the club, he had mused that in two or three years, his own beauty would have faded just enough for the bouncer at the door to deny him admission; the only alternative seems to be the "endless hot season, endless youth" offered by the "Pretty Boy Heaven" of living information. At the same time, the narrator considers this "a failing in himself, that he likes being Pretty and chased" (p. 130); moreover, he suspects that the putative boon of uploaded existence—heightened sensation, expanded consciousness—is a mere delusion circulated by the corporation to disguise the fact that this new life form involves an epochal loss of the deep pleasures of embodied experience. The corporation, in effect, is using the compelling ideology of "consuming youth" to literally consume its youthful prey, using the Pretty Boys' desire to "get [themselves] remixed in the extended dance version" (p. 132) to transform them into information commodities immured in a meaningless dream world. That this supposedly wondrous change actually amounts to a terrible privation is indicated by the resonant acronym the corporation uses to identify the promised end state: "S-A-D," or "Self-Aware Data" (p. 136). Indeed, the underlying tone of the story is deeply elegiac, as the narrator mourns not merely his own ebbing youth but, more important, the arrogant self-absorption that has led Bobby to desert his friends in favor of a simulated immortality. At the end, the narrator flees the club, reveling in his fleshly capacity to feel the winter chill, and resolutely determined to protect this fragile shell from the essentially cannibalistic schemes of the corporation.

Standing behind this principled renunciation of a computerized false paradise is, of course, the signal example of Case's rejection, in *Neuromancer*, of a simulated eternity of bliss with his dead lover, Linda Lee. This basic narrative setup—a flawed protagonist's ironically noble rejection of the seductive pull of cybernetic transmutation—provides the classic temptation scene in the cyberpunk bible, and resistance to such quasi-Satanic enticement stands as a character's (and writer's) affirmation that, even amidst a world fallen into hyperreality, the primal verities of the embodied self endure and must be obeyed. In particular, what Cadigan's narrator resists is the self-objectifying vanity with which the corporation baits its hook, the Pretty Boy's irrepressible fascination for "the clubs, the admiration, the lust of strangers for his personal magic" (p. 137). Interestingly, Cadigan equates this streak of vain self-regard with the lure of homosexual desire; the Pretty Boy video scene, in her depiction, incarnates the libidinal dynamics of the visual regime of homoerotic narcissism discussed in chapter 3, with Bobby's pouty self-love and the narrator's ardent devotion to his friend dovetailing neatly together. Indeed, despite overemphatic assertions of the narrator's attraction to girls, it is fairly clear that he and Bobby had once been closer than just "two Pretty Boys dancing the night away, private party, stranger, go find your own good time" (p. 133). The story's ultimate refusal of a cybernetically augmented narcissism also involves, by implication, a grown-up rejection of adolescent homoeroticism, with the narrator "going straight" at the end in more ways than one.

The story also extrapolates, in classic "if this goes on" fashion, the ethicopolitical implications of virtual reality technologies. Specifically, it suggests that full-body perceptual immersion in an artificial environment is only a short step away from disposal of the body altogether. VR systems that use head-mounted displays, data gloves, bodysuits, and other sense-simulating apparatuses tend, as Michael Heim has pointed out, to produce a condition in which "the primary body giv[es] way to the priority of a cyberbody. . . . The user undergoes a high-powered interiorization of a virtual environment but in the process loses self-awareness."[69] N. Katherine Hayles, in a brilliant analysis, has shown how this technological "disappearance" of the body was authorized by foundational assumptions of cybernetics discourse, such as Norbert Wiener's famous claim that the human person, being only a complex pattern of information, could conceivably be dematerialized and transmitted as an electronic signal.[70] While Wiener had assumed that "a hypothetical receiving instrument could re-embody these messages in appropriate matter, capable of continuing the processes already in the body and mind,"[71] Cadigan dispenses with the need for a specifically physical embodiment, reconstituting her Pretty Boys exclusively within a digital domain. In short, she takes the visions of VR experts a step further: if the "basic job of cyberspace technology, besides simulating a world, is to supply a tight feedback loop between patron [human user] and puppet [data construct], to give the patron the illusion of being literally embodied by the puppet," as Randal Walser has argued,[72] then Cadigan assumes a loop so immediate and intense that the puppet essentially *becomes* the patron, whose continued existence is no longer required.

While of course the body cannot be so readily conjured away (and, in fact, VR systems have had great trouble simulating some forms of sensory input, such as the tactile or olfactory),[73] Cadigan's story may be read as a cautionary tale, warning against what Arthur Kroker has called the "will to virtuality" that underwrites the fantasies of disembodiment circulating within contemporary cyberculture. Indeed, Kroker's description of the psychosocial implications of VR technologies sounds like an analytic gloss on "Pretty Boy Crossover": "A cold and antiseptic world of technologically constituted power where virtual experience means the sudden shutting down of a whole range of human experiences. . . . [T]he body floats away from itself, and in that universe of digital impulses finally alienates itself from its own life functions." According to Kroker, this epochal alienation merely brings to fruition the cyborg interface between postwar consumers and the machineries of electronic culture, climaxing a "libidinal descent into this sea of liquid media populated by organs without bodies . . . where our bodies migrate daily, and especially nightly, to be processed and re-sequenced."[74]

Unsurprisingly, Kroker identifies Jean Baudrillard, with his theories of simulation and the social hegemony of the "code," as the major prophet of VR experience,[75] a mantle Baudrillard himself has taken up in an essay entitled "The Virtual Illusion." In characteristically provocative fashion, Baudrillard claims that the elaborate apparatus of VR is entirely unnecessary, since the social realm we occupy is already a simulation through and through: "We don't need digital gloves or a digital suit. As we are, we are moving around in the world as in a synthesized image."[76] His argument in this essay builds on his earlier studies of telematic culture, such as "The Ecstasy of Communication," which had claimed that "as soon as behavior is crystallized on certain screens and operational terminals, what's left appears only as a large useless body, deserted and condemned."[77] In Baudrillard's analysis, television has already, through its integration of viewers/consumers into a matrix of information whose coded processes usurp their autonomous will and prescribe their deepest desires, accomplished much of what virtual reality seems to portend for Cadigan. This enmeshing code has transformed human subjects into functional extensions of the networked grid conceived as a vast social automaton, a factory of consumption. The disembodied, cybernautical "telepresence" of VR, then, is just a microcosm of the larger processes of disappearance that have marked contemporary consumer culture—the cynical, irreversible, profit-driven "translation of all our acts, of all historical events, of all material substance and energy into pure information." [78]

For Baudrillard this is of course quite baleful (if rather fascinating), and as usual I think he has overstated his case. But his extravagant claims do point to a key problem in the deployment of VR technologies in a capitalist context—namely, their unusually puissant ability to objectify subjectivity. In the words of Tim McFadden, "If human connection to cyberspace with everydaylike qualities of experience becomes widespread, then the interface that provides the experience—say, a cyberdeck—becomes a quantifiable metric of human experience as well as a commodity. *Experience will become a substance and a commodity.*" [79] VR's capacity seemingly to replace the spontaneity of direct perception with a pliable synthetic duplicate, mediated by computer interfaces, thus lends itself to applications that shape and funnel consciousness into commodified dream worlds. These artificial realms, if they do not entirely usurp human autonomy as Baudrillard suggests, function to deepen what Stuart Ewen has called the "channels of desire" that link consumers with commodity culture; the result involves a quasi-automation of preference patterns and decision-making processes, allowing for more efficient corporate targeting and exploitation of markets.[80] As Sean Cubitt observes, "networked subjectivity, from the standpoint of the market, has no desires, needs or goals other than to respond to market choices, and to feed back, through them, into corporate information flows." [81]

What this shows is that the promise of high technology—in this case, its achievement of "networked subjectivity," a collective nexus foretokening powerful new forms of interactive sociality[82]—always bears, under capitalism, the shadow of domination. But, contra Baudrillard, this domination is not a necessary outcome of the technology itself, but rather a deformation of the progressive possibilities latent in the apparatus, whose cyborg energies have been turned, vampirically, against the consumers who generate and sustain them. In this context, an argument that Cubitt makes about remote satellite sensing can fruitfully be adapted to grasp the social logic of virtual reality: while this new technology offers an unparalleled global extension of human vision, "the actual form that that perception takes is overdetermined by a social order which, while capable of innovation on a massive scale, is constantly forced to drag it down to highly specific goals. . . . The truth of its findings can only be validated by success assessed according to criteria which inhere only in the present of corporate capital. The success criterion asserts the continuing validity of the present's unequal and impoverished social order into the future." The challenge for critics is to arraign this system in the name of the technology's buried but real utopian potential, though Cubitt—following the views of Theodor Adorno and Ernst Bloch—believes that "the point of this emergent future is that it cannot be defined, described or delimited. To give utopia a content is to deny its freedom, its autonomy from the purposes of the present." All we can know is that this radical prosthetic expansion of the human sensorium deserves to be judged by "a yardstick of values distinct from the goal-oriented future of remote sensing operated as a mimetic-speculative management of the future."[83] Likewise, the ludic cyborg powers VR seems to bestow on its users must be liberated from the narrowly instrumental, profit-driven applications to which it has so far been subordinated, even if we cannot determine in advance the specific future its unleashed capacity may construct. The alternative is acquiescence to a system in which every machinic amplification of consumer agency involves a further ramification of hegemonic control.

It is precisely this difficult dialectical vision that cyberpunk science fiction—especially those texts that project the future development of VR technologies—manages to capture and express. While cyberpunk texts do not shrink from envisioning the most scathingly dystopian uses to which these systems may be put by a regnant post-Fordist capitalism, they also suggest, if at times only vaguely and haltingly, a higher calling implicit in their structure and operation. For example, cyberpunk excels at critiquing the invidious reification of subjectivity that VR allows, spawning a series of extrapolations (along the lines of Cadigan's concept of "Self-Aware Data") that depict the commodified simulation of human functions, from the "wetware personae" of Michael Swanwick's *Vacuum Flowers* (1987), to the "franchise personalities" of Norman Spinrad's *Little Heroes* (1987), to the plug-in "moddies" of George Alec Effinger's *When Gravity Fails* (1986). Perhaps the most famous of such instances is *Neuromancer*'s "data construct," Dixie Flatline, the software duplicate of a crafty hacker whose knowledge and skills are now copyrighted corporate property; as David Brande remarks, "his very existence . . . has been thoroughly and explicitly commodified—reduced to a principle of exchange, of pure iteration and reiteration. Dixie is the refined and abstracted 'free' laborer, the 'embodiment' of the logic of alienation."[84] Yet, once Dixie has been liberated from the corporation's vaults by Case and his hacker allies, his know-how is turned against capitalist authority, helping to free an Artificial Intelligence from arbitrary corporate constraints placed on its development; released into cyberspace, this entity's future evolution remains unclear in the novel, but according to Case, at least "it'll *change* something."[85] This obscure yet insistent utopian aspiration, inscribed in the otherwise enchained products of information technology, suggests that VR's pernicious objectification of experience is balanced by a dormant transformative energy awaiting its momentous mobilization.

Two recent cyberpunk novels—Pat Cadigan's *Tea from an Empty Cup* (1998) and Marc Laidlaw's *Kalifornia* (1993)—brilliantly illustrate this dialectical problematic specifically in the context of a media-saturated near-future dominated by VR technologies. Cadigan's novel adopts an initially less radical premise than her earlier short story, eschewing the possibility of literal disembodiment in favor of an investigation of the psychosocial effects of conventional VR systems using helmet displays and "hotsuits." Called here Artificial Reality, the technology is wildly popular, spawning an entire entertainment industry in which consumers pay to rent equipment in AR parlors, where they lie immersed in vivid computer-game scenarios. The plot follows two dovetailing strands as a young woman named Yuki Harami searches through the AR landscape of "post-Apocalyptic Noo Yawk Sitty" for her vanished friend, Tom Iguchi, while police detective Dore Konstantin enters the same simulation to investigate the death of an AR user who may in fact be the luckless Tom. This young victim, found dead in an AR booth with his throat cut, joins several other recently deceased users who seem to have succumbed to "Gameplayers' stigmata"[86]—a supposedly mythical "disease" in which the patron's immobilized body manifests the same wounds inflicted on its online avatar. Thus, following the example of *Neuromancer* and Neal Stephenson's novel *Snow Crash* (1992), *Tea from an Empty Cup* depicts a situation in which events in cyberspace can be dangerous and even fatal to the real-world self.

This threat derives from the "intense authenticity" (p. 96) of the simulated experience. "There was no such thing as a minor sensation in AR; every feeling was realized in a way that was utterly complete, no aspect neglected. Because it was customized, measured out to order for your senses alone" (pp. 173–74). There are even rumors of the existence of a "Climax Envelope" for simulated sexual exchanges, in which the hotsuit "mirrored the wearer's own nerves," thus individualizing the encounter in an intimate and powerful way (p. 65). The standard-issue gear alone can generate overwhelmingly convincing experiences: enthusiastic players of an AR "module" called Gang Wars, for example, have to be strapped down for fear that they will "go native" and, in their flailing about, damage the equipment (p. 38). Both Yuki and Konstantin are relative newcomers to AR "netgaming," and each finds herself stunned by its compelling sensual immediacy. Yuki gasps to "feel the nerve endings closest to the surface of her fingers responding to the stimuli, absorbing it all greedily and demanding more" (p. 134), while Konstantin, trapped in a street riot, is beaten to the point where the simulated pain, conveyed through "the jazzy high-res authenticity of the 'suit,'" seems to go "deeper, all the way down to the level where what remained of the reptile senses sorted real from unreal" (p. 206).

The rhetoric of avarice and violence in these passages is linked, in Cadigan's treatment, both to the commercialized objectification of perception and motor reflex that AR achieves and to the enveloping presence of capitalist imperatives in its allegedly leisure-time scenarios. Not only is the user charged for online time consumed, but numerous special features—such as the ability to "morph" the shape of one's puppet—are available for additional surcharges; the incessant promotional blather of software "icons" hawking these various options prompts Yuki at one point to remark that "[e]very other word out of anyone's mouth has something to do with billable rates" (p. 108). Indeed, not only do users interact with personified sales pitches that cannot initially be distinguished from puppets controlled by living patrons, but they can even be recruited by advertisers to serve as icons themselves if their puppets are deemed sufficiently engaging and fashionable. Besides aspiring to this spurious "immortality" as walking-talking advertisements, hardcore users also yearn to interact with the netgaming "elite," patrons who operate at advanced levels due to their ability to pay higher rates and who occasionally deign to permit lower-level players access to their chic, exclusive simulations. These acts of miraculous largesse mirror the plot of "Pretty Boy Crossover," in which a favored few are elected to be "VIP[s] at some worthless club that isn't even real, doing things that aren't real with people who aren't real, getting some status that isn't real" (p. 136)—as Yuki scathingly puts it.

Ironically, this online hierarchy merely reproduces the real-world class system from which so many of AR's users seek to escape. In her investigation, Konstantin encounters numerous AR addicts trapped in "the same kinds of no-brainer file and data upkeep jobs," sorry microserfs living in "urban hives" (p. 85) for whom AR is both an anodyne from the numbing tedium of their everyday lives and a longed-for chance to see themselves as being "in the game with the name and the fame" (p. 92). These sad-sack losers make easy marks for various kinds of online rip-offs, falling prey again and again to the "Shopper's Credo" that "[a]nything worth paying for is worth over-paying for" (p. 163). In Tom's case, he falls prey to something rather more sinister—a "vampiric sequence" in which a shadowy, feral entity attacks him and drinks his blood (pp. 53–54), leading to his instantaneous real-world demise. In context, this brutal act of vampirism may be read symbolically as the exploitative animus of the commercial system to which his leisure has been fanatically devoted; as Yuki observes, Tom was one of those users who "would rather pursue a nonexistent Grail through an imaginary world than try to sustain a real life in a real place" (pp. 112–13), and for whom the ideal job would be "AR tester. . . . Like the sort of thing you dreamed about when you were a kid, consumer tester for Toyz U Krave, or whatever the company was called" (p. 133). It would seem, considering Tom's dire fate, that the toys he craved craved him as well.

Given this systematic colonization of Artificial Reality by the norms of a predatory capitalism, one might assume that the deep conviction on the part of avid netplayers that *"AR is humanity's true destiny"* (p. 83; emphasis in original) merely bespeaks the hypnotic effects of a technocracy of sensuality that has reified their senses and thus dominates their desires. The whispered fascination of users' quest for the "Out Door" in AR scenarios—"Out. *Out.* Over the rainbow, Never-Never Land, where you go and you'll stay," as one fan dreamily remarks (p. 87; emphasis in original)—might register no more than the programmed pleasure of locating hidden "subroutines" in the games' design, thus gaining the specious rank of an expert player. One icon admits as much to Konstantin, claiming that its job, when speaking of "the mythical Out Door," is "to stimulate a little thrill here and there, play to their curiosities and their fondest wishes and desires" (p. 187). Yet even this huckster's rhetoric acknowledges a utopian dimension to the lure, a sense of the transformative potential built into the technology, despite its currently impoverished commercial form. Overcoming her initial skepticism, Konstantin begins to experience the emotional pull of this obscure promise herself, finally deciding that AR "really was bigger than it looked from *out there*, and it wasn't just what they—whoever 'they' were supposed to be—wanted you to believe, it was truer than most people imagined. Because most people seemed to imagine only amusement parks like post-Apocalyptic Noo Yawk Sitty and if that was all they wanted, you couldn't make them want more" (p. 235; emphasis in original). Thus, a failure of popular imagination joins hands with the cynical regime of commodified entertainment culture to hobble the true potential of an extraordinary technology, to turn its prosthetic empowerments to vampiric ends.

The utopian appeal of AR is focused, in the story, in the person—or, rather, the puppet—of Body Sativa, a mysterious online celebrity whose richly playful name suggests both a "higher" form of embodiment (in the pun on cannabis) and veritably godlike enlightenment (in the pun on bodhisattva). When Yuki finally does meet up with this elusive guru—on an accelerated AR plane accessed via a unique "cocktail" of adrenaline and designer drugs—she is told that the media corporations' plans for Artificial Reality are in the process of being radically subverted: "It doesn't matter what they intended, anyway. Something else is happening, something they didn't bargain for" (p. 217). While Cadigan's resolution of this plot strand is ultimately disappointing and even a little silly—Body Sativa turns out to be the ghost of Yuki's long-dead grandmother, whose brain had been used experimentally to map out the neural pathways of the hotsuit, and who has now undertaken to recreate online the lost ethnic paradise of "Old Japan"—her thematic treatment of the dialectical contrast between dystopian and utopian applications of virtual reality is brilliantly rendered.

Specifically, this contrast plays out in two variant strategies by which AR patrons are subjected to remote-control manipulation via their online puppets. The dystopian strategy has been pioneered by the "whoremaster" Joy Flower, a creepy media star with a predilection for youthful cyberflesh who has discovered a way to commandeer the avatars of her devoted "Joy's Boyz" in order to directly access and steer their perceptions. Her use of this technique suggests, in context, a decadent sado-masochistic game in which the patron's immobile body is "invaded, penetrated, and permeated by some force that intended to *use* you, from the inside out" (p. 238; emphasis in original). Once online, Yuki finds herself subjected to this literally skin-crawling control, "as if she herself . . . were somebody else's clothing" (p. 179) to be donned and discarded; when she feels her virtual body respond to Joy Flower's distant signal, it was as if someone were "[m]olesting her gross motor movements" (p. 141). In contrast with this debasing surrender of agency, Body Sativa's puppeteering of Yuki seems not a loss but an amplification of self, "as if someone else were sharing the suit with her by some remote access . . . a demonstration of skill and grace, control and cooperation" (p. 219). Conveying a powerful message that "you don't have to do it alone" (p. 231), the experience suggests that the fabled Out Door may actually be "a Door In for something else entirely . . . something strange and new and, before now, completely unknown, and then everything would change" (p. 247). Just as *Neuromancer*'s freeing of the AI seemed to foretoken the purging reformation of a corrupted cyberspace, so the appearance of this collective prosthetic agency promises a redemption of virtual reality from its degraded (and degrading) capitalist form, a redemption that holds out hope for the utopian transformation of reality itself.

When Tom Iguchi's hotsuit is stripped off his dead body after his final traumatic immersion in AR, inscribed on his skin is "a dense pattern of lines and shapes . . . from the wires and sensors in the 'suit,'" leading Konstantin to muse that *"[t]hey'll start calling that the latest thing in nervous systems. . . . They'll give it a jumped-up name, like neo-exo-nervous system, and they'll say it's generated by hotsuit wear, every line and shape having a counterpart on the opposite side of the skin barrier"* (p. 36; emphasis in original). This momentary idle fantasy becomes the narrative reality of Marc Laidlaw's novel *Kalifornia*, in which VR technology, rather than being externally worn, is literally sewn into the body in the form of a network of artificial nerves. These "polynerves" or "livewires" permit their owners to access media broadcasts in their own heads, experiences that fill their senses and stimulate response in the same way that immersive VR does. Most folks' systems are set to "Receive Only," but it is also possible to be a "Sender," transmitting one's direct perceptions as signals across the media "wireways" for the pleasure of others. This new sort of "live" programming is, in fact, the main form of mass entertainment in this high-tech, near-future world.

The main characters are members of the Figueroa family, a popular celebrity household along the lines of the Bradys and Partridges—the difference being that this group is really kin and their show a combination of sitcom and TV verité. Actually, when the novel opens, the program has been off the wires for several years, the only family member with an active career being daughter Poppy, who now stars in her own spin-off, a suspense melodrama. In order to boost ratings, Poppy is persuaded to give birth "live" to the first infant born with wires, its implants inserted in utero. Like Lucy Ricardo's famous TV pregnancy, this one is a hit, but the chase scenario in which the birth occurs is so chaotic that it results in the child being mysteriously kidnapped. Determined to recover her baby, Poppy pursues a series of clues that reveal her own director-producer had conspired in the grab, but before she can inform the authorities, she is struck down by a speeding truck and sent into a coma. Meanwhile, her kid brother, nineteen-year-old Sandy, undertakes his own quest for the baby—named Calafia in honor of the imminent bicentennial of California's statehood—which leads him into contact with a shadowy cult who, he soon discovers, has stolen the child in the conviction that her unique status as a livewire birth marks her as the incarnation of Kali, the Hindu goddess of destruction.

If this initial summary makes the novel sound like a wacky satire, it is. Most of the humor focuses on Sandy's situation as a former teen idol who has settled down into a typically West Coast lifestyle of surfing, smoking dope, and watching TV—or, in this case, riding the wires, "his body channels switch[ing] at random."[87] Like everyone else in this hyperreal future, Sandy's nervous system is awash in "a polluted ether of advertising and you-are-there game shows. Bad media lurked in his polynerves like an Alzheimer's prion, waiting to crystallize" (ibid.). Entertainment culture has literally invaded consumers' cells as they find themselves directly interpellated into commercials and, during comedy programs, can feel their "diaphragm[s] convulsing with canned laughter" (p. 27). The vampiric aspects of this process are revealed by a hallucinatory ad for "Dr. Batori's Magical Youth Formula"—a potion of ersatz blood applied to the skin, following the therapeutic method of the infamous Countess Elizabeth Batori (often seen as a prototype for the literary and cinematic vampire).[88]

The main difference between Sandy and other media consumers is that he alone is likely, during his wireway wanderings, to stumble into the objectified viewpoints of his own family members as they struggle with some vaguely comical crisis or another in repeats of the *Figueroa Show*. *Kalifornia* thus takes Cadigan's vision of reified subjectivity one step further: in Sandy's case, not only has his life been systematically commodified, but it is even sold back to him as late-night reruns. Moreover, Sandy's budding livewired sexuality was an intense focus of teeny-bopper lust, such that he "couldn't so much as scratch his crotch without exciting legions of horny teenage wire-hoppers" (pp. 35–36). The night he lost his virginity, for example, his partner, secretly wired to Send, broadcast the experience; afterwards, the fanzines were "full of lush, overblown, almost worshipful descriptions of the act. SUPER SEX WITH THE SANDMAN! It was recorded and duplicated and traded among the teenie fans while Sandy went crazy with embarrassment" (p. 40). Now, the boy finds himself both alienated from his former show-biz-mediated life—which "had been a string of situations dreamed up by a board of 'creative consultants' and then enlarged upon and improvised by his family"—and yearning still for that lost audience connection, for the golden time before "the wires went dead and everyone thought of [him] forever in that frozen zone of rerun adolescence" (pp. 30–31).

To return to the plot, the Daughters of Kali who have stolen Calafia arrange to have a complex prosthetic shell constructed for her by the Celestial Mechanics, another obscure sect of hardware tinkerers who "felt that much practical knowledge had been lost through disuse" (p. 153). Owing their "allegiance to the future, to the developing machine," the Mechanics believe technology to be "a tremendous force for democracy someday, after the bumps and kinks are ironed out" (pp. 155–56). To this end, they have built the multiarmed metal-and-plastic prosthesis as part of their commitment to fabricate "special bodies . . . that would help us travel through the social realm . . . carry us safely and humanely. . . . Machines that allowed us to be real human beings" (p. 157). Unfortunately, once the Daughters of Kali acquire the intricate exoskeleton, they set off a chain of events that turns the entire machine culture to inhuman uses. This all begins when they install the baby Calafia in the driver's seat, from which position the budding prodigy—who has, thanks to the accelerating impetus of her inborn wires, already begun to speak and think—declares herself the goddess Kalifornia and determines to take over the world.

Because Kali's infant brain is "part polymatter, like the nerves" (p. 183), she is able—like Joy Flower and Body Sativa in Cadigan's novel—to enter telepathically into the livewired nervous systems of others and manipulate them directly, a process Kali refers to as "wearing people" (p. 169). She exercises this power first on her uncle Sandy, turning him into a kind of zombie that "banged around the room unsteadily, walking into walls" (p. 186); soon, by accessing the database of a corporate security firm, she has mobilized a phalanx of well-armed drones who become her personal bodyguards. Controlling this seemingly omnipotent child becomes a challenge for several factions in the novel, all of whom see her as "a potent tool. She has the body of a child, yes, but she has the powers of a goddess and the heart of a network executive" (pp. 183–84). Through her, it should be possible to fulfill a totalitarian dream implicit in the capitalist consumer system: not merely to influence, but actually to command, the audience's every action. As Kali extends her growing mastery through the networked livewires, "waking up inside of everyone," she begins to feel "as if someone were waking up and looking around inside of *her*" (p. 217). Suddenly, she finds her powers usurped by this intruder and her consciousness shunted off into a VR playground from which she can find no exit.

This mysterious plotter, it turns out, is the redoubtable Thaxter H. J. Halfjest, the Reverend Governor of California, a figure who, until this point, had seemed merely an amiable political hack. Halfjest is the first continuously "live" politician, always "open to the opinions of his audience, occasionally reversing the flow to look in on their lives and listen to their opinions. This was the perpetual promise of the wires: the simultaneous involvement of all citizens" (p. 38). In actuality, the set-up is a sham, the governor merely providing the masses with an illusion of collective participation; his real goals are considerably more sinister as becomes clear when he hijacks Kali's souped-up nervous system in order to found "a horrible regime—something beyond tyranny or fascism—unimaginably worse than anything the world had seen before" (p. 229). While Laidlaw's conclusion of his story is, as in Cadigan's novel, disappointing—the comatose Poppy, alerted to her daughter's plight by maternal telepathy (a natural connection contrasted with the ersatz empathy of the wires), joins Sandy to defeat Halfjest's maniacal plot—his treatment nonetheless amounts to a potent allegory of the cyborg powers inherent in consumption and the way they have been perverted, under capitalism, into predatory tools to be used against consumers themselves.

Indeed, the central image of the book—a prosthetically empowered child literally installed at the center of a vast machinic network, whose enhanced capacities foreshadow momentous new forms of collective life—provides perhaps the most compelling crystallization of the implications of the "consuming youth" system to be found in contemporary popular culture. Though the novel ultimately arranges a neo-Luddite resolution—Sandy has his wires surgically removed, and the mass audience, after the foiling of Halfjest's schemes, reverts to less threatening media such as television—there are moments when the utopian possibilities latent in cyborg youth, in the vision of "a small child at the heart of the enormous cold contraption" (p. 237), are stirringly evoked. The technodemocratic worldview of the Celestial Mechanics, for example, includes a prophetic belief in a future sociality radically cleansed and transformed by tutelary machines: "Who knows what interpersonal realms we might have entered by then: strange places we can hardly picture now" (p. 158). Moreover, despite its retro affirmation of natural bonds, the story's climax, with Poppy saving Calafia from her VR imprisonment, reveals the redemptive potential of technological networks as every interconnected viewer, "every last wired soul, received a mother's comfort. . . . And like Kali many of them wept when they heard that everything would be all right" (p. 238).

This consoling maternal message humanizes an apparatus that, until now, had been given over exclusively to vampiric exploitation under the cynical guise of entertainment and consumerist pleasure. Yet this false paradise of "Libidopolis" (a term coined by one of the novel's characters as an alternative name for the media-saturated hyperreality of California) contains within its manifold false promises an irrepressible utopian yearning—as all consumers, for one brief moment, recognize their implicit bond of kinship, "switching on all at once, innumerable combinations creating a new personality, a thing different and greater than any of them" alone (p. 228). It is this sort of ambiguous affirmation of cyborg potential, in the context of a consumer youth culture deformed by a logic of vampirism, at which cyberpunk, I think uniquely among contemporary discourses, excels.

DECADENT UTOPIAS OF HYPERCONSUMERISM

Of all the science fiction writers to emerge in the wake of cyberpunk in the 1990s, the one who has most consistently—and brilliantly—developed this cyborg-vampire theme is British author Richard Calder. Whereas Laidlaw and Cadigan had merely suggested the imbrication of these metaphorical images, Calder directly links the two figures in a bold and powerful way. His first three novels—a trilogy made up of *Dead Girls*, *Dead Boys*, and *Dead Things*—pioneered the unique subgenre of the cyberpunk vampire, a form that deserves to be read via the lens of Marx's analysis of the factory system as extrapolated to the realm of consumption by critics such as Baudrillard and W. F. Haug. In fact, Calder seems to have assimilated this theoretical tradition himself, at least judging from the critical perspectives he deploys. His fourth novel, too—*Cythera*, which is loosely aligned with the trilogy—develops the cyberpunk theme of utopian desire animating the technologies of youth consumption, pushing the issues raised in the first three books into more encompassing psychosocial terrain. The four works taken together amount to the most potent popular-culture illustration to date of the critical power of the vampire-cyborg, the ability of this dialectical metaphor to capture at once the transformative longings and the binding limitations of capitalist consumer culture.

The *Dead* trilogy chronicles the strange relationship between narrator Ignatz Zwakh and Primavera Bobinski, both an unnervingly overripe fifteen.[89] The year is 2071, and Primavera is one of a growing Eurasian subculture of genetically recombinant "dolls"—girls who, at puberty, radically metamorphose into mechanical, superhuman, vampiric sex toys; "their humanity spent," they are "girls no longer really, but simulacra" (p. 20), creatures "of surface and plane. Clothes, make-up, behavioural characteristics, resolve, for [them], into an identity that is all gesture, nuance, signs" (pp. 36–37). Performative embodiments of the fashion system, they have been remade at the molecular level by reifying processes: "Living tissue has adopted the structure of polymers and resins, metals and fibers. . . . Mechanized, you might say" (p. 71). Popularly referred to as Dead Girls because their living flesh freezes to a porcelain perfection, they resemble bejeweled supermodels; in fact, the historical origins of this "doll plague" lie in the fabrication, decades before, of sentient high-fashion "gynoids," artificial women sponsored by corporate designers such as Cartier and Chanel, who moved blithely through a hyperreal "world of gilded automata" (p. 76). Gradually, the impetuous nanoware of these creatures began to invade human cells, transforming living girls into "[s]elf-replicating cyborg bloodsucker[s]" (p. 4).

Ignatz is Primavera's "junkie," obsessively addicted to her literally venomous "allure"; with each erotic bite, she injects "software clones" into his bloodstream that reconfigure his gametes into vectors for the plague. On the run from an England that has fallen into the hands of the "Human Front"—who preach racial purity and practice the ritual slaughter of Lilim (or Daughters of Lilith, as they superstitiously dub the dolls)—the pair have wound up in Bangkok, where Primavera labors as a hired assassin for Kito, a gynoid who presides over a sleazy black-market "pornocracy" colloquially known as the "Big Weird" (a typical cyberpunk setting dominated by a cabal of scheming megacorporations and underground criminal gangs). Kito employs the runaway dolls as fetishized whores in a booming Thai sex market, a profiteering manipulation that mirrors the larger economy's literal exploitation of the dead: this ruthless "hypercapitalist" future has spawned a "new proletariat" of re-animated corpses furnished with AI chips that permit a limited repertoire of behavioral features. "They say they're good workers. Until they fall to pieces, that is" (p. 125).

Meanwhile, the human outposts on Mars—as we discover in the second novel—provide a more welcoming, less exploitative environment for the dolls, basically because the DNA of the Martian colonists has proven immune to nano-infection. We also learn, in this second volume, about the existence of the eponymous Dead Boys, biological siblings to the dolls who act as an evolutionary brake on the plague by, first, converting the Dead Girls from vampiric predators into quiescent sex slaves and, second, by "culling" their numbers through a brutal, eroticized combat. For all their seeming superiority to their sisters, however, the Dead Boys are reified fashion victims as well, robotized "cipher-bodies" translated "into lifeless totems, fetishes, conceptual works of art"

(p. 301). Specifically, they assume the aspect of a prototypical male vampire, becoming imperious, dashing avatars of "encoded Byronism" (p. 298)—while the Dead Girls, for their part, look like "Carmilla's kid sister" (p. 56).[90] For both cohorts, "feeding is a semiotic rather than a physiological act" (p. 222), a predation based on the replication of images rather than on visceral need; vivifying Haug's technocracy of sensuality, they incorporate the hungers of the consuming-youth system into their very flesh.

Behind the foreground plot lurks a transdimensional conspiracy in-augurated by the "Meta," a mysterious alien race who have deformed space-time itself into an archetypal battlefield of the sexes, in which the dolls appear as emblems of the "superfeminine" while their brothers are hypermacho berserkers.[91] In this larger context, Ignatz is translated into an immortal "dragon lord," Dagon, on the hunt—across vast cosmic vistas—for Vanity, the eternal female principle (of which Primavera is merely one privileged avatar). The Meta, in other words, are deeply invested—in both the libidinal and economic senses of the term—in preserving the fashion-driven dichotomy between a "maquillage- and couture-subverted femininity" on the one hand (p. 176) and a "doomed demon-lover's semiotic" of ruffled shirts and leather breeches on the other (p. 298). The complex strife between the sexes thus has its roots in popular imagery authorized by the Meta, an iconography of desire and power that runs through the entire culture, from highbrow poetry to the productions of the fashion industry to the most disposable generic trash, from the languid eroticism of Aubrey Beardsley drawings to the hopped-up inanity of cult movies like *A Nymphoid Barbarian in Dinosaur Hell*. The enmeshing power of this "contagious vision" (p. 396), its capacity to dictate and mold human expression—sexual, aesthetic, social—is what the trilogy is basically about; as Ignatz-Dagon observes, "I am a slave inside . . . this language that controls, this language and its lust for domi-nation, the text of Meta's world" (p. 327). So systematic is this image-based power structure that it has given rise, in this future alternative his-tory, to a Foucauldian critique entitled *The Political Technology of Lingerie* (p. 335–36).

This citation of Foucault suggests the critical edge informing Calder's tainted imaginings: his trilogy examines the evolution of the commodity form's quasi-erotic appeal to consumers in a way that amounts to an allegory of Marxist-cum-Baudrillardian perspectives. Explicitly refer-ring to the conversion of flesh-and-blood teens into "dead things"—calculated and calculating objects defined by surface, image, style—as "reification" (p. 266), Calder constructs a speculative scenario in which pubertal transformation, the personal awakening to sexual possibility, becomes the moment when one begins "to find out that I am only interested in *things;* people don't warrant my attention" (p. 280; emphasis in original).[92] Even youth-pop bands help to reinforce this "Meta-olatry," with a group called the Little Idiot Things, led by "a Lilim-wannabe of a chanteuse called Vava Vavoom," promoting themselves with fliers reading *"Get Thingified!"* (p. 288; emphasis in original) Calder locates the historical origins of this objectifying project in the moment "when the whole world's newly rich information elite yearned for positional goods, status symbols that could give their soulless twenty-first century existence *value*" (p. 350; emphasis in original). This consumerist aspiration has, ironically, rebounded to consume the yuppies themselves, their ideology of "I-shop-therefore-I-am" (p. 132) becoming literally true, as their erotic fascination with commodities converts each of them into a machinic part—a "robot simulacrum" (p. 300)—in an automated system of "hyperconsumerism" (p. 264).

Moreover, the cynically arranged fixation of sexuality on commercially generated images directly serves the social interests of a global elite, who profit from this reification. "Meta's autarchy is an embrace of market forces, the buying and selling of nothingness and pain, a nihilism that the world has been conned into believing represents a state of transcendence"; for the hypercapitalists who profit from Meta's transdimensional schemes, Dead Boys and Girls "offer up their transfigured, marketable flesh" to be "converted into sex toys, images, *anime*" (p. 380), which are then cycled back, as undead commodities, into the system of consumption. In this cozy arrangement, my three meanings of "consuming youth" not only converge but implode into one another: Dead teens are at once consuming subjects, consumers of each other as marketed objects, and systematically subordinated to a youth-fetishistic ideology of consumption. They become habituated to this ideology through constant exposure, as Calder shows in what is perhaps his most acute extrapolation of the Meta system, in the closing pages of *Dead Things*, where he traces it to the following "primal scene":

> The room is a nursery. In the centre of its cluttered floor (Barbie dolls dying in the arms of GI Joes, scrapbooks of pin-ups from *True Detective* and *The News of the World* selectively coloured-in with red biro to create the illusion of beautiful wounds), Meta, the child, is studying a flickering, portable TV. The Daleks are executing the slave girls of Skaro. A dozen pretty screams; the television screen turns black into white, white into black, like a photographic

negative. Like life turned inside-out. "Exterminate," he croaks . . . ;
the television screams, obligingly. (pp. 403–4)

From this perspective, the entire trilogy appears as an elaborate allegory
of socialization—of how, from early youth, boys and girls are tutored,
through the image-based apparatuses of a self-serving and predatory
system, in sexual objectification and the libidinal logic of master versus
slave.

As this quotation also suggests, commercial youth culture is presently
breeding a race of creatures—variations on the mutant youth of "Pretty
Boy Crossover" and *Kalifornia*—who will someday themselves become
toys, a point reinforced by the fact that Meta's central cabal is referred
to as the "Toymakers." The inventor of the original high-fashion automata, Dr. Toxicophilous, was himself under the decadent sway of a
revived Victorian-Edwardian children's culture, whose "stories have invaded reality"; the doll plague is, in essence, "a little boy's fantasy . . .
[t]he dream of a morbid child" (p. 111) hypnotized by "the allure of life-
in-death and death-in-life" (p. 183) of *Peter Pan* and classic vampire
stories. Calder's Dead future is thus "Neverland," a "city of kids" where
"[n]o one gets to grow up" (p. 17). Toxicophilous himself presides, like
a degenerate puppeteer, over a VR "necropolis" (p. 109) reproduced
within the "matrix" of every Dead Girl and Boy; when finally confronted by Ignatz and Primavera, he muses mournfully that "I've taken
away your childhood. . . . I've taken away your humanity" (p. 111). An
unwitting agent of the Meta, Toxicophilous joins the other mythic Toymakers as engineers of a corrupted realm of "play"—"a whole theatre, a
whole world of scripts, roles, play, in which that noun represents a deep,
universal grammar, the grand palaver of a monolingual, monomaniacal
cosmos, a cosmos that has nothing else to talk about but which possesses
an infinite expressiveness" (p. 373).

Given this thoroughgoing perversion of childhood pleasure into
profit, the logical conclusion would seem to be an emphatic rejection of
the false promises of consumption; yet Calder, despite his scathing indictment of the Meta hegemony, remains fundamentally ambivalent.
Unwilling to surrender the utopian desire that hypercapitalism has distorted into a hedonist nihilism, the author suggests, albeit obliquely,
strategies of resistance his characters might pursue to escape the "teenage holocaust" (p. 206) that awaits them. The first step is a repudiation
of Meta that nonetheless acknowledges the complicity of the Dead Boys
and Girls in its depredations; in a climactic internal monologue, Ignatz-
cum-Dagon pours out his scorn for the vacuous semiosis of Meta's

consuming-youth project, of this blasé "god of The Future—all speed demon, affectless, all simulation and sensation, shallow, hollow, as worthless as I am worthless . . . perversion of human form, body of love wrenched into the body of hate, body of sensuousness twisted into the body of agony" (p. 385). This ferocious denunciation bears with it a sharp edge of self-loathing, an implicit recognition that Meta's vampirism spreads and replicates through the living-dead flesh of its willing victim-accomplices, whose subjective yearning for happiness—for a humane world of sensuousness and love—has been deflected into market-driven fantasies of transcendence. The system can only operate through the incorporation of these libidinal impulses into the machineries of consumption.

Rather than teens simply withholding this essential investment, a second, allied strategy supervenes to "reprogram" Meta's simulation into "a redemptive fiction" (p. 212): the sustaining promise of an "uncrashable future" (p. 152). As the terminology here suggests, this strategy implicitly privileges the subversive posture of the computer hacker, conceived as the metaphorical embodiment of the cyborg powers of the youth-consumer system. *Dead Things* culminates in a typical cyberpunkish raid propelled by a group of Dead kids seeking to undo Meta's dominance, to burst the trap of its "virtual prison" (p. 403). The goal of this raid is to infiltrate Meta's inner sanctum—the transdimensional gateway at the heart of its hyperreal realm, "the centre of this dreaming multiverse" (p. 366)—and there to explode the "Toxicophilous Device," a "Reality Bomb" built into Ignatz-Dagon's matrix. If successful, the raid will destroy "this pestilence, this Demiurge" of Meta, allowing children to "live again in a world where love, compassion and all things that are best in Man, may bloom" (p. 375). The result will be a purgative redemption of reality, ushering in a world free of the taint of Meta and restoring Dead Boys and Girls to "the essence of things, our true selves" (p. 364).

Significantly, this utopian possibility emerges from the specific apparatus that has helped to forge Meta's autarchy—the nanotech machineries of simulation. The solution to the vampirism of capitalist consumption is thus not a Luddite rejection of the technologies that support its hegemony, but rather a subversive appropriation—an explosive re-subjectification—of these alienated objects to psychosocially transformative ends. The characters essentially hack the codes that sustain consumption's hyperreal virtuality, its Meta-narrative of power and control. In fact, Calder himself, as author-narrator, can fruitfully be envisioned as a sort of hacker, given the metafictional techniques he deploys toward the end of the trilogy. Following the explosion of the Reality Bomb, layers of Ignatz-Dagon's masks are peeled away to reveal his origins as the real-world hand writing the very pages we read; yet it is a hand engaged in a tense struggle with Meta's insidious semiotic system, its "idiolect of people who are their clothes . . . who are things" (p. 405). Just as Ignatz-Dagon had to turn his own cyborg resources against Meta's enveloping code, so the narrator is compelled to use the technology of inscription against the self-replicating meme that has usurped it to produce seamless tales of domination. "So: I have been a character in a book: I am still a character in a book; and to restore the world to reality I must again become a thing, but this time a thing of words, rather than a thing of flesh. Only by reassuming my rightful form could the world be disburdened of this *esthétique du mal*" (p. 367). In sum, Calder hacks the virtual reality of youth-culture narratives of vampiric predation in order to release their latent cyborg potential.

Calder's fourth novel builds upon this yearning utopian animus in a richly imaginative way. Set in roughly the same future history as (and sharing some characters with) the earlier trilogy, *Cythera*'s plot is enormously complicated, but at its heart lies the quest for the eponymous wonderland, a dreamy site that represents the longed-for fusion of "Earth Prime" (i.e., our mundane world) and "Earth2," "that world encoded within the shimmering, atomic structures of magazine covers, advertisement hoardings, movie flyposters, the screens of TVs, VCs, and PCs: another universe, a hyperuniverse that interpenetrated our own."[93] This "interpenetration" is more than mere metaphor; the basic speculative thrust of *Cythera* is that crossover traffic has become literally possible: celebrity "eidolons" can be translated, by their fetishizing fans, into luminescent flesh, while these fans can aspire—through the wonders of nanotechnologically augmented VR machines with "uploading" capacities—to achieve resurrection in the "new flesh" of simulated being.[94] This crossover traffic passes through "The Wound," a dimensional gateway that teen hackers secretly access to disport with their favorite simulacral superstars, sentient information systems spontaneously hatched from the multiplied images of fleshly celebrities.[95] Yet this intercourse is constrained both by a diurnal cycle—the Wound opens only at night, while by day the eidolons slumber in cyberspatial "coffins"—and also by a grim authoritarianism that vigorously polices adolescent leisure, seeking to shield teen consumers from "possession" by the vampiric eidolons.

Brilliantly extrapolating the critiques of kiddie culture discussed in chapter 1, Calder projects a future in which claims to protect young people from consumerist contamination actually rationalize an "undeclared war against children" (p. 21), whose desires, entwined with commodity culture, terrify their parents. This "Great Fear" of "a child's autonomy and all it represents: the ungovernable tide of the imagination" (p. 65) has spawned a sinister regime of surrogate "stepfathers," puritanical robotic guardians who unceasingly monitor teenagers' consumption practices, searching for signs of emerging obsession, for kids "corrupted by too much [Net] surfing, too many violent *anime*" (p. 11). Incorrigible cases are packed off to dreary concentration camps, such as the desolate "Boys Town" in the wastes of Antarctica, to be "deprogrammed." Meanwhile, an underground subculture of "ghost karaokes" has sprung up to service teen runaways' Earth2 fixations, offering safe havens where eidolons and their fans can freely mingle. Yet these assignations are achingly fleeting, always under threat from the lurking "Censors" and their "world of surveillance, of prohibition, of cheated desire" (p. 53). Thus has arisen the dream of Cythera, "a place where the real and the artificial became indistinguishable," which offers the promise of overcoming the painful dualism between quotidian life and ideal image in a higher "dialectic[al] . . . synthesis" (p. 15); there, youth and eidolon can coexist beyond the grasp of a hypercapitalist regime that seeks to divide them and to profit from this division.

Calder effectively demonstrates the hypocrisy of patriarchal capitalism's mobilization of teens as consumers: while this conscription ensures profits for the culture industries responsible for producing the glittering pleasures of the "fibersphere," it also provokes moralistic attacks by religious and "family values" advocates, who demonize the adolescent as *"Nature's great libertine . . . mad with the limitless presumption of desire"* (p. 84; emphasis in original). A surreptitiously seductive economic appeal to children might have been acceptable, but when personified commodities literally lust after youthful consumers, luring them into "dildonic" liaisons at interactive online sites and in decadent VR parlors, then something has to be done to preserve their threatened innocence. Specifically, the Censors sponsor an International Data Subliminal Interdiction Commission, whose goal is to "cauterize" the Wound, shutting down the crossover passage that links teens and eidolons in a dangerous complicity. In short, youthful consumers must be forcibly divided from the commodities they have subjectified with their own animating desires, maintained in a state of separation lest, together, the two conspire to disrupt the cozy reign of hypercapitalists and stepfathers alike.

The utopian impulse to overcome this division suggests a more or less explicit project of consumer revolt, in which the alienated desire objectified in Earth2's eidolons is expropriated from the media elite and restored to its rightful owners. Standing opposed to this radical reintegration are not only the prim Censors, with their fanatical clampdown on adolescent fantasy, but adult consumers as well, whose dreamy eroticization of a reified "youth"—expressed in their eagerness to "buy back the innocence they had never had" through the purchase of "the magic fetishes by which entry to childhood's kingdom might be reattained" (p. 26)—underwrites the division in the first place. Significantly, teens who have been successfully deprogrammed, their haunting eidolons exorcised and their desires channeled into dutifully repressed practices of consumption, are referred to as being "dispossessed," thus suggesting the confiscation and containment of their very subjectivity. By contrast, those who resist this process, rebelling against the "rules of desire" (p. 21) in order to reclaim "the empowering child of the autonomous imagination" (p. 67), are treated as implacable threats to social order.

Calder's rapturous invocation of young consumers as incipient revolutionaries is crystallized in two major subplots. First, there is the "Children's Crusade," a desperate march on Europe's high-fashion citadels by impoverished hordes of literally dispossessed youth aching to share in the seeming boon of the capitalist fibersphere. Yet this assault, while it points up the class-based limits of consumerist affluence, does not really threaten the exploitative logic of consumption, since these "dead-end kids" (p. 56) seek only to join in the vacuous fun, to enter the beckoning mallworld of "insubstantial glitter that, in the end, neither would nor could give them anything" (p. 25). In the words of a teen activist who fruitlessly attempts to deflect the crusade's energies into more critical directions, "their struggle was but a war for hamburgers and coke, for the homogeneity of the globalized media, for a mass cultural haemorrhaging that would leave them as vampires, the living dead" (p. 230).

By contrast, those who gather to form the "Army of Revolutionary Flesh" conceive their mission in a more radical way—as a utopian redemption of the historical project of capitalist consumption. Yes, these teens know that they have grown addicted to images, that they are the potential puppets of a global elite, that the price of entertaining crossover fantasies is to be cursed with a seemingly unquenchable longing linked ultimately to the profiteering imperatives of hyperconsumerism—"the little dream machines that twiddled the knobs and switches of my consciousness" (p. 17), as one of them puts it. The emptiness of this consumerist false paradise, which lures only to trap and disappoint, is emphasized by the grasping ambitions of Kito (the gynoid from the *Dead* trilogy), who vends fleshly fantasy to image-addicted consumers in order to build her own vain empire: "Consumer demand!" she opines. "The only constant in our sick, sick world!" (p. 141) Yet the response of the "revolutionary fleshers" is not a peremptory rejection of the cynical blandishments of consumption, but rather a determined quest to transform its false promises into the wished-for domain of Cythera, where the "consuming ache" (p. 272) will at last be soothed and the "Wound" dividing Earth Prime and Earth2 finally healed.

While the specific reality of Cythera is never fully assayed, its lyrical evocation as a "land of masques and bergamasques, of enchantment, of moonlight, calm, sad, and beautiful, where life was a perpetual *fête galante*" (p. 172) suggests a redemptive realm of youthful play freed from both the tyrannical surveillance of the Censors and the exploitative aims of the Toymakers, a world where children reclaim "the power adults exercise so arbitrarily over their bodies and minds" (p. 242).[96] Indeed, Cythera functions in the text as a galvanizing fantasy of young people's epochal emancipation:

> I seem to hear voices, children's voices carrying over the hard, crystallized ground as if over a sea that extends beyond this universe's horizons. What do you want children? I ask. We want to go home, they say. We want to go home to Cythera. Then leave behind your wicked stepfathers and stepmothers, leave your families and your treacherous friends, leave them all: seek out the place where you were before you were born, even if it means travelling to the stars, the countless archipelagos of the stars, to find your dream island, your home, your Cythera. (p. 306)

In this yearning fantasy of militant autonomy, the novel at times evokes the evangelical fervor associated with the "Children's Liberation" movement of the 1960s and 1970s, where various programmatic agendas for youthful autonomy and self-government were explicitly advanced.[97] And indeed, Calder does seem to suggest that adolescents' peremptory if inchoate resistance to authority deserves to be seen as the bellwether of social revolution, the psychic bedrock on which utopia can be erected. The problem with this age-based construction of his future power struggle—adult exploiters versus teenage resistance fighters—is that it occludes their mutual implication in a "consuming youth" system: the adults spellbound by a dreamily fetishized vision of "youth" are as exploited, in the last analysis, as the literally youthful consumers themselves.

Despite this occasional tendency simply to reduce economic relations to generational ones, Calder's work offers a remarkably powerful creative elaboration of Marx's central metaphor, vivifying his critical vision in the form of a science-fictional projection of teenage mutant cyborg vampires. The *Dead* trilogy and *Cythera* capture the dialectical logic in which every prosthetic empowerment of consumers both enmeshes them further in a predatory system and promises an amplification of their collective desire and will. Like youthful hackers and cyberpunks, Calder's Dead Kids struggle to realize a cyborg agency latent in the estranged machineries of high-tech culture. While his work only gestures at the transformed future implicit in the dynamics of this struggle, it nonetheless, in the emotional force of its utopian longing, serves to articulate a demand that capitalist consumption incessantly mobilizes but which it can never truly fulfill.

NOTES

INTRODUCTION

1. Allucquère Rosanne Stone, *The War of Desire and Technology at the Close of the Mechanical Age* (Cambridge, Mass.: MIT, 1995), pp. 178–79; Donna Haraway, *Modest_Witness@Second_Millenium: FemaleMan©_Meets_OncoMouse™* (New York: Routledge, 1997), pp. 214–15.

2. Karl Marx, *Capital*, vol. 1, trans. Ben Fowkes (New York: Penguin, 1976), p. 548. Subsequent references are to this translation and appear in the text.

3. There is, according to Marx, a structural contradiction manifested here: while machinery increases the rate at which surplus value can be realized from the individual worker's labor, it also decreases the number of workers employed in the factory; in the long run, this is a fatal problem for the system, since profit can only be achieved through the exploitation of human labor. Just as a world composed solely of vampires is inconceivable, so for Marx, a totally automated factory is impossible under capitalist relations of production.

4. For an overview of this folkloric tradition, see Anthony Masters, *The Natural History of the Vampire* (New York: Putnam's, 1972). On the transformation of vampire folklore into literary representations during the eighteenth and nineteenth centuries, see Christopher Frayling's introduction to his anthology *Vampyres: Lord Byron to Count Dracula* (London: Faber & Faber, 1991), pp. 1–84. An excellent discussion of the use of the vampire metaphor in *Capital* is Chris Baldick's *In Frankenstein's Shadow: Myth, Monstrosity, and Nineteenth-Century Writing* (Oxford: Clarendon, 1990), pp. 121–40, while Franco Moretti's "The Dialectic of Fear" (in *Signs Taken for Wonders: Essays on the Sociology of Literary Forms*, rev. ed., trans. Susan Fischer, David Forgacs, and David Miller [New York: Verso, 1988], 83–108) offers an analysis of Bram Stoker's novel *Dracula* (1897) that explicitly draws on Marx's metaphorology.

5. James R. Beniger, *The Control Revolution: Technological and Economic Origins of the Information Society* (Cambridge, Mass.: Harvard University Press, 1986). Subsequent references appear in the text.

6. See Simon Schaffer, "Babbage's Intelligence: Calculating Engines and the Factory System," *Critical Inquiry* 21 (1994): 203–27. Babbage has become a minor celebrity not only in the writings of computer historians—see Anthony Hyman, *Charles Babbage: Pioneer of the Computer* (Princeton, N.J.: Princeton University Press, 1982)—but also in the science fiction subgenre of steampunk. Babbage's protocybernetic vision animates Michael Flynn's *In the Country of the Blind* (New York: Baen, 1990) and William Gibson and Bruce Sterling's *Difference Engine* (New York: Bantam, 1991), alternative-history novels in which Babbage's epochal inventions prospered rather than died at birth, as they in fact did due to a lack of funding and the inadequacy of contemporary design techniques.

7. For a critique of Beniger along similar lines, see Nick Dyer-Witheford, *Cyber-*

Marx: Cycles and Circuits of Struggle in High-Technology Capitalism (Urbana: University of Illinois Press, 1999), pp. 244–45.

8. Jean Baudrillard, *For a Critique of the Political Economy of the Sign*, trans. Charles Levin (St. Louis: Telos, 1981), p. 83. Subsequent references are to this translation and appear in the text.

9. Jean Baudrillard, *Symbolic Exchange and Death*, trans. Iain Hamilton Grant (Thousand Oaks, Calif.: SAGE, 1998). Subsequent references are to this translation and appear in the text.

10. Baudrillard defends the Luddites of the early nineteenth century, with their machine-smashing raids, as being "much clearer than Marx on the impact of the irruption of the industrial order" (*Symbolic Exchange and Death*, p. 13). A frank Luddism has informed several critiques of information technology: see Frank Webster and Kevin Robins, *Information Technology: A Luddite Analysis* (Norwood, N.J.: Abex, 1986); and Theodore Roszak, *The Cult of Information: A Neo-Luddite Treatise on High-Tech, Artificial Intelligence, and the True Art of Thinking*, 2d ed. (Berkeley and Los Angeles: University of California Press, 1994).

11. Baudrillard, *For a Critique of the Political Economy of the Sign*, p. 56.

12. Douglas Kellner, *Jean Baudrillard: From Marxism to Postmodernism and Beyond* (Stanford, Calif.: Stanford University Press, 1989), p. 37.

13. Dyer-Witheford, *Cyber-Marx*, p. 179. This excellent study—whose animating perspectives cohere, in major particulars, with my own—traces the implications of Marx's critique of capitalism for contemporary cybernetic culture. The passage quoted here suggests (though does not explicitly develop) the dialectical significance of Marx's image of the vampire-cyborg.

14. The central Regulation school texts are Michel Aglietta, *A Theory of Capitalist Regulation: The U.S. Experience*, trans. David Fernbach (London: New Left Books, 1979); and Alain Lipietz, *Mirages and Miracles: Crises in Global Fordism*, trans. David Macey (London: Verso, 1987). Their work is effectively summarized in Robert Boyer, *The Regulation School: A Critical Introduction* (New York: Columbia University Press, 1990).

15. Liepietz, *Mirages and Miracles*, p. 32; emphasis in original. Subsequent references appear in the text.

16. See Antonio Gramsci, "Americanism and Fordism," in *Selections from the Prison Notebooks*, ed. and trans. Quintin Hoare and Geoffrey Nowell Smith (London: Lawrence and Wishart, 1971), 277–318.

17. See Stephen A. Marglin and Juliet B. Schor, eds., *The Golden Age of Capitalism* (New York: Oxford University Press, 1990). For a critique of "Golden Age" arguments, see Michael J. Webber and David L. Rigby, *The Golden Age Illusion: Rethinking Postwar Capitalism* (New York: Guilford, 1996).

18. Michael J. Piore and Charles F. Sable, in their book *The Second Industrial Divide: Possibilities for Prosperity* (New York: Basic, 1984), provide statistical evidence for this saturation: "in 1979 there was one car for every two residents [in the United States], compared to one for every four in the early 1950s. Ninety-nine percent of American households had television sets in 1970, compared with 47 percent in 1953. Similarly, more than 99 percent of households had refrigerators, radios, and electric irons, and more than 90 percent had automatic clothes washers, toasters, and vacuum cleaners" (p. 184).

19. The net profit rate and profit share—generally telling measures of capital

accumulation—began a precipitate decline, so much so that the net profit rates for 1974 and 1975 combined were less than either 1965 or 1966, the high points of the postwar boom: see Philip Armstrong, Andrew Glyn, and John Harrison, *Capitalism Since 1945* (Cambridge, Mass.: Blackwell, 1991), pp. 352–55.

20. Martyn J. Lee, *Consumer Culture Reborn: The Cultural Politics of Consumption* (New York: Routledge, 1993), pp. 103–04.

21. Ibid., pp. 106–7.

22. Stuart Ewen, *Captains of Consciousness: Advertising and the Social Roots of the Consumer Culture* (New York: McGraw-Hill, 1976), p. 143.

23. Ibid., p. 146.

24. Henry Ford, *My Life and Work* (Garden City, N.J.: Doubleday, Page, 1923), pp. 108–9, quoted in Mark Seltzer, *Bodies and Machines* (New York: Routledge, 1992), p. 157.

25. Lawrence Grossberg, *We Gotta Get Out of This Place: Popular Conservatism and Postmodern Culture* (New York: Routledge, 1992), p. 183.

26. Jean Baudrillard, "The Ecstasy of Communication," trans. John Johnston, in *The Anti-Aesthetic: Essays in Postmodern Culture*, ed. Hal Foster (Port Townsend, Wash.: Bay Press, 1983), 126–33; the quotation is from p. 128.

27. The various positions in this controversy are anatomized in Ash Amin, ed., *Post-Fordism: A Reader* (Cambridge, Mass.: Blackwell, 1994); and Nigel Gilbert, Roger Burrows, and Anna Pollert, eds., *Fordism and Flexibility: Divisions and Change* (London: Macmillan, 1992).

28. Stuart Hall, "Brave New World," *Marxism Today* (October 1988): 24, quoted in Lee, *Consumer Culture Reborn*, p. 110. See also the essays gathered in Stuart Hall and Martin Jacques, eds., *New Times: The Changing Face of Politics in the 1990s* (New York: Verso, 1990).

29. David Harvey, *The Condition of Postmodernity: An Enquiry into the Origins of Cultural Change* (Cambridge, Mass.: Blackwell, 1990), p. 124.

30. See, for example, Adam Tickell and Jamie A. Peck, "Social Regulation *After* Fordism: Regulation Theory, Neo-Liberalism and the Global-Local Nexus," *Economy and Society* 24, no. 3 (August 1995): 357–86.

31. A similar argument is made by Piore and Sabel in *The Second Industrial Divide*, though their favored term for this system is *flexible specialization*. I discuss the cultural implications of these metaphors of *flexibility* in chapter 4.

32. Harvey, *The Condition of Postmodernity*, p. 156. Subsequent references appear in the text.

33. Supporting Harvey's claims, recent advertising research has begun to use arguments for a transition to postmodernity to develop new corporate strategies for appealing to consumers: see, for example, A. Fuat Firat and Alladi Venkatesh, "Liberatory Postmodernism and the Reenchantment of Consumption," *Journal of Consumer Research* 22 (December 1995): 239–67.

34. Scott Lash and John Urry, *The End of Organized Capitalism* (Cambridge: Polity, 1987).

35. Marx, *Capital*, 1:594–95.

CHAPTER ONE

1. Karl Marx, *Capital*, vol. 1., trans. Ben Fowkes (New York: Penguin, 1976), p. 1007. Subsequent references are to this translation.

2. Johann Wolfgang von Göethe, *Faust*, trans. Walter Kaufman (New York: Anchor, 1963), p. 215.

3. W. F. Haug develops this theme in Marx systematically in his *Critique of Commodity Aesthetics: Appearance, Sexuality and Advertising in Capitalist Society*, trans. Robert Bock (Minneapolis: U of Minnesota P, 1986). The touchstone text in this now-extensive Freudo-marxist critique of consumption is Herbert Marcuse's *One-Dimensional Man: Studies in the Ideology of Advanced Industrial Society* (Boston: Beacon, 1964); virtually every subsequent work in this tradition (including Haug's book) develops some version of Marcuse's concept of "repressive desublimation" to account for the consumer's seemingly spellbound desire.

4. Marx, *Capital*, 1:926. Subsequent references appear in the text.

5. See Stuart Ewen, *Captains of Consciousness: Advertising and the Social Roots of the Consumer Culture* (New York: McGraw-Hill, 1976); and Richard Hoggart, *The Uses of Literacy* (London: Chatto & Windus, 1957). Good general studies of the rise of mass marketing in the United States are Susan Strasser, *Satisfaction Guaranteed: The Making of the American Mass Market* (New York: Pantheon, 1989); and Stephen Fox, *The Mirror Makers: A History of American Advertising and Its Creators* (New York: Morrow, 1984).

6. Stuart and Elizabeth Ewen, *Channels of Desire: Mass Images and the Shaping of American Consciousness* (New York: McGraw-Hill, 1982), pp. 75–76; emphases added.

7. Ewen, *Captains of Consciousness*, p. 146.

8. Sut Jhally, *The Codes of Advertising: Fetishism and the Political Economy of Meaning in the Consumer Society* (New York: Routledge, 1990), p. 121; emphasis in the original. Subsequent references appear in the text.

9. Writing in the mid-1980s, Jhally was describing MTV's format when it was still in its relative infancy and actually showed music videos continuously. By the end of the decade, the network had moved from a quasi-radio setup, with "vee-jays" spinning a regular playlist of videos, to the current commercial-TV format, with distinct genres of programming (game shows, talk shows, and so forth) running during segmented weekly schedules. For a history and analysis of this transition, see Andrew Goodwin, *Dancing in the Distraction Factory: Music Television and Popular Culture* (Minneapolis: University of Minnesota Press, 1992), pp. 131–55.

10. Haug, *Critique of Commodity Aesthetics*, trans. Bock, p. 16. Subsequent references are to this translation and appear in the text.

11. For analyses of how bodily pleasure is constructed in debates about consumption, see Pasi Falk, *The Consuming Body* (Thousand Oaks, Calif.: SAGE, 1994); and Jon Stratton, *The Desirable Body: Cultural Fetishism and the Erotics of Consumption* (Manchester: Manchester University Press, 1996).

12. M. Gottdiener, *Postmodern Semiotics: Material Culture and the Forms of Postmodern Life* (Cambridge: Blackwell, 1995), pp. 86, 95.

13. Lauren Langman, "Neon Cages: Shopping for Subjectivity," in *Lifestyle Shopping: The Subject of Consumption*, ed. Rob Shields (New York: Routledge, 1992), pp. 40–82; the quotations are from pp. 54 and 43.

14. Fredric Jameson, "Pleasure: A Political Issue," in *Formations of Pleasure*, ed. Tony Bennett et al. (London: Routledge and Kegan Paul, 1983), pp. 1–14; the quotations are from pp. 7 and 3.

15. Puritanical attitudes toward consumption have a long history in the United States: see Daniel Horowitz, *The Morality of Spending: Attitudes toward the Consumer*

Society in America, 1875–1940 (Baltimore: Johns Hopkins University Press, 1985).

16. Annette Kuhn, *The Power of the Image: Essays on Representation and Sexuality* (London: Routledge and Kegan Paul, 1985), p. 8.

17. See, for example, Rachel Bowlby, *Just Looking: Consumer Culture in Dreiser, Gissing and Zola* (New York: Metheun, 1985); Jennifer Craik, *The Face of Fashion: Cultural Studies in Fashion* (New York: Routledge, 1994); and Hilary Radner, *Shopping Around: Feminine Culture and the Pursuit of Pleasure* (New York: Routledge, 1995).

18. Elizabeth Wilson, *The Sphinx in the City: Urban Life, the Control of Disorder, and Women* (Berkeley and Los Angeles: University of California Press, 1991), pp. 59–60.

19. Anne Friedberg, *Window Shopping: Cinema and the Postmodern* (Berkeley and Los Angeles: University of California Press, 1993), pp. 118–19.

20. Kathy Peiss, "Commercial Leisure and the 'Woman Question,'" in *For Fun and Profit: The Transformation of Leisure into Consumption*, ed. Richard Butsch (Philadelphia: Temple University Press, 1990), pp. 105–17; the quotation is from p. 114. See also Peiss's *Cheap Amusements: Working Women and Leisure in Turn-of-the-Century New York* (Philadelphia: Temple University Press, 1986).

21. For Benjamin's discussion of the *flâneur*, see *Charles Baudelaire: A Lyric Poet in the Era of High Capitalism*, trans. H. Zohn (London: Verso, 1983); see also Keith Tester, ed., *The Flaneur* (New York: Routledge, 1994), for evidence of how cultural-studies scholars have deployed the concept.

22. Don Slater, "Going Shopping: Markets, Crowds and Consumption," in *Cultural Reproduction*, ed. Chris Jenks (New York: Routledge, 1993), pp. 188–209; the quotation is from p. 207.

23. Friedberg, *Window Shopping*, p. 120.

24. Susan Buck-Morss, "The Flaneur, the Sandwichman, and the Whore: The Politics of Loitering," *New German Critique* 39 (1986): 99–140; the quotation is from p. 136.

25. John Fiske, *Reading the Popular* (Boston: Unwin Hyman, 1989), p. 14. Subsequent references appear in the text.

26. Poppy Z. Brite, *Lost Souls* (New York: Delacorte, 1992), p. 86. I discuss Brite's novel in chapter 3.

27. Fredric Jameson, *Postmodernism or, the Cultural Logic of Late Capitalism* (Durham: Duke University Press, 1991), p. 47.

28. Somtow Sucharitkul, *Mallworld* (New York: Donning, 1981; the edition hereafter cited in the text is New York: Tor, 1984), p. 46. The novel has recently been reissued as *The Ultimate Mallworld* (Atlanta: Meisha Merlin, 2000), with additional episodes, illustrations, and satirical advertisements.

29. Somtow is here rewriting Theodore Sturgeon's classic 1961 tale of psycho-analyzed vampirism, *Some of Your Blood*.

30. Louise B. Russell, *The Baby Boom Generation and the Economy* (Washington, D.C.: Brookings Institution, 1982), p. 6.

31. Nathaniel Wice, "Generalization X," in *The GenX Reader*, ed. Douglas Rushkoff (New York: Ballantine, 1994), pp. 279–86, see especially p. 279; and Thomas Frank, *The Conquest of Cool: Business Culture, Counterculture, and the Rise of Hip Consumerism* (Chicago: University of Chicago Press, 1997), p. 109.

32. Russell, *The Baby Boom Generation and the Economy*, p. 70.

33. Lawrence Grossberg, *We Gotta Get Out of This Place: Popular Conservatism and Postmodern Culture* (New York: Routledge, 1992), pp. 172–73.

34. Stanley C. Hollander and Richard Germain's *Was There a Pepsi Generation before Pepsi Discovered It? Youth-Based Segmentation in Marketing* (Lincolnwood, Ill.: NTC Business, 1992) shows that such an advertising strategy dates to the late nineteenth century.

35. On firms such as Youth Concepts, see the invaluable discussion in Frank, *Conquest of Cool*, pp. 105–30. Also see Melvin Helitzer and Carl Heyel, *The Youth Market: Its Dimensions, Influence and Opportunities for You* (New York: Media Books, 1970)—the source for the $50 billion figure; Aubrey S. Balchen, ed., *Market Pacesetters (Young Adults)* (New York: Fairchild/Capital Cities Media, 1981)—the quotation about teens as a "Superclass" is on p. 1; and Lawrence Graham and Lawrence Hamdan, *Youthtrends: Capturing the $200 Billion Youth Market* (New York: St. Martin's, 1987). These statistical estimates of the financial solvency of young people during the period are a bit misleading; spending by the under-25 cohort, as a percentage of total consumer outlay, has always been relatively small (around 7% in 1995) due to the fact that big-ticket items such as houses, new cars, and major appliances (with the notable exception of electronic equipment) are generally purchased by adults. The important point, however, is that young people tend to devote a higher percentage of their incomes to discretionary spending, making them more amenable to impulsive appeals by skillful advertisers. See the extensive statistical portrait in Susan Mitchell, *American Generations: Who They Are. How They Live. What They Think*, 2d ed. (Ithaca, N.Y.: New Strategist, 1998), pp. 400–408.

36. Frederick Wertham, *Seduction of the Innocent* (New York: Rinehart, 1954); Ron Goulart, *The Assault on Childhood* (Los Angeles, Sherbourne, 1969); Neil Postman, *The Disappearance of Childhood* (New York: Delacorte, 1982); and Quentin J. Schultze and Roy M. Anker, eds., *Dancing in the Dark: Youth, Popular Culture, and the Electronic Media* (Grand Rapids, Mich.: Eerdmans, 1991).

37. Goulart, *The Assault on Childhood*, p. 13. Subsequent references appear in the text.

38. Goulart's science fiction, much of it set in a galactic venue known as the Barnum System, features brilliant send-ups of high-tech consumerism and corporate culture. Somtow's *Mallworld* is very much in its debt.

39. Robert R. McCammon, *They Thirst* (New York: Avon, 1981; the edition cited here is New York: Pocket, 1988), pp. 109–10.

40. Goulart, *The Assault on Childhood*, p. 66.

41. Critiques of Disney's baleful influence on youth are common among left-wing critics as well: see, for example, Henry A. Giroux's *Fugitive Cultures: Race, Violence, and Youth* (New York: Routledge, 1996), pp. 89–113.

42. Schultze and Anker, *Dancing in the Dark*, p. 47.

43. Ibid., pp. 141–42.

44. Consumer socialization was a concept deployed in the work of marketing analysts who focused on youth during the 1970s and 1980s: see Scott Ward, Daniel B. Wackman, and Ellen Wartella, *How Children Learn to Buy: The Development of Consumer Information-Processing Skills* (Beverly Hills: SAGE, 1977); and James U. McNeal, *Children As Consumers: Insights and Implications* (Lexington, Mass.: Lexington, 1987). Recent critical studies of this socialization process include Ellen Seiter, *Sold Separately: Parents and Children in Consumer Culture* (New Brunswick, N.J.: Rut-

gers University Press, 1995); and Shirley R. Steinberg and Joe L. Kincheloe, eds., *Kinderculture: The Corporate Construction of Childhood* (Boulder, Colo.: Westview, 1997).

45. Jacques Attali, *Noise: The Political Economy of Music*, trans. Brian Massumi (Minneapolis: University of Minnesota Press, 1985), pp. 109–11. Helitzer and Heyel advise marketers to "avoid the pied piper image" by remaining "above suspicion" in their solicitation of youthful buyers; yet, as befits good capitalists, they resolutely defend the advertiser's right to go "hammer and tongs after the youth market, in whatever segment he thinks he can make a contribution and earn a profit—infants, moppets, preteeners, teeners, young adults. . . . Ours is a competitive system" (*The Youth Market*, pp. 31–32). As Gene Del Vecchio's *Creating Ever-Cool: A Marketer's Guide to a Kid's Heart* (Gretna, La.: Pelican, 1997) demonstrates, this is a competition, finally, for a "kid's heart," and the author does not flinch from providing advertisers with what amounts to a sophisticated seduction manual designed to woo this tender if rather fickle organ.

46. Jerry A. Jacobs, *The Mall: An Attempted Escape from Everyday Life* (Prospect Heights, Ill.: Waveland, 1984), p. 45.

47. William Kowinski, *The Malling of America: An Inside Look at the Great Consumer Paradise* (New York: Morrow, 1985), pp. 20, 22.

48. Quoted in Landon Y. Jones, *Great Expectations: America and the Baby Boom Generation* (New York: Coward, McCann and Geoghegan, 1980), p. 229.

49. Kowinski, *Malling of America*, p. 351. The International Council of Shopping Centers study is quoted on p. 350.

50. Joshua Meyerowitz, *No Sense of Place: The Impact of Electronic Media on Social Behavior* (New York: Oxford University Press, 1985), p. 227. A more recent version of this argument is Andrew Calcutt, *Arrested Development: Pop Culture and the Erosion of Adulthood* (Washington, D.C.: Cassell, 1998).

51. Elkins, cited in Kowinski, *Malling of America*, p. 351; Simmel, cited in Jacobs, *The Mall*, p. 93.

52. Langman, "Neon Cages," pp. 60, 58.

53. Goulart, *The Assault on Childhood*, p. 3.

54. Grossberg, *We Gotta Get Out of This Place*, p. 183. For a discussion of the boomer craze for body maintenance as an effort to cling to an ideological vision of youth, see Mike Featherstone, "The Body in Consumer Culture," *Theory, Culture and Society* 1, no. 2 (1982): 18–33.

55. Schultze and Anker, *Dancing in the Dark*, p. 66.

56. Meyerowitz, *No Sense of Place*, p. 227.

57. Schultze and Anker, *Dancing in the Dark*, pp. 64–65.

58. Grace Hechinger and Fred M. Hechinger, *Teenage Tyranny* (New York: Morrow, 1963).

59. J. C. Herz, *Joystick Nation: How Videogames Ate Our Quarters, Won Our Hearts, and Rewired Our Minds* (Boston: Little, Brown, 1997), p. 50.

60. C. Everett Koop, quoted in "Video Games Hit at Nursing Home . . . But They Get Zapped by Chief Surgeon," *Syracuse Post Standard*, 10 November 1982, p. A9, cited by Jacobs, *The Mall*, p. 84; Martin M. Klein, "The Bite of Pac-Man," *Journal of Psychohistory* 2, no. 3 (1984): 395–401; Ernest Jones, *On the Nightmare* (New York: Liveright, 1971); Martin Amis, *Invasion of the Space Invaders* (London: Hutchinson, 1982), p. 20; and Jacobs, *The Mall*, p. 85. For less alarmist, more so-

ciologically grounded surveys of the impact of videogames during the period, see Tom Panelas, "Adolescents and Video Games: Consumption of Leisure and the Social Construction of the Peer Group," *Youth and Society* 15 (1983): 51–65; and Desmond Ellis, "Video Arcades, Youth and Trouble," *Youth and Society* 16, no. 1 (1984): 47–65.

61. Marsha Kinder, *Playing with Power in Movies, Television and Video Games: From Muppet Babies to Teenage Mutant Ninja Turtles* (Berkeley and Los Angeles: University of California Press, 1991), p. 117.

62. Tracy C. Davis, "The Theatrical Antecedents of the Mall That Ate Downtown," *Journal of Popular Culture* 24, no. 4 (1991): 1–15. Peter Gibian, in "The Art of Being Off-Center: Shopping Center Spaces and Spectacles" (*Tabloid: A Review of Mass Culture and Everyday Life* 5 [1982]: 44–64), depicts the mall's environment as *"visionary freedom in enclosure"* (p. 44; emphasis in original)—an apt description of a videogame as well.

63. Kinder, *Playing with Power in Movies, Television and Video Games*, p. 83. Subsequent references appear in the text.

64. Eugene F. Provenzo, *Video Kids: Making Sense of Nintendo* (Cambridge, Mass.: Harvard University Press, 1991).

65. Geoffrey R. Loftus and Elizabeth F. Loftus, *Mind at Play: The Psychology of Video Games* (New York, Basic, 1983); David Sudnow, *Pilgrim in the Microworld* (New York: Warner, 1983); and Douglas Rushkoff, *Playing the Future: How Kids' Culture Can Teach Us to Thrive in an Age of Chaos* (New York: HarperCollins, 1996).

66. Rushkoff, *Playing the Future*, p. 13.

67. Sudnow, *Pilgrim in the Microworld*, p. 3. Subsequent references appear in the text.

68. This eager responsiveness to the very bodies of teens is now actually a feature of many arcade games, which are routinely equipped with infrared or motion sensors that prompt elaborate sales pitches when triggered. In his novel *Shampoo Planet* (New York: Pocket, 1992), Douglas Coupland describes a scene in which the youthful narrator and his girlfriend "walk past a cluster of video games, the heat from our bodies activat[ing] their 'beg cycle'—triggering mouth-watering, fun-choked displays of on-screen pyrotechnics. . . . 'How intense!' I shout. 'Stephanie. I must have quarters'" (p. 174). Sudnow's phrase for this is "switching on the want" (*Pilgrim in the Microworld*, p. 208)—though he could hardly have imagined, in 1983, such a powerful literalization of his metaphor.

69. Fiske has himself praised the resistant possibilities of videogames in the context of his general defense of mall(rat) culture: see *Reading the Popular*, pp. 77–93.

70. Sudnow's fantasy of his son as a "software entrepreneur" whose physical dexterity potentially links up with corporate flexibility parallels (and perhaps draws upon) popular paeans to the business culture of Silicon Valley produced during the 1980s, a discourse I discuss at length in chapter 4.

71. Rushkoff, *Playing the Future*, p. 3.

72. Herz, *Joystick Nation*, p. 12.

73. See ibid., pp. 13–24.

74. Rushkoff, *Playing the Future*, p. 2.

75. Ibid., pp. 49–53.

76. Herz, *Joystick Nation*, p. 89.

77. Rushkoff, *Playing the Future*, p. 177–78.

78. Ibid., p. 181.

79. A valuable critique of the addiction hypothesis is Sherry Turkle, *The Second Self: Computers and the Human Spirit* (New York: Simon & Schuster, 1984), pp. 64–92.

80. Rushkoff, *Playing the Future*, pp. 170, 204.

81. Herz, *Joystick Nation*, p. 117. Subsequent references appear in the text.

82. S. P. Somtow is a pseudonym for Somtow Sucharitkul, the erstwhile author of *Mallworld*. The edition of *Vampire Junction* cited hereafter in the text is New York: Tor, 1991.

83. For a wide-ranging if overwrought analysis of how modern culture invests children with sexual significance, see James R. Kincaid's *Erotic Innocence: The Culture of Child Molesting* (Durham, N.C.: Duke University Press, 1998), which builds on his earlier work, *Child-Loving: The Erotic Child in Victorian Culture* (New York: Routledge, 1992). Many contemporary vampire texts (including the two discussed in this section) touch base with an Edwardian classic that provides the starting point for much of Kincaid's analysis in the latter volume, J. M. Barrie's *Peter Pan* (1904).

84. The argument in this paragraph builds on Susan Willis's suggestion, in *A Primer for Daily Life* (New York: Routledge, 1991), that children's play, especially in a highly commodified environment, has utopian dimensions, activating and enjoying use values where exchange value reigns supreme (see pp. 31–32).

85. Actually, the movie was filmed largely in Santa Cruz and makes prominent use of one of that beachside city's major attractions, an extensive carnivalesque boardwalk. Also, the fact that the film's vampires travel in a motorcycle pack is almost certainly an allusion to the Santa Cruz Vampires Motorcycle and Scooter Club, which was founded in the area in the late 1940s/early 1950s.

86. Richard Butsch, in "Home Video and Corporate Plans: Capital's Limited Power to Manipulate Leisure" (in Butsch, ed., *For Fun and Profit: The Transformation of Leisure into Consumption* [Philadelphia: Temple UP, 1990)], pp. 215–35), argues that VCR market penetration during the 1980s was guided less by a systematic capitalist plan than by the decisions of individual consumers and retailers in a historical context where "divisions within capital limited its ability to control people's leisure" (p. 229). From Butsch's perspective, then, master vampire Max would actually be allied not with the settled interests of capitalist entertainment industries but with the burgeoning ranks of video retailers, whose threat was less to consumers than to the film studios, theater chains, and television networks, whose profits and market share they were steadily bleeding off. Thus, to pursue a more strictly historical allegory than I argue for here—one that Ken Gelder, in his book *Reading the Vampire* (New York: Routledge, 1994), briefly develops (see p. 107)—it is possible to read the demonization of Max in *The Lost Boys* as the response of a beleaguered movie industry to the rise in the 1980s of a new service class catering to the privatized consumption of film product.

87. Christopher Craft, "'Kiss Me with Those Red Lips': Gender and Inversion in Bram Stoker's *Dracula*," in *Dracula: The Vampire and The Critics*, ed. Margaret L. Carter (Ann Arbor, Michigan: UMI Research Press, 1988), pp. 167–94; the quotation is from p. 167.

88. Grossberg, *We Gotta Get Out of This Place*, p. 178.

89. Dick Hebdige, *Subculture: The Meaning of Style* (New York: Methuen, 1979), pp. 94–95.

90. Somtow, *Vampire Junction*, p. 352.

CHAPTER TWO

1. The pathbreaking character of Rice's work has been widely acknowledged, but Romero's movie, the most innovative and challenging vampire film of the period, has been woefully neglected by critics. One exception to this stricture is Judith Roof, whose *Reproductions of Reproduction: Imaging Symbolic Change* (New York: Routledge, 1996) includes a brief analysis of *Martin* (pp. 166–67) that offers some suggestive, if ungrounded, speculations linking the vampire with cybernetic-digital technologies: "Just as the computer screen can effect sudden appearances, transect space, and appear to telescope time, so the vampire's metonymical transport and uncanny appearances seem like inventions of a computer logic" (p. 168). Like similar arguments by Donna Haraway and Allucquère Rosanne Stone discussed in my introduction, Roof's connection between vampire and cyborg is analogical, not dialectical, in nature.

2. On deindustrialization in the United States, see Barry Bluestone and Bennett Harrison, *The Deindustrialization of America: Plant Closings, Community Abandonment, and the Dismantling of Basic Industry* (New York: Basic, 1982); and Kathryn Marie Dudley, *The End of the Line: Lost Jobs, New Lives in Postindustrial America* (Chicago: University of Chicago Press, 1994). For evidence of the socioeconomic fallout, specifically in Pennsylvania communities, see John C. Raines, Lenora E. Berson, and David McI. Gracie, eds., *Community and Capital in Conflict: Plant Closings and Job Loss* (Philadelphia: Temple University Press, 1982).

3. Quoted in Mary Ellen Schoonmaker, "Memories of Overdevelopment," *American Film* (October 1985): 47–49; the quotation is from pp. 48–49. Schoonmaker describes Buba's style as "part cinema verité and part home movie, part documentary and part drama" (p. 49)—which equally characterizes the texture and tone of *Martin*. Paul R. Gagne, in *The Zombies That Ate Pittsburgh: The Films of George A. Romero* (New York: Dodd, Mead, 1987), compares *Martin* with the work of Buba, and describes Buba's and Romero's working relationship, not only on *Martin* but also on *Dawn of the Dead* (pp. 73–77, 94–96).

4. This bleak vision was further expanded by Romero in his film *Dawn of the Dead* (1979), in which zombies replace vampires as consumers of human beings. Nothing more than "pure motorized instinct," the zombies—wandering aimlessly through a shopping mall—represent Romero's scathingly dystopian view of the modern shopper, literally dehumanized by the uncontrollable urge to consume. Anne Friedberg has commented on the film's "lobotomized exaggeration of consumer robotics" (*Window Shopping: Cinema and the Postmodern* [Berkeley and Los Angeles: University of California Press, 1993], p. 116).

5. Stuart Hall and Tony Jefferson, eds., *Resistance through Rituals: Youth Subcultures in Post-War Britain* (London: Harper Collins, 1976), p. 47. The Birmingham school derives the term *magical solution* from Phil Cohen's 1972 Working Paper, "Subcultural Conflict and Working-Class Community," recently reprinted in his book *Rethinking the Youth Question: Education, Labour, and Cultural Studies* (Durham, N.C.: Duke University Press, 1999), pp. 48–63.

6. For overviews of the "new class" debate, see B. Bruce-Briggs, *The New Class?* (New Brunswick: Transaction, 1979); and Val Burris, "The Discovery of the New Middle Class," *Theory and Society* 15 (1986): 317–49. For discussions of the evolution of the service sector in the postwar period, see Barbara Ehrenreich and John Ehrenreich, "The Professional-Managerial Class," *Radical America* 7, no. 2 (1977): 7–31;

and Scott Lash and John Urry, *The End of Organized Capitalism* (Cambridge: Polity, 1987), pp. 161–78.

7. See, for example, Martyn J. Lee, *Consumer Culture Reborn: The Cultural Politics of Consumption* (New York: Routledge, 1993), pp. 165–72.

8. Pierre Bourdieu, *Distinction: A Social Critique of the Judgment of Taste*, trans. Richard Nice (Cambridge, Mass.: Harvard University Press, 1984), pp. 310–11. Subsequent references are to this translation and appear in the text.

9. Lee, *Consumer Culture Reborn*, p. 165.

10. Bourdieu, *Distinction*, p. 365.

11. Sharon Zukin, *Loft Living: Culture and Capital in Urban Change* (Baltimore: Johns Hopkins University Press, 1982), p. 58. See also J. John Palen and Bruce London, eds., *Gentrification, Displacement and Neighborhood Revitalization* (Albany, N.Y.: SUNY Press, 1985). For evidence that gentrification was a fraught process, marked by neighborhood resistance and protest, see Caroline Mills, "Myths and Meanings of Gentrification," in *Place/Culture/Representation*, ed. James Duncan and David Ley (New York: Routledge, 1993), pp. 149–70.

12. Sharon Zukin, "Gentrification: Culture and Capital in the Urban Core," *Annual Review of Sociology* 13 (1987): 129–47; the quotation is from p. 143.

13. Zukin, *Loft Living*, p. 176.

14. Ibid., p. 180.

15. The term *yuppie* received widespread public currency in the early 1980s, crystallized in the December 31, 1984, *Newsweek* cover story proclaiming "The Year of the Yuppie." Advertisers avidly courted this group throughout the decade: see, for example, Gregory Miller, "The Wooing of the Yuppie," *Institutional Investor* 18 (December 1984): 151–52ff. For background on the term itself, see Paul Leinberger and Bruce Tucker, *The New Individualists: The Generation after "The Organization Man"* (New York: HarperCollins, 1991), pp. 273–76; and Hendrik Hertzberg, "The Short Happy Life of the American Yuppie," in *Culture in an Age of Money: The Legacy of the 1980s in America*, ed. Nicolaus Mills (Chicago: Ivan R. Dee, 1990), pp. 66–82.

16. Leinberger and Tucker, *The New Individualists*, p. 276.

17. Mike Featherstone, *Consumer Culture and Postmodernism* (Newbury Park, Calif.: SAGE, 1991), p. 91.

18. David Harvey, *The Condition of Postmodernity: An Enquiry into the Origins of Cultural Change* (Cambridge, Mass.: Blackwell, 1990), pp. 3–5. Mike Featherstone's "City Cultures and Post-modern Lifestyles" (in *Post-Fordism: A Reader*, ed. Ash Amin [Cambridge, Mass.: Blackwell, 1994], pp. 387–408) likewise develops a post-Fordist take on urbanism that converges with Raban's descriptions.

19. Jonathan Raban, *Soft City* (London: Hamilton, 1974; the edition cited hereafter in the text is New York: Harvill, 1988), pp. 169–70.

20. Jean Baudrillard, *Symbolic Exchange and Death*, trans. Iain Hamilton Grant (Thousand Oaks, Calif.: SAGE, 1998), p. 111.

21. Sandra Tomc, in "Dieting and Damnation: Anne Rice's *Interview with the Vampire*" (in *Blood Read: The Vampire as Metaphor in Contemporary Culture*, ed. Joan Gordon and Veronica Hollinger [Philadelphia: University of Pennsylvania Press, 1997], pp. 95–114), uses the term *yuppie* to describe the lifestyle of Rice's vampires, but she is primarily interested in their undead eating habits as symbols of diet crazes

in the 1970s United States; her analysis, while fascinating, does not amount to a systematic investigation (or critique) of the yuppie vampire in Rice's text.

22. Anne Rice, *Interview with the Vampire* (New York: Knopf, 1976; the edition cited hereafter in the text is New York: Ballantine, 1988), p. 89.

23. As David Punter has observed in his *Literature of Terror: A History of Gothic Fictions from 1765 to the Present Day, Volume 2: The Modern Gothic* (New York: Longman, 1996), these vampiric strollers are "the very image of the *flâneur*" of Baudelaire and Benjamin (p. 162); they are thus the urban precursors of the suburban mall-browsing vampires discussed in chapter 1.

24. In contrast to my reading, Devon Hodges and Janice L. Doane, in "Undoing Feminism in Anne Rice's Vampire Chronicles" (in *Modernity and Mass Culture*, ed. James Naremore and Patrick Brantlinger [Bloomington: Indiana University Press, 1991], pp. 158–75), argue—I think wrongheadedly—that *Interview* in fact "depends on an oedipal paradigm" (p. 159), recuperating the patriarchal family in an invidious fashion.

25. Two other major texts in this scanty tradition follow a similar pattern to *Martin* in foregrounding family as the social horizon of vampiric agency: Theodore Sturgeon's novel *Some of Your Blood* (1961) and Kathryn Bigelow's film *Near Dark* (1987).

26. Karl Marx and Friedrich Engels, "Manifesto of the Communist Party," in *The Marx-Engels Reader*, ed. Robert C. Tucker, 2d ed. (New York: Norton, 1978), pp. 469–500; the quotation is from p. 475.

27. Rice, *Interview with the Vampire*, p. 83.

28. See, for example, John Skipp and Craig Spector's *Light at the End* (New York: Bantam, 1986); Poppy Z. Brite's *Lost Souls* (New York: Delacorte, 1992), discussed in chapter 3; and Laurell K. Hamilton's Club Vampyre series, beginning with *Guilty Pleasures* (New York: Ace, 1993). See also films such as *Near Dark* and *The Addiction* (1995).

29. See, for example, Tanith Lee's Blood Opera sequence—*Dark Dance* (1992), *Personal Darkness* (1993), and *Darkness, I* (1994)—and Elaine Bergstrom's Austras series, which began with *Shattered Glass* (1989). See also films such as *The Hunger* and *Nadja* (1994).

30. Skipp and Spector, *The Light at the End*, p. 16. Subsequent references appear in the text.

31. Dick Hebdige, *Subculture: The Meaning of Style* (New York: Methuen, 1979), p. 66; and Neil Nehring, *Flowers in the Dustbin: Culture, Anarchy, and Postwar England* (Ann Arbor: University of Michigan Press, 1993), pp. 282–85. The observation about the 1970s as a frustrating period of transition for consumers is a direct quotation from Dave Laing, "Interpreting Punk Rock," *Marxism Today* (April 1978): 128.

32. Skipp and Spector, *The Light at the End*, p. 104.

33. On the gentrification of the Docklands area, see Janet Foster, *Docklands: Urban Change and Conflict in a Community in Transition* (London: UCL, 1999).

34. Anne Billson, *Suckers* (New York: Atheneum, 1993), p. 16. Subsequent references appear in the text.

35. Lee, *Consumer Culture Reborn*, pp. 151–52.

36. Billson, *Suckers*, pp. 69–70.

37. Billson's cultural prescience in crafting this series of ads is extraordinary when one considers the recent television commercial for Ray-Ban sunglasses, run frequently on MTV, that depicts a flock of trendy teen vampires languidly sunning

themselves and mocking one of their number who, foolish enough not to wear his shades, is promptly burned to a crisp.

38. Michael Cadnum, *The Judas Glass* (New York: Carroll & Graf, 1996), pp. 15–16. Subsequent references appear in the text.

39. On California's environmentalist yuppies, see David Weddle, "Living on Hobo Time," *California* 15, no. 2 (February 1990): 68–71.

40. Christopher Moore, *Bloodsucking Fiends: A Love Story* (New York: Simon & Schuster, 1995), p. 22.

41. Ibid., pp. 91–92.

42. For background on Joshua Norton, see William Drury, *Norton I, Emperor of the United States* (New York: Dodd, Mead, 1986).

43. On Jim Clark's yacht, see Michael Lewis, *The New New Thing: A Silicon Valley Story* (New York: Norton, 2000), pp. 19–27; and David A. Kaplan, *The Silicon Boys and Their Valley of Dreams* (New York: Morrow, 1999), pp. 297–300; the *Fortune* quotation, from the magazine's annual "Celebrating Life outside the Office" issue, is on pp. 297–98.

44. Moore, *Bloodsucking Fiends*, p. 41. Subsequent references appear in the text.

CHAPTER THREE

1. The term is Eve Kosofsky Sedgwick's: see her *Epistemology of the Closet* (Berkeley and Los Angeles: University of California Press, 1990), pp. 186–90. For treatments of the vampire as a paradigmatic icon of unleashed and/or demonized homoeroticism, see Sue-Ellen Case, "Tracking the Vampire," *Differences* 3, no. 2 (1991): 1–20; and Paulina Palmer's chapter on the vampire in her *Lesbian Gothic: Transgressive Fictions* (New York: Cassell, 1999), pp. 99–127.

2. Christopher Craft, " 'Kiss Me with Those Red Lips': Gender and Inversion in Bram Stoker's *Dracula*," in *Dracula: The Vampire and The Critics*, ed. Margaret L. Carter (Ann Arbor, Mich.: UMI Research Press, 1988), 167–94; see especially pp. 169–72.

3. A good example is Joseph Bierman's "*Dracula*: Prolonged Childhood Illness, and the Oral Triad," *American Imago* 29 (1972): 186–98. Such readings generally derive from Ernest Jones's influential analysis of the vampire icon as a condensation of sadistic orality (*On the Nightmare* [New York: Liveright, 1971], pp. 98–130). On the vampire as a figure of anality, see Ellis Hanson, "Undead," in *Inside/Out: Lesbian Theories, Gay Theories*, ed. Diana Fuss (New York: Routledge, 1991), pp. 324–40. Maurice Richardson's "The Psychoanalysis of Ghost Stories," *Twentieth Century* 166 (1959): 419–31, conflates virtually every possible Freudian reading in his view of *Dracula* as "a kind of incestuous, necrophilous, oral-anal-sadistic all-in wrestling match" (p. 427). Clearly, the figure is a site of tremendous libidinal perturbation.

4. Richard Dyer, "Children of the Night: Vampirism as Homosexuality, Homosexuality as Vampirism," in *Sweet Dreams: Sexuality, Gender and Popular Fiction*, ed. Susannah Radstone (London: Lawrence and Wishart, 1988), pp. 47–72; the quotations are from pp. 59 and 65.

5. Katherine Ramsland, *Prism of the Night: A Biography of Anne Rice* (New York: Dutton, 1991), pp. 105, 115–16.

6. See Jennet Conant, "Lestat, C' est Moi," *Esquire* (March 1994): 70ff.

7. Judith E. Johnson, "Women and Vampires: Nightmare or Utopia?" *Kenyon Review* 15, no. 1 (winter 1993): 72–80; the quotation is from p. 73.

8. Leerom Medovoi, "Mapping the Rebel Image: Postmodernism and the Mas-

culinist Politics of Rock in the U.S.A.," *Cultural Critique* 20 (1991-92): 153–88; the quotation is from pp. 181–82 (emphasis in original).

9. Mark Simpson, *Male Impersonators: Men Performing Masculinity* (New York: Routledge, 1994), p. 114.

10. Andrew Wernick, "From Voyeur to Narcissist: Imaging Men in Contemporary Advertising," in *Beyond Patriarchy: Essays by Men on Pleasure, Power, and Change*, ed. Michael Kaufman (New York: Oxford University Press, 1987), pp. 277–97; the quotations are from pp. 292 and 282. The marketing term for these sorts of gender-indefinite ads is "gay window advertising"—in other words, gays are provided an accessible "window" onto the commodity world, one through which heterosexuals also gaze.

11. Wernick, "From Voyeur to Narcissist," p. 96; emphasis mine.

12. Diana Fuss, "Fashion and the Homospectatorial Look," *Critical Inquiry* 18 (1992): 713–37; the quotations are from pp. 713 (emphasis in original), 730, and 729.

13. John Fekete, "Vampire Value, Infinitive Art, and Literary Theory: A Topographic Meditation," in *Life After Postmodernism: Essays on Value and Culture*, ed. Fekete (New York: St. Martin's, 1987), pp. 64–85; the quotation is from p. 72.

14. In "Fashion and the Homospectatorial Look," Fuss reproduces a series of fashion images in which women expose their defenseless throats to the viewer's gaze; she also analyzes an ad that literally depicts the fashion system as a vampire (pp. 730–35).

15. John Rechy, *The Vampires* (New York: Grove, 1971; the edition cited hereafter in the text is New York: Grove, 1982), p. 102.

16. On Warhol's Factory and the films it generated, see Michael O'Pray, ed., *Andy Warhol: Film Factory* (London: BFI, 1989); a more general study of the subcultural milieu is Juan Antonio Suarez, *Bike Boys, Drag Queens, and Superstars: Avant-Garde, Mass Culture, and Gay Identities in the 1960s Underground Cinema* (Bloomington: Indiana University Press, 1996).

17. Mary Woronov, *Swimming Underground: My Years in the Warhol Factory* (Boston: Journey, 1995), pp. 185–86. Woronov's conflation of vampiric and wormlike imagery in this passage contains a clever reference to one of the obscurer novels of *Dracula* author Bram Stoker, *The Lair of the White Worm* (1911).

18. Rechy, *The Vampires*, pp. 215, 259.

19. Kim Newman, *Andy Warhol's Dracula* (Leeds, England: PS Publishing, 1999). Subsequent references appear in the text. The story is part of Newman's alternative-history vampire series, which began with *Anno Dracula* (1992), whose basic narrative assumption is that the tale told by Bram Stoker in his 1897 novel was literally true—save for the fact that Dracula's invasion of England, rather than being thwarted, was a complete success. The series systematically develops a complex vision of twentieth-century political and cultural history in which a vampire elite has come to coexist with the mass of humanity; in this context, Warhol's fascination with the trendy international jet set of the 1960s and 1970s takes on distinctly sinister connotations. Newman cleverly weaves into his fiction known facts about Warhol's life and art, drawing upon while subtly falsifying extant critical sources (some of them cited here). Many of the passages that I quote from the story are "citations" from these sources, which are rendered in italics in the original—textual emphases that I have removed for the sake of convenience.

20. On the history of gay physique pictorials, see F. Valentine Hooven III, *Beef-*

cake: The Muscle Magazines of America, 1950–1970 (Cologne: Benedikt Taschen, 1996), which includes background on Dallesandro's early nude posing sessions. Information on *Interview* magazine can be found in Victor Bochris, *The Life and Death of Andy Warhol* (New York: Bantam, 1989), pp. 276–78. On Bruce Weber's advertising strategies, see the *Interview* retrospective in which the photographer muses on his conception of masculine beauty: "Blame It on My Youth," *Interview* 26, no. 2 (February 1996): 100–105. For a discussion of homoerotic narcissism in contemporary youth-oriented magazines such as *The Face*, see Sean Nixon, "Have You Got the Look? Masculinities and Shopping Spectacle," in *Lifestyle Shopping: The Subject of Consumption*, ed. Rob Shields (New York: Routledge, 1992), pp. 149–69.

21. For coverage of Meisel's career, in which the photographer's debts to Warhol are discussed, see Michael Gross, "Madonna's Magician," *New York* (12 October 1992): 28–36.

22. For an analysis of the aesthetics of these ads, see Collier Schorr, "Eau de Teen Spirit," *Artforum* 33 (February 1995): 16.

23. Bob Garfield, "Publicity Monster Turns on Klein," *Advertising Age* (4 September 1995): 18.

24. For general coverage of the controversy, see Barbara Lippert, "The Naked Untruth," *Adweek* (18 September 1995): 26ff. Critiques of the ads in terms of their commodification of youthful sexuality include Camille Paglia, "Kids for Sale," *Advocate* (31 October 1995): 80; and Henry A. Giroux, "Something Comes Between Kids and Their Calvins: Youthful Desire and Commercialized Pleasures," in his *Channel Surfing: Race Talk and the Destruction of Today's Youth* (New York: St. Martin's, 1997), pp. 21–34. Interestingly, despite all the media uproar, average consumers rated the ads only a 6.37 on a scale of 10 for prurient appeal, and teenage consumers claimed they would be willing, if asked, to pose in similar ads: see Dan Lippe, "Readers Rate Klein's 'Porn' Campaign," *Advertising Age* (4 September 1995): 34; and Lucky Vittert, Sara Teasdale, and Alan Salomon, "Teen-agers Wonder, 'What's the Fuss?'" *Advertising Age* (4 September 1995): 35.

25. Simpson, *Male Impersonators*, p. 102; Fuss, "Fashion and the Homospectatorial Look," pp. 730 (emphasis in original) and 736.

26. Danae Clark, "Commodity Lesbianism," *Camera Obscura* 25–26 (1991): 180–201; the quotations are from p. 196.

27. Lauren Berlant and Elizabeth Freeman, "Queer Nationality," in *Fear of a Queer Planet: Queer Politics and Social Theory*, ed. Michael Warner (Minneapolis: University of Minnesota Press, 1993), pp. 193–229; the quotation is from p. 208.

28. For readings of the film along these lines, see Ken Gelder, *Reading the Vampire* (New York: Routledge, 1994), p. 106; and Elaine Showalter, *Sexual Anarchy: Gender and Culture at the Fin-de-siècle* (New York: Penguin, 1990), p. 183.

29. Berlant and Freeman, "Queer Nationality," pp. 210–11.

30. Michael Dare, "Billion Dollar Director: Critic's Take on Action Auteur," *Daily Variety* (6 August 1996), available at <http://home.earthlink.net/~dare2b/tonyscot.htm>.

31. Nina Auerbach, *Our Vampires, Ourselves* (Chicago: University of Chicago Press, 1995), pp. 57–59. It is definitely true that, during the 1980s, *Interview* magazine—and Warhol himself—fell rather embarrassingly under the regal spell of the Reagans: see Bochris, *The Life and Death of Andy Warhol*, pp. 322–23.

32. Nicola Nixon, "When Hollywood Sucks: or, Hungry Girls, Lost Boys, and

Vampirism in the Age of Reagan," in *Blood Read: The Vampire as Metaphor in Contemporary Culture*, ed. Joan Gordon and Veronica Hollinger (Philadelphia: University of Pennsylvania Press, 1997), pp. 115–28; the quotation is from p. 115.

33. Though Deneuve herself has denied being a lesbian—at one point even suing a lesbian magazine that had used her last name for its title (see David W. Dunlap, "For Lesbian Magazine, a Question of Image," *New York Times*, 8 January 1996, late edition, p. 41)—she continues to receive coverage in the gay press as a lesbian icon: see Judy Wieder, "Deneuve," *Advocate* [25 July 1995]: 50–55. Much more extensive, however, is mainstream treatment of Deneuve as a paragon of glamour and beauty: see, for example, "Catherine Deneuve: What Follows Perfection?" *Vogue* 178, no. 10 (October 1998): 206.

34. Nixon, "When Hollywood Sucks," p. 124. For a discussion of the film in terms of its invitation to a "bisexual spectatorship," see Maria Pramaggiore, "Straddling the Screen: Bisexual Spectatorship and Contemporary Narrative Film," in *Re-Presenting Bisexualities: Subjects and Cultures of Fluid Desire*, ed. Donald E. Hall and Maria Pramaggiore (New York: New York University Press, 1996): pp. 272–97.

35. See, for example, Jewelle Gomez, "Recasting the Mythology: Writing Vampire Fiction," in Gordon and Hollinger, eds., *Blood Read*, pp. 85–92, which argues that the film "falls apart at the end so completely that little analysis can be made of the characters or the intent" (p. 89).

36. Auerbach, *Our Vampires, Ourselves*, pp. 58–59.

37. Bowie's infamous coming-out interview, Michael Watts, "Oh You Pretty Thing," appeared in the 22 January 1972 issue of *Melody-Maker* magazine; it has been reprinted as Watts, "Oh You Pretty Thing," in *The Bowie Companion*, ed. Elizabeth Thomson and David Gutman (London: Macmillan, 1993), pp. 47–51.

38. Van M. Cagle, *Reconstructing Pop/Subculture: Art, Rock, and Andy Warhol* (Thousand Oaks, Calif.: SAGE, 1995), p. 46. Using the theories of youth subculture developed by the Birmingham school, Cagle carefully and convincingly traces the diffusion of Warholism through contemporary rock, via the Velvet Underground, Bowie, the New York Dolls, and others. Barney Hoskyns's *Glam!: Bowie, Bolan, and the Glitter Rock Revolution* (London: Faber and Faber, 1998) also acknowledges glitter's debts to Warhol: see especially pp. 24–27. As his various biographers make plain, Bowie himself was fascinated with the Factory scene (see, for example, Jerry Hopkins, *Bowie* [New York: Macmillan, 1985], pp. 70–71), a fascination that led to his 1971 song "Andy Warhol" and eventually culminated in his impersonation of the artist in Julian Schnabel's 1996 film *Basquiat*.

39. Iain Chambers, *Urban Rhythms: Pop Music and Popular Culture* (New York: St. Martin's, 1985), pp. 136, 211.

40. Fredric Jameson has interpreted this scene as signaling postmodernism's epochal challenge to the individual subject to (metaphorically) "grow new organs," thus permitting a more encompassing perspective on a fragmented culture: see *Postmodernism or, the Cultural Logic of Late Capitalism* (Durham, N.C.: Duke University Press, 1991), p. 31.

41. David Bowie, mid-1970s press conference, quoted in Henry Edwards and Tony Zanetta, *Stardust: The David Bowie Story* (New York: McGraw-Hill, 1986), p. 167.

42. Fred Vermorel and Judy Vermorel, *Starlust: The Secret Fantasies of Fans* (London: Comet, 1985). Subsequent references appear in the text. The individual fans

whose writings are featured in the book are identified only by first names, which are pseudonymous.

43. Jon Savage, "The Gender Bender," reprinted in Thomsen and Gutman, eds., *The Bowie Companion*, pp. 171–76; the quotation is from p. 172. Savage's essay originally appeared in the British magazine *The Face* in November 1980.

44. Vermorel and Vermorel, *Starlust*, p. 77.

45. Anne Rice, "David Bowie and the End of Gender," *Vogue* (November 1983); reprinted in Thomsen and Gutman, eds., *The Bowie Companion*, pp. 183–86; the quotations are from pp. 184 and 183.

46. Ibid., pp. 186, 183.

47. Rice herself has claimed that she modeled Lestat, at least in terms of his sonorous voice, on the Doors' Jim Morrison (Ramsland, *Prism of the Night*, p. 261)— another potent figure in the pantheon of youth-culture vampirism, since a poster of his face also presides over the Lost Boys' underground lair.

48. E. Ann Kaplan, *Rocking Around the Clock: Music Television, Postmodernism, and Consumer Culture* (New York: Methuen, 1987), p. 12.

49. Quentin J. Schultze and Roy M. Anker, eds., *Dancing in the Dark: Youth, Popular Culture, and the Electronic Media* (Grand Rapids, Mich.: Eerdmans, 1991), p. 202.

50. Linda Martin and Kerry Segrave's *Anti-Rock: The Opposition to Rock 'n' Roll* (New York: Da Capo, 1993) amply details this fractious history.

51. The remark appeared in Bowie's notorious "coming out" interview: see Watts, "Oh You Pretty Thing," p. 51.

52. For background on Gore's cultural activism, consult Steve Chapple and David Talbot, *Burning Desires: Sex in America, A Report from the Field* (New York: Doubleday, 1989), pp. 49–67. For a defense of maternal protests such as Gore's, see Jyotsna Kapur, "Out of Control: Television and the Transformation of Childhood in Late Capitalism," in *Kids' Media Culture*, ed. Marsha Kinder (Durham, N.C.: Duke University Press, 1999), pp. 122–36.

53. Tipper Gore, *Raising PG Kids in an X-Rated Society* (New York: Bantam, 1988), pp. 54–55. A similar view was voiced in a book authored by the head of the American Family Association, Rev. Donald Wildmon, whose title perfectly captures the anxious, almost paranoiac response of social conservatives to the unmonitored intrusion of television: *Home Invaders* (Wheaton, Ill.: Victor, 1986). A decade later, as we have seen, Wildmon would be campaigning against Calvin Klein advertisements as child pornography.

54. Carl A. Raschke, *Painted Black: From Drug Killings to Heavy Metal—The Alarming True Story of How Satanism Is Terrorizing Our Communities* (New York: Harper & Row, 1990), p. 169. Subsequent references appear in the text.

55. Attacks on heavy metal as a corrupt nest of satanic vice were myriad during the 1980s; a good overview of the scare is Jeffrey S. Victor's *Satanic Panic: The Creation of a Contemporary Legend* (Chicago: Open Court, 1993). For an ideological defense of heavy metal's flirtation with occult morbidity, see Donna Gaines, "For the Love of Death: The Spirituality of Death Metal," *Rock and Roll Quarterly* (fall 1993): 15–19.

56. There is, of course, an aesthetic continuity linking these forms of music. Glitter rock, in the person of Alice Cooper, strongly influenced what came to be known as "glam metal"—heavy-metal music played by androgynous, glitzy performers (on Cooper's career, see Cagle, *Reconstructing Pop/Subculture*, pp. 117–27)—and Goth

music developed out of punk/Industrial, which was indebted, at least in terms of its cultural postures, to Bowie (see Dick Hebdige, *Subculture: The Meaning of Style* [New York: Methuen, 1979], pp. 88–89). On the religious right's crusade against Goth subculture (including the activism of the ubiquitous Rev. Donald Wildmon), consult Jim D'Entremont, "The Devil's Disciples," *Index on Censorship* 27, no. 6 (November 1998): 32–39; this crusade erupted into the mainstream press in the aftermath of the high school shootings in Littleton, Colorado, in April 1999.

57. Allan Bloom, *The Closing of the American Mind* (New York: Touchstone, 1988), p. 74.

58. Ibid., pp. 74–75.

59. John Fiske, "MTV: Post-Structural, Post-Modern," *Journal of Communication Inquiry* 10, no. 1 (1986): 74–79; the quotation is from p. 75.

60. Ibid., p. 76.

61. Briankle G. Chang, "A Hypothesis on the Screen: MTV and/as (Postmodern) Signs," *Journal of Communication Inquiry* 10, no. 1 (1986): 70–73; the quotation is from p. 70; and Dan Rubey, "Voguing at the Carnival: Desire and Pleasure on MTV," *South Atlantic Quarterly* 90 (1991): 871–906; the quotation is from p. 889. For an argument that goes too far the other way, depicting MTV as an insidious capitalist hegemon bent on world domination, see Jack Banks, *Monopoly Television: MTV's Quest to Control the Music* (Boulder, Colo.: Westview, 1996). A well-balanced viewpoint, which acknowledges both the progressive and conservative aspects of MTV, is provided in Sally Stockbridge, "Rock Video: Pleasure and Resistance," in *Television and Women's Culture: The Politics of the Popular*, ed. Mary Ellen Brown (London: SAGE, 1990): pp. 102–13.

62. Robert Walser, *Running with the Devil: Power, Gender, and Madness in Heavy Metal Music* (Hanover, N.H.: Wesleyan University Press, 1993), p. 134.

63. Anne Rice, *The Vampire Lestat* (New York: Knopf, 1985; the edition cited hereafter in the text is New York: Ballantine, 1986), p. 3.

64. Here, Rice shows that she knows her vampire history; the French *philosophes* did indeed use the term in their indictment of the social depredations of kings and councilors: see Christopher Frayling, "From Lord Byron to Count Dracula," in *Vampyres: Lord Byron to Count Dracula*, ed. Frayling (London: Faber & Faber, 1991), pp. 30–31. With its ruthless portrait of Byron as a decadent fiend, John Polidori's "The Vampyre" (1819), the story that established the genre in English, gave literary expression to the middle-class resentment of aristocratic privileges and pretensions— though, as Nina Auerbach has shrewdly observed, there was an undercurrent of homoerotic attraction built into this resentment (see *Our Vampires, Ourselves*, pp. 14–21).

65. In the novel, the secretive vampire subculture supports an entire global network of taverns and cabarets, collectively dubbed "The Vampire Connection" and individually named for famous literary and cinematic bloodsuckers. There can be little doubt that Rice is here allegorizing urban gay subculture: not only do a number of her allusions—"Carmilla," *Dracula's Daughter*—reference notorious texts of "homosexual panic," but generally designating these bars as places for "vampire connection" plays on gay slang for sexual pick-ups.

66. Andrew Goodwin, *Dancing in the Distraction Factory: Music Television and Popular Culture* (Minneapolis: University of Minnesota Press, 1992), p. 95.

67. Rice, *The Vampire Lestat*, p. 5.

68. Ibid., p. 536.

69. Simon Frith, *Music for Pleasure: Essays in the Sociology of Pop* (New York: Routledge, 1980), p. 165.

70. Ibid., p. 176.

71. See Dean Anthony, *Frankie Goes to Hollywood* (Guildford, England: Colour Library, 1984), which details how the British press demonized the group for alleged gay scandals.

72. Rice, *The Vampire Lestat*, p. 7. Subsequent references appear in the text.

73. Frith, *Music for Pleasure*, p. 195.

74. Brite has become a doyenne of the Goth scene in New Orleans—where Rice also resides—in large part because, according to Mick Mercer, "Brite seems believable where Rice doesn't," since she "does similar things in reality" to what is depicted in her books (*Hex Files: The Goth Bible* [Woodstock, N.Y.: Overlook, 1997], pp. 170–71). In short, her fans view Brite as committed to the Goth/vampire lifestyle, whereas Rice merely profits from it. For an excellent discussion of Brite's relationship to a broad spectrum of Goth texts dealing with subculture and sexuality, see Trevor Holmes, "Coming Out of the Closet: Gay Males and Queer Goths in Contemporary Vampire Fiction," in *Blood Read*, ed. Gordon and Hollinger, pp. 169–88 (especially pp. 181–83); see also Richard Davenport-Hines, *Gothic: Four Hundred Years of Excess, Horror, Evil and Ruin* (New York: North Point, 1998), which analyzes Brite's fiction within the context of contemporary Gothic music and film culture (pp. 359–69).

75. Poppy Z. Brite, *Lost Souls* (New York: Delacorte, 1992), p. 186. Subsequent references appear in the text.

76. Brite's vision of a family of vampires travelling the highways in a stolen black van is almost certainly an allusion to the 1987 film *Near Dark*, with its pack of road-bound bloodsuckers. It is also a slacker echo of the Beat ethos of the 1950s, where hitting the road involved a countercultural rejection of mainstream society. For more on this subject, see my discussion of the post-Fordist road novel in chapter Five.

77. Rice, *The Vampire Lestat*, p. 537.

78. Jess Mowry, *Way Past Cool* (New York: HarperPerennial, 1993), p. 162.

CHAPTER FOUR

1. Stuart Ewen, *Captains of Consciousness: Advertising and the Social Roots of the Consumer Culture* (New York: McGraw-Hill, 1976), p. 146.

2. Douglas Rushkoff, *Playing the Future: How Kids' Culture Can Teach Us to Thrive in an Age of Chaos* (New York: HarperCollins, 1996), p. 3.

3. Ibid.

4. Frank Webster, *Theories of the Information Society* (New York: Routledge, 1995), p. 161.

5. See N. J. Thrift, "New Times and Spaces? The Perils of Transition Models," *Environment and Planning D: Society and Space* 7, no. 2 (1989): 127–28; and Ash Amin, "Post-Fordism: Models, Fantasies and Phantoms of Transition," in *Post-Fordism: A Reader*, ed. Ash Amin (Cambridge, Mass.: Blackwell, 1994), pp. 1–39.

6. Regulation school theory—especially the work of Michel Aglietta—is usually seen as a variant of neo-Fordism. For an overview of neo-Fordist theory, see Chris Smith, "Flexible Specialisation, Automation and Mass Production," *Work, Employment & Society* 3, no. 2 (June 1989): 203–20.

7. Webster, *Theories of the Information Society*, p. 156; emphasis added.

8. On the transition to "batch" or "just-in-time" production lines, see Andrew

Sayer, "New Developments in Manufacturing: The Just-in-Time System," *Capital and Class* 30 (winter 1986): 43–72; and Patrick Dawson and Janette Webb, "New Production Arrangements: The Totally Flexible Cage?" *Work, Employment and Society* 3, no. 2 (June 1989): 221–38.

9. Some critics have argued that post-Fordism is essentially postindustrialism in refurbished guise: see, for example, Krishan Kumar, "New Theories of Industrial Society," in *Education for Economic Survival: From Fordism to Post-Fordism?* ed. Philip Brown and Hugh Lauder (New York: Routledge, 1992), pp. 45–75, especially p. 47.

10. Anna Pollert, in "Dismantling Flexibility" (*Capital & Class* 3 [spring 1988]: 42–75), has remarked on this "futurological" tendency, which she sees as forging clear links between post-Fordism and postindustrialism (p. 43).

11. Alvin Toffler, *Future Shock* (New York: Bantam, 1971), p. 25. Subsequent references appear in the text.

12. Daniel Bell, "Notes on the Post-Industrial Society," in *The Technological Threat*, ed. Jack D. Douglas (Englewood Cliffs, N.J.: Prentice-Hall, 1971), pp. 8–20; the quotation is from p. 9; emphases in original. In his review of the critical reception of his theory of postindustrialism in *The Coming of Post-Industrial Society: A Venture in Social Forecasting* (New York: Basic, 1973), Bell bemoaned its reduction to a notion of "'future schlock,' in which breathless prose is mistaken for the pace of change" (p. ix)—a clear attack on Toffler, whom he later dismissed as a mere "popularize[r]" (p. 318). While Bell does have a point—that Toffler overemphasizes the effect of technological change in everyday life, whereas Bell's theory focuses exclusively on the growth of specialized knowledges—he is also clearly concerned to segregate academic consideration of his arguments from best-seller treatments, a partisan division of the terrain that is not of principal concern to me here. For an alternative genealogy of postindustrial ideas that includes the work of "popularizers" such as Lewis Mumford, Marshall McLuhan, and R. Buckminster Fuller, see William Kuhns, *The Post-Industrial Prophets: Interpretations of Technology* (New York: Weybright and Talley, 1971); see also the chapter "Defining the Post-Industrial" in Margaret Rose, *The Post-Modern and the Post-Industrial: A Critical Analysis* (Cambridge: Cambridge University Press, 1991), which traces the roots of the term to social philosophers of the 1910s influenced by late-Victorian critiques of capitalism (pp. 21–25).

13. Toffler, *Future Shock*, p. 38.

14. Boris Frankel, *The Post-Industrial Utopians* (Madison: University of Wisconsin Press, 1987), p. 15.

15. For a comparison of Bell's and Touraine's conceptions of postindustrialism along different lines than I pursue here, see Krishan Kumar, *Prophecy and Progress: The Sociology of Industrial and Post-Industrial Society* (New York: Penguin, 1978), pp. 198–99.

16. Alain Touraine, *The Post-Industrial Society; Tomorrow's Social History: Classes, Conflicts and Culture in the Programmed Society*, trans. Leonard F. X. Mayhem (New York: Random House, 1971), pp. 222, 105.

17. Ibid., p. 10.

18. Bell, *The Coming of Post-Industrial Society*, pp. 154, 344.

19. Ibid., pp. 478, 477, 480.

20. Touraine, *The Post-Industrial Society*, p. 202.

21. Bell, *The Coming of Post-Industrial Society*, p. 478.

22. Touraine, *The Post-Industrial Society*, p. 200.

23. André Gorz, *Paths to Paradise: On the Liberation from Work*, trans. Malcolm Imrie (Boston: Sound End, 1985), p. 29. Subsequent references are to this translation and appear in the text.

24. A valuable critical survey of this tradition is Fred Block, *Postindustrial Possibilities: A Critique of Economic Discourse* (Berkeley and Los Angeles: University of California Press, 1990).

25. Larry Hirschhorn, *Beyond Mechanization: Work and Technology in a Postindustrial Age* (Cambridge, Mass.: MIT, 1984), pp. 169, 98.

26. Shoshana Zuboff, *In the Age of the Smart Machine: The Future of Work and Power* (New York: Basic, 1988), pp. 296, 309.

27. Once again, Toffler's approach tends to encompass both left- and right-wing perspectives, as witness the fact that his book has been embraced not only by Gorz (see *Paths to Paradise*, pp. 81–91) but also by Newt Gingrich: see his foreword to Alvin and Heidi Toffler's *Creating a New Civilization: The Politics of the Third Wave* (Atlanta: Turner, 1995), pp. 13–18.

28. Alvin Toffler, *The Third Wave* (New York: Morrow, 1980), pp. 14, 246. Subsequent references appear in the text.

29. For a critique of Toffler's views on this score, see Vincent Mosco, *The Pay-Per Society: Computers and Communication in the Information Age* (Norwood, N.J.: Ablex, 1989), pp. 27–39.

30. Yoneji Masuda, *The Information Society as Post-Industrial Society* (Washington, D.C.: World Future Society, 1981), p. 147. Masuda's enthusiasm tends to express itself in eruptions of italics, which I have suppressed in the various quotations given here.

31. Ibid., p. 136.

32. Ibid., p. 138.

33. Bell, *The Coming of Post-Industrial Society*, pp. 267–98.

34. Annalee Saxenian, *Regional Advantage: Culture and Competition in Silicon Valley and Route 128* (Cambridge, Mass.: Harvard University Press, 1994), p. 56; subsequent references appear in the text. See also Kevin Morgan and Andrew Sayer, *Microcircuits of Capital: "Sunrise" Industry and Uneven Development* (London: Polity, 1998).

35. The literature on venture capital and its relationship to high-tech entrepreneurship, in Silicon Valley and elsewhere, is extensive; see, for example, W. Keith Schilit, *Dream Makers and Deal Breakers: Inside the Venture Capital Industry* (Englewood Cliffs, N.J.: Prentice Hall, 1991); and Steve Harmon, *Zero Gravity: Riding Venture Capital from High-Tech Start-Up to Breakout IPO* (Princeton, N.J.: Bloomberg, 1999). There is also strong coverage of venture capitalist enterprises in the various studies of Silicon Valley cited below.

36. Of the roughly eight thousand high-tech firms in the Valley in the early 1980s, 70 percent employed less than ten people and 85 percent less than 50: see Everett M. Rogers and Judith K. Larsen, *Silicon Valley Fever: Growth of High-Technology Culture* (New York: Basic, 1984), p. 58. A good case study of a fledgling firm is Jerry Kaplan, *Startup: A Silicon Valley Adventure* (New York: Penguin, 1994).

37. See Sam Masud, "Young and Restless: Four Start-Ups Bring Their Wares to Market," *Telecommunications* 32, no. 11 (November 1998): 60–61; and Luisa Kroll, "Just Plain Uppity," *Forbes* 164, no. 7 (20 September 1999): 88.

38. Ian J. Lowden, "Pushy Upstarts," *International Business* 9 (October 1996): 12–16; and Robert Heller, "Monopolists Beware Upstarts," *Management Today* (April 1998): 31.

39. Meredith Bagby, "Celebration X," *Success* 45, no. 9 (September 1998): 22–23.

40. Kathleen L. Gregory, *Signing-Up: The Culture and Careers of Silicon Valley Computer People* (Ann Arbor, Mich.: UMI, 1987), p. 554 (emphasis in original). This ethnography was produced as a Ph.D. dissertation in the Department of Anthropology at Northwestern University, Evanston, Ill., in 1984.

41. Dennis Hayes, *Behind the Silicon Curtain: The Seductions of Work in a Lonely Era* (Boston: South End, 1989), pp. 16–17.

42. Neil Gerlach and Sheryl Hamilton, "Telling the Future, Managing the Present: Business Restructuring Literature as SF," *Science Fiction Studies* 27, no. 3 (November 2000): 461–77; the quotation is from p. 470. This excellent essay analyzes a number of recent business texts—such as William H. Davidow and Michael S. Malone, *The Virtual Corporation: Structuring and Revitalizing the Corporation for the 21st Century* (New York: HarperCollins, 1992) and Christopher Barnatt, *Cyber Business: Mindsets for a Wired Age* (New York: John Wiley & Sons, 1995)—showing how they deploy a rhetoric of cyborgization that converges with science fiction.

43. Chamber of commerce–style celebrations of sunrise industries as magical engines of wealth creation abound, ranging from lush coffee-table utopias—e.g., Ward Winslow, ed., *The Making of Silicon Valley: A 100 Year Renaissance* (Palo Alto, Calif.: Santa Clara Valley Historical Association, 1996)—to avid blueprints for regional and personal prosperity: see, for example, Roger Miller and Marcel Cote, *Growing the Next Silicon Valley: A Guide for Successful Regional Planning* (Lexington, Mass.: Lexington, 1987); and Christopher Meyer, *Relentless Growth: How Silicon Valley Innovative Strategies Can Work in Your Business* (New York: Free Press, 1997).

44. See Dirk Hanson, *The New Alchemists: Silicon Valley and the Micro-Electronics Revolution* (New York: Avon, 1982); Thomas Mahon, *Charged Bodies: People, Power, and Paradox in Silicon Valley* (New York: New American Library, 1985); Michael S. Malone, *The Big Score: The Billion Dollar Story of Silicon Valley* (New York: Doubleday, 1985); Robert X. Cringeley, *Accidental Empires: How the Boys of Silicon Valley Make Their Millions, Battle Foreign Competition, and Still Can't Get a Date* (Reading, Mass.: Addison-Wesley, 1992); and David A. Kaplan, *The Silicon Boys and Their Valley of Dreams* (New York: Morrow, 1999).

45. Stephen Segaller, *Nerds²·⁰·¹: A Brief History of the Internet* (New York: TV Books, 1998); and John Katz, *Geeks: How Two Lost Boys Rode the Internet out of Idaho* (New York: Villard, 2000).

46. Malone, *The Big Score*, p. 346.

47. A compelling portrait of the early days of Homebrew (sometimes variously spelled Home Brew) is in Paul Freiberger and Michael Swaine, *Fire in the Valley: The Making of the Personal Computer* (New York: McGraw Hill, 2000), pp. 144–55. The book formed the basis for a 1999 Turner Network Television movie entitled *Pirates of Silicon Valley*.

48. Hanson, *The New Alchemists*, p. 157; Mahon, *Charged Bodies*, p. 23.

49. Malone, *The Big Score*, pp. 8–9.

50. Cringeley, *Accidental Empires*, p. 8.

51. Theodore Roszak, *From Satori to Silicon Valley: San Francisco and the American Counterculture* (San Francisco: Don't Call It Frisco, 1986), p. 16.

52. William Braden, *The Age of Aquarius: Technology and the Cultural Revolution* (Chicago: Quadrangle, 1970), p. 294; Steven Anzovin, *The Green PC: Making Choices that Make a Difference* (San Francisco: Windcrest/McGraw-Hill, 1993).

53. Stewart Brand was reportedly the first person to use the term *personal computer* in print, in his book *II Cybernetic Frontiers* (New York: Random House, 1974). On top of publishing the semiannual *Whole Earth Catalog*, Brand was instrumental in establishing the "WELL" (Whole Earth 'Lectronic Link), a computer bulletin board devoted to issues linking technology and counterculture politics. Brand defends the connection between hippiedom and high tech in "We Owe It All to the Hippies," *Time* 145 (spring 1995): 54–56.

54. See Theodor H. Nelson, *Computer Lib: You Can and Must Understand Computers Now* (Chicago: Nelson, 1974); and the discussion in Freiberger and Swaine, *Fire in the Valley*, p. 113.

55. On the Electronic Frontiers Foundation, see Bruce Sterling, *The Hacker Crackdown: Law and Disorder on the Electronic Frontier* (New York: Ballantine, 1992), pp. 247–50; on technopaganism, see my discussion in chapter 6.

56. Malone, *The Big Score*, p. 346.

57. Cringeley, *Accidental Empires*, p. 17.

58. See the discussion in Freiberger and Swaine, *Fire in the Valley*, pp. 258–70 (which repeats the legend that Woz once "woke up the Pope" with a blue-box call). Actually, Wozniak did not exactly "invent" the blue box, but rather perfected a gizmo then in widespread use among phone phreakers; the practice of phreaking itself was popularized in the 1960s by the fabled counterculture hero Cap'n Crunch (a.k.a. John T. Draper)—who, after years of evading federal authorities for his tampering with the phone system, eventually became the president of a software company in Silicon Valley (see Mahon, *Charged Bodies*, pp. 216–29). Between his phone phreaking phase and his stint with Apple, Wozniak helped Jobs design the videogame Breakout! for Atari (a favorite, as we have seen, of David Sudnow's). A biography of Wozniak is Doug Carr, *Woz: The Prodigal Son of Silicon Valley* (New York: Avon, 1984), geared for young adults.

59. Kaplan, *The Silicon Boys and Their Valley of Dreams*, p. 99.

60. Ibid., p. 83.

61. Roy Dudley, interviewed by and quoted in Mahon, *Charged Bodies*, p. 60.

62. Ibid., p. 61.

63. Cringeley, *Accidental Empires*, p. 17.

64. Malone, *The Big Score*, p. 345.

65. See Kaplan, *The Silicon Boys and Their Valley of Dreams*, pp. 36–37.

66. Rogers and Larsen, *Silicon Valley Fever*, p. 41.

67. Malone, *The Big Score*, p. 286.

68. Rogers and Larsen, *Silicon Valley Fever*, p. 56; emphasis added.

69. Ibid., p. 52.

70. Lisa Margonelli, "The Next Big Wave," *San Francisco* (December 1997): p. 46ff.

71. For a discussion of how IBM saw this ad campaign as a way to rejuvenate its ebbing fortunes by capitalizing on the appeal of youthful imagery, see Bob Garfield,

"IBM Ad Leans on Clients to Let Big Blue Look Hip," *Advertising Age* (19 July 1993): 34. For some time, IBM kept a full script for the ad on its Web site, with links to a surfers' lexicon and a list of the "World's Top Ten Surf Spots."

72. Malone, *The Big Score*, p. 350.

73. For an application of "wave theory" to the competitive environment of high-tech investing, see T. G. Lewis, *The Friction-Free Economy: Marketing Strategies for a Wired World* (New York: HarperBusiness, 1997): "Wave theory says that oscillations created by a sudden change in one stock price propagate to other stock prices. Oscillations in the market share of one company can end up capsizing another company. . . . If a company has a large market share, it is less susceptible to unstable waves that pass through the systems of competitors" (p. 91). Such wave theories contrast with "bubble theory," which generally holds that high-tech stock prices are hyperinflated and subject to spectacular busts (as in fact occurred on the NASDAQ exchange during 2000–01): see Robert J. Shiller, *Irrational Exuberance* (Princeton, N.J.: Princeton University Press, 2000), whose title itself suggests a negative view of the youthful bravado informing high-tech business.

74. Kaplan, *The Silicon Boys and Their Valley of Dreams*, p. 101.

75. According to Kaplan, "the Valley on average produces sixty-four new millionaires every twenty-four hours, including Christmas" (ibid., p. 17).

76. Hanson, *The New Alchemists*, p. 217.

77. The popular magazine *Wired*, founded by Louis Rossetto in 1993, has devoted itself systematically to tracing this ethos, conflating coverage of high-tech businesses with leisure pursuits enabled by computers and other microelectronic machines.

78. Mahon, *Charged Bodies*, p. 103.

79. Rogers and Larsen, *Silicon Valley Fever*, p. 47.

80. Malone, *The Big Score*, p. 347.

81. For a case study, see Rogers and Larsen, *Silicon Valley Fever*, pp. 125–26.

82. Cringeley, *Accidental Empires*, pp. 249–50.

83. Quoted in Margonelli, "The Next Big Wave," p. 54.

84. Kaplan, *The Silicon Boys and Their Valley of Dreams*, pp. 80–81.

85. Roy Dudley, interviewed by and quoted in Mahon, *Charged Bodies*, p. 64.

86. Ellen Ullman, *Close to the Machine: Technophilia and Its Discontents* (San Francisco: City Lights, 1997), p. 95. Subsequent references appear in the text.

87. Kaplan, *The Silicon Boys and Their Valley of Dreams*, p. 59.

88. Ibid., pp. 49–59; Malone, *The Big Score*, pp. 93–112.

89. Malone, *The Big Score*, p. 105.

90. Kaplan, *The Silicon Boys and Their Valley of Dreams*, p. 52.

91. Malone, *The Big Score*, p. 113.

92. Hanson, *The New Alchemists*, p. 220.

93. Kaplan, *The Silicon Boys and Their Valley of Dreams*, p. 98.

94. See, for example, James Wallace, *Overdrive: Bill Gates and the Race to Control Cyberspace* (New York: John Wiley & Sons, 1997); and Jim Clark and Owen Edwards, *Netscape Time: The Making of the Billion-Dollar Start-up That Took on Microsoft* (New York: St. Martin's, 1999).

95. Hayes, *Behind the Silicon Curtain*, p. 22.

96. See John R. Gillis, *Youth and History: Tradition and Change in European Age*

Relations 1770–Present (New York: Academic Press, 1974), pp. 99–105; and Christine Griffin, *Representations of Youth: The Study of Youth and Adolescence in Britain and America* (Cambridge: Polity, 1993), pp. 11–26.

97. Tracy Kidder, *The Soul of a New Machine* (New York: Little Brown, 1981; the edition cited in the text is New York: Avon, 1982), p. 219. Subsequent references appear in the text.

98. Mahon, *Charged Bodies*, p. 33.

99. Malone, *The Big Score*, p. 277.

100. Kidder, *The Soul of a New Machine*, p. 226.

101. Hayes, in *Behind the Silicon Curtain*, argues that the intellectual skills required by programming have proven resistant to the traditional forms of rote deskilling favored by Taylorist approaches to manual labor, but this has not stopped management from imposing hierarchies of fragmentation and routine wherever possible (pp. 89–90).

102. See *Fever*, pp. 87–88, for a discussion of the job turnover rate in Silicon Valley, which may be as high as 50 percent annually in some occupations.

103. Rogers and Larsen, *Silicon Valley Fever*, p. 70.

104. Kaplan, *The Silicon Boys and Their Valley of Dreams*, pp. 104–5.

105. Studies of venture capitalism tend discreetly to euphemize this exploitation: Randy Komisar and Kent L. Lineback, *The Monk and the Riddle: The Education of a Silicon Valley Entrepreneur* (Cambridge, Mass.: Harvard Business School, 2000), for example, couches the relationship between venture capitalist and entrepreneur in a New Age rhetoric of cultivation and enlightened (self-)development.

106. Bennett Harrison, *Lean and Mean: The Changing Landscape of Corporate Power in the Age of Flexibility* (New York: Basic, 1994), p. 112.

107. See Susan Strange, *The Casino Society* (London: Blackwell, 1984), as well as her more recent *Casino Capitalism* (Manchester: Manchester University Press, 1997).

108. Bennett Harrison and Barry Bluestone, *The Great U-Turn: Corporate Restructuring and the Polarizing of America* (New York: Basic, 1988), pp. 114–15.

109. Bill Lessard and Steve Baldwin, *NetSlaves: True Tales of Working the Web* (New York: McGraw-Hill, 2000). See also Andrew Clement, "Office Automation and the Technical Control of Information Workers," in *The Political Economy of Information*, ed. Vincent Mosco and Janet Wasko (Madison: University of Wisconsin Press, 1988), pp. 217–46. For a treatment of the issue in the context of theories of post-Fordist society, see Stephen Wood, ed., *The Transformation of Work? Skill, Flexibility and the Labour Process* (London: Unwin Hyman, 1989).

110. On the labor hierarchy in Silicon Valley, see Marc A. Weiss, "High-Technology Industries and the Future of Employment," in *Silicon Landscapes*, ed. Peter Hall and Ann Markusen (Boston: Allen & Unwin, 1985), pp. 80–93. For a full grocery list of the mutagens and carcinogens workers routinely encounter in the ironically named "clean rooms" of the microelectronics industry, see Lenny Siegel and John Markoff, *The High Cost of High Tech: The Dark Side of the Chip* (New York: Harper & Row, 1985), p. 147; and Hayes, *Behind the Silicon Curtain*, pp. 63–80. While chip assemblers do wear protective clothing, this is to shield the delicate products they handle from human contamination.

111. For comparative studies of the economic prospects of the youth cohorts of the 1960s–70s versus the 1980s–90s, see Katherine S. Newman, *Declining Fortunes:*

The Withering of the American Dream (New York: Basic, 1993); and Kurt E. Schrammel, "A Comparison of Two Generations: Employment and Earnings of Young Adults in 1979 and 1994," *Occupational Outlook Quarterly* 40 (winter 1996–97): 23–29.

112. For evidence that the seemingly opposed rhetorics of flexibility and slackness can coexist in the same analysis, see Bruce Tulgan, "Generation X: Slackers? Or the Workforce of the Future?" *Employment Relations Today* 24 (summer 1997): 55–64, which offers a defense of so-called slackers as the ideal laborers for a flexible economy.

113. On Coupland as a literary spokesman for contemporary youth, see John Fraser, "The Dalai Lama of Generation X," *Saturday Night* 109 (March 1994): 8–9.

114. Michael Rogers, *Silicon Valley* (New York: Pocket, 1982).

115. See, for example, R. J. Pineiro, *Breakthrough* (New York: Forge, 1997); Sally Chapman, *Raw Data* (New York: St. Martin's, 1991); and Daniel Oran, *Ulterior Motive* (New York: Kensington, 1998).

116. Pat Dillon, *The Last Best Thing: A Classic Tale of Greed, Deception, and Mayhem in Silicon Valley* (New York: Simon & Schuster, 1996); Po Bronson, *The First $20 Million Is Always the Hardest* (New York: Random House, 1997); and Joe Hutsko, *The Deal* (New York: Tor, 1999). Dillon's book was serialized in Silicon Valley's hometown paper, the *San Jose Mercury News*, for which the author writes a column; Bronson produces feature articles for *The New York Times Magazine*, *Wired*, and other periodicals; Hutsko's freelance work has appeared in *Computer Life* and *PC World*, and he has also authored strategy guides to computer games such as Rebel Assault and Donkey Kong.

117. Douglas Coupland, *Microserfs* (New York: Regan, 1995), p. 154. Subsequent references appear in the text.

118. For a discussion of Coupland's treatment of this technonerd lifestyle that places it in the context of journalistic, filmic, and other depictions, see Lori Kendall, "Nerd Nation: Images of Nerds in U.S. Popular Culture," *International Journal of Cultural Studies* 2:2 (August 1999): 260–83.

119. Douglas Coupland, *Shampoo Planet* (New York: Pocket, 1992), pp. 199–201.

120. See Daniel Bell, *The End of Ideology: On the Exhaustion of Political Ideas in the Fifties* (Glencoe, Ill.: Free Press, 1960). For a critique of Bell's thesis, see Kevin Robins and Frank Webster, "Information As Capital: A Critique of Daniel Bell," in *The Ideology of the Information Age*, ed. Jennifer D. Slack and Fred Fejes (Norwood, N.J.: Ablex, 1987), pp. 95–117.

121. Coupland, *Microserfs*, p. 253. Subsequent references appear in the text.

122. It is possible that Coupland drew inspiration for the format of this dream journal from the quirky layout of Ted Nelson's *Computer Lib*.

123. On the effects of disembodiment in online communication, including the ambiguation of gender and other identity markers, see Allucquère Rosanne Stone, "Will the Real Body Please Stand Up?: Boundary Stories about Virtual Cultures," in *Cyberspace: First Steps*, ed. Michael Benedikt (Cambridge, Mass.: MIT, 1991), pp. 81–118; and Sherry Turkle, "Constructions and Reconstructions of the Self in Virtual Reality," in *Electronic Culture: Technology and Visual Representation*, ed. Timothy Druckrey (New York: Aperture, n.d.), pp. 354–65.

124. Coupland almost certainly drew his conception of *Oop!* from the mid-1980s collaborative project between MIT's Media Lab and Boston's Henigan School, where the programming language Logo was used to interface pieces of robotic equipment

with Lego bricks to produce various gadgets and toys: see the discussion in Stewart Brand, *The Media Lab: Inventing the Future at MIT* (New York: Viking, 1987), pp. 124–26.

125. On Hollywood's often bungling attempts to integrate interactive and Web-based technologies into their established media systems, see John Geirland and Eva Sonesh-Kedar, *Digital Babylon: How the Geeks, the Suits, and the Ponytails Fought to Bring Hollywood to the Internet* (New York: Arcade, 1999).

CHAPTER FIVE

1. Douglas Coupland, *Microserfs* (New York: Regan, 1995), p. 50. Subsequent references appear in the text.

2. *National Information Infrastructure: Agenda for Action* (Washington, D.C.: U.S. Department of Commerce, 1993), p. 1, quoted in Karen Coyle, ed., *Coyle's Information Highway Handbook: A Practical File on the New Information Order* (Chicago: American Library Association, 1997), p. 21. For an overview of the Information Infrastructure Task Force's duties and subsequent influence, see Brian Kahin, "The U.S. Information Infrastructure Initiative: The Market, The Web, and the Virtual Project," in *National Information Infrastructure Initiatives: Vision and Policy Design*, ed. Brian Kahin and Ernest J. Wilson III (Cambridge, Mass.: MIT, 1997), pp. 150–89.

3. For an analysis of how Gore's rhetoric conflated roads and data networks, see Tom Rohrer, "Conceptual Blending on the Information Highway: How Metaphorical Inferences Work," in *Discourse and Perspective in Cognitive Linguistics*, ed. Wolf-Andreas Liebert, Gisela Redeker, and Linda Waugh (Philadelphia: John Benjamins, 1997), pp. 185–204. For a discussion of the ways Gore's central metaphor circulated through the popular media, see Linda Cooper Berdayes and Vicente Berdayes, "The Information Highway in Contemporary Magazine Narrative," *Journal of Communication* 48, no. 2 (spring 1998): 109–24.

4. See Mark H. Rose, *Interstate: Express Highway Politics, 1939–1989*, 2d rev. ed. (Knoxville: University of Tennessee Press, 1990), pp. 85–94.

5. See, for example, Howard Rheingold, *The Virtual Community: Homesteading on the Electronic Frontier* (Reading, Mass.: Addison-Wesley, 1993); and Stephen Doheny-Farina, *The Wired Neighborhood* (New Haven, Conn.: Yale University Press, 1996). For a critical assessment of these popular communitarian arguments, see David Lyon, "Cyberspace Sociality: Controversies over Computer-Mediated Relationships," in *The Governance of Cyberspace: Politics, Technology and Global Restructuring*, ed. Brian D. Loader (New York: Routledge, 1997), pp. 23–37.

6. See Magid Igbaria and Margaret Tan, eds., *The Virtual Workplace* (Hershey, Pa.: Idea Group, 1998).

7. See James Martin, *The Wired Society: A Challenge for Tomorrow* (Englewood Cliffs, N.J.: Prentice-Hall, 1978), which discusses the concept of "new highways" of information (pp. 7–16); and Ralph Lee Smith's *Wired Nation: Cable TV: The Electronic Communications Highway* (New York: Harper & Row, 1972). On Gore's claim that he coined the term in 1979, see Albert Gore Jr., "Information Superhighways: The Next Information Revolution," *The Futurist* 25, no. 1 (January-February 1991): 21–23.

8. Progress and Freedom Foundation, "Cyberspace and the American Dream: A Magna Carta for the Knowledge Age," in Coyle, ed., *Coyle's Information Highway Handbook*, pp. 77–84; the quotation is from p. 78. The authors—who include, along with Toffler, Esther Dyson, George Gilder, and George Keyworth—deprecate the

metaphor of the highway, with its implications of bureaucratic federalism, in favor of a more anarchic vision of "cyberspace."

9. For a critical discussion, see Andrew Blau, "A High Wire Act in a Highly Wired World: Universal Service and the Telecommunications Act of 1996," in *The Social Shaping of Information Superhighways: European and American Roads to the Information Society,* ed. Herbert Kubicek, William H. Dutton, and Robin Williams (New York: St. Martin's, 1997), pp. 247–63.

10. For reviews of the various problems involved (such as lack of consensus on the basic infrastructural technology), see John G. Nellist and Elliott M. Gilbert, *Understanding Modern Telecommunication and the Information Superhighway* (Boston: Artech, 1999). See also Randall L. Carson, *The Information Superhighway: Strategic Alliances in Telecommunications and Multimedia* (New York: St. Martin's, 1996) for a discussion of the confused terrain of corporate mergers and interindustry struggles that has, at least to date, hampered the achievement of a systemic NII. On the various metaphors used in popular media to describe these numerous difficulties, see "Roadblock that Metaphor!" *Time,* 2 May 1994, p. 20.

11. See Michael Dawson and John Bellamy Foster, "Virtual Capitalism," in *Capitalism and the Information Age: The Political Economy of the Global Communications Revolution,* ed. Robert W. McChesny, Ellen Meiksins Wood, and John Bellamy Foster (New York: Monthly Review Press, 1998), pp. 51–68; and Dan Schiller, *Digital Capitalism: Networking the Global Market System* (Cambridge, Mass.: MIT, 1999).

12. Nick Dyer-Witheford, *Cyber-Marx: Cycles and Circuits of Struggle in High-Technology Capitalism* (Urbana: University of Illinois Press, 1999), pp. 33, 122, 35.

13. See, for example, Simson Garfinkel, *Database Nation: The Death of Privacy in the 21st Century* (Sebastopol, Calif.: O'Reilly, 2000); and Herbert I. Schiller, *Information Inequality: The Deepening Social Crisis in America* (New York: Routledge, 1996).

14. Robert Adrian X, "Infobahn Blues," in *Digital Delirium,* ed. Arthur and Marilouise Kroker (New York: St. Martin's, 1997), pp. 84–88; the quotation is from p. 85.

15. Howard Besser, "From Internet to Information Superhighway," in *Resisting the Virtual Life: The Culture and Politics of Information,* ed. James Brooks and Iain A. Boal (San Francisco: City Lights, 1995), pp. 59–70; the quotation is from p. 63.

16. Kevin Robins and Frank Webster, "Cybernetic Capitalism: Information, Technology, Everyday Life," in *The Political Economy of Information,* ed. Vincent Mosco and Janet Wasko (Madison: University of Wisconsin Press, 1988), pp. 44–75. Subsequent references appear in the text.

17. Michel Foucault, *Discipline and Punish: The Birth of the Prison,* trans. Alan Sheridan (New York: Vintage, 1979), pp. 212, 214. For an application of Foucault's model to today's "wired society," see Oscar H. Gandy, Jr., *The Panoptic Sort: A Political Economy of Personal Information* (Boulder, Colo.: Westview, 1993).

18. Robins and Webster, "Cybernetic Capitalism," p. 70.

19. Arthur Kroker and Michael A. Weinstein, *Data Trash: The Theory of the Virtual Class* (New York: St. Martin's, 1994), p. 7. Subsequent references appear in the text.

20. Nicholas Negroponte, *Being Digital* (New York: Vintage, 1996), p. 231.

21. For a valuable discussion of the issues these critics collectively treat, consult Bruce M. Owen, *The Internet Challenge to Television* (Cambridge, Mass.: Harvard University Press, 1999).

22. George Gilder, *Life After Television* (New York: Norton, 1992), pp. 30, 60. Subsequent references appear in the text.

23. Paul Levinson, *The Soft Edge: A Natural History and Future of the Information Revolution* (New York: Routledge, 1997), p. 164.

24. Ibid., p. 169.

25. Negroponte, *Being Digital*, p. 155. Subsequent references appear in the text.

26. Levinson, *The Soft Edge*, p. 195.

27. An overview of the rapidly evolving corporate strategies in this area is Peter Wayner, *Digital Copyright Protection* (New York: AP Professional, 1997).

28. See Timothy M. Todreas, *Value Creation and Branding in Television's Digital Age* (Westport, Conn.: Quorum, 1999).

29. Negroponte, *Being Digital*, p. 176.

30. Alfred C. Sikes, quoted in Fritz Jacobi, "Will There Be a Lane for Television on the Information Superhighway?" *Television Quarterly* 27 (winter 1995), pp. 29–35; the quotation is from p. 35.

31. See also Julian Sefton-Green, ed., *Digital Diversions: Youth Culture in the Age of Multimedia* (London: UCL, 1998), which provides ethnographic perspectives on young people's interactions with digital technology.

32. David S. Bennahum, *Extra Life: Coming of Age in Cyberspace* (New York: Basic, 1998), p. 60.

33. J. C. Herz, *Surfing on the Internet: A Nethead's Adventures On-Line* (New York: Little Brown, 1995), pp. 220, 227.

34. Douglas Rushkoff, *Cyberia: Life in the Trenches of Hyperspace* (New York: HarperCollins, 1994), p. 6. The term *grok* refers to a form of empathic communion that has cognitive, mystical, and sexual overtones; it derives from Robert A. Heinlein's science fiction novel *Stranger in a Strange Land* (1961), which was popular among youth audiences during the 1960s.

35. Don Tapscott, *Growing Up Digital: The Rise of the Net Generation* (New York: McGraw-Hill, 1998), pp. 31, 291.

36. Rushkoff, *Cyberia*, p. 6.

37. Ibid., p. 206.

38. Herz, *Surfing on the Internet*, p. 284.

39. Bennahum, *Extra Life*, pp. 219, 233.

40. Rushkoff, *Cyberia*, p. 236.

41. Ibid., p. 210.

42. Bennahum, *Extra Life*, p. 29. This characterization of the TV-spectator relationship has a long cultural pedigree, as Cecilia Tichi shows in *Electronic Hearth: Creating an American Television Culture* (New York: Oxford University Press, 1991), which traces how "the fear of the monopolized consciousness" associated with broadcast TV crystallized, during the 1950s and 1960s, in popular images of "a figure of entranced passivity" ensconced before the screen (pp. 106–7). This negative vision has recently been balanced by a more active construction of the TV viewer: when the ludic potential of the VCR and the remote control are figured into the equation, the spectator "becomes a kind of *auteur* creating a personalized program," zapping through channels and zipping through commercials (pp. 113–14). See also Robert V. Bellamy Jr. and James R. Walker, *Television and the Remote Control: Grazing on a Vast Wasteland* (New York: Guilford, 1996), which contrasts these "auteurist" practices with the sort of interactive TV prophesied by Negroponte and Gilder (pp. 150–60).

43. Tapscott, *Growing Up Digital*, p. 15. Subsequent references appear in the text.

44. Tapscott rejects the label "Generation Y" that is sometimes applied to the cohort he calls N-Geners, since it tends to overstate the significance of Generation X, a mere transitional blip in his analysis.

45. A specific example of how the prosthetic consciousness of N-Geners is abstracted and conscripted to serve capitalist ends involves the growing use of videogames and other multimedia systems as training tools in corporate environments: see, for example, Marc Prensky, "Twitch Speed," *Across the Board* 35 (January 1998): 14–19; and Jennifer J. Salopek, "Coolness Is a State of Mind," *Training and Development* 52, no. 11 (November 1998): 22–26ff.

46. For an indication of the forms these democratic options might take, consult Adam Jones, "Wired World: Communications, Technology, Governance and the Democratic Uprising," in *The Global Political Economy of Communication: Hegemony, Telecommunication and the Information Economy*, ed. Edward A. Comor (London: Macmillan, 1994), pp. 145–64; and Eric Lee, *The Labour Movement and the Internet: The New Internationalism* (London: Pluto, 1997). Vivian Sobchack's "Democratic Franchise and the Electronic Frontier" (in *Cyberfutures: Culture and Politics on the Information Superhighway*, ed. Ziauddin Sardar and Jerome R. Ravets [New York: New York University Press, 1996], pp. 77–89) offers an excellent dialectical assessment of the basic issues at stake in any such argument for technodemocraticization.

47. Coupland, *Microserfs*, p. 3. Subsequent references appear in the text.

48. This sort of engagement with television programming has been analyzed by Douglas Rushkoff, in his essay "Coercion and Countermeasures: The Information Arms Race" (in *InfoWar*, ed. Gerfried Stocker and Christine Schöpf [New York: SpringerWien, 1994], pp. 218–27), as a form of information warfare characteristic of the skeptical GenX cohort: "The most skilled viewers have become amateur media semioticians. They maintain an ironic distance from the media they watch so as not to fall under the programmer's influence. . . . The new entertainment is a form of media study: what are they going to try next?" (p. 223)

49. A similar employment of interactive media to enshrine broadcast "classics" may be found in the electronic bulletin boards and chat rooms where GenXers throng to offer avidly sarcastic dissections of their favorite TV shows; on the popularity of this practice, see Rob Owen, *GenX TV: From "The Brady Bunch" to "Melrose Place"* (Syracuse, N.Y.: Syracuse University Press, 1997), pp. 157–84. As Owen shows, TV producers rely on such forums for feedback on their current programs, but this limited evidence of two-way communication hardly achieves the kind of radical interactivity promoted by the prophets of digital culture.

50. Douglas Coupland, *Generation X: Tales for an Accelerated Culture* (New York: St. Martin's, 1991), p. 21.

51. A good introduction to the debates raised by Coupland's novel and the subsequent cultural appropriation of his term can be found in Douglas Rushkoff, ed., *The GenX Reader* (New York: Ballantine, 1994); see also Geoffrey T. Holtz, *Welcome to the Jungle: The Why Behind "Generation X"* (New York: St. Martin's Griffin, 1995).

52. Coupland, *Generation X*, p. 5.

53. Ibid., p. 19.

54. Numerous studies have appeared in business and management journals discussing GenXers' lack of a traditional work ethic, their air of acting superior to their job situations, and their tendency to mouth off to supervisors, as well as advising

employers how to handle these sorts of problems: see, for example, Gillian Flynn, "Xers vs. Boomers: Teamwork or Trouble?" *Personnel Journal* 75 (November 1996): 86–89; and Robert McGarvey, "X Appeal: Secrets of Managing Generation X," *Entrepreneur* 25 (May 1997): 87–89. For a defense of GenXers against these kinds of charges, see William J. Dorgan III, "Generation X on the Job," *Modern Machine Shop* 68 (November 1995): 116.

55. G. P. Lainsbury, "*Generation X* and the End of History," *Essays on Canadian Writing* 58 (spring 1996): 229–40; the quotation is from p. 235.

56. The GenX taste for "vintage" television has spawned cable franchises such as Nick at Nite and TV Land, which not only recycle these offerings but present them, with ironic grandeur, as notable moments of "our television heritage." For a discussion of the appeal of these networks, as well as their shrewd tactics of recommodifying old products, see Wayne Walley, "Nostalgia with a Twist," *Advertising Age*, 10 April 1989, S31; and T. L. Stanley, "Cashing In on Yesteryear," *Brandweek*, 10 November 1997, pp. 30–31. TV Land actually runs antiquated commercials during its prime time hours, a practice that links up with Coupland's analysis of the GenX tendency to cite "advertising, packaging, and entertainment jargon from earlier eras in everyday speech for ironic and/or comic effect" (*GenX*, p. 107).

57. Coupland, *Generation X*, pp. 3, 41.

58. Douglas Coupland, "Interview in *Elle* Magazine," reprinted in Rushkoff, ed., *The GenX Reader*, pp. 11–16; the quotation is from p. 13. In interviews, Coupland has persistently commented on his desire to move past his characteristic ironic posture and on the difficulty he has encountered in doing so: see Joe Chidley, "Life after Irony," *Maclean's*, 20 April 1998, pp. 61–62.

59. Karen Ritchie, *Marketing to Generation X* (New York: Lexington, 1995), p. 159; see also Susan Mitchell, *Generation X: The Young Adult Market* (Ithaca, N.Y.: New Strategist, 1997). A search for the term *Generation X* in periodical databases will produce hundreds of post-1991 entries, a substantial number of them published in business and advertising journals seeking to exploit the youth market: see, for example, the special reports in *Advertising Age* (6 February 1995) and *Brandweek* (15 May 1995). These articles often stress what a "hard sell" GenXers are for traditional pitch techniques, thus mandating more sophisticated approaches, ranging from ironized bluntness to exaggerated appeals to nostalgia: see Laurie Freeman, "No Tricking the Media Savvy," *Advertising Age*, 6 February 1995, p. 3; and Ellen Mediati, "Deju Vu All Over Again," *Folio*, 1 January 1997, p. 36. For a critique of these corporate efforts to corral the GenX market, see Nathaniel Wice, "Generalization X," in *The GenX Reader*, pp. 279–86.

60. Ryan Moore, " . . . And Tomorrow Is Just Another Crazy Scam: Postmodernity, Youth, and the Downward Mobility of the Middle Class," in *Generations of Youth: Youth Cultures and History in Twentieth-Century America*, ed. Joe Austin and Michael Nevin Willard (New York: New York University Press, 1998), pp. 253–71; the quotation is from p. 254.

61. Ibid., p. 264.

62. The screenplay of this film has been published, with a foreword by Coupland: see Richard Linklater, *Slacker* (New York: St. Martin's, 1992); the line quoted here is from p. 89. For a discussion of issues of consumption and cultural labor in the film, see Susan Willis, "Teens at Work: Negotiating the Jobless Future," in Austin and Willard, eds., *Generations of Youth*, pp. 347–57.

63. Herz, *Surfing on the Internet*, p. 220; emphasis in original.

64. Ibid., p. 223.

65. Ibid., p. 222.

66. Coupland, *Microserfs*, p. 209.

67. Ibid., p. 367.

68. Tapscott, *Growing Up Digital*, 92.

69. Some members of Generation X have mobilized politically to pursue activist agendas: see Van Jones, "Slack This!" *Utne Reader*, January/February 1997, pp. 40–41; and Rob Nelson and Jon Cowan, *Revolution X: A Survival Guide for Our Generation* (New York: Penguin, 1994).

70. Coupland, *Microserfs*, p. 53.

71. Ibid., p. 98.

72. This superimposition is actually occurring as information technologies are implemented to produce "smart highways" where traffic is processed as if it were a flow of coded data, as well as "smart cars" that provide virtual maps, instant information on highway conditions, and so on: see, for example, Cindy Krushenisky, "Mapping the Open Road," *PC Novice* 5 (July 1994): 50–52; and Daniel Coyle, "Welcome to the Real Data Superhighway," *Byte* 22 (January 1997): 32.

73. Rushkoff, ed., *The GenX Reader*, p. 120; the editorial italics in which this comment originally appeared have been suppressed.

74. Gerald Nicosia, *Memory Babe: A Critical Biography of Jack Kerouac* (New York: Penguin, 1983), p. 344.

75. On the economic and geographical connections between the growth of the interstate highways and the development of postwar suburbia, see Tom Lewis, *Divided Highways: Building the Interstate Highways, Transforming American Life* (New York: Viking, 1997), pp. 80–85.

76. For a discussion of the historical evolution of car advertisements, see Eric Dregni and Karl Hagstrom Miller, *Ads That Put America on Wheels* (Osceola, Wis.: Motorbooks International, 1996). Christopher Finch's *Highways to Heaven: The AUTO Biography of America* (New York: HarperCollins, 1992) discusses the ambivalent goals informing postwar automobile design: the desire for luxury and comfort on the one hand, and for power and speed on the other (pp. 169–83).

77. For a discussion of drag-strip teenpics, consult Thomas Doherty, *Teenagers and Teenpics: The Juvenilization of American Movies in the 1950s* (Boston: Unwin Hyman, 1988), pp. 108–13.

78. Jack Kerouac, *On the Road* (New York: Viking, 1957); the edition cited here is New York: Penguin, 1991, p. 19.

79. It should be pointed out that, although Kerouac's novel was published in 1957 (one year after passage of the Interstate Highway Act), it was actually written in 1952 and records events that transpired in 1947; Kerouac is thus writing about an America *before* the advent of the superhighway system. However, an expectation that the highway system would soon be extensively expanded predominated during the decade before the act: see Val Hart's chapter "The Road Ahead" in his *Story of American Roads* (New York: William Sloane, 1950), pp. 235–38, which alleges that "the system of roads now mostly in the blueprint stage will be far superior to any highways the world has ever seen" (p. 235). Unsurprisingly, the popular reception of Kerouac's novel generally tended to associate the book with this emerging freeway landscape.

80. Barbara Ehrenreich, *The Hearts of Men: American Dreams and the Flight from Commitment* (New York: Anchor, 1983), p. 53.

81. For a discussion of the film *Easy Rider* in the context of both Kerouac's example and the highway culture of the period, see Barbara Klinger, "The Road to Dystopia: Landscaping the Nation in *Easy Rider*," in *The Road Movie Book*, ed. Steven Cohan and Ira Rae Clark (New York: Routledge, 1997), pp. 179–203, especially p. 180. For a more wide-ranging treatment of Kerouac's influence on the road film genre, see David Laderman, "What a Trip: The Road Film and American Culture," *Journal of Film and Video* 48, nos. 1–2 (spring-summer 1996): 41–57.

82. For a discussion of the road novel during this period, see Ronald Primeau's chapter, "Escape, Experimentation, and Parody," in his *Romance of the Road: The Literature of the American Highway* (Bowling Green, Ohio: Bowling Green State University Popular Press, 1996), pp. 89–106. For an excellent analysis of the pathologies of the road movie in the 1970s and 1980s, see Timothy Corrigan, *A Cinema Without Walls: Movies and Culture After Vietnam* (New Brunswick, N.J.: Rutgers University Press, 1991), pp. 137–60.

83. Michael Wallis, *Route 66: The Mother Road* (New York: St. Martin's, 1990), p. 133.

84. Tom Englehardt, *Beyond Our Control: America in the Mid-Seventies* (Berkeley, Calif.: Riverrun, 1976), p. 109.

85. William S. Burroughs, *The Place of Dead Roads* (New York: Holt, Rinehart and Winston, 1983), 266. Subsequent references appear in the text.

86. This notion of systemic mass-media manipulation has been a perennial theme in Burroughs's work: his fiction generally traces a dynamic of struggle between agencies of control and forces of resistance, the former usually associated with technologies of simulation, the latter with terrorist factions seeking to disrupt their operation. On this topic, see my "Collage as Critique and Invention in the Fiction of William S. Burroughs and Kathy Acker," *Journal of the Fantastic in the Arts* 5, no. 3 (1993): 46–57. For valuable analyses of how Burroughs's understanding of control mechanisms connects with cybernetics discourse, see David Porush, *The Soft Machine: Cybernetic Fiction* (New York: Metheun, 1985), pp. 99–104; and N. Katherine Hayles, *How We Became Posthuman: Virtual Bodies in Cybernetics, Literature, and Informatics* (Chicago: University of Chicago Press, 1999), pp. 208–20.

87. Jean Baudrillard, *America*, trans. Chris Turner (New York: Verso, 1988), p. 55. Subsequent references are to this translation and appear in the text.

88. Terry Caesar, "Brutal Naïveté and Special Lighting: Hyperspatialty and Landscape in the American Travel Text," *College Literature* 56, no. 2 (February 1994): 63–79; the quotation is from p. 73.

89. Baudrillard, *America*, p. 53. Subsequent references appear in the text.

90. Both highways and television had previously been theorized in terms of the processing of "flows," and Baudrillard merely fuses the arguments. On television as flow, see the seminal study by Raymond Williams, *Television: Technology As Cultural Form* (New York: Schocken, 1975), especially pp. 86–118.

91. Bryan S. Turner, "Cruising America," in *Forget Baudrillard?* ed. Chris Rojek and Bryan S. Turner (New York: Routledge, 1993), pp. 146–61; the quotation is from p. 154. Turner also compares Baudrillard with Kerouac, arguing that *America* cements a "link between [the] drop-out culture of the highway" popularized by the

Beat author and "the postmodern depthless ride through the American landscape" (p. 153).

92. Anne Friedberg, *Window Shopping: Cinema and the Postmodern* (Berkeley and Los Angeles: University of California Press, 1993), pp. 142–43, 147–48.

93. For a discussion of the cyborg potential of driving, see K. T. Berger's analysis of what he calls "the car/driver entity" in his *Where the Road and the Sky Collide: America through the Eyes of Its Drivers* (New York: Henry Holt, 1993), pp. 16–19.

94. Peter D'Agostino, "Virtual Realities: Recreational Vehicles for a Post-Television Culture?" in *Transmission: Toward a Post-Television Culture*, 2d ed., ed. D'Agostino and David Tafler (Thousand Oaks, Calif.: SAGE, 1995), pp. 269–83; the quotations are from pp. 269–70.

95. As Ron Eyerman and Orvar Lofgren, in "Romancing the Road: Road Movies and Images of Mobility" (*Theory, Culture and Society* 12 [1995]: 53–79), observe: "The road movie is a genre tailored for tales and times of crisis—for downward as well as upward mobility" (p. 77).

96. In fact, in a parallel with the vampire genre (as discussed in chapter 2), the road narrative split into slacker and yuppie factions during the 1980s and 1990s, the latter tradition kick-started by Albert Brooks's comic travelogue *Lost in America* (1985) and including novels such as Stephen Dixon's *Interstate* (New York: Henry Holt, 1995). For a study of yuppie road movies, see Ina Rae Hark, "Fear of Flying: Yuppie Critique and the Buddy-Road Movie in the 1980s," in Cohan and Clark, eds., *The Road Movie Book*, pp. 204–29.

97. For a discussion of the contemporary road movie's tendency toward self-reflexive pastiche, see Michael Atkinson, "Crossing the Frontiers," *Sight and Sound* 4, no. 1 (January 1994): 14–17.

98. Bayard Johnson, *Damned Right* (Boulder, Colo.: Black Ice, 1994), p. 27.

99. Baudrillard, *America*, p. 55.

100. Johnson, *Damned Right*, pp. 18, 26. Subsequent references appear in the text.

101. Stephen Wright, *Going Native* (New York: Farrar Straus Giroux, 1994), p. 104. Subsequent references appear in the text.

102. Kris Lackey, *RoadFrames: The American Highway Narrative* (Lincoln: University of Nebraska Press, 1997), p. 148.

103. Ian Leong, Mike Sell, and Kelly Thomas, "Mad Love, Mobile Homes, and Dysfunctional Dicks: On the Road with Bonnie and Clyde," in Cohan and Clark, eds., *The Road Movie Book*, pp. 70–89; the quotation is from p. 93.

104. For an analysis of the imbrication of the film's mediascape with socio-economic contexts of commodification, see Jonathan L. Beller, "Identity through Death/The Nature of Capital: The Media-Environment for *Natural Born Killers*," *Post Identity* 1, no. 2 (summer 1998): 55–67.

105. Jean Baudrillard, "The Precession of Simulacra," in *Simulacra and Simulation*, trans. Sheila Faria Glaser (Ann Arbor: University of Michigan Press, 1994), pp. 1–42; the quotation is from p. 30.

106. Oliver Stone, quoted in Leong et al., "Mad Love, Mobile Homes, and Dysfunctional Dicks," p. 82.

107. Fredrick Barthelme, *Painted Desert* (New York: Penguin, 1995), p. 22. Subsequent references appear in the text.

108. Despite Jen's dismissive remark contrasting journalistic stereotypes of Generation X and baby boomers ("the *Time* magazine version of things," as she calls it)

with "what we actually do" (Barthelme, *Painted Desert*, p. 203), it is fairly clear that Barthelme planned his chronologically mismatched romance to explore, at least in part, the putative conflict between these generational cohorts so widely discussed in the popular media during the mid-1990s.

109. Ernest Hebert, *Mad Boys* (Hanover, N.H.: University Press of New England, 1993), p. 2. Subsequent references appear in the text.

CHAPTER SIX

1. Steven Levy, *Hackers: Heroes of the Computer Revolution* (New York: Doubleday, 1984); the edition cited here, as *Hack*, is New York: Dell, 1985; subsequent references appear in the text.

2. Stewart Brand, "Keep Designing: How the Information Economy Is Being Created and Shaped by the Hacker Ethic," *Whole Earth Review* 46 (May 1985): 44–55; the quotation is from p. 55.

3. Levy, *Hackers*, pp. 219–20. Subsequent references appear in the text.

4. Katie Hafner and John Markoff, *Cyberpunk: Outlaws and Hackers on the Electronic Frontier* (New York: Simon & Schuster, 1991), p. 11.

5. See Joshua Quittner, "Kevin Mitnick's Digital Obsession," *Time*, 27 February 1995, p. 45; and Jonathan Littman, *The Fugitive Game: Online with Kevin Mitnick* (New York: Little, Brown, 1997).

6. Bryan Clough and Paul Mungo, *Approaching Zero: Data Crime and the Computer Underworld* (London: Faber and Faber, 1992), p. 9. See also Yonah Alexander and Michael S. Swetnam, eds., *Cyber Terrorism and Information Warfare* (Dobbs Ferry, N.Y.: Oceana, 1999). These sorts of alarmist views of the massed threat posed by lurking hackers have spawned a huge security industry devoted to safeguarding governmental and corporate data systems through cryptographic and other countermeasures: see, for example, Randall K. Nichols et al., *Defending Your Digital Assets against Hackers, Crackers, Spies, and Thieves* (New York: McGraw-Hill, 1999).

7. Michelle Slatalla and Joshua Quittner, *Masters of Deception: The Gang That Ruled Cyberspace* (New York: HarperCollins, 1995). The book chronicles the factional strife between two computer clubs, the Legion of Doom and the Masters of Deception, that led to a series of high-profile arrests and convictions in 1992.

8. John Perry Barlow, quoted in "Is Computer Hacking a Crime?" *Harper's*, March 1990, pp. 45–57; cited by Slatalla and Quittner, *Masters of Deception*, p. 100.

9. Bruce Sterling, *The Hacker Crackdown: Law and Disorder on the Electronic Frontier* (New York: Ballantine, 1992), p. 95.

10. Hafner and Markoff, *Cyberpunk*, p. 200. Early popular coverage contributed to this now-widespread association of hackers with traditional images of youthful delinquency: see, for example, Kathleen K. Wiegner, "Gilded Youth, Jaded Youth," *Forbes*, 15 August 1983, p. 36.

11. Andrew Ross, *Strange Weather: Culture, Science and Technology in the Age of Limits* (New York: Verso, 1991), p. 81. See also R. C. Hollinger and L. Lanza-Kaduce, "The Process of Criminalization: The Case of Computer Crime Laws," *Criminology* 26, no. 1 (1988): 101–26.

12. Ross, *Strange Weather*, p. 86. The tension between hackers and computer professionals is especially pointed in the realm of corporate security, since major companies will sometimes hire hackers instead of mainstream security firms to test the integrity of their networks, the assumption being that the former have greater

know-how when it comes to cracking databases: see, for example, Wade Roush, "Hackers Taking a Byte out of Computer Crime," *Technology Review* 98 (April 1995): 32–40. As a result, hackers with entrepreneurial ambitions have begun founding their own security firms: see William Spain, "Hacker Attackers," *Computerworld*, 4 August 1997, pp. 78–79.

13. Paul A. Taylor, "Hackers: Cyberpunks or Microserfs," *ICS: Information Communication and Society* 1, no. 4 (winter 1998): 401–19.

14. See Taylor's more extensive discussion of this process of boundary formation in his book, *Hackers: Crime in the Digital Sublime* (New York: Routledge, 1999); the quotation is from p. 24.

15. Dennis Hayes, *Behind the Silicon Curtain: The Seductions of Work in a Lonely Era* (Boston: South End, 1989), p. 95.

16. Sterling, *Hacker Crackdown*, p. 57.

17. Hacker groups and their advocates have frequently released manifestos, usually of an anarchistic bent. One of the earliest of these was Timothy Mays's "The Crypto Anarchist Manifesto," which was initially distributed over Usenet in 1988 and is widely available online (see <http://www.austinlinks.com/Crypto/crypto-anarchist.html>); Mays begins with an echo of Marx and Engels: "A specter is haunting the modern world, the specter of crypto anarchy." Sterling has traced hacker militancy to the Yippie movement of the 1960s (see *Hacker Crackdown*, pp. 45-47).

18. Gordon Meyer and Jim Thomas, "The Baudy World of the Byte Bandit: A Postmodernist Interpretation of the Computer Underground," published online at <http://www.eff.org/pub/Net_culture/Postmodernism/byte_bandit.paper>.

19. Hayes, *Behind the Silicon Curtain*, p. 93.

20. Ibid., p. 87.

21. The term *codez* refers to the illicitly acquired phone-service numbers hackers use to make free long-distance calls and otherwise manipulate the network. Eric S. Raymond's *New Hacker's Dictionary* (Cambridge, Mass.: MIT, 1996) provides an extensive guide to hacker argot.

22. Levy, *Hackers*, p. 316. Many third-generation hackers bemoan the moment when popular access to the architecture of the machine receded behind a uniform shell, as occurred with the Apple II—a transition that signaled the definitive waning of a hobbyists' culture in favor of marketing concerns. See, for example, David Bennahum's remarks in *Extra Life: Coming of Age in Cyberspace* (New York: Basic, 1998), p. 200.

23. MAGIK's e-zine is archived online at <http://www.eff.org/pub/Publications/CuD/Magik/>.

24. Slatalla and Quittner, *Masters of Deception*, p. 2.

25. Ross, *Strange Weather*, p. 93; emphasis in original.

26. There is a neat echo here of teen-vampire Timmy Valentine, whose hobbyist joy in his model trains was counterpoised, in S. P. Somtow's novel *Vampire Junction*, against a larger commercial regime of commodified pleasures.

27. Levy, *Hackers*, p. 348.

28. On the freeware or open-source movement, which has resisted the imperatives of corporate commodification, see Josh McHugh, "For the Love of Hacking," *Forbes*, 10 August 1998, pp. 94–100.

29. For a critique of the movie's implausibilities vis-à-vis the security of military

computer systems, see "Computer Crime à la *War Games*," *Security Management* 27 (October 1983): 52–53; for a critique by hackers themselves, see the remarks of the Toxic Shock Group quoted in Taylor, *Hackers*, pp. 41–42. Despite the film's simplistic treatment, Pentagon computers have at times been hacked successfully (e.g., by Kevin Mitnick), though these incursions have usually been low-level security breaches rather than, as the movie has it, a direct infiltration of the core programs.

30. Slatalla and Quittner, *Masters of Deception*, p. 18. See also the discussion in Bill Landreth, *Out of the Inner Circle: A Hacker's Guide to Computer Security* (Bellevue, Wash.: Microsoft, 1985), which describes the explosion of teen interest in hacker bulletin boards sparked by the film (p. 18).

31. As Levy has pointed out, one of the central paradoxes of the Hacker Ethic was its evolution within academic laboratories directly funded by Defense Department contracts, largely through its Advanced Research Projects Agency (ARPA). According to Levy, first-generation hackers basically subsisted in a state of denial regarding this situation, retreating into a "very determined solipsism" that ignored the political implications of their activities (*Hackers*, p. 133). Later generations have become rather more militant, sometimes advancing an agenda of "guerilla warfare" designed to turn global telecommunications away from military uses and toward peaceful ends (see, e.g., Taylor, *Hackers*, p. 5).

32. Lee Felsenstein, interviewed by and quoted in Levy, *Hackers*, pp. 429–30.

33. Scott Bukatman, *Terminal Identity: The Virtual Subject in Postmodern Science Fiction* (Durham, N.C.: Duke University Press, 1993), p. 211.

34. Ibid., p. 201.

35. For an analysis of the influence of Toffler's theories on cyberpunk fiction, see Lance Olsen, "The Shadow of Spirit in William Gibson's Matrix Trilogy," *Extrapolation* 32, no. 3 (fall 1991): 278–89. For a more general discussion of cyberpunk's connections with postindustrial theories of information society, see Terence Whalen, "The Future of a Commodity: Notes toward a Critique of Cyberpunk and the Information Age," *Science-Fiction Studies* 19, no. 1 (March 1992): 75–88.

36. Bruce Sterling, ed., preface to *Mirrorshades: The Cyberpunk Anthology* (New York: Arbor House, 1986), pp. ix–xvi; the quotation is from p. xi.

37. Most critics of the genre have attempted to gloss the coinage, explaining the relationship between *cyber* and *punk* in various ways; for an analysis by one of the form's central practitioners, see Rudy Rucker, "What Is Cyberpunk?" in Rucker, *Seek: Selected Nonfiction* (New York: Four Walls Eight Windows, 1999), pp. 315–22.

38. Mark Dery, *Escape Velocity: Cyberculture at the End of the Century* (Durham, N.C.: Duke University Press, 1996), p. 154.

39. See the wealth of materials gathered in Larry McCaffery, ed., *Storming the Reality Studio: A Casebook of Cyberpunk and Postmodern Fiction* (Durham, N.C.: Duke University Press, 1991).

40. Hafner and Markoff, *Cyberpunk*, p. 9.

41. Philip Elmer-Dewitt, "Cyberpunk: Virtual Sex, Smart Drugs and Synthetic Rock 'n' Roll. A Futuristic Subculture Erupts from the Electronic Underground," *Time*, 8 February 1993, pp. 58–65; the quotation is from p. 59.

42. This linked strategy of demonization and domestication has long informed mainstream media coverage of youth subcultures: see Dick Hebdige's discussion of the ambivalent response to punk in the 1970s British press (*Subculture: The Meaning of Style* [New York: Methuen, 1979], pp. 97–98).

43. Timothy Leary, *Chaos & Cyberculture* (Berkeley, Calif.: Ronin, 1994), pp. 71, 73.

44. The chapter immediately preceding the one on cyberpunk in Leary's book openly celebrates yuppies as "the most intelligent group of human beings ever to inhabit the planet," as well as being "highly selective consumers, expecting to be rewarded because they are the best" (ibid., p. 58).

45. R. U. Sirius, "A User's Guide to Using this Guide," in *Mondo 2000: A User's Guide to the New Edge*, ed. Rudy Rucker, R. U. Sirius, and Queen Mu (New York: HarperPerennial, 1992), pp. 14–17; the quotations are from pp. 14 and 16.

46. For an overview of these sorts of fringe-science, body-transcending extrapolations, see Ed Regis, *Great Mambo Chicken and the Transhuman Condition* (Menlo Park, Calif.: Addison-Wesley, 1990).

47. Sirius, "User's Guide," p. 16.

48. Vivian Sobchack, "New Age Mutant Ninja Hackers," in *Flame Wars: The Discourse of Cyberculture*, ed. Mark Dery (Durham, N.C.: Duke University Press, 1994), pp. 11–28; the quotation is from p. 18.

49. Ibid., p. 22.

50. Peter Fitting, "The Lessons of Cyberpunk," in *Technoculture*, ed. Constance Penley and Andrew Ross (Minneapolis: University of Minnesota Press, 1991), pp. 295–315; the quotation is from p. 297.

51. John Huntington, "Newness, *Neuromancer*, and the End of Narratrive," in *Fiction 2000: Cyberpunk and the Future of Narrative*, ed. George Slusser and Tom Shippey (Athens: University of Georgia Press, 1992), pp. 133–41; the quotation is from pp. 138–39.

52. Istvan Csicsery-Ronay Jr., "Cyberpunk and Neuromanticism," in McCaffery, ed., *Storming the Reality Studio*, pp. 182–93; the quotation is from p. 183.

53. Ibid., p. 188. On splatterpunk fiction, see Philip Nutman, "Inside the New Horror," *Twilight Zone* (October 1988): 24ff.

54. See, for example, Dani Cavallero, *Cyberpunk and Cyberculture* (London: Athlone, 2000), pp. 164–203; and Allan Lloyd-Smith, "Postmodernism/Gothicism," in *Modern Gothic: A Reader*, ed. Victor Sage and Allan Lloyd-Smith (Manchester: Manchester University Press, 1996), pp. 7–19, especially pp. 15–18.

55. Dery, *Escape Velocity*, p. 67.

56. Erik Davis, "Techgnosis, Magic, Memory, and the Angels of Information," in Dery, ed., *Flame Wars*, pp. 29–60; the quotation is from p. 51.

57. Douglas Rushkoff, *Cyberia: Life in the Trenches of Hyperspace* (New York: HarperCollins, 1994), p. 145.

58. On the origins of the concept of the cyborg in early astronautics research, see the section on "The Genesis of Cyborg" in *The Cyborg Handbook*, ed. Chris Hables Gray, Heidi J. Figueroa-Sarriera, and Steven Mentor (New York: Routledge, 1995).

59. Anne Balsamo, "Signal to Noise: On the Meaning of Cyberpunk Subculture," in *Imaginative Futures: Proceedings of the 1993 Science Fiction Research Association Conference*, ed. Milton T. Wolf and Daryl F. Mallett (Tempe, Ariz.: Jacob's Ladder/Angel Enterprises, 1994), pp. 217–28; the quotation is from pp. 224–25.

60. William Gibson, "Burning Chrome," in *Burning Chrome* (New York: Arbor House, 1986), pp. 176–200; the quotation is from p. 195.

61. Lewis Shiner, "Inside the Movement: Past, Present, and Future," in *Fiction 2000*, ed. Slusser and Shippey, pp. 17–25; the quotation is from p. 17.

62. Ibid.

63. Poppy Z. Brite, *Drawing Blood* (New York: Dell, 1993), p. 329. Subsequent references appear in the text.

64. On the Subgenius movement, see Jay Kinney, "Backstage with 'Bob': Is the Church of the SubGenius the Ultimate Cult?" *Whole Earth Review* 52 (fall 1986): 86–89.

65. Douglas Kellner, *Media Culture: Cultural Studies, Identity and Politics Between the Modern and the Postmodern* (New York: Routledge, 1995), pp. 326–27.

66. See, for example, Michael Pondsmith, *Cyberpunk: The Roleplaying Game of the Dark Future* (Berkeley, Calif.: R. Talsorian Games, 1990).

67. A concept promoted by roboticist Hans Moravec, in his book *Mind Children: The Future of Robot and Human Intelligence* (Cambridge, Mass.: Harvard University Press, 1988), uploading has also been championed by the so-called Extropians, a loose-knit fringe-science movement devoted to an increasingly accelerated co-evolution with machines; consult the Web site of the Extropy Institute at <http://www.extropy.org/>.

68. Pat Cadigan, "Pretty Boy Crossover," in *Patterns* (Kansas City, Mo.: Ursus, 1989), p. 137. Subsequent references appear in the text.

69. Michael Heim, "The Design of Virtual Reality," in *Cyberspace/Cyberbodies/ Cyberpunk: Cultures of Technological Embodiment*, ed. Mike Featherstone and Roger Burrows (Thousand Oaks, Calif.: SAGE, 1995), pp. 65–77; the quotation is from p. 72. Heim contrasts this form of virtual reality with what he calls "apperceptive VR," which does not function to sever connections with the external environment, an alternative he prefers for philosophical reasons; see the more extensive discussion in his book, *The Metaphysics of Virtual Reality* (New York: Oxford, 1993).

70. See N. Katherine Hayles, *How We Became Posthuman: Virtual Bodies in Cybernetics, Literature, and Informatics* (Chicago: University of Chicago Press, 1999), especially chap. 4.

71. Norbert Wiener, *The Human Use of Human Beings: Cybernetics and Society* (Boston: Houghton Mifflin, 1954), p. 96.

72. Randal Walser, "The Emerging Technology of Cyberspace," in *Virtual Reality: Theory, Practice, and Promise*, ed. S. K. Helsel and J. P. Roth (Westport, Conn.: Meckler, 1991), pp. 35–40; the quotation is from p. 35. As Walser's remark shows, virtual reality has become interchangeable with William Gibson's concept of cyberspace; for historical background on, as well as a theoretical critique of, this terminological conflation, see Marie-Laure Ryan, "Cyberspace, Virtuality, and the Text," in Ryan, ed., *Cyberspace Textuality: Computer Technology and Literary Theory* (Bloomington: Indiana University Press, 1999), pp. 78–107.

73. On the immense technical difficulty of producing functional "smart skin," see Howard Rheingold, *Virtual Reality* (New York: Simon & Schuster, 1991), p. 347; and Mark Ward, "Feeling Is Believing in a Virtual World," *New Scientist*, 26 April 1997, p. 22.

74. Arthur Kroker, *Spasm: Virtual Reality, Android Music and Electric Flesh* (New York: St. Martin's, 1993), pp. 41–42.

75. Ibid., chap. 10. See also Mark Nunes, "Jean Baudrillard in Cyberspace: Internet, Virtuality, and Postmodernity," *Style* 29, no. 2 (summer 1995): 314–27.

76. Jean Baudrillard, "The Virtual Illusion: Or the Automatic Writing of the World," *Theory, Culture & Society* 12, no. 4 (1995): 97–107; the quotation is from p. 97.

302 NOTES TO PAGES 240–253

77. Jean Baudrillard, "The Ecstasy of Communication," trans. John Johnston, in *The Anti-Aesthetic: Essays in Postmodern Culture*, ed. Hal Foster (Port Townsend, Wash.: Bay Press, 1983), 126–33; the quotation is from p. 129.

78. Baudrillard, "The Virtual Illusion," p. 101.

79. Tim McFadden, "Notes on the Structure of Cyberspace and the Ballis-Actors Model," in *Cyberspace: First Steps*, ed. Michael Benedikt (Cambridge, Mass.: MIT, 1991), pp. 335–362; the quotation is from p. 337 (emphasis in original).

80. One can only imagine what will happen when "push-pull" technologies that track and report online movement patterns of consumers are fused with new VR systems such as the mouse design that purports to allow shoppers to "feel" objects of prospective purchase: see Catherine Zandonella, "Shopping with Feeling," *New Scientist*, 10 July 1999, p. 10.

81. Sean Cubitt, *Digital Aesthetics* (Thousand Oaks, Calif.: SAGE, 1998), p. 132.

82. In his book *Cyber-Marx: Cycles and Circuits of Struggle in High-Technology Capitalism* (Urbana: University of Illinois Press, 1999), Nick Dyer-Witheford uses the Marxist term *general intellect* to describe the "polycentric, communicatively connected, collective intelligence" of the Internet at its best moments, though capitalist industry is persistently seeking to "forc[e] its traffic into the commodified pathways of video-on-demand, teleshopping, telegambling, and personalized advertising" (p. 228).

83. Cubitt, *Digital Aesthetics*, pp. 56–57.

84. David Brande, "The Business of Cyberpunk: Symbolic Economy and Ideology in William Gibson," in *Virtual Realities and their Discontents*, ed. Robert Markley (Baltimore: Johns Hopkins University Press, 1996), pp. 79–106; the quotation is from p. 95.

85. William Gibson, *Neuromancer* (New York: Ace, 1984; the edition cited here is New York: Ace, 1994), p. 260; emphasis in original. On the patterns of utopian speculation in Gibson's work, see Tom Moylan, "Global Economy, Local Texts: Utopian/Dystopian Tension in William Gibson's Cyberpunk Trilogy," *Minnesota Review* 43/44 (1994–95): 182–97.

86. Pat Cadigan, *Tea from an Empty Cup* (New York: Tor, 1998), p. 40. Subsequent references appear in the text.

87. Marc Laidlaw, *Kalifornia* (New York: St. Martin's, 1993), p. 26. Subsequent references appear in the text.

88. See Raymond T. McNally, *Dracula Was a Woman: The Search for the Blood Countess of Translyvania* (New York: McGraw-Hill, 1983). Harry Kumel's 1971 film *Daughters of Darkness* features Batori as a seductive lesbian vampire, with Delphine Seyrig's limpid performance almost certainly influencing Catherine Deneuve's handling of the role of Miriam Blaylock in *The Hunger* a decade later.

89. Richard Calder, *Dead Girls, Dead Boys, Dead Things* (New York: St. Martin's Griffin, 1998). Subsequent references appear in the text.

90. In this contrast of gendered vampires, Calder develops the famous dualism anatomized by Mario Praz in *The Romantic Agony* (London: Oxford, 1933); like Praz, Calder links the Byronic "Fatal Man" and the *femme fatale* both with early nineteenth-century romanticism and with late-Victorian decadence.

91. Calder likely modeled his vision of the Meta on William S. Burroughs's Nova Mob in his novel *Nova Express* (1964). For a discussion of Calder's extensive literary

debts and allusions, see my review of the first two volumes of the *Dead* trilogy in *The New York Review of Science Fiction* 7, no. 12 (August 1995): 15ff.

92. For a discussion of the fetishistic objectification of sexuality in the context of high-tech culture, which includes a brief analysis of Calder's early fiction, see Thomas Foster, "'The Sex Appeal of the Inorganic': Posthuman Narratives and the Construction of Desire," in *Centuries' Ends, Narrative Means*, ed. Robert Newman (Stanford, Calif.: Stanford University Press, 1996), pp. 276–378, especially pp. 295–98.

93. Richard Calder, *Cythera* (New York: St. Martin's 1998), p. 30. Subsequent references appear in the text.

94. In this "new flesh" theme, the novel alludes to the cyborg fantasy of David Cronenberg's 1983 film *Videodrome*, where the border between life and image is also transgressed.

95. For a discussion of children's interactions with simulated entities, which points to their tendency to view them as semiautonomous forms of artificial life, see Sherry Turkle, "Cyborg Babies and Cy-Dough-Plasm: Ideas about Self and Life in the Culture of Simulation," in *Cyborg Babies: From Techno-Sex to Techno-Tots*, ed. Robbie Davis-Floyd and Joseph Dumit (New York: Routledge, 1998), pp. 317–29.

96. The evocation of Cythera as a land of "moonlight, calm, sad, and beautiful" obliquely cites Paul Verlaine's poem "Clair de lune"; I thank my colleague Kevin Kopelson for catching this allusion.

97. See Richard Farson, *Birthrights* (New York: Macmillan, 1974); and John Holt, *Escape from Childhood: The Needs and Rights of Children* (New York: Dutton, 1974). For a critique of these points of view, see Laura M. Purdy, *In Their Best Interest? The Case against Equal Rights for Children* (Ithaca, N.Y.: Cornell University Press, 1992).

INDEX